HIDDEN CONVERSATIONS

The communicative approach to psychoanalytic therapy, pioneered in the 1970s by Robert J. Langs, an American analyst, has aroused much controversy among analysts. Langs implies that psychotherapy is often harmful, with the words of a patient unconsciously revealing an unsatisfatcory experience to the analyst. He raises many questions which analytical practitioners find hard to accept or resolve.

Hidden Conversations introduces Langs's radical reinterpretation of psychoanalysis by presenting and expanding his ideas in new and accessible ways. It is the first clear account of the theories underlying Langs's approach, placing them within the context of the history of psychoanalysis and showing, for example, that Freud nearly "discovered" the communicative approach in the late 1890s, and that in the 1930s Ferenczi also anticipated the approach.

David Livingstone Smith illustrates the communicative approach with a wealth of practical, clinical examples, including verbatim accounts of communicative psychoanalytical sessions and a commentary on the unconscious processes underlying them. He also explores the philosophical underpinnings of psychoanalysis, providing critiques of conventional concepts such as "transference" and responding to philosophical objections to psychoanalytic theory.

In *Hidden Conversations* **David Livingstone Smith** asserts that many psychotherapists and psychoanalysts are unwittingly damaging to their patients. He argues therefore, that all psychoanalysts should look seriously at the communicative approach, and his book will be of great interest and value to all analysts and psychotherapists willing to subject their own work to self-scrutiny.

Other Books by David L. Smith

Approaching Psychoanalysis:
An Introductory Course

Books by Robert Langs

Clinical Practice and the Architecture of the Mind

Clinical Workbook for Psychotherapists

Death Anxiety and Clinical Practice

Doing Supervision and Being Supervised

Empowered Psychotherapy:
Teaching Self-Processing

The Evolution of the Emotion-Processing Mind

Ground Rules in Psychotherapy and Counselling

Science Systems and Psychoanalysis

Orders: Tel: +44 (0)20 8969 4454; Fax: +44 (0)20 8969 5585
Email: shop@karnacbooks.com; Internet: www.karnacbooks.com

HIDDEN CONVERSATIONS

AN INTRODUCTION TO COMMUNICATIVE PSYCHOANALYSIS

Second Edition

David Livingstone Smith

KARNAC

LONDON   NEW YORK

First published in 1991 by Routledge, London

Reprinted in 1999 by
Rebus Press, London

Reprinted in 2004 by
H. Karnac (Books) Ltd.
6 Pembroke Buildings
London NW10 6RE

British Library Cataloguing in Publication Data
A C.I.P. for this book is available from the British Library

ISBN: 1 85575 312 X
www.karnacbooks.com

Printed & bound by Antony Rowe Ltd, Eastbourne

To Benjamin and Sasha

I have made many beginnings and thrown out many suggestions . . . I can hope that they have opened up a path to an important advance in our knowledge. Something will come of them in the future.

Sigmund Freud

A theory that cannot be mortally endangered cannot be alive.

Rushton

Foreword to the 1999 Edition

One of Freud's greatest achievements was to notice the extent to which we routinely deceive both ourselves and one another. According to the communicative approach to psychoanalysis described in this book, each of us has the unconscious capacity to perforate these layers of duplicity. Unconsciously we all possess x-ray vision. Thus we all understand the raw messages lurking behind the polite façade.

Psychotherapists deceive just as much as anybody else. In particular, psychotherapists deceive themselves about the degree to which they deceive and exploit their patients. This is not an unanalysed pathological residue of infantile conflict. It is entirely natural, and of enormous concern to those seeking help from psychotherapists. As soon as a person enters psychotherapy their x-ray vision is focused on the psychotherapist. Unconsciously, patients monitor every move that their therapists make. These perceptions are expressed indirectly, by means of encoded narratives.

Since the first publication of this book in 1991, experience has taught me that it is unbearable for the majority of psychotherapists and psychoanalysts to look in the mirror that their patients hold up to them. Ironically, it is usually only students, who do not yet have an idealised professional self-image to protect, who are able to tolerate high levels of unconscious meaning. The theories and techniques of psychoanalysis and psychotherapy seem largely constructed out of practitioners' defensive needs.

My exploration of the wider scientific literature since the first publication of *Hidden Conversations* has received corroboration from some surprising sources. One of these is the work of Robert Trivers, a biologist, on the evolution of deception and self-deception (Trivers, 1985). Human beings, it seems, have evolved a propensity to exploit one another. Criminality, dishonesty and infidelity are extremely widespread features of human life. A great deal of this exploitation is covert, and covert exploitation requires deception. However, deception creates stress in the deceiver: The liar must maintain strict vigilance in order to avoid letting the cat out of the bag. As lie-detection technology has taught us, even the most skilful liar betrays himself through *involuntary* stress reactions. Trivers argues that Mother Nature's solution to this problem is to render deception unconscious. If we are not conscious of our exploitative and deceitful engagements with others we will not display signs of bad faith. We lie to ourselves in order to more effectively lie to others. Trivers argues that the evolution of ever more subtle methods of deception should favour the evolution and ever more incisive methods of detection until this spiralling evolutionary arms race reaches a point of equilibrium. Communicative psychoanalytic theory demonstrates that natural selection has fashioned a subtle mechanism for the detection of exploitation and deceit, thus corroborating and extending Trivers' hypothesis (Smith, 1998; 1999).

Communicative psychoanalytic theory claims that there are two fundamental modes of communication and thinking, the narrative and non-narrative modes. This hypothesis has received support from the work of a number of investigators (Bruner, 1986; Bucci, 1997; Paivio, 1986). Donald (1991), a paleopsychologist, describes the narrative mode as perhaps the most ancient and fundamental mode of verbal communication. Communicative psychoanalysis has the potential to enrich the work of these investigations by throwing light on the unconscious function of the narrative mode.

While Robert Langs was extending and refining his groundbreaking ideas on unconscious communication in psychoanalysis, a cognitive psychologist named Robert Haskell was independently reaching some very similar conclusions about the nature of non-conscious metaphoric communication. Taking his data primarily from small group meetings, Haskell developed sophisticated empirical methods for demonstrating how narrative themes map onto emotionally significant events in the here-and-now (Haskell, 1987a, 1987b, 1987c, 1988, 1989a, 1989b, 1990, 1991). Haskell (1999) has acknowledged the close relationship between Langs' findings and his own work on what he calls 'sub-literal' communication.

The investigation of the implications of these new developments must be reserved for a future volume, as must the examination of more recent contributions to the communicative corpus. The present book must remain a practical and theoretical introduction to what is perhaps the most radical, disturbing and neglected approach to contemporary psychoanalysis.

Contents

Foreword

Robert Langs, MD

This is for me a most auspicious occasion. For many years now I have waited for a follower of the communicative approach to step forward and speak out, to aid me in carrying the burden of developing a convincing literature from our vantage point. And here at last David Smith has had the courage and wisdom to do just that, and to take the approach and his readers into places — historical, philosophical, and clinical — where none of us have likely visited before. While this itself is a marvellous contribution to the psychoanalytic and psychotherapeutic literatures (if such a distinction can any longer be maintained), David has accomplished far more. In bringing a direct and forthright challenge to current psychoanalytic ideas and practice, he has given all of us — orthodox and free thinkers alike — a rare opportunity to question our beliefs and convictions, and to take a candid second look. Informed self-reflection is a nearly lost mode of thought in today's world of rigid thinking and action, yet here David insists that we think and frankly reconsider the entire purview of the psychoanalytic perspective in the hope of making us better theoreticians and clinicians. This is a stunning achievement, founded as it is in the history of Freud's writings and the psychoanalytic movement, and extended into the work of contemporary practitioners. And I, for one, am especially impressed with the manner in which communicative clinical precepts emerge as the logical and compelling resolution to many of the clinical dilemmas and misconceptions that David tries to resolve. Rare is the book so well informed in so many directions, and even more rare is the book that can truly make a difference in how a reader thinks and works. But this is the achievement of *Hidden Conversations*; it will be well to read it slowly, contemplate long its diverse ideas, and allow it to move you forward with its originality and practicality.

Acknowledgements

I owe a great debt of gratitude to my wife, Emmy van Deurzen-Smith, without whose faith, encouragement, and unshakeable support this book would never have been conceived, let alone brought to completion. Her intellectual and spiritual influence pervades these pages.

I would also like to thank Robert Langs for his tireless reading and annotation of draft chapters, and his innumerable helpful comments and criticisms.

Setting out to write one's first book is a daunting prospect. I owe thanks to Giovanni Trombi for his moral support and enthusiastic reception of my first tentative efforts.

Without the cooperation of my students and supervisees who have courageously shared their clinical work with me, I would never have had the opportunity to test the communicative theory against uncontaminated data. They have also kept me on my toes; forcing me to think and rethink my position on a number of vital issues. I would like to specifically thank Sonia Appleby, Tamar Avgar, Fatos Erguven, Gigi Gatti, Carol Holmes, Linda Martin, Lucia Moja, Renate Ogilvie, Elizabeth Sani, Freddie Strasser, and Derrek Williamson. Very special thanks are due to Dr Arthur Jonathan and Alessandra Lemma.

I cannot finish without thanking Anna David for photocopying draft chapters and correcting my German spellings. I must also thank Jinny Gray for helping me combat writer's fatigue with a constant supply of strong coffee and gallows humor.

Last but not least, I would like to thank Edwina Welham, my editor, for the real support she gave to the writing of this book. She made it possible for me to say what I wished to say directly and without compromise.

Introduction

'Begin at the beginning,' the King said gravely, 'and go on till you come to the end: then stop.'

Lewis Carroll

It was Victor Calef, a San Francisco psychoanalyst, who started me on the journey that has led to the writing of this book. In 1979 I was working as a psychotherapist of a broadly Freudian persuasion. Whilst thumbing through the *Journal of the American Psychoanalytic Association* in a London Library, my eyes settled upon a review that Calef had written of Robert Langs's *The Bipersonal Field* which struck me as quite the most vitriolic review that I had ever come across in that normally staid publication.

Several weeks later I found myself in Dillon's University Bookshop opening a heavy tome by Langs entitled *The Listening Process*, fully prepared to sneer derisively at its contents. I was quite taken aback by what I found: this was like no other book on psychoanalysis that I had ever read. After some hesitation I purchased the volume, took it home, and read it compulsively from cover to cover. Over the next few years I caught up with Langs's earlier work and kept up with the new publications which were flowing from his typewriter with bewildering rapidity. I experimented with Langs's approach to psychotherapy and found that it *worked*. My enthusiasm waxed to near fanaticism, as family and colleagues kept a watchful eye on my psychological equilibrium.

In 1983 I wrote to Langs, enquiring about others in Europe who were using the *communicative approach* to psychoanalysis that he had developed. I was surprised to learn that there were very few people in the field of psychoanalysis who found Langs's work worth their while. In London there was only one other person, Dr Maureen Gledhill, who was using the approach. In Italy there were two active proponents of the approach, Giovanni Trombi and Dr Maria Gina Meacci, who had gathered a small following. The communicatively orientated Society for Psychoanalytic Psychotherapy, which consisted almost entirely of Americans, numbered only about 200 members.

Langs's work was being given the cold shoulder, and I wanted to understand why. I did not expect everyone to *agree* with the theory or practice the technique. Although I had reached the conclusion that the future of psychoanalysis as an applied science lay in the hands of communicative analysts, I did not assume that others would or should regard it in the same way. However, I was puzzled by the fact that, with very few exceptions, the issues Langs had raised were not being debated in the literature.

It seemed to me that the problem lay mainly in the defensive needs of the psychoanalytic community and, to a lesser extent, in the way that Langs had presented his discoveries.

There can be no doubt that communicative psychoanalysis is almost invariably experienced by therapists and analysts as deeply threatening. As far as I can see, there are two reasons for this. The first is intellectual. If Cioffi (1975) is right (and I think he is) in asserting that psychoanalysts consistently attempt to evade the challenge of falsification, then any vigorous rival paradigm that actually welcomes scientific scrutiny must, I think, necessarily be experienced as intensely persecutory. To lock horns with such a rival can be dangerous, as fatal wounds may be incurred. Far better to turn away and deny the very existence of the new theory. Second, on the more personal level, psychoanalysts are taught to believe that they are considerably more 'healthy' than their patients. There is tremendous pressure – both psychological and institutional – to fall in with this way of thinking. Psychoanalysts are, on the whole, blind to their own madness and embrace an elaborate system of theories and technical principles which serve to keep self-awareness at bay. To point out the intellectual and spiritual nakedness of a profession which has always prided itself on its integrity and moral superiority is bound to arouse terror and anguish among its proponents. To admit to such reactions, however, would amount to implicitly concurring with the communicative diagnosis. It seems that Kraus's well-known epigram that psychoanalysis is itself the disease for which it pretends to be the cure is more profoundly true than even its author realized.

Given these considerations, it is hard to see how psychoanalysts *en masse* could have responded in any way other than they in fact have done to the communicative approach.

During the earliest phase of Langs's career as a psychoanalytic theorist he presented his innovative theories as addenda to classical Freudian analysis. In spite of this modest approach, many of Langs's erstwhile colleagues responded with irrational vehemence. This led to a second phase of Langs's writing, during the early 1980s, which was highly polemical. Langs's embattled stance during this period led him to express his ideas in a way which offended the sensibilities of many of his readers. After 1985 Langs's writing became less polemical as he began to develop his approach as an entity entirely distinct from conventional psychoanalysis and started to immerse himself in empirical research into the psychotherapeutic interaction. What I take to be a difficulty in Langs's presentation of his ideas during the 'middle' period mentioned above could readily be used as a pretext for rejecting their very core and essence.

Between 1980 and 1986 Langs distinguished in his writings between 'Truth Therapy' and 'Lie Therapy'. Truth Therapy was limited to communicative therapy, properly executed, while Lie Therapy denoted all other approaches. As the word 'lie' suggests a deliberate, if not necessarily conscious, *evasion* of the truth, the concept of 'Lie Therapy' presupposes that non-communicative practitioners deliberately seal over truths which would be evident to them if they refrained from this mendacious behavior. Implicitly, this turns ignorance into a moral failing and produces what Popper (1963) has called the 'conspiracy theory of falsehood': the view that truth is obvious unless actively covered over. According to this view ignorance can only prevail when people conspire – in defense of some vested interest – to conceal truth. Of course, the truth or falsehood of propositions about the human mind are rarely self-evident. The truth does not lie around waiting to be picked up. We have to *work* at the truth, evaluating competing hypotheses against objective evidence and discarding those that do not stand up to the test.

From this perspective a Lie Therapist would be one who is in bad faith, who comes to the rational conclusion that belief in a theory is warranted by the evidence but who deliberately chooses to ignore this conclusion. Another form of intellectual dishonesty – a form of Lie Therapy if you will – is expressed in the refusal to even consider the relative virtues of rival theories in an objective fashion. Such a person then clings dogmatically to a point of view which he or she makes no effort to question. Thus, the mere fact that a person advocates a certain *type* of therapy does not automatically mark them out as a Lie or a Truth Therapist. The crucial variable is one's readiness to bring beliefs before the higher court of evidence.

I think that in impugning people's beliefs, rather than their attitudes toward the *evaluation* of their beliefs, Langs did his own work a disservice and opened himself to the unjustified charge of dogmatism.

The present volume, then, is an effort to present a broadly based introduction to the communicative approach to a wide audience. It includes a critique of some of the most central concepts of what I call, after Kuhn, 'normal psychoanalysis' (see Chapter 5, note 5). Although I have sincerely made every effort to be fair to my theoretical adversaries I have at times expressed myself rather forcefully, and I fear that some may find this forthrightness offensive. Science thrives on criticism and diversity of opinion, so I invite those who take issue with me to respond.

In the first part of the book, comprising the first four chapters, I lay the groundwork for the introduction of Langs's work through demonstrating the scientific poverty of fundamental psychoanalytic concepts.

In Chapter 1, I discuss Freud's 'seduction theory' and its abandonment. I argue, *contra* critics like Masson (1984) and Krüll (1986), that Freud was entirely justified in discarding this dubious conjecture but also argue, this time against the Freudians, that the fantasy-based theory with which Freud eventually replaced it, and which became a cornerstone of psychoanalytic theory, is also deeply problematic. In the years between the abandonment of the seduction theory and the entrenchment of the fantasy theory, Freud advanced a third theory which he called the theory of 'screen memories'. In later psychoanalytic writings Freud used the term 'screen memories' to denote those memories from childhood which cover over repressed infantile memories. Between 1897 and 1899, however, Freud used the term to designate those memories from childhood which serve as symbolic expressions of unconsciously perceived here-and-now issues. I show that Freud avoided applying this theory to his clincial data (he apparently confined its use to his own self-analysis), probably because it would have led him to the conclusion that his patients unconsciously and justifiably perceived him as sexually abusing and assaulting them. Had Freud persisted in his investigation of screen memories instead of taking refuge in the hypothesis of unconscious phantasy, he would have discovered the central insight of communicative psychoanalysis.

Freud's decision to base psychoanalysis on the concept of phantasy has had important practical ramifications. One of these has been establishment and entrenchment of the theory of transference, which states that patients' attitudes towards their analysts are primarily based on childish phantasies. According to this view, the analyst is always viewed through a haze of illusion stemming from patients' repressed emotional life. In Chapter 2 I take a long critical look at the concept of transference and conclude that it is deeply and probably irreparably incoherent. I follow this with a potted history of the concept of countertransference, which I conclude has been used in a highly defensive way by the psychoanalytic profession. (My style of argumentation in this chapter was inspired by the incomparable Daniel Dennett. It is, alas, only a pallid imitation of Dennett's tremendous verve, wit, and intellectual agility.)

In the screen-memory theory, Freud implicitly proposed that the concept of unconscious perception is a viable alternative to the notion of unconscious phantasy. Chapter 3 traces the history of the theory of unconscious perception in Freud's later work. I cite experimental support for the concept of unconscious perception and show how this theory can provide a satisfactory rejoinder to Sartre's critique of Freud's model of the mind in *Being and Nothingness*. The chapter concludes with a reconsideration of a published clinical presentation by M. Masud Khan in light of the theory of unconscious perception.

Chapter 4 presents the ideas of those analysts coming after Freud but before Langs who have explored the clinical significance of unconscious perception. As well as summarizing the contributions made by Little, Klein and the post-Kleinians, Balint, and Searles I also discuss aspects of the work of Sandor Ferenczi and R.D. Laing which form part of this psychoanalytic tradition.

The second part of the book, containing Chapters 5 through 10, describes the communicative approach to psychoanalysis and traces out some of its theoretical, therapeutic, and philosophical implications.

Chapter 5 introduces Langs's work, giving a summary of how the communicative approach has developed and how the psychoanalytic Establishment has responded to it.

Chapter 6 describes the communicative theory of the mind and human communication. This is brought to life by means of a reinterpretation of a published transcript of a psychoanalytic session with a psychotic adolescent boy, which shows just how radical a difference communicative theory makes to the understanding of the psychotherapeutic process.

Chapter 7 gives an account of Langs's theory of the 'frame' or psychotherapeutic environment. I trace out the history of this concept from Freud, through Milner and Winnicott, to the present day and give clincial examples of departures from the secure frame and their consequences for the patient.

Chapter 8 describes how communicative theory forms the basis for a constructive psychotherapeutic technique, and contains a full account of the principles for formulating unconscious meaning, intervening, and evaluating one's interventions. This is illustrated with numerous clinical examples.

Chapter 9 consists of two practically verbatim accounts of communicative psychoanalytic sessions with a running commentary on the unconscious dimensions of these interactions.

Finally, Chapter 10 tackles the thorny issue of the scientific status of psychoanalysis. Summarizing the seminal arguments of Nagel, Popper, Cioffi, and Grünbaum which cast grave doubt upon the scientific claims made on behalf of psychoanalysis, I go on to show how the communicative approach is able to conform to stringent post-Popperian standards of scientificity and can, therefore, open itself to objective scientific scrutiny.

Throughout the text the terms 'psychoanalysis' and 'psychotherapy' will be used synonymously unless the context shows that a clear differentiation between the two is being made.

Part I

The psychoanalytic background

1 Seduction

*Science does not rest upon solid bedrock. The bold structure of its
theories rises, as it were, above a swamp.*

Popper

Although the communicative approach is a relatively recent development within psychoanalysis, important stands of communicative
theory were prefigured in some of Freud's earliest work on unconscious mental processes. This aspect of Freud's early work is not
widely known. It was not incorporated into Freud's later psychoanalytic theorizing. Indeed, there is no reference to this aspect of his
work in any of Freud's accounts of the origins of psychoanalysis in
spite of the fact that it played a major role in his self-analysis and
played an important role in Freud's thinking during the late 1890s.

Between the years 1896 and 1899 Freud wrestled with fundamental
theoretical issues which were to determine the substance and subsequent course of development of classical psychoanalysis and its off-
shoots. After his initial collaboration with Breuer, Freud had gone on
to advance, in 1896, his highly unpopular seduction theory of psychoneurosis. This theory stated that hysterical symptoms were caused by
unconscious memories of childhood sexual traumas – 'seductions' by
adults or older children. Little more than a year later, in September
1897, Freud began seriously to question the validity of this proposition, and during the closing years of the nineteenth century he
gradually came to replace the seduction theory with the idea that
hysterical symptoms were caused by repressed infantile sexual
phantasies rather than memories of real experiences. The theory based
on the purported causal role of wishful infantile phantasies became a
cornerstone of psychoanalytic theory.

What has gone unnoticed, largely because Freud himself expunged
it from the record, is the fact that between 1897 and 1899 Freud

advanced a third theory of the nature of unconscious mental contents and their impact upon neurotic behavior. Instead of stressing the importance of *past* events – whether memories or phantasies – this theory gave primary importance to the unconscious perception of *here-and-now* emotional realities. In advancing this theory Freud came within a hair's breadth of formulating the communicative approach to psychoanalysis which Robert Langs developed over eighty years later.

I believe that Freud's decision to abandon this theory in favor of a theory based on hypothetical infantile phantasies has had many important ramifications and has led psychoanalysis down a false, scientifically sterile path. In the present chapter I will support this contention by reconsidering the transformations undergone by psychoanalytic theory during the late 1890s.

In recent years there has been considerable controversy surrounding Freud's abandonment of the seduction theory. Several authors (Blamary 1978; Levinson 1981; Masson 1984; Krüll 1986; Miller 1986) have contested Freud's verdict, some even going as far as to describe Freud's theoretical reorientation as caused by a 'failure of nerve' in the face of social dissapproval. In common with these writers I will find much to criticize in Freud's adoption of the phantasy theory. Instead of criticizing him for exchanging a disturbing truth for a comforting falsehood, however, I will argue that Freud traded one falsehood for another at the very point in his scientific career when he could most easily have entertained a fruitful alternative to both. Freud's decision was a fateful one and, as I will show in subsequent chapters, it cast a long shadow over the future development of psychoanalysis.

THE RECEIVED VIEW

Some of the most penetrating scholarly work on this period of Freud's development has been undertaken by Schimek,[1] whose findings are reported in a paper entitled 'Fact and fantasy in the seduction theory: a historical review' (Schimek 1985). Most scholars interested in this phase of Freud's career have relied on one or another of Freud's later, retrospective accounts of his theoretical transition. There are six such retrospective accounts in Freud's writings (Freud 1905a, 1906, 1914b, 1917c, 1925, 1933) Schimek shows not only that these six accounts differ from one another in important respects, but that they collectively bear only a tenuous relationship to the facts reported in Freud's original papers on the seduction theory published in 1896 and emerging in his contemporaneous correspondence with his friend and confidente Wilhelm Fliess.

Let us examine the bones of the seduction theory while leaving aside for the moment the issues of evidential support and scientific methodology. The seduction theory was advanced in three papers published during the spring of 1896: 'Heredity and the aetiology of the neurosis' (Freud 1896a), 'Further remarks on the neuro-psychoses of defence' (Freud 1896b), and 'The aetiology of hysteria' (Freud 1896c). Freud set out in these papers the thesis that hysteria, obsessional neurosis, and paranoia were caused by the repression of traumatic memories of childhood sexual experiences. Freud believed that the 'seduction' – at the hands of an adult or older child – must occur prior to the age of eight or ten to produce a neurotic outcome (Freud 1896a). The main seducers are given as nursemaids, domestic servants, governesses, and other children (usually brothers) (Freud 1896b). Freud also included brutal sexual assault by strangers as a neurotic pathogen (Freud 1896c). Although he is now notorious for having implicated fathers in scenes of infantile seduction, fathers are not in fact mentioned in any of the 1896 papers. The father as seducer appears only in Freud's correspondence with Fliess and only after December 1896. There are only three clincial vignettes in the entire Freud–Fliess correspondence featuring fathers in this role.

Freud describes hysteria as stemming from a 'pre-sexual sexual shock' passively endured prior to the age of five, believing that during this 'first period of childhood . . . the mnemic residues are not translated into verbal images' (Freud 1887–1904: 230) – hence the 'body language' of conversion symptoms. He argues that obsessional neurosis is caused by the repressed memory of an infantile sexual experience in which the child actively participated (Freud believed that for a child to participate actively in a seduction, he or she had to have previously endured a seduction passively – a seduction which precociously awakened sexual impulses in the child). In order for these experiences to serve as pathogenic agents, Freud had to find a way to bridge the temporal gap between the original sexual trauma and the outbreak of neurotic symptoms typically occurring only years later in early adulthood. For Freud the original seduction has relatively little effect at the time, but its 'psychical trace' (memory) is retained. Later, at puberty, the onset of sexual maturity awakens the memory from its dormant state.

Thanks to the change due to puberty, the memory will display a power which was completely lacking from the event itself. *The*

memory will operate as though it were a contemporary event. What happens is, as it were, *a posthumous action by a sexual trauma.*
(Freud 1896a: 154)

The reinforcement of the memory at puberty is described as a necessary but not a sufficient cause for the eruption of neurotic symptoms. The pathogenic memory thus activated must remain *unconscious* in order to produce a pathological effect. The symptoms of neurotic illness are substitutes for memories of infantile traumas. 'Their traces', Freud remarks, 'are never present in concious memory, only in the symptoms of the illness' (Freud 1896b: 166). The therapeutic strategy that Freud adopted, then, was to try to raise the repressed memories into consciousness: 'With our patients those memories are never conscious; but we cure them of their hysteria by transforming their unconscious memories into conscious ones' (Freud 1896c: 211).

Freud began seriously to question the validity of the seduction theory in September 1897 (Freud 1897–1904: 264) and gradually abandoned it over the following few years, not making a public retraction until the publication of the 'Three essays on the theory of sexuality' (Freud 1905a) and more decisively in 'My views on the part played by sexuality in the aetiology of the neuroses' (Freud 1906). In the latter paper Freud presented his reasons for abandoning the seduction theory in considerable detail and, for the first time, described the infantile scenes of seduction as products of his patients' imaginations: '. . . I was unable to distinguish with certainty between falsifications made by hysterics in their memories of their childhood and traces of real events' (Freud 1906: 274).

As Schimek (1985) points out, Freud embellished this account in his paper 'On the history of the psycho-analytic movement' (Freud 1914b), adding that his patients themselves 'ascribed their symptoms to passive sexual experiences in the first years of childhood' (p. 17) and goes on to remark that: 'If hysterical subjects traced back their symptoms to traumas that are fictitious, then the new fact which emerges is precisely that they create such scenes in *fantasy*' (ibid.).

By 1914, therefore, Freud was stating that his patients themselves attributed their symptoms to infantile seductions.[2] In the 'Introductory lectures on psycho-analysis' (1917c) Freud adds that girls regularly blame their fathers for seducing them in infancy. It is not until the publication of 'An autobiographical study' in 1925 that Freud proclaimed that the fantasies of seduction are imaginary fulfillments of incestuous wishes. Once again he presents his patients as leading him astray with their stories of seduction.

The majority of my patients reproduced from their childhood scenes in which they were sexually seduced by some grown-up person. With female patients the part of the seducer was almost always assigned to their father. I believed these stories, and consequently supposed that I had discovered the roots of the subsequent neurosis. . . . If the reader feels inclined to shake his head at my credulity, I cannot altogether blame him.

(Freud 1925: 34)

Eight years later, in the 'New introductory lectures on psychoanalysis' Freud made his final statement on the subject, which is generally treated as the definitive account: 'Almost all my women patients told me that they had been seduced by their father. I was driven to recognize in the end that these reports were untrue' (Freud 1933: 120).

To summarize, therefore, in the years following his repudiation of the seduction theory Freud stated and reiterated the view that his patients had presented fallacious memories of infantile sexual abuse to him, had attributed their neurotic symptoms to the experiences of abuse, and that he had wrongly given credence to these phantasies and their purported etiological significance. We can now go on to investigate to what extent this rendition of the events is consistent with the accounts presented in the most fundamental sources: the three papers of 1896 and Freud's letters to Fliess.

UNCONSCIOUS MEMORIES

As we have seen, Freud believed that traumatic memories had to be *unconscious* in order to act as neurotic pathogens. In all of the 1896 papers the crucial traumatic memories supposedly responsible for neurotic symptoms are explicitly described as being unconscious, as being walled off from conscious awareness by an 'enormous resistance' (Freud 1896a: 153). Freud believed that if such memories are retained *consciously* they cannot eventuate in neurotic symptoms. Arguing with an imaginary critic who objects to the seduction theory on the grounds that many normal adults recall experiences of infantile seduction, Freud counters by saying:

This objection has no weight. . . . According to our understanding of the neurosis, people of this kind *ought* not to be hysterical at all, or at any rate, not hysterical as a result of the scenes which they consciously remember. With our patients, those memories are never conscious. . . . From this you will perceive that the matter is not merely one of the existence of the sexual experiences, but that a psychological precondition enters in as well. The scenes must be present as *unconscious memories*; only so long as, and in so far as, they are unconscious are they able to create and maintain hysterical symptoms.

(Freud 1896c: 211)

In treatment these recollections emerge in piecemeal fashion in response to therapeutic intervention: 'patients never repeat these stories spontaneously, nor do they ever in the course of treatment suddenly present the physician with the complete recollection of a scene of this kind' (Freud 1896a: 153).

In fact, as Freud makes clear, the scenes of seduction can only be discovered in an indirect, inferential manner, like an unknown language which must be 'decyphered and translated' in order to yield 'undreamed of information' (Freud 1896c: 192). This reveals the first of several important misrepresentations of the facts found in Freud's later accounts of the seduction theory. Freud's patients never *told* him that they had been abused as children. He *inferred* the existence of purely unconscious memories of seduction.

The most important methodological question presenting itself at this juncture is this: On what basis did Freud infer the existence of unconscious memories of seduction? Freud is not very explicit about this point. He tells us that the scenes were 'reproduced' by his patients in treatment. Of what did these reproductions consist? We know from remarks already quoted that they did not involve direct, conscious verbal reports of memories. The techical use of the term 'reproduction' was already established in Freud's writings by 1896. In Breuer and Freud's 'Studies on hysteria' published a year earlier, Breuer describes reproductions as 'mnemic symbols' of earlier traumatic experiences (Freud and Breuer 1895), to which Freud harks back, in the third of the 1896 papers. 'Symbols', in the Freud–Breuer sense, are mental representations or acts which serve as substitutes for the expression of unconscious ideas. Thus, Freud's 'reproductions' are proxies for the unconscious scenes of seduction. In Freud's most explicit passage about the reproduction of repressed scenes he states that his patients 'suffer under the most violent sensations, of which they are ashamed and which they try to hide' (Freud 1896c: 204). After winnowing all of the available evidence Schimek (1985) concludes that the reproductions involved 'visual scenes, often of hallucinatory intensity, accompanied with strong display of affect, physical sensations and motoric gestures' (943).

Freud makes a point of emphasizing in each of the 1896 papers that his patients did not experience these events as memories ('they have no feeling of remembering the scenes' – Freud 1896c: 204). It was Freud, then, and not his patients, who connected the scenes with hypothetical unconscious memories of sexual abuse. Freud's later statements to the effect that his patients told him that they remembered having been seduced as children are flatly contradicted by the evidence. Far from being the case of a naive researcher credulously believing the stories of seduction offered up to him by his patients,

> Freud's conclusion that hysteria always requires the occurrence of sexual abuse in early childhood was not based directly on patients' reports and conscious memories, but involved a great deal of selective interpretation and reconstruction. The reconstructions presupposed a complex set of hypotheses and assumptions and were based on a wide variety of not clearly specified data.
>
> (Schimek 1985: 138)

The manner in which Freud elicited reproductions from his patients further undermines the plausibility of the seduction hypothesis. During this period of his career Freud deployed what he called the method of 'pressing and insisting'. Placing his hand on a patient's forehead, he would apply physical pressure and admonish her to produce the required memories. Freud regarded this incessant pressure as necessary for provoking the reproductions: 'One only succeeds in awakening the psychical trace of a precocious sexual event under the most energetic pressure of the analytic procedure, and against an enormous resistance' (Freud 1896a: 153).

Freud emphasized that his patients yielded to his interventions only reluctantly. It was only under 'the strongest compulsion of the treatment' (Freud 1896c: 204) that his patients could be induced to reproduce the scenes. He also made it clear, to both his readers and his patients, that only certain types of reproduction were acceptable: 'If the first discovered scene is unsatisfactory, we tell our patient that this experience explains nothing, but that behind it, there must be a more significant, earlier experience' (Freud 1896c: 195–6).

If his earlier writings are anything to go by, Freud would not allow his patients to move away from topics which he felt possessed a hidden sexual significance, and would consistently lead them back 'in spite of all their protestations' to the infantile scenes (Freud 1894: 57). He could even resort to threats when patients 'resisted' his interpretations of their material in terms of childhood sexual abuse. One such instance is described in a letter to Fliess.

When I thrust the explanation [that she had been seduced] before her, she was at first won over, then she committed the folly of questioning the old man [her alleged seducer] himself, who at the very first intimation exclaimed indignantly 'are you implying that I was the one?' and swore a holy oath to his innocence.

She is now in the throes of the most vehement resistance, claims to believe him. . . . I have threatened to send her away and in the process convinced myself that she has already gained a good deal of certainty which she is reluctant to acknowledge.

(Freud 1887–1904: 220–1)

A letter to Fliess shows that as early as November 1895, Freud had unacknowledged doubts about the validity of the seduction theory which he publicly advanced with such bravado. 'Today', Freud wrote, '. . . one of the cases gave me what I expected . . . and . . . strengthened my confidence in the validity of my psychological constructions' (ibid.: 149). Freud's longing for confirmation ('gave me what I expected') is coupled with a reference to wavering confidence and an admission of the highly conjectural nature of his hypotheses ('constructions'). This uncertainty was certainly warranted, for nowhere in the 1896 papers or the correspondence with Fliess does Freud present evidence consistent with his own scientific canons which supports the seduction hypothesis! In order to substantiate this theory scientifically Freud would first have had to establish that the events described as 'reproductions' that were enacted in his consulting room were, in fact, disguised and symbolized memories of repressed memories of sexual abuse. Second, Freud would have had to establish that the said unconscious memories were causally necessary for the emergence of psychoneurotic symptoms. Freud, I will argue, was unable to accomplish the first task, much less the second.

In 'Heredity and the aetiology of the neuroses' (1896a) – the first of the three 1896 papers – Freud simply presents his theory with no attempt to provide evidential justification. The second paper, 'Further remarks on the neuropsychoses of defense' (Freud 1896b), gives a fairly extended account of a case of chronic paranoia in an attempt to show that this disorder shares the same specific etiology as hysteria and obsessional neurosis. The patient, Frau. P, experienced delusions of persecution, visual hallucinations of naked bodies, and heard voices which described her actions, threatened and reproached her. In response to Freud's questions, she reported memories of her brother and herself showing themselves naked to one another prior to bed.

Freud conjectured that Frau. P had had an incestuous relationship
with her brother during infancy and reports that he:

> . . . succeeded in getting her to reproduce the various scenes in
> which her sexual relationship with her brother (which had certainly
> lasted at least from her sixth to her tenth year) had culminated. . . .
> After we had gone through this series of scenes, the hallucinatory
> sensations and images had disappeared, and (up to the present, at
> any rate) they have not returned.
>
> (Freud 1896b: 180)

Impressive as this vignette seems at first glance, it is actually of no
evidential value. It should be noted that Freud first conjectured the
seduction and then applied his highly pressured interventionist
approach to compel Frau. P to 'reproduce' them. Freud is silent about
just what the reproductions consisted of, so it is impossible to assess
the plausibility of this interpretation of them. The reported therapeutic success, which might have lent credibility to the theory, was
undermined by a footnote which Freud added to the paper in 1922 in
which Freud admits that he had written up this case while his patient
was still in treatment:

> Very shortly after, her condition became so much more serious that
> the treatment had to be broken off. She was transferred to an insti-
> tution and there went through a period of severe hallucinations and
> had all the signs of dementia praecox [i.e. schizophrenia].
>
> (Freud 1896b: 180–1)

According to Freud's own principles the reproduction and
conscious assimilation of scenes of infantile seduction should have
made it *impossible* for this patient to remain ill (much less decompen-
sate). By these canons the ultimate failure of the treatment of Frau. P
must count *against* the validity of the seduction theory as applied to
this case.

In the third 1896 paper, 'The aetiology of hysteria', Freud responds
to some obvious criticisms of the seduction theory. After remarking
that patients do not experience the reproduced scenes as memories of
childhood events and that they therefore withold belief from his
constructions, Freud rather perversely assures the reader that the
repudiation of his interpretations 'seems to provide conclusive proof'
(204) of the seduction theory on the grounds of 'Methinks the lady
doth protest too much'!

Freud next attempts to counter the charge of suggestion.[3] An examination of Freud's accounts of his method shows the plausibility of

this accusation. We have already seen how Freud used 'the strongest compulsion of the treatment' to induce his patients to reproduce the scenes, how he dismissed those reproductions which did not fit his requirements, and how he punished patients who did not believe in his reconstructions. Freud also reports that he would regularly *warn* his patients beforehand that the required scenes would emerge in treatment (Freud 1896c). On occasion he asserted to his patients that they *must* have been seduced in infancy purely on the basis of his belief in his own theory. In a letter to Fliess dated 2 May 1897, for example, Freud writes of a hysterical patient who retained conscious memories of experiences of sexual abuse dating from late childhood. Freud told her that 'similar and worse things must have happened in her earliest childhood, and she could not find it incredible' (Freud 1887–1904: 238). In 'The aetiology of hysteria' Freud writes, in defense of his methods, that he 'never yet succeeded in forcing on a patient a scene I was expecting to find, in such a way that he seemed to be living through it' (1896c: 205). As this amounts to an admission by Freud that he attempted to steer his patients toward the expected findings, it supports the very criticism that Freud is anxious to neutralize.

Freud next goes on to specify some points in favor of the reality of the reproductions. He mentions 'the uniformity which they exhibit in certain details' and the description by patients of certain events which they regarded as 'harmless' because they did not understand their real significance (1896c: 205). Any probative value that these points could conceivably possess is vitiated by the total lack of supporting data.

Freud then presses on to 'another and stronger proof' (ibid.). This proof amounts to an argument equating truth with coherence:

> It is exactly like putting together a child's picture-puzzle: after many attempts, we became absolutely certain in the end which piece belongs in the empty gap. . . . In the same way, the contents of the infantile scenes turn out to be indispensible supplements to the associative and logical framework of the neurosis.
>
> (ibid.)

Once again no clinical data is provided for the reader's scrutiny. Freud argues from a personal sense of conviction rooted in the intellectual satisfaction provided by the seduction theory. The seduction theory offers a sense of coherence, of 'fit', but although coherence is a precondition of truth it does not vouchsafe it. In the absense of detailed clinical data the reader is in a position neither to confirm nor to contest Freud's conclusion.

Finally, Freud moves on to the 'really unassailable' proof: independent conformation. He provides what he takes to be two examples of this, stating that these are the *only* two instances of independent confirmation that he had encountered in a total sample of eighteen cases. Clearly, these two cases must be strong enough to support the entire weight of the seduction theory. In the first example, the brother of one of Freud's patients confirmed to him that he had indeed had a sexual relationship with his sister. However, Freud notes that the brother confirmed specific scenes dating only from later childhood which, according to the theory, can have no bearing on the patient's hysteria. Freud states that the brother confirmed that there had been earlier sexual scenes but that the lack of detailed information made it impossible to link these with the reproductions that occurred in therapy. At the most, then, this example might support the contention that at least some reproductions could support accurate inferences about real events. Given that there is no data presented, though, the reader must take this on faith. The second instance involved two of Freud's patients whom Freud believed had had sexual relations simultaneously with the same man during their childhood, and who shared an identical symptom based on their common traumatic experiences. Again, no data are provided. One would need to know how it was that Freud reached his conclusions in order to even begin to assess his claim.

As scientific support for the seduction theory the evidence marshaled in 'The aetiology of hysteria' is very weak. If we turn now to the other collection of contemporary documents dealing with the seduction theory, Freud's letters to Fliess, we find that nothing of real probative value appears here either. On 22 December 1897, for example, he writes to Fliess that a hysterical patient reported to him that she observed her mother having a hysterical fit, from which Freud reconstructs that the mother had been anally raped as a child, and offers this up as possessing evidential value! (Freud 1887–1904: 288–9). On 28 April 1897 he reports on a patient who possessed a *conscious* memory of sexual abuse dating from age ten or twelve. Freud informed her that similar and worse things must have happened in her earlier years, which she evidently took on faith (238). On 3 January 1897 he describes how he had 'won a patient over' to the seduction hypothesis only to see her change her mind when the alleged seducer denied the accusation (220–1). In the same letter Freud presents what appears to be a third instance of independent confirmation. A patient had traveled to his own home town 'in order to ascertain the reality of the things he remembered . . . he received full confirmation from the seducer' (219). Unfortunately, as we read further we find that this turns out to be a third-hand anecdote related to Freud by a Mrs F who had heard it from a professor Sulz (or Petz – Freud wasn't sure) who had possibly heard it from the former patient himself. Even the well-known case of Katherina published in *Studies on Hysteria* does not fulfill Freud's theoretical requirements. Katherina, a young woman whom Freud met while hiking in the mountains, suffered from hysterical symptoms. In a one-off session Freud uncovered a sexual trauma which he claimed to be of pathogenic importance. However, Katherina's was a *conscious* memory of a seduction which occurred at the age of *fourteen*, violating the specifications set out in the seduction theory on two counts. Furthermore, the memory was not 'reproduced' in Freud's special sense of the word: it was directly reported. Freud needed to infer the causal significance of the seduction but not, as the theory required, the existence of the event itself.

Freud first expressed disbelief in the seduction theory in a now famous letter to Fliess dated 21 September 1897. Public retraction of the theory was deferred for seven years. The reasons that Freud gives for his loss of faith in the theory are much more frank and explicit than those offered to the public in his 'official' retraction in a paper on the etiology of hysteria published in 1906 (Freud 1906). Freud lists eight reasons for rejecting the seduction theory. The first four are on therapeutic grounds: he mentions that he had never been able to bring any analysis to a real conclusion and notes that patients who for a period of time had been most 'gripped' by analysis ended up 'running away', lamenting that the complete therapeutic successes that he had counted on never materialized and adding that there were plausible alternative explanations for those successes which did occur. The next two objections are epidemiological: Freud felt that the incrimination of the father in every case of psychoneurosis was rather unlikely (he had by this time tightened up his original formulation of the theory to stipulate that the future psychoneurotic is invariably seduced by his or her father) and he found it implausible that the sexual abuse of children was as widespread as the theory suggests (as seduction was held to be a necessary but not a sufficient cause of psychoneurosis, the actual incidence of seduction would have to be greater than the incidence of neurosis). Finally, Freud moves on to epistemiological objections to the theory. He mentions that 'there are no indications of reality in the unconscious, so that one cannot distinguish between truth and fiction' (264). All of the preceeding points take on greater credibility and poignancy in light of Freud's final criticism:

. . . the consideration that in the most deep-reaching psychosis the unconscious memory does not break through, so that the secret of childhood experiences is not disclosed even in the most confused delirium. If one thus sees that the unconscious never overcomes the resistance of the conscious, the expectation that in treatment the opposite is bound to happen, to the point that the unconscious is completely tamed by the conscious, also diminishes.

(ibid.: 265)

Freud's exaggerated confidence in the seduction theory had collapsed, and he courageously spelled out the hard truth of why the theory is not scientifically justified. Freud did not reject the notion of unconscious mental contents or the causal significance he had previously attached to them. His letter emphasizes that the hypothetical pathogenic contents that he had imagined to exist unconsciously in his patients were scientifically unwarranted and unvalidated conjectures. Freud's rejection of the theory was a sound scientific move, for as we have seen the seduction theory had precious little evidence to commend it. Those writers who view the retraction of the seduction theory as an act of intellectual cowardice (for example, Masson 1984) cannot have carefully considered what would have counted as evidential support for the seduction theory as Freud conceived it. Freud 'did not suppress clear and unambiguous evidence' (Schimek 1985: 939): he followed his scientific conscience by calling into question an unsupported and highly fanciful theory, in spite of the fact that he was deeply enamoured with it.

Freud equivocated for several years before finally consigning the seduction theory to oblivion. This process may well have been hastened by Leopold Löwenfeld, a psychiatrist who was sympathetically disposed toward Freud's early work and with whom Freud frequently corresponded. A passage from a book published by Löwenfeld in 1899 states that:

By chance, one of the patients on whom Freud used the analytic method came under my observation. The patient told me with certainty that the infantile sexual scene which the analysis had apparently uncovered was pure fantasy and had never really happened to him.

(Löwenfeld 1899: 195)[4]

SCREEN MEMORIES

It is well known that Freud came to regard the 'reproductions' that took place in analysis not as disguised memories of real infantile experiences, but as disguised memories of infantile *phantasies*. It is less well known that during the period when Freud had lost confidence in the seduction theory but had not yet definitely adopted the phantasy theory as a replacement for it, he seriously considered the proposition that infantile memories – and their reproduction in analysis – are actually representations of *contemporary* significance that have been projected back into infancy. The very first reference to this thesis appears in the letter to Fliess dated 21 September 1897. After running through the reasons why he has lost faith in the seduction theory Freud remarks: 'It seems once again arguable that only later experiences give the impetus to phantasies, which [then] hark back to childhood' (Freud 1887–1904: 265).

In a letter of 7 July 1898 Freud approaches the issue in greater detail:

> A new experience is projected back into the past so that the new persons become aligned with the old ones, who become their proto-types. The mirror image of the present is seen in the fantasied past, which then prophetically becomes the present.
>
> (ibid.: 320)

And again on 3 January 1899 we find Freud writing that: 'A small bit of my self-analysis has . . . confirmed that fantasies are products of later periods and are projected back from what was then the present into earliest childhood' (ibid. 338).

This 'small bit of self analysis' was written up in a paper entitled 'Screen memories' (Freud 1899; see also Kris, in Freud 1887–1904). This disguised autobiographical account of the analysis of an early memory was written during the week before Whitsun 1899. Freud describes the subject of his observations as 'a man of university education, aged thirty-eight' (Freud 1899: 309) who recounts a childhood memory of a sloping meadow full of dandelions.

> Three children are playing on the grass. One of them is myself (between the ages of two and three); the two others are my boy cousin, who is a year older than me, and his sister, who is almost exactly the same age as I am. We are picking the yellow flowers and each of us is holding a bunch of flowers we have already picked. The little girl has the best bunch; and, as though by mutual agreement, we – the two boys – fall on her and snatch away her flowers. She runs up the meadow in tears and as a consolation the peasant woman [who was standing outside her cottage] gives her a big piece of black bread. Hardly have we seen this than we throw the flowers

away, hurry to the cottage and ask to be given some bread too. And
we are in fact given some; the peasant woman cuts the loaf with a
long knife. In my memory the bread tastes quite delicious – and at
that point the scene breaks off.

(ibid.: 311)

The man recounting the anecdote is puzzled as to why he remembers
it. He also notes that there is 'something not quite right' about the
scene: the colour yellow is disproportionately prominent and the
pleasant taste of the bread is greatly exaggerated. Freud then asks the
man – who is actually himself – when it was that he first became aware
of this memory. The man then recalls how he first remembered this
scene when, as a youth of seventeen, he revisited the town where he
had lived before the age of four. On that occasion the family with
whom he was lodging had a fifteen-year-old daughter with whom he
fell passionately in love. After a few days' acquaintance the girl went
off to boarding school which brought the lad's longings 'to a really
high pitch'. He began fervently to wish that he had never left his home
town, for then he could already have lived in the girl's presence for
years. When the two of them first met she had been wearing a yellow
dress. The second spontaneous emergence of the memory into consciousness occurred three years later on the occasion of the young
man's visit to an uncle and the two cousins who featured in the scene
with the dandelions. This family had also left the young man's birth-
place, and had become prosperous in a far-distant city (these were, in
fact, Freud's relations living in Manchester, England). The uncle had
conspired with the young man's father to persuade him to abandon
his studies in university for something more practical, to marry his
female cousin and to settle down with her in the city where the uncle
lived.

Freud links the yellow flowers which are reproduced with such
intensity in the memory from childhood with the girl with whom the
man had fallen in love: the girl with the yellow dress. The memory of
the exquisitely delicious country bread, then, could be linked to
thoughts about the pleasure it would have afforded him to marry her.
The theme of throwing away the flowers for the bread seemed linked
as well to the plot to get the young man to give up his studies and settle
down: 'You were to give up your impractical ideals and take on a
"bread and butter" occupation, were you not?' (315).

The content of the memory, Freud argued, was intimately tied to
the context of its recollection. This does not mean that the memory is
ungenuine:

> You [unconsciously] selected it [the memory] from innumerable others of a similar or another kind because, on account of its content (which in itself was indifferent) it was well adapted to represent the two phantasies, which were important enough to you.
>
> (ibid.: 315)[5]

After some theoretical discussion, the man relates the theme of snatching the girl's flowers to his suppressed adolescent desire to deflower her. In complete harmony with his various remarks on this subject in the Fliess correspondence, Freud goes on to say that 'the slipping away of repressed thoughts and wishes into childhood memories' is something that one finds 'invariably happening in hysterical patients' (317). Later he expresses the point with even greater force: 'You have accepted my assertion that *every suppressed phantasy of this kind tends to slip away into a childhood scene* (ibid.: 318, emphasis added). The process of 'slipping away' requires a bridge between the suppressed thoughts and the childhood memory.

> Once a point of contact of this kind has been found – in the present instance it was the deflowering, the taking away of the flowers – the remaining content of the phantasy is remodelled with the help of every legitimate intermediate idea – take the bread as an example – till it can find further points of contact with the childhood scene.
>
> (ibid.: 318)

In other words, Freud hypothesized that this particular memory had been activated by suppressed ideas ('phantasies') which it expressed indirectly and symbolically.[6]

As we have seen, this theory was first mooted by Freud in the letter to Fliess announcing the abandonment of the seduction theory. In the letter, the theory of screen memories is presented as an *alternative* to the seduction theory. As an alternative explanation of the seduction theory data – patients' 'reproductions' in analysis – the screen-memory approach would assert that the strange and disturbing sensations, affects, images, and hallucinations experienced by Freud's patients were disguised expressions of their unconscious perceptions of Freud and his interventions.

We have seen how Freud developed and deployed the screen-memory theory in his self-analysis. How did he use it to interpret and reinterpret material produced by his patients? The first and perhaps the clearest account of this comes from Leopold Löwenfeld's *Psychic Obsessions*. Löwenfeld states that:

According to the current views of the author [Freud], the symptoms of compulsion neurosis do not originate directly from real sexual experiences, but from phantasies which attach themselves to these experiences. The latter accordingly form intermediary links between memories and pathological symptoms.

(Löwenfeld 1903: 296)[7]

Löwenfeld goes on to quote from a letter that he had received from Freud:

'As a rule it is the experiences of puberty which have a harmful effect. In the process of repression these events are fantasied back into early childhood following the pathways of sexual impressions accidentally experienced during the illness or arising from the [sexual constitution]'.

(ibid.)

In this passage the theory of screen memories is expanded into a theory of psychopathology. Contemporary triggers evoke unconscious reactions which become associated with infantile memories. As a result of the new investment of psychical energy, these memories become pathogenic. This account is basically consistent with discussions in the Fliess correspondence and Freud's 'Screen memories'. However, there is a very important omission in this transformation of the theory. If the context of recollection – or reproduction – is the key to understanding the unconscious significance of an infantile memory, it would follow that if infantile memories are reproduced in analysis then there must be something about the contemporary analytic situation which these memories symbolically portray.

By 1906 the concept of screen memories had undergone a more drastic transformation: 'I have learned to explain a number of phantasies of seduction as attempts at fending off memories of the subject's *own* sexual activity (infantile masturbation)' (Freud 1906: 274). Here screen memories are understood as later transformations of early memories in order to ward off other early memories. They are no longer regarded as possessing any *contemporary* significance, and the crucial role of the context of recollection in the original theory has fallen entirely by the wayside. This concept of screen memories became generally accepted within the psychoanalytic community. The *locus classicus* of the remodelled theory is the case of the 'Rat Man' published three years later:

If we do not wish to go astray in our judgement of their historical reality, we must above all bear in mind that people's 'childhood memories' are only consolidated at a later period, usually at the age of puberty; and that this involves a complicated process of remodelling, analogous in every way to the process by which a nation constructs legends about its early history. It at once becomes evident that in his phantasies about his infancy the individual as he grows up *endeavours to efface the recollection of his auto-erotic activities*; and this he does by exalting their memory-traces to the level of object-love, just as a real historian will view the past in the light of the present.

(Freud 1909: 206)

Ironically, these words can be read as a confession. In his later accounts of the abandonment of the seduction theory Freud certainly strove to 'efface the recollection' of the real events and construct a 'legend' about the early history of psychoanalysis. Likewise, Freud gradually effaced his original theory of screen memories. Although he held to this theory for at least one-and-three-quarter years – from September 1897 to Whitsun 1899 – and in spite of the fact that Freud originally advanced the theory to explain the occurrence of 'reproductions' in analysis, Freud never used the theory in an entirely consistent manner when applying it to clinical data. *He never used the theory of screen memories to explain why particular infantile memories 'spontaneously' emerge in psychoanalysis.* Furthermore, by eliminating the causal role originally imputed to the context of recollection he made it virtually impossible for analysts to re-open the question.

Why did Freud falsify the record regarding the seduction theory and, simultaneously, theoretically diminish the causal significance of the here-and-now as a trigger for unconscious mental processing? Let us consider what conclusions Freud would have reached if he had both retained the screen-memory theory and preserved an accurate record of the seduction-theory episode. So far as can be pieced together, the 'reproductions' evoked by Freud in his early patients must have had features suggesting the themes of seduction, sexual abuse, and assault. The original theory of screen memories would have understood this to signify that Freud's patients unconsciously experienced the psychoanalytic process itself as a form of seduction, sexual abuse and assault because the *content* of a screen memory (seduction) covertly portrays unconsciously discerned properties of the here-and-now (the analytic situation) evoking it. The theory of screen memories would therefore 'retrodict' that there was something about the analytic situation, the way that Freud interacted with his patients, that provoked just these ideas to come to the fore.

As seduction, incest, and (rather less frequently) assault were regular features of the 'reproductions', the premises of the theory would lead one to the conclusion that Freud's patients unconsciously perceived *him* as behaving in a seductive, incestuous, and assaultive manner. To put it bluntly: the acceptance of the screen-memory theory leads to the conclusion that Freud's patients unconsciously felt that Freud seduced them, assaulted them, and engaged them in perverse forms of sexual behavior. The screen-memory theory would explain the indirect expression of these perceptions in the following way. First, Freud's patients perceived the sexual and assaultive properties of his behavior; next, because of the highly disturbing implications of this, the perceptions were rendered unconscious; after being repressed, the unconscious representations of Freud's behavior would 'slip away' into childhood scenes – that is, their cathexis would be displaced on to a memory or set of memories possessing some thematic affinity to the repressed ideas. Finally, after this internal process is completed, the reinforced childhood memory springs 'spontaneously' to mind either directly as a recollection or indirectly as a 'reproduction'.[9]

This application of Freud's theory is by no means a strained or far-fetched exercise. Freud formulated the theory of phantasy precisely because he recognized the implausibility of the seduction etiology as a sufficient explanation for his clinical data. Furthermore, he explicitly described hysterical productions as screen memories, and, in 1899, used all of the hypothetical intrapsychic processes specified in the pre-ceding paragraph to explain the genesis of screen memories. Masson (1984: 142) compares Freud to 'a dogged detective, on the track of a great crime'. Had Freud applied his own hypotheses more systematic-ally to the clinical data at his disposal he would have reached the unsettling conclusion that the perpetrator of the 'great crime' – the seducer, the rapist – *was he himself*. There can be no doubt that this would have been an enormously difficult insight for Freud to bear. This, in turn, may go a long way toward explaining why Freud effaced the historical record of the seduction theory, avoided applying the theory of screen memories consistently to his own data, and modified the screen-memory theory so as to eliminate the crucial semantic/causal role of contemporary reality. It may be that in order to keep on exploring the unconscious domain Freud had to distance himself from the implications of his own thinking in order to extricate himself from the unsavory causal role in which the screen-memory theory would place him.

But are these conclusions even prima facie plausible? I think that they are. I have already described how Freud had to apply physical and psychological pressure on his patients to induce them to produce the desired 'reproductions'. Reiff (1959) conveys this nicely in his description of Freud's treatment of Dora, a young hysteric whom Freud saw for several months in 1899.

> Dora expressed disbelief [in Freud's interpretations]. Freud applauds his own persistence; he speaks of using facts against the patient and reports how he overwhelmed Dora with interpretations, pounding away at her argument, until 'Dora disputed the facts no longer'.
>
> (p. 82)[8]

Imagine yourself as one of Freud's patients in 1896. You are a young woman who is disabled by severe psychiatric symptoms that no one around you can – or even tries to – understand. Your illness elicits scorn more readily than compassion. You are visited repeatedly at home by a young male doctor who expresses a sympathetic interest in your condition and holds out some hope of a cure. He instructs you to lie down and, while massaging your forehead, he begins to tell you to produce recollections. When you are silent he interrupts, asking 'What did you see?' or 'What occurred to you?'. Sometimes things come up that you do not want to tell him, but he insists that you *must* tell him *everything*. It soon becomes apparent that for some reason this man is almost exclusively interested in the details of your earlier sexual experiences. Recounting these to a male stranger is difficult: it violates your sense of propriety. Still, you force yourself to comply with his demands in the hope of finding some deliverance from your illness. Often you produce memories which he discounts as unsatisfactory, urging you to produce earlier memories. As he pushes you to relate more and more sexual memories you begin to find scenes flashing across your mind that seem quite alien to you. They are images of assault, sexual violation, and exploitation. You begin to experience powerful feelings of revulsion. The doctor keeps on massaging you and pressing you for more. He is clearly pleased with what you are giving him now, and tells you that the images and feelings of distress that you are experiencing are actually memories of your uncle sexually abusing you when you were four years old. You are shocked. You tell him that he is wrong. You tell him that such a thing never happened and that the things you are experiencing don't seem like memories at all, but he insists that you are deceiving yourself.

This fictional vignette is based on information given by Freud in his 1896 papers and the correspondence of that period, and we do not require a speculative theory of infantile seduction or an even more speculative theory of the Oedipus complex to make sense of the patient's imagery. *We need look no further than Freud's interaction with his patient to form a plausible hypothesis about why she 'spontaneously' became preoccupied with issues of seduction, abuse, and exploitation.*

It may well be that if Freud had followed this pathway he would not have been emotionally capable of persisting in his research. If this is true we can count ourselves lucky that Freud veered toward phantasy rather than reality, the past rather than the present, patients' 'transferred' relationships with their parents rather than their real relationships with their analysts. Had Freud turned away from his quest completely we would be unable to benefit from the brilliant insights, intuitions, and hypotheses that he has bequeathed to us. But for every such gift there is a cost. Freud's fateful decision has made it difficult for his heirs to radically examine their real influence over what their patients say and do in their consulting rooms.

In this respect the contrast between Freud and his one-time colleague and mentor Joseph Breuer is instructive. It was Breuer who stumbled upon the mode of therapy which was transformed by Freud into psychoanalysis. In the early 1880s Breuer was treating a severely hysterical young woman known pseudonymously as 'Anna O' (her real name was Bertha von Pappenheim: she later became one of the first German social workers and a leading light in the women's movement). Breuer removed her various symptoms, one by one, through hypnotic regression and catharsis. The patient seemed to be progressing satisfactorily when, as Jones (1953) recounts, Breuer became aware of her sexual preoccupation with him and decided to cut short the treatment. That evening he received an urgent call to come to Anna's bedside. Breuer asked her what was the matter, to which she replied 'Now Dr Breuer's child is coming!' Anna, it seemed, was in the throes of hysterical labor. Breuer, deeply shaken, placed her in an hypnotic trance and fled. Anna soon relapsed and was institutionalized (Sulloway 1979). As Breuer gave up the practice of psychotherapy, it seems likely that he took the sexual dynamics of his relationship with Anna quite seriously, and it is reasonable to conclude that he felt that there was something not quite right about what was developing between himself and his patient. Breuer abandoned Anna – and psychotherapy generally – instead of delving more deeply into what had occurred. Unlike Breuer, Freud was able to persist and attempt to unravel the nature of the therapeutic relationship. However, as Szasz (1963) has suggested, he was enabled to do this through the invention of 'transference': the theory that patients' reactions to their therapists are based upon anachronistic infantile phantasies and are quite out of touch with reality. The concept of transference is the undisputed centerpiece of psychoanalytic clinical theory. It has provided analysts, down through the decades, with a unique tool for theoretically absenting themselves from the analytic situation.

> For the patient, the frightening or shameful impulses were not to be taken seriously: they were quite unreal and illusory. . . . For the therapist there was considerable safety in the belief that he had done nothing to stimulate the patient's fantasies and impulses.
>
> (Langs 1982b: 111–12)

Freud's first theory of screen memories has in effect been a lost psychoanalytic legacy. Over the decades analysts such as Ferenczi, Little, Searles, Laing, and other (including Freud himself) have rediscovered fragments of that legacy. However, psychoanalysis had to wait for over seventy years until Robert Langs, a classically trained American psychoanalyst, was to stumble upon the screen-memory approach to understanding clinical data and, for the first time, apply it consistently, refine and develop it. The results were deeply unsettling: so unsettling, in fact, that they turned Langs's erstwhile Freudian colleagues against him.

Before looking at Langs's discoveries in detail, we will need to consider, among other things, the theory of transference that was built over the abandoned theory of screen memories. This will be the subject of Chapter 2.

2   The distorting mirror

The mirror cracked from side to side;
'The curse has come upon me', cried
The Lady of Shallot.

                                    Tennyson

In this chapter I will critically evaluate the psychoanalytic theory of
transference and, somewhat less thoroughly, do the same to the theory
of countertransference. Transference is at the very heart of psychoanalytic theory and technique. It is almost universally regarded –
within the profession – as an indispensable concept for understanding
the analytic process (as well as numerous extra-clinical phenomena),
and the 'analysis of transference' is believed to be the most important
component of analytic technique. In short, the concept of transference is securely entrenched, and attempts to dislodge it are normally
greeted with an attitude of amused incredulity that anyone would seek
to question such a patently self-evident phenomenon.

I am going to fly in the face of tradition and consensus. I will
advance the claim that the interaction between patient and analyst
cannot possibly be understood in terms of transference and that the
concept of transference, when pinned down and closely scrutinized,
turns out to be either vacuous or trivial.

One standard rejoinder to this type of objection is the assertion that
although some psychoanalysts possessing a somewhat fanatical and
blinkered turn of mind have taken the perfectly acceptable notion of
transference to absurd extremes, there is surely nothing wrong with a
more modest, mellow use of the concept. So long as one recognizes
such factors as 'rapport', the 'working alliance', or even 'unconscious
perception' – so the argument goes – it is perfectly all right to bring in
an innocent notion of transference as well. I will oppose this view. I
want to shift the burden of proof on to the shoulders of the transference apologists and require them to show that when they use the

concept of transference they are using it to denote some intelligible phenomenon or process.

A second popular rejoinder to my attack is the claim that of course the classical Freudian concept of transference is wrong headed, but psychoanalysis has 'come a long way since Freud'. This putative advance over Freud's supposedly primitive formulation of the theory turns out, on close inspection, to be no such thing. As I will show, these 'advances' usually turn out to be either mystifications or trivializations of the concept of transference. Freud, to his credit, invented the concept of transference because of a real scientific need for a term to denote a special process not covered by ordinary language, and he defined this special term quite precisely.

I think that psychoanalysts should feel uncomfortable when using the term 'transference', and it is uncomfortable to me that they do not feel uncomfortable. I will therefore try to show that a glib invocation of this concept – without careful consideration of its validity – is not compatible with scientific conscience.

Freud introduced the term 'transference' (Übertragung) in *Studies on Hysteria* (Freud and Breuer 1895), noting that some patients experience the work demanded of them in psychotherapy as a personal sacrifice which is only compensated by the special attention paid to them by the physician. 'Transference' disrupts this positively toned doctor–patient relationship and therefore – with this type of patient – disrupts the treatment. Transference itself is described as the association by the patient of distressing ideas arising in the treatment with the person of the analyst. The patient is said to make a 'false connection' (302) between an idea appropriate to some past, extra-therapeutic situation and the analyst. Freud illustrates the emergence of such a false connection as follows:

> In one of my patients the origin of a particular hysterical symptom lay in a wish, which she had had many years earlier and had at once relegated to the unconscious, that the man she was talking to at the time might boldly take the initiative and give her a kiss. On one occasion at the end of a session, a similar wish came up in her about me. She was horrified at it, spent a sleepless night, and at the next session, though she did not refuse to be treated, was quite useless for work. After I had discovered the obstacle and removed it, the work proceeded further; and lo and behold! The wish that had so much frightened the patient made its appearance as the next of her pathogenic recollections.
>
> (ibid.: 302–3)

If we are to understand precisely what Freud means by the term 'transference' here we must pay careful attention to the notion of 'false connection', because transference is described twice in *Studies on Hysteria* as an instance of false connection. As is often the case, Freud uses this perfectly ordinary sounding term in a specifically technical sense.

> There seems to be a necessity for bringing psychical phenomena of which one becomes conscious into causal connection with other conscious material. In cases in which true causation evades conscious perception one does not hesitate to make another connection, which one believes although it is false. It is clear that a split in the content of consciousness must greatly facilitate the occurrence of 'false connections' of this kind.
>
> (Freud and Breuer 1895: 67, n.1)

Freud goes on to recount a 'typical' example of a false connection. His patient, Frau. Emmy von N., took a lukewarm hip bath daily as part of her medical treatment. On one occasion Freud attempted to convince her to take a cool hip bath instead, as he considered it more refreshing. Emmy countered this with the assertion that cool hip baths invariably made her depressed. Nonetheless, Freud managed to sway her. The day after this patient had taken the cool hip bath, Freud found her in a state of melancholy which she attributed to having followed Freud's recommendation. However, under hypnosis she confessed that her low spirits were really to do with worries about her brother's safety (her brother lived in Santo Domingo, which at the time was in the throes of a revolution). Emmy had evidently repressed her concerns about her brother but the associated mood of sadness found its way into consciousness and was causally misattributed to the cool hip bath.

Given that Freud uses the term 'false connection' to denote a kind of causal fallacy, we can turn once more to Freud's example of transference from *Studies on Hysteria* with an improved understanding of what is implicit in the account. When Freud says that his patient made a false connection between the man in her past by whom she wanted to be boldly kissed and himself, he must mean – if he is using his own jargon consistently – that his patient believed that he, Freud, *was responsible for her desire to be kissed by him*. Freud, of course, regarded this as an illusion. He believed that an old wish appropriate to an old situation had been stirred up by the treatment procedure. The patient, he believed, became conscious of the wish denuded of its true cause in the past and then unconsciously confabulated that he,

Freud, had caused this desire to arise in her. In other words, Freud held that his patient's view that something occurring in the here-and-now of the interaction between them was causing her to want a kiss from him was *false*: the true cause lay in the past. Freud believed that his own role was merely catalytic.

The early theory of screen memories certainly possesses conceptual links with the notion of false connections. Like false connections, screen memories are said to involve a causal fallacy: the subject does not understand the true contemporary cause for the evocation of an early memory, although he or she does not necessarily seize upon a false cause to explain it. This family resemblance makes the 1897–9 theory of screen memories a close relation of the theory of transference.

The next description of transference appears in *The Interpretation of Dreams* (Freud 1900). Here Freud speaks of transference as an intrapsychic process essential to the formation of dreams, but emphasizes that his understanding of the role of transference in dreams was an extrapolation from 'the psychology of the neuroses' (263). Freud invokes the concept of transference in his dream theory to explain how it is that an unconscious wish is able to find disguised expression through a dream and why it is that dreams typically incorporate memories of experiences from the preceding day (the *'day residues'*). In answering these two questions, Freud advances a theory of transference as the hypothetical intrapsychic process causally mediating between unconscious wish and conscious cognition and behavior.

Freud makes a fundamental distinction between two systems within the mind. The unconscious mental system is sealed off from conscious awareness and contains urgent, conflict-laden infantile wishes. The preconscious system, on the other hand, contains all of those mental contents that can readily be brought to conscious awareness.

> We learn . . . that an unconscious idea is as such quite incapable of entering the preconscious and it can only exercise any effect there by establishing a connection with an idea which already belongs to the preconscious, by transferring its intensity onto it and getting itself 'covered' by it. . . . The preconscious idea, which thus acquires an undeserved degree of intensity, may either be left unaltered by the transference, or it may have a modification forced upon it, derived from the idea which effects the transference.
>
> (ibid.: 562–3)

Freud's 1900 concept of transference is a conceptual descendant of the notion of 'deferred action' in the seduction theory and is, to all intents and purposes, identical to the process hypothesized in 'Screen memories' to link contemporary unconscious concerns with infantile memories. In both accounts an unconscious idea finds disguised expression through reinforcing a preconscious memory, which 'screens' or 'covers' its unconscious instigator. In both cases the pre-conscious idea may or may not undergo alteration as a result of its unconscious reinforcement, and also, in both cases, the link between unconscious and preconscious mental contents is often determined by homonyms and verbal similarities.

In *The Interpretation of Dreams* Freud picks out transference as the mechanism *par excellence* by means of which unconscious ideas impact upon the conscious mind. Unconscious ideas are described as displaying a 'need for transference' (563).

There is one aspect of this theory of transference, however, which stands out in bold contrast to the theory of screen memories advanced a year previously: the 'transference of intensity' described in *The Interpretation of Dreams* is said to invariably proceed from a more archaic to a less archaic idea. The wishes seeking expression through a mode of transference are, according to this theory, always infantile in origin and are transferred on to 'recent material' (573). By late 1899, when this work was actually published, there was no room in Freud's theory of the mind for a concept of unconscious interpretations of *contemporary* events finding disguised expression through the evoca-tion of early memories. Freud stipulated that transference does not flow backwards from recent material, and the 'fantasied past' was no longer seen – as it had been in 1898 – as 'the mirror image of the present' (Freud 1887–1904: 320).

Although the focus is certainly different, there is considerable conceptual continuity between the original 1895 account of transfer-ence and the version presented in Freud's dream book. In fact, it would appear that the latter is a sophisticated hypothetical explana-tion of the clinical data offered in *Studies on Hysteria*. The theory of 1900 explains the observations of 1895 by postulating that the patient's preconscious mental representation of the analyst receives an 'intensity' displaced from an unconscious idea. The person of the analyst then (allegedly) becomes a 'cover', then, for an unconscious representation of the patient's father, mother, or other infantile figure.

The next important Freudian text that deals with the concept of transference is Freud's case presentation of Dora (Freud 1905b). Here he abandons the rather broad metapsychological definition of *The Interpretation of Dreams* and opts for a more narrowly clinical characterization of the process. In *The Interpretation of Dreams* transference is described as a *process*. In the Dora case Freud uses the term in the plural – 'transferences' rather than 'transference' – to denote structures rather than processes. Transferences are described as 'a special class of mental structures' which are 'for the most part unconscious' (116). They are 'facsimiles' of unconscious infantile material (ibid.). Freud's use of the term 'facsimiles' here clearly echoes his use of the term 'reproductions' in the 1896 papers on the seduction theory, and it has the same basic function of signifying the indirect (inferred) expression of unconscious ideas. The transferences are seen as unconscious mental structures replacing some earlier individual with the person of the physician.

Freud emphasizes in the paper on Dora that transferences are difficult to detect because they are unconscious. This reveals an important ambiguity that had entered Freud's theorizing by 1905. In the 1900 version of the theory, transference is described as a causal linkage between unconscious and preconscious contents which was *in principle* unobservable. In describing transferences as 'structures', however, it sounds as though Freud is viewing transferences as *contents* of the mind which, although unconscious, are only contingently so (in other words, it is possible to render them conscious). Freud seems to be using the term 'transference' for both the process by means of which unconscious ideas interact with preconscious ideas and for the amalgam of unconscious and preconscious representations which is supposed to result from this process. If we understand transferences as the end products of an unconscious process of displacement they are indeed only contingently unconscious as Freud (1905b) states.

At this point in Freud's theorizing there has been no suggestion that transference creates a false or illusory picture of the analyst. Freud stresses in *The Interpretation of Dreams* that the unconscious ideas select specific preconscious ideas because of their appropriateness for particular unconscious concerns. He mentions that the preconscious ideas may – but need not – be distorted by the impact of transference. This principle is not contradicted in the 1905 discussion. Indeed, Freud comments that: '. . . [the transferences] may even become conscious by cleverly taking advantage of some real peculiarity in the physician's person or circumstances and attaching themselves to that' (Freud 1905b: 116). In Freud's *Five Lectures on Psycho-Analysis* (1910) the tone changes. Freud seems to return to the use of 'transference' to designate a process rather than a content, reverting to the singular form of the word. He also asserts that: 'The patient . . . directs towards the physician a degree of affectionate feeling (mingled, often enough, with hostility) *which is based on no real relation between them'* (51).

In all of Freud's later writings on the subject the notion of transference is understood, basically, as an intrapsychic process giving rise to illusion. For example, he writes in 'The dynamics of the transference' (Freud 1912a) that:

> The unconscious impulses do not want to be remembered in the way that the treatment desires them to be, but endeavour to reproduce themselves in accordance with the timelessness of the unconscious and its capacity for hallucination. Just as happens in dreams, the patient regards the products of the awakening of his unconscious impulses as contemporaneous and real; he seeks to put his passions into action without taking any account of the real situation.

> (ibid.: 199)

To recapitulate, Freud mainly used the concept of transference to designate a hypothetical intrapsychic process. This hypothetical process was invoked to explain why it was that patients became emotionally preoccupied with their analysts. 'Transference' thus served, in Freud's clinical theory, as a term for the *cause* of these phenomena: i.e. Freud came to believe that his patients experienced such intense emotional responses to him because of a displacement of psychic energy away from an unconscious parental image and on to a preconscious representation of himself. The clear distinction between the explanatory hypothesis and the phenomenon that it is intended to explain, which became obscured in the clinical discussion of the treatment of Dora, makes it possible to approach the theory of transference in a scientific spirit. It allows one, in principle, to pit rival causal hypotheses against one another in order to determine which best accounts for the phenomenon under consideration. It is also a constant reminder that one's hypothesis is, after all, only a hypothesis and as such is merely a part of what Freud called the 'speculative superstructure of psycho-analysis, any portion of which can be abandoned or changed without loss or regret the moment its inadequacy has been proved' (Freud 1925: 32–3). The transference hypothesis is, in principle, theoretically expendable. To abandon the concept would not entail the abandonment of the idea that patients form powerful emotional bonds with their analysts, or even necessarily the rejection of the hypothesis that infantile experiences are causally relevant to the formation of these emotional attachments. To abandon the concept of transference would simply mean that one would no longer *explain* these phenomena in terms of the displacement of emotional intensity (or its hypothetical substrate, psychic energy) from an unconscious representation of a past figure on to a preconscious representation of a contemporary person.

Unfortunately psychoanalysts soon lost sight of the crucial distinction between *explanandum* and *explanans* in the theory of transference (following Freud's bad example in the Dora case). Transference became equated with a set of observable clinical phenomena. Modes of behavior or relatedness were held up as 'examples' of transference. The hypothsized cause became conceptually merged with the effect.

Perhaps an analogy from physics will make clear the bizarre implications of this situation. We know that the sensation of heat is caused by the agitation of the molecules composing the hot object. Thus, when we say that some object is hot, we can go on to explain this state of affairs by saying that its constituent molecules are agitated. But imagine touching a frying pan and crying out in distress 'Those molecules are really moving!'. This absurd conflation of cause (molecular agitation) and effect (the sensation of being burnt) is considerably more sound than analysts' talking about 'transference phenomena', as the explanation of heat in terms of molecular activity is much better established than is the explanation of a patient falling in love with her psychoanalyst in terms of the displacement of psychical energy from an unconscious representation of her father. However, talk of 'transference phenomena' has something in common with the frying-pan fallacy: both confuse cause with effect.

The conceptual confusion haunting the theory of transference sometimes make it difficult to debate the issue of the validity of this theory with transference apologists. To say that one does not believe in transference is taken as the denial of the existence of a well-attested phenomenon rather than of a hypothetical (and by definition unobservable) process of causal transmission.

The muddle surrounding the theory of transference shows up clearly in, for example, Gellner's (1985) treatment of the topic. For Gellner, 'There is an almost comic contrast between the overwhelming and genuine evidence for this one phenomenon and the sketchy, dubious evidence for most other psychoanalytic ideas' (54). Why does the otherwise sceptical Gellner regard the theory of transference as so clearly true? The answer to this is revealed by his use of the term 'phenomenon'. Gellner is treating transference as a phenomenon rather than as a theory purporting to explain phenomena. Although he uses the term 'transference', he is not really using this in properly psychoanalytic (explanatory) sense. This becomes quite clear as Gellner elaborates his position.

What this marvel of a generalization [the concept of transference] says is: when a person, self-identified as a patient, comes in repeated and sustained contact with a person whom he recognizes as a doctor or therapist, and the latter listens to the deliberately unstructured confessions of the former, and only occasionally and tentatively offers interpretations of them – in brief, if the two comport themselves as the therapeutic technique recommends – then the latter will develop very strong, and in the main, initially and on the surface, positive feelings about the therapist, accept his authority, and so on.

(ibid.: 54)

It should be obvious that the definition of transference proffered by Gellner is in fact no such thing, it is an empirical generalization about the behavior of psychoanalytic patients which has no explanatory component and entails no conception of hypothetical processes. The observations offered by Gellner *might* be explained in terms of trans-ference, but they cannot be *equated* with transference. Gellner's logical error, which is quite widespread in the literature dealing with psychoanalysis, is analogous to setting out to explain the physical causes of heat by describing how to fry an egg.

An objection to the line of argumentation that I am pursuing, frequently voiced by present-day advocates of the theory of transfer-ence, states that my conception of transference is an unduly limited and anachronistic one derived from Freud's early work which takes no account of the 'great advances' made by psychoanalytic theorists since Freud's day. Let us pause, then, to consider these new, improved notions of transference. Once such revised conception identifies trans-ference with the patient's 'total attitude' to the analyst. It is obvious that this formulation of transference is scientifically worthless. It makes 'transference' a mere synonym for an ordinary term with no explanatory value, and a misleading synonym at that (there is nothing being 'transferred' from one psychic locality to another). Another alternative formulation, apparently first advanced by Glover (1955), identifies transference with *all* the ways that the patient brings his or her past experiences to bear on present-day realities. This would include unconscious displacement – the classical 'transference' – but also more. According to this view transference would include general-izations made on the basis of earlier experiences, distortions wrought by infantile defenses, developmental arrests, and so on. This concep-tion of transference loses all specificity. Instead of denoting a specific causal process, a lawful relationship between unconscious mental contents and their derivatives, 'transference' is defined as a functional state: anything is transference if it is an example of past impacting on present experience. Any instantiation of this program is considered as transference. This concept begs the original – and still vital – Freudian question which the original theory of transference was put forward to answer: '*How* is unconscious influence transmitted?' Freud wanted a theory to explain how highly charged repressed ideas could find disguised expression through the preconscious domain. In other words, he wanted to understand how to explain 'Freudian' phenomena – neurotic symptoms, dreams, and parapraxes – as the by-products of unconscious mental contents. The scientific role of the theory of transference can only be obscured by making its extension a whole class of disparate psychological processes.

CAN TRANSFERENCE BE DISTINGUISHED FROM NON-TRANSFERENCE?

If transference, in the Freudian sense, is to be a meaningful theoretical concept it must be possible to distinguish transference from non-transference. Making this crucial distinction turns out to be difficult if not impossible. Greenson's *The Technique and Practice of Psychoanalysis* (1967) is a standard textbook on classical Freudian theory of technique, a sourcebook for the classical interpretation of psychoanalytic clinical concepts. Greenson addresses the question of differentiating transference from non-transference and presents the standard Freudian criterion for accomplishing this.

According to Greenson, transference is a distinctive type of human relationship involving the experience of wishes, feelings, drives, phantasies, defenses, and attitudes toward another person which 'do not befit that person and which actually apply to another' (152–3). Transference attitudes 'befit' a past relationship rather than a present relationship (153). Transference is therefore intrinsically anachronistic. According to Greenson, it is usually the patient who transfers on to the analyst rather than vice versa. He stresses that the factor distinguishing transference from non-transference is *inappropriateness*. It is the inappropriateness of transference reactions that marks them off as anachronistic. Attitudes which are 'mature', 'realistic', or 'in accord with the circumstances' cannot be regarded as transferential (156).

Given that any judgement about whether or not something is a manifestation of transference hinges on an evaluation of its appropriateness, it is possible to imagine two types of clinical scenario flowing from this: either (a) both patient and analyst agree that the patient's attitude toward the analyst is inappropriate, or (b) the analyst regards the patient's attitude as inappropriate while the patient considers it appropriate (the other option involving the appropriateness of the *analyst's* behavior being called into question is logically possible but is, alas, unlikely to be taken seriously by most practicing analysts). In either case there must be some plausible procedure for reaching a rational conclusion: it must, in the interest of the theory of transference, be possible to classify the patient's attitudes as either appropriate or inappropriate. It is this very possibility that I will now call into question.

First we must establish just what 'appropriate' means in the context of the theory of transference. For Greenson, appropriate would appear to signify something like 'accurate', 'realistic', or 'adaptive'. An appropriate idea about the analyst, then, would be an idea warranted by the analyst's actual behavior. Thus, for example, if an analyst behaves in an irritable manner it would be appropriate, and not transferential, for his patients to regard him as bad tempered. According to this view, appropriate emotions would be those that follow on from such realistic perceptions (for example, fearing to attend sessions conducted by an irascible analyst).

How can the appropriateness of the patient's attitudes thus defined be determined? The most obvious and by far the most naive approach to this problem is the simple appeal to self-awareness. If, for example, a patient were to assert that her analyst wished to seduce her, the analyst – invoking the criterion of self-awareness – could just peer into his own psyche and, finding no desire to seduce his patient, conclude that her belief about him is inappropriate. This approach is fundamentally incompatible with psychoanalytic theory, the most basic proposition of which is that our most puissant and insistent desires lie beyond the scope of introspection. Freud's chilly anti-Cartesianism is committed to the notion that human beings are unable to know their deepest emotional yearnings directly. The appeal to psychic transparency, to unmediated self-awareness, cannot be entertained coherently by someone who also accepts the Freudian theory of the unconscious mind, for this approach to the problem of 'appropriateness' presupposes that the contents of one's mind are directly disclosed to consciousness.[1]

The idea that we cannot be directly acquainted with aspects of our own inner nature, our wishes and dreads, provides the *raison d'être* for the whole psychoanalytic enterprise. Psychoanalysis *needs* the disjunction between conscious and unconscious realms to justify its own existence. It would therefore be a curious spectacle to witness a psychoanalyst underwriting his view that a patient's impression of him is inappropriate because he has measured the patient's view of him against his own view of himself and found the former wanting! And yet, variations of this strategy are used, at least implicitly, by many analysts. For example, Freud writes that at a particular point in his treatment the Rat Man felt compelled to heap 'the grossest and filthiest abuse' upon Freud and his family (Freud 1909: 209). While doing this the Rat Man would get up from the couch and roam about the room. The Rat Man explained his physical restlessness in terms of delicacy of feeling (he couldn't bear saying such horrible things about Freud while lying there comfortably on his sofa). Freud suggested a transference interpretation that the Rat Man unconsciously regarded him as his father and consequently avoided Freud's proximity for fear of getting a beating. In accord with his own canons, Freud could only regard the Rat Man's behavior as transferential if he believed it to be unwarranted in its contemporary context. For Freud the Rat Man *really* dreaded a thrashing at the hands of his father and was 'inappropriately' transferring this primal terror on to his analyst. As Margaret Little (1951) notes, to label a patient's behavior as transference implicitly denies that behavior has a basis in here-and-now reality. In so far as Freud regarded the Rat Man's behavior as a vestige of his relationship with his father, he would regard him as unjustified in thinking that he, Freud, harbored violent impulses toward him.

On the face of it the appeal to the data of introspection is inadequate for underwriting the theory of transference. A second line of defense in the face of this cul-de-sac is to claim that although the patient in analysis is unable to consciously access his innermost desires and fears, and hence requires psychoanalytic assistance, the analyst *is* relatively transparent to himself. If insightfulness is unequally distributed in this manner an analyst could reasonably invoke his own superior self-awareness with impunity while simultaneously securing the privilege of making interpretations to benighted patients. But what could account for this (alleged) difference between analyst and patient? What could have brought about the analyst's psychological transformation? The answer offered by psychoanalysts is the momentous experience of the training analysis. All psychoanalysts and virtually all psychoanalytic psychotherapists are required to undergo a lengthy and intensive personal analysis as an essential part of their training. It is this training analysis which is supposed to render the candidate fit to psychoanalyze or conduct psychotherapy with others.

Gellner (1985), tongue in cheek, describes the process as the removal of an inner veil of unknowing, suggesting that:

> It is now possible to spell out the tacit theory which underlies, and which alone can explain and justify, the wild eccentricity of psycho-analytical training and the habitual dogmatism of analysts. The training analysis is the central and essential part of the training of an analyst *because* (so the theory runs) in the course of it the trainee learns to penetrate and neutralize the internal obstacles to his own vision. To do so is the very essence of an analysis. Hence, if the analysis is successful and the inner barriers are down, objects are clearly and easily visible to the mind. Veil-removal is a sufficient condition of knowledge. There is no further problem.
>
> (ibid.: 84)

The notion that psychoanalysts have attained anything even remotely approximating direct self-knowledge by virtue of their training analyses or any other process is absurdly easy to refute. Given that psychoanalysts of all persuasions claim to have knowledge of certain universal aspects of our unconscious mental life (such as the Oedipus complex, mechanisms of defense, oral sadism, and so on) and given that such universals must, by definition, be found in the mental composition of all psychoanalysts (because psychoanalysts are human beings), it follows that there should be near-complete consensus among psychoanalysts about the nature of the human mind. If the mind were indeed an open book to those who are fully analyzed, most theoretical disputes could be settled with a momentary recourse to introspection. If one analyst were to say that the core of the Oedipus complex is oral (as Klein did) and another were to counter-assert that the Oedipus complex is basically phallic (as Freud did) there would be no need for bellicosity or for attempts to win over the opposition by marshaling clinical evidence. Both parties to the dispute could just look inside of themselves, focus in on the Oedipus complex and note what its characteristics are! But this idealized picture bears no resemblance to the real history of a profession that has been characterized by petty and acrimonious theoretical debates and immense differences of opinion about basic theoretical concepts. The notion of the well analyzed analysts who can look straight into themselves is contradicted by the proliferation of psychoanalytic 'schools' advancing mutually exclusive doctrines. The fact that there are Freudians (of several distinct flavors), Kleinians, Kohutians, American object-relationists, British object-relationists, Lacanians, culturalists, and so many other depth-psychological factions belies the pretensions of the veil-lifting theory. Unconscious mental contents and processes can never be directly perceived: they must always be inferred (Freud 1940).

Even so, the transference apologist might promote his or her argument through making a concession. Even if we grant that the analyst does not in fact possess an unhindered inner gaze, it might be argued that the analyst is *still* in an epistemically privileged position by virtue of the fact that patients are given insufficient information on which to base sound conclusions about their analysts. Analysts are supposed to be anonymous to their patients. Why? To cultivate an 'analyzable transference'. 'The doctor', wrote Freud, 'should be opaque to his patients and, like a mirror, should show them nothing but what is shown to him' (Freud 1912b: 118).

Freudian opacity is designed to safeguard the transference. As Greenson (1967) describes it:

> The analyst's personal values and preferences should not intrude into the analysis. . . . It is the consistent neutrality of the analyst . . . that makes it possible for the patient's distorted and unrealistic reactions to become demonstrable as such. . . . Only in this way can the patient's transference reactions come into clear focus so that they can be singled out and distinguished from more realistic reactions.
>
> (272)

And later:

> There is no doubt that the less the patient really knows about the psychoanalyst, the more easily he can fill in the blank spaces with his own fantasies. Furthermore, the less the patient actually knows about the analyst, the easier it becomes for the analyst to convince the patient that his reactions are displacements and projections.
>
> (274)

It is to Greenson's credit that after having set out this tidy scheme, he immediately calls its absolute validity into question, reminding us that the analyst's incognito is 'at best . . . only a relative matter' (274) and that everything that an analyst says and does, including the way that he or she chooses to furnish the consulting room, reveals personal information. Furthermore 'many patients are extremely intuitive and pick up a good deal of knowledge about their analyst' from the clues that he or she provides (275). Sooner or later 'all patients get to know a goodly amount about their analyst in reality' (ibid.). These points are illustrated by an amusing anecdote recounting how one of Greenson's patients was able to correctly deduce Greenson's political affiliation.

I asked him how he knew I was a liberal and anti-Republican. He then told me that whenever he said anything favourable about a Republican politician, I always asked for associations. On the other hand, whenever he said anything hostile about a Republican, I remained silent as though in agreement. Whenever he attacked Roosevelt, I would ask him who did Roosevelt remind him of, as though I was out to prove that hating Roosevelt was infantile.

(Greenson 1967: 273)

One must concede, then, that patients can draw accurate inferences about their analysts on the basis of minimal and implicit information. The anonymity of the analyst, no matter how impeccable, does not preclude that his or her patients may come to valid conclusions. Even if this were not the case, incidentally, it would be logically fallacious to argue that an incorrect conclusion reached by a patient about an analyst must be attributed to the operation of transference. It might more plausibly be attributed to an inference based on too limited and partial a fund of information, or to a cognitive error. The mere fact that a conclusion is faulty says nothing about the *cause* of the error. I will leave this dimension of the argument to one side, though, in order to pursue the more radical and, I think, philosophically interesting question of whether or not a psychoanalytic frame of reference enables one to distinguish between transference and non-transference in a coherent fashion.

It is but a short step from Greenson's observations to the admission that patients' perceptions of their psychoanalysts might, if unflattering, be dismissed by those analysts as 'inappropriate'. It is logically possible that the Rat Man accurately inferred that Freud wished to harm him and that Freud, disavowing this wish, labeled the Rat Man's insight as a 'transference fantasy'.

There seems to be only one more strategy for attempting to preserve the psychoanalyst's privilege of stamping patient's attitudes and actions with the judgement of inappropriateness. At first glance this strategy seems completely unassailable – an impression that crumbles away upon closer inspection. Let us agree for the sake of the argument that analysts' knowledge of their own minds – their dispositions, attitudes, desires, and so on – is quite imperfect and that this commits us to the admission that patients' statements about their analysts' psyches are difficult to evaluate with certainty. There remains another class of statements made by patients about their analysts which appear to be self-evidently true or false: namely, statements about their analysts' outer, public behavior and circumstances. For example, when Greenson's patient guessed that he was a liberal, Greenson did not need to engage in a process of introspection in order to evaluate the truth of falsity of this proposition. He knew the answer straight away, and was immediately able to decide that his patient's remark was not an expression of a transference fantasy. It was a well-reasoned, appropriate inference. It would seem to follow that if Greenson's patient had guessed wrongly – i.e. if Greenson was actually a Republican – it would have given Greenson epistemic licence to conclude that this was an 'inappropriate' and hence transferential vision of him (I am intentionally ignoring the fallacy, mentioned above, of jumping to conclusions about the cause of a cognitive error).

Let us imagine that this patient *had* guessed wrongly and that Greenson was instantly aware, with absolute certainty, that his patient's representation of him did not accord with reality. Employing his own criteria, Greenson would probably have gone on to conclude that this error was a manifestation of transference, i.e. that the error was caused by the displacement of an infantile unconscious attachment. Now, how would Greenson proceed to tease out the unconscious mental content responsible for the transference fantasy? One thing that is certain is that he would not assume that the error was a *direct* expression of the unconscious mind. As a Freudian, Greenson is committed to the idea that unconscious mental contents express themselves only indirectly through encoded derivatives. He would not confine himself to the manifest content of the error and assume that it meant that an important figure from the patient's early life must have been a liberal. Greenson would begin with the assumption that the patient's image of him as a liberal is a *disguised* representation of an unconscious, infantile mental representation, and would therefore seek out the *latent* meaning of the transference. He would try to infer this on the basis of the patient's associations to the notion of being a liberal. Let us imagine, for the sake of the argument, that this patient associated liberalism with concepts of social justice and that, as a child, this patient had felt that his father had treated him unfairly with respect to his sister. The notion that Greenson was a liberal might then be understood as the disguised expression of an infantile wish to be loved by his father: to be given at least the same amount of affection as his sister received. It is the *symbolic* value of the 'transference fantasy' which is of importance here, and the manifest fact that the patient's father was *not* a liberal does not invalidate the Freudian hypothesis. The relationship between an 'inappropriate' idea and its unconscious sources is regarded as an altogether more subtle and convoluted matter.

This hypothetical example illustrates an important implicit premise that is endemic to psychoanalytic thinking about so-called transference phenomena: the idea that if an attitude of the patient toward the analyst is manifestly inappropriate to the contemporary situation, it must therefore be latently inappropriate to the contemporary situation. Although widely taken for granted as a necessary truth, this idea is obviously open to empirical testing and, possibly, refutation. There is no strictly logical reason why a manifestly inappropriate idea could not flow from a latently appropriate idea. The belief that 'transference' attitudes must be latently inappropriate flows from the Freudian assumption that the unconscious part of the mind is incapable of making realistic inferences about the nature of external reality. The notion that the unconscious mind is capable only of wishing, fantasizing, and hallucinating has little (if any) empirical support in its favour and, as I will show in Chapter 3, the opposing thesis that the unconscious mental system is capable of deploying sophisticated cognitive and perceptual processes is well supported by experimental psychology and cognitive science. Thus, if one does not take on board as an article of faith the Freudian idea that the unconscious part of the mind is intrinsically autistic it leaves one open to explore the possibility that so-called inappropriate ideas are not, on a deeper level, inappropriate at all.

If the Freudian assumption is bracketed, the argument that false statements about publicly verifiable aspects of the analyst's behavior must be attributed to the operation of transference begins to boomerang. The notion that a manifestly incorrect idea about the analyst must be an expression of a latent fantasy (as opposed to a latent perception or inference) – i.e. that the unconscious denotation of the manifest idea must be something inappropriately anachronistic – is an arbitrary judgement. The latent meaning of the 'transference' might at least in principle be an accurate and realistic though unconscious representation of the analyst: there is no apparent reason for assuming that because an idea is unconscious it must therefore be inaccurate.

Returning to our adaptation of Greenson's example, let us imagine that the patient associated liberalism with an undisciplined approach to government and that, prior to the session described, the analyst had extended the patient's session by five minutes. The remark that the analyst was a liberal could then be taken as a disguised, encoded expression of a valid perception that the analyst's management of the preceding session was rather undisciplined. The idea that the analyst was a liberal, then, turns out to be merely superficially inappropriate. The judgement of inappropriateness rests entirely on the manifest content of the patient's statement. When analyzing the 'inappropriate' idea as transference, however, analysts do not confine themselves to the manifest dimension. It follows from all of this that the argument that an incorrect statement about the analyst's outer life must be inappropriate, an argument which at first glance seemed quite unassailable, is based on a double standard: latent, unconscious meaning can be invoked when analyzing an attitude assumed to be transferential, but the possibility that this latent meaning expresses an appropriate perception of the analyst is theoretically foreclosed.

I have tried to show that the classical Freudian account of transference is beset with deep and perhaps insurmountable problems. Given the centrality of the analysis of transference to Freudian practice, this diagnosis, if correct, is quite damaging to clinical psychoanalysis. I will now go on to consider, somewhat more briefly, the Kleinian alternative to the Freudian theory of transference. The Achilles heel of the Freudian account is the seeming impossibility of distinguishing transference from non-transference. The Kleinian formulation undercuts this problem by regarding transference as a component of everything that a patient does in analysis (indeed, of everything anyone does anywhere). There is yet hope, then, that the concept of transference may be salvaged in its Kleinian incarnation.

I have been unable to locate a discussion of transference in the Kleinian literature that comes anywhere near the clarity and explicitness of Greenson's presentation. This may be due to the fact that the Freudians have, at least ideologically, remained faithful to the scientific ideal which demands that hypotheses be empirically justified. Greenson's presentations can be seen in this light as a scientifically clumsy effort to supply evidence supporting the transference hypothesis. Kleinian analysts seem on the whole to be less concerned with the scientific evaluation of their doctrines than with the interpretative possibilities that they offer. Because I must rely on writings which strike me as rather ambiguous there is some possibility that my understanding of what the Kleinians mean by 'transference' will be inaccurate. If I do not do justice to the Kleinian theory I would certainly welcome some Kleinian writer to set me right and clarify the essential issues.

The Kleinian concept of transference cannot be understood in isolation from the theory of unconscious phantasy held by that school. According to Isaacs (1943), in a seminal paper on this topic, phantasy is the mental representation of instinct (by 'instinct' she presumably means '*trieb*' – 'drive'). The dramatis personae of unconscious phantasies are termed 'internal objects', which are mental representations of people or parts of people (breast, penis, and so on) believed to be housed inside of oneself in an 'inner world'. This internal world is understood to be a rather bizarre place because of the extraordinarily primitive character of the inhabitants and their behavior. The inner world of phantasied objects is believed, by Kleinian theorists, to be remarkably complex from very early on in life.

Transference, in the distinctly Kleinian sense of the concept, is the process of assimilating external reality to the prototypes of internal objects and internal object relations. In other words, transference is the externalization of unconscious phantasy, Spillius (1988: 6) writes that:

> The emphasis of Klein and her successors of the pervasiveness of transference is derived from Klein's use of the concept of unconscious phantasy, which is conceived as underlying all thought, rational as well as irrational, rather than there being a special category of thought and feeling that is rational and appropriate and therefore does not need analysing, and a second kind of thought and feeling which is irrational and unreasonable and therefore expresses transference and needs analysing.

The sense of the word 'underlying' in this passage is not altogether clear, but what seems to be meant is that unconscious phantasy influences, in an important way, all thought. It follows from this that transference is ubiquitous, cannot be demarcated from non-transference, and is not intrinsically irrational or inappropriate.[2] Transference is, in this view, an ongoing *dimension* of all of the patient's thoughts, actions, communications, and emotions. Within the analytic setting, then, the analyst will inevitably be assimilated to the patient's inner phantasy world, and this transference on to the analyst will be derivatively expressed in all of the patient's free associations irrespective of whether they show a conscious preoccupation with the analyst. Transference is not episodic. It is 'a relationship in which something is going on all the time' (Joseph 1985: 69).

A second important characteristic of the Kleinian concept is that it ascribes to transference a basically endopsychic origin. The unconscious phantasies which are projected as transference originate, for the most part, during the first half of the first year of extra-uterine life and give the human mind its fundamental structure. Klein (1930) even went as far as to suggest that unconscious phantasies were inherited. Also, although an unconscious phantasy may be evoked by an external stimulus, the logic of the theory dictates that this stimulus will invariably be assimilated to a phantasy. This proposition entails that transference can be understood only in so far as the corresponding unconscious phantasies are understood. Fortunately, according to Klein, the unconscious phantasy repertoire of human beings is very limited indeed, consisting mainly of the themes of sexuality, destruction, and reparation portrayed concretely in terms of interaction between mouth, breast, penis, feces, and a few other body parts. Armed with a knowledge of these ultimate phantasies, the Kleinian analyst of transference seems basically concerned with (a) determining which unconscious phantasy best fits the clinical material (the possibility that the material does not fit with any unconscious phantasy is not considered a valid option) and (b) interpreting the material accordingly.

Here is an example of transference analysis taken from a paper by Segal (1967). Segal recounts how a candidate opened the first session of his training analysis with the announcement that he wished to obtain a psychoanalytic qualification as rapidly as possible. He then went on to mention some digestive troubles that he had been experiencing and then, in a different connection, mentioned cows. Segal promptly interpreted this, informing her analyzand that the cow represented her analyst, and that he wanted to empty her greedily of her 'analysis-milk' in the minimum time possible.

To formulate a Kleinian transference interpretation it is necessary only to know what the basic unconscious phantasies are and to understand how they can be thematically linked with the patient's analytic material.

Now, given the all-pervasive character of these (hypothetical) unconscious phantasies, it is difficult to understand how they could have been isolated in the first place. If, as it seems, one can only access unconscious phantasy through its transferential or transference-like manifestations and, at the same time, if transference can only be understood as such by virtue of a prior understanding of unconscious phantasy, then it sounds as though the whole theoretical edifice is built upon a viciously circular, self-validating, and unfalsifiable manner of thinking. To put it differently: within the Kleinian system there is no way in which the concept of unconscious phantasy – and hence transference – can be called into question. Unconscious phantasy is *presupposed*. It is an indispensable premise, rather than an empirical conclusion. As Gedo (1988: 94) notes:

In fact, Klein never indicated *how* she had reached her hypotheses. . . . Klein made no effort to develop inductive propositions on the basis of her clinical observations. On the contrary, she classified all the phenomena she encountered in working with the patient according to a detailed set of predetermined categories.

It now becomes possible to make a sharp philosophical distinction between the Freudian and the Kleinian approaches. According to Greenson, the Freudian, it is necessary to determine whether or not a given piece of behavior is a manifestation of transference using fairly definite if fallacious criteria. It is only after this has been established that one can hypothesize about what it is that the patient is transferring on to the analyst. According to the Freudian approach, then, it is not possible to know *a priori* that something is being transferred. The procedure is inductive in spirit. In contrast to this, Klein's method is deductive and rationalistic rather than empirical in inspiration. By beginning with a limited set of hypothetical unconscious phantasies, which she holds to be human universals, Klein goes on to assimilate the manifest content of the patient's communications to these. A valid deductive argument depends upon the truth of its premises to guarantee the truth of its conclusion. Faith is inadequate to epistemically underwrite claims to knowledge. Unfortunately, there seems to be only a circular and evidentially unjustified 'validation' for Kleinian hypotheses about transference. One might anticipate that this system of thought – oblivious as it appears to be to issues of falsification and evidence – would give rise to a rather dogmatic attitude. This seems inevitable for an approach which contains no method (or even incentive) for questioning its own premises. In fact both Kernberg (1980) and Gedo (1988) have commented on the dogmatic streak in the Kleinian attitude. Gedo (1988) describes how in her *Narrative of a Child Analysis* (Klein 1961):

> Klein responded to the patient's failure to accept interpretations in the fifth session with a barrage of arguments in which she arbitrarily asserted that all the patient's subsequent associations confirmed her prior statements. When, in the next session, the boy reported that he had been afraid to return, Klein interpreted . . . that he wanted to have intercourse with her (pp. 35–6). Under the circumstances, most analysts would have considered the possibility that the child might simply have been frightened by her insistence on interpretations that made no sense to him. Some weeks after this incident, when the patient expressed doubt that Klein knew everything about him and made *only* valid interpretations, she understood these statements as signs of his paranoid mistrust (pp. 111–12).
>
> (Gedo 1988: 91)

Bion (1955) gives a rather chilling example of the excesses to which such an approach tends to lead one. Reporting on two interviews with a schizophrenic patient, Bion reports that in the first session the patient picked a tiny piece of skin from his face and then said that he felt quite empty. Bion then confidently informed this unfortunate man that the piece of skin was his penis, that he had therefore torn out his penis, and that all of his insides had come out with his penis (hence the feeling of emptiness). The patient, not surprisingly, expressed some confusion in reponse to this remark, which Bion appears to have attributed to his thought disorder. In the second session the patient remarked that he could not find any food, to which Bion replied, 'You feel that it has all been eaten up' (229). The patient then goes on to say that he feels unable to buy new clothes and that his socks are full of holes, which Bion attributes to the skin-picking episode of the previous day. He 'interprets' this to the patient, who then says that despite the numerous holes, the socks constrain his feet. Bion then tells him:

> Not only did you tear out your own penis but also mine. So today there is no interesting food – only a hole, a sock. But even this sock is made of a mass of holes, all of which you made and which you have joined together to constrict, or swallow and injure, your foot.
>
> (ibid.)

Laing (1983), commenting on this presentation, points out, to my mind appropriately, that:

> It is difficult to imagine what the patient could say that could tell Bion anything he does not think he knows. . . . It is difficult to imagine anything anyone could say which could possibly reveal to Bion that his constructions could be wrong, or that they are a grinding machine that reduces any sense to nonsense. It is difficult to fathom the difference between Bion's psychoanalytic phantasies and what is usually called a psychotic delusional system.
>
> (ibid.: 52)

COUNTERTRANSFERENCE

It is instructive to compare the history of the concept of transference in psychoanalytic thought with that of *countertransference*. Since the introduction of the concept in 1895 the basic operational meaning of transference has remained reasonably constant: it has always been understood to refer to the hijacking of a conscious relationship by archaic, primitive, and infantile unconscious concerns. In contrast to this, the concept of countertransference has become liberalized to such a great extent that it has virtually lost its original self-critical significance.

Freud first mentions countertransference in 1910, a good fifteen years after the début of transference. From the beginning Freud equated countertransference with the way analysts' blind spots, complexes, and inner resistances hamper their effective psycho-analytic functioning (Freud 1910, 1912b, 1915a). For Freud, counter-transference amounted to the inappropriate expression of the analyst's 'psychopathology' within the psychoanalytic arena. He seems to have retained this concept of countertransference for the remainder of his life. Thus, in spite of being in some sense a concep-tual counterpart of transference, the notion of countertransference was from its inception understood as pertaining to a broader range of phenomena. It should also be noted that in its pristine form counter-transference was intended as a classificatory rather than an explana-tory concept. Countertransference could not be invoked as a cause or an explanation of behavior. It corresponded, rather, to certain forms of behavior in themselves.

It is clear that Freud included in countertransference more than the analyst's transference . . . to his patient. While it is true that the patient may come to represent a figure of the analyst's past, the countertransference might arise simply because of the analyst's inability to deal appropriately with those aspects of the patient's communications and behavior which impinge on inner problems of his own. Thus if a psychoanalyst had not resolved problems con-nected with his own aggression, for example, he might need to placate his patient whenever he detected aggressive feelings or thoughts towards him in the patient. Similarly, if the analyst is threatened by his unconscious homosexual feelings, he may be unable to detect any homosexual implications in the patient's material; or, indeed, he may react with undue irritation to homo-sexual thoughts or wishes in the patient, may sidetrack the patient onto another topic, etc.

(Sandler *et al.* 1973: 63)

In its original sense, countertransference introduced a kind of democracy into psychoanalysis. The patient had no monopoly on neurosis. Not only was the analyst seen to suffer from neurotic problems, but it was also recognized that he or she was prone to import these conflicts into the psychoanalytic situation and consequently damage or obstruct therapeutic work with patients.

In Chapter 1 of this volume I suggested that the original version of Freud's theory of screen memories was never consistently applied to psychoanalytic data and was in effect repudiated and forgotten by Freud and his heirs largely because of their emotional unreadiness for a full confrontation with their own destructive impact upon their patients. What I have said so far about the theory of transference is consistent with this conjecture, for retaining the concept of transference requires one to idealize analysts' capacity for self-awareness and to denigrate patients' ability to perceive the implications of analysts' behavior accurately. The theory of transference entails that the analyst, *qua* analyst, occupies an epistemically privileged position *vis-à-vis* the patient by virtue of the training analysis which has supposedly vastly refined and enhanced his or her introspective abilities. Historically, it was the recognition of the existence of countertransference that led to the requirement that all analysts undergo a training analysis.

The democracy introduced with the concept of countertransference runs counter to the self-congratulatory, defensive spirit of the theory of transference. The reader unfamiliar with the history of psychoanalysis might venture to predict, or rather retrodict, that the original concept of countertransference would not be permitted to stand for long without being softened or modified in a way consistent with the ethos of omniscient analysts and purblind patients. These anticipations are borne out by the later history of psychoanalysis.

It was not long after Freud's death that the attrition of his concept of countertransference got under way. In 1939 Michael and Alice Balint published an influential paper arguing for a 'broader' understanding of countertransference. The Balints used 'countertransference' to designate everything that the analyst does which reveals his or her individual personality (Balint and Balint 1939). The way that an analyst ends a session, arranges the cushions on the couch, and expresses interpretations are all manifestations of countertransference. The Balints discuss how psychoanalysts' personal peculiarities inevitably influence the 'analytic atmosphere' but somehow end up asserting that although one would expect this to have some variable impact on analytic outcome,

> Curiously enough, this does not seem to be so. Our patients, with very few exceptions, are able to adapt themselves to most of these individual atmospheres and to proceed with their own transference, almost undisturbed by the analyst's countertransference.
>
> (ibid.: 206)

This is reassuring news. Although 'countertransference' is much more pervasive than had previously been recognized it apparently has little to do with analysts' psychopathology. Countertransference is reduced to style and idiosyncrasy, and is therefore quite harmless.

After 1939 countertransference came out of the closet. Prior to this period it seems to have been regarded as a cardinal analytic sin to be dealt with by further analysis (Freud 1937). As the profession began hesitantly to admit that countertransference is inevitable it simultaneously dulled the cutting edge of the concept. By the late 1940s Sharpe (1947) could write that, for an analyst to experience countertransference is just a manifestation of his or her humanity, which is necessary for being a good analyst (are bad analysts non-human?). Annie Reich wrote four years later that without the presence of countertransference one would have no aptitude or interest in analyzing people (Reich 1951). For Little (1960) empathy with the patient, a prerequisite for analytic work, is caused by countertransference (which has obviously become a causal/explanatory concept), while for Money-Kyrle (1956) empathy *is* a form of countertransference. By the late 1950s, therefore, the concept of countertransference had swallowed up numerous constructive components of the analytic attitude. The old foe had become a friend indeed. Who in their right mind would want to renounce or disavow a countertransference thus defined?

This theoretical trend reached its apogee in the work of Paula Heimann. Heimann's brief paper 'On countertransference' (1950) is widely hailed as a modern classic on psychoanalytic technique. A personal friend of Klein who was, as she herself put it, 'seduced' into analysis with her (Heimann, quoted in Grosskurth 1985: 381), Heimann published the paper as a gesture of independence. Although Heimann's theory of countertransference was avidly taken up by the British psychoanalytic community, Klein, with uncharacteristic level-headedness, remained firmly skeptical. In essence, Heimann regarded countertransference as a creation by the patient. The patient evokes emotional responses in the analyst which express the patient's unconscious conflicts and desires. The analyst's countertransference is, as it were, a product of his or her unconscious access to the patient's inner world. Rather than being a consequence of the analyst's psychological problems, as Freud would have it, countertransference has become an expression of the *patient's* problems. The analyst need only examine the reactions which have, so to speak, been thrust upon her by her unconscious sensitivity to have material for drawing inferences about her patient's unconscious issues.

This concept is well illustrated in a presentation by Khan (1963) which I will analyze in greater detail in Chapter 3. Khan describes how Peter, an eighteen-year-old patient, had been referred to him by a psychiatrist because of his parents' anxieties about Peter not sitting his exams. Peter agreed to begin once-weekly therapy with Khan and soon fell into complete silence. He remained silent for six consecutive sessions. Finding this situation rather annoying, Khan describes his own desire to shake Peter out of his torpor, the sheer torture of sitting hour after hour with a silent patient and his ongoing feelings of despair. Readers unfamiliar with psychoanalytic thinking will find nothing extraordinary in Khan's reactions to Peter. Surely, it is only natural to feel frustration in such a situation. But Khan is not content with so pedestrian an understanding. He asserts that his reactions to Peter's silence were *really* expressions of Peter's unconscious emotions. Khan confidently informs us that his frustration and despair were actually the emotions felt by 'child-Peter'. In other words, Khan did not believe that his reactions had anything to do with his personal limitations. Instead, he regarded them as evidence of his virtually telepathic sensitivity.

Heimann's idealization of the psychoanalyst's powers typified a trend in psychoanalysis which had been present, in the background, for decades but which had been held in check by the prevailing view of countertransference as something fundamentally undesirable. As far back as 1919, in fact, Ferenczi had stated that an analyst's distractability during a session is caused by the emptiness and futility of the patient's associations when he or she is in a state of resistance. In other words, an analyst gets bored because the patient is boring. The analyst's boredom is, to paraphrase Heimann, a creation of the patient. Ferenczi even goes so far as to say that it is of no consequence if in such situations the analyst falls asleep, because as soon as the patient utters something truly meaningful the analyst will automatically wake up! (Ferenczi 1919).

The concept of countertransference was introduced fifteen years after transference had entered the analytic literature. In contrast to the voluminous literature on transference, little was written on countertransference until the 1940s. As the acceptance of the idea of the inevitability of countertransference became more widespread, the original uncomplimentary connotations of the concept were attenuated. By the 1950s countertransference was widely regarded as a manifestation of analysts' unconscious sensitivity to their patients rather than as an expression of their personal limitations, defenses, and neurotic conflicts. With this development the one theoretical concept designed to restrict the pretensions to omniscience which seem to be so tempting for psychoanalysts was stripped of its critical power. Why did this occur? And why have psychoanalysts clung so steadfastly to the theory of transference, making it a cornerstone of clinical theory for more than eight decades? Both trends fit into a larger pattern in the evolution of psychoanalytic theory. Freud's quick abandonment of the original screen-memory theory some time around the turn of the century enabled him to avoid seriously enquiring into his own seductive and assaultive impact on his patients, while the roughly simultaneous development of the theory of transference made it possible for Freud to dismiss his patients' impressions of him as mere fantasies.[3] In spite of the defensive function of this theory (Szasz 1963), psychoanalysts were still able to use the notion of countertransference to call themselves into question. However, after Freud's death the concept of countertransference gradually became modified, while the Kleinian theory of transference gained considerable ground. Taken together, these factors conspired to justify an analytic stance of virtual omniscience and an immunity to the sort of disciplined self-criticism that is essential to the growth of any real science. Far from being, as Freud described it, the last great blow to human narcissism, psychoanalysis has become a bastion of grandiosity.

A second reason why psychoanalysts have retained the dubious theory of transference is more purely theoretical: they have not been aware of a workable alternative. The complex reasons for this and the presentation of what I believe to be a workable alternative will be taken up in Chapter 3.

3 An unimaginable substratum

Facts do not cease to exist because they are ignored.

Aldous Huxley

In my discussion of the Freudian theory of transference in Chapter 2, I noted that psychoanalysts foreclose the possibility that so-called transference phenomena are in fact derivatives of accurate unconscious perceptions. That psychoanalysts do not entertain a theory of unconscious perception is not a mere oversight on their part. It is deeply rooted in the philosophy of mind to which Freud subscribed. In the present chapter I will place Freud's philosophical position within its historical context[1] and then go on to show why it is that the neglected concept of unconscious perception is, in truth, a very powerful alternative to the theory of transference.

The dichotomy between the concepts of the conscious and unconscious parts of the mind seems not to have been an issue prior to the Cartesian revolution of the early seventeenth century. The ancient Greeks did not make the distinction at all. Their main word for the mind, or soul – *psyche* – denoted a life force and was neutral with respect to consciousness. This view persisted through the medieval Aristotelian tradition until Descartes came on the scene. Descartes denied that the soul was the animating principle of the body and, in contradiction to the Aristotelians, placed it instead in a separate ethereal domain. Along with the spiritualization of the soul Descartes propounded a theory that the soul is transparent to itself. This view is clearly summarized in a letter from Descartes to Mersenne:

> As to [the proposition] *that nothing can be in me, that is, in my mind, of which I am not conscious*, I have proved it in the *Meditations*, and it follows from the fact that the soul is distinct from the body and that its essence is to think.
>
> (Kenny 1970: 90)

When psychology began to differentiate itself from philosophy during the nineteenth century, many of its tenets were modeled on the basis of Cartesian assumptions. In *Psychology from an Empirical Standpoint* (1874), Brentano advocated the use of a mental process which he called *Wahrnemung* (inner perception) for the study of mental events. Brentano took pains to distinguish *Wahrnemung* from *Beobachtung* (inner observation). *Beobachtung* is the act of focusing directly on some mental content or event, as though one were studying a specimen under a microscope. Brentano cautioned psychologists against this procedure because he believed that it must inevitably alter the mental phenomenon being studied. *Wahrnemung*, on the other hand, involves a more subtle, indirect approach; looking at the mind, as it were, out of the corner of one's eye (Lyons 1986). Brentano's recommendations were seized upon by Wundt, who created the *introspectionist* school of psychology. Introspectionism was the first full-blown school of experimental psychology. Wundt sought to make introspection scientifically serviceable, and in order to accomplish this he had to use experimental subjects trained in introspective data gathering, hedging the introspective process about with strictly controlled and quantitatively monitored conditions. Wundt presented stimuli to subjects using a tachiscope and carefully measured reaction times. As James (1890: 192–3) jocularly summed up:

> This method taxes patience to the utmost, and could hardly have arisen in a country whose natives could be *bored*. . . . There is little of the grand style about these new prism, pendulum and chronograph-philosophers. They mean business, not chivalry.

Notwithstanding its businesslike intentions, the ponderous introspectionist program proved scientifically sterile. This, combined with powerful philosophical reservations about the value of introspection for scientific psychology (Comte 1830–42; James 1980) ushered in the decline of introspectionism and the birth of vigorous new anti-Cartesian paradigms for psychology: behaviorism and psychoanalysis. The behaviorist strategy, which was based on the work of Pavlov in Russia and was launched by Watson in the United States in 1913, involved avoiding the inner life of human beings altogether.

The behaviorists confined their attention to observable phenomena in the hope of elaborating a truly objective psychological science, decrying other orientations as 'mentalistic'. Psychoanalysis chose the less radical route of limiting the scope of introspection by inferring the existence of causally potent unconscious mental processes. These unconscious processes and contents can, according to the psychoanalytic theory, never be directly apprehended. Freud's final statement on this subject summarizes the psychoanalytic research program quite concisely.

> The processes with which it [psychoanalysis] is concerned are in themselves just as unknowable as those dealt with by other sciences, by chemistry or physics, for example; but it is possible to establish the laws which they obey and to follow their mutual relations and interdependencies. . . . In short, to arrive at what is described as an 'understanding' of the field of natural phenomena in question.
>
> (Freud 1940: 158)

Freud saw mental processes as 'in themselves unconscious' (Freud 1915b: 171) and to be studied by indirect inference rather than direct introspective access. Freud's whole approach is therefore profoundly anti-Cartesian. It undercuts the idea of privileged access to one's own inner life that is so central to the Cartesian and neo-Cartesian paradigms.[2] Freud's anti-Cartesian stance, however, was never total. Although he often stated that all mental processes are in the first instance unconscious he exempted the phenomenon of perception from this otherwise all-embracing constraint.[3]

Statements yoking perception to consciousness can be found in Freud's earliest psychological writings. There are several such references in his correspondence to Fliess. In the 1895 'Project for a scientific psychology', he states quite explicitly that:

> Consciousness is the subjective side of one part of the physical process in the nervous system, namely of the ω [perceptual] processes; and the omission of consciousness does not leave psychical events unaltered but involves the omission of the contribution from ω [perceptual neurones].
>
> (Freud 1950: 311)

Five years later in *The Interpretation of Dreams* (Freud 1900) this view is revised somewhat. The conscious system and the perceptual system are now differentiated from one another, and information is seen as flowing into the conscious system from the perceptual system. Freud suggests that this information can be 'revised' before entering consciousness, which implies that he was toying with the idea of non-conscious perception during this period, but in the end concludes that perceptual information must pass through the conscious mental system before being passed into the unconscious mental system.

In 'A metaphysical supplement to the theory of dreams' (1917b)

Freud reverts to the identification of perception and consciousness found in the 1895 'project':

> In *The Interpretation of Dreams* we were already led to a decision to regard conscious perception as the function of a special system. . . . We may regard this system, which is there called the *Pcpt.*, as coinciding with the system *Cs.*, on whose activity becoming conscious usually depends.
>
> (Freud 1917b: 232)

So close was the relationship between perception and consciousness in Freud's 1917 metapsychology that he designated this double-barreled system by the single abbreviation *Cs. (Pcpt.)*. By 1923 this had become the hyphenated *Pcpt.-Cs.* (Freud 1923).

Freud's curious limiting of perception to conscious perception not only ran against his own dogged insistence that the mental should not be limited to the conscious, it actually introduced unnecessary problems into the texture of his model of the mind. In Chapter 7 of *The Interpretation of Dreams* Freud presented his first published model of the mind: the so-called 'reflex-arc' model. This model pictures the mind as an apparatus extended in space with a terminal at each end (see Figure 1). The terminal at the left end of the apparatus is the perceptual terminal, and the terminal to the right is the motor terminal. Input into the apparatus occurs at the perceptual terminal, passes through a sequence of mnemonic (memory) systems, and is discharged by the motor terminal as output. Freud uses the metaphor of a camera ('compound optical instrument') to describe the first stages of this process. The perceptual terminal, like the lens of a camera, remains unmodified by the information that it receives while the mnemonic systems, like a series of photographic plates, retain traces of the input. Information (to use the more modern equivalent of Freud's 'innervation') passes through the perceptual 'lens' to be inscribed upon and analyzed by the mnemonic systems and finally passes through to the motor terminal to produce some form of activity. Freud has good reason to associate consciousness with the motor terminal, for the conscious mind controls voluntary movement. Some information passing through the apparatus will never reach the conscious, motor end: its passage will be blocked by an internal filter ('censorship') and will be retained in an unconscious mental system. Other information will pass into the 'preconscious' region of the mind near the motor end of the apparatus where it will be potentially available for conscious registration.

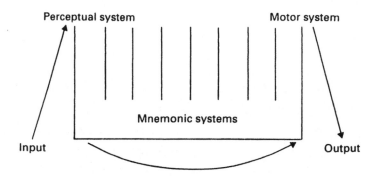

Figure 1   Freud's reflex-arc model

On close inspection this model reveals a serious inconsistency. As I have already described, Freud felt, in 1900, that the perceptual system fed its information directly into the conscious system. The perceptual system is on the left-hand side of the apparatus. But Freud has already identified the conscious mental system with the motor terminal (at the right side). In other words, consciousness appears twice, at opposite ends of the model. In the first four editions of the book Freud completely ignores this difficulty. It was not until the fifth edition which was published in 1919 that Freud appended a footnote explaining that:

> If we attempt to proceed further with this schematic picture, in which the systems are set out in linear succession, we should have to reckon with the fact that the system next beyond the pcs [preconscious] is the one to which consciousness must be ascribed – in other words, that *Pcpt. = Cs.*
>
> (Freud 1900: 541)

Erdelyi (1974, 1985) shows that Freud was constrained by his insistence on tying consciousness to perception, and considers this to be 'inconsistent with the overall dynamic thrust of psychoanalytic thinking' (Erdelyi 1985: 125). He proposes the alternative of detaching the perceptual system and making perception neutral with respect to consciousness. This opens the possibility of perceptual information passing directly to the unconscious system without having first traversed the conscious system.

This modification offers four additional advantages over the original model. First, it is consistent with experimental evidence which cannot be otherwise explained within the Freudian framework.

Second, it can incorporate *Freudian* hypotheses which are inconsistent with the standard model. Third, it provides a solution for a paradox generated by the first model: Sartre's Paradox: and fourth, it enables the Freudian model to incorporate and extend certain Kleinian findings.

The debate about the validity of the concept of unconscious perception in experimental psychology has been extremely contentious, in spite of the fact that masses of work has been done testing the hypothesis with generally favorable results. The experimental case for the existence of unconscious perception has been carefully documented by Dixon (1971). Accounts delving less deeply into the minutiae of experimental protocol can be found in Erdelyi (1985) and Kline (1984, 1988b). Commenting on the reluctance of psychologists to embrace the idea of subliminal perception despite powerful supporting evidence, Dixon remarks that:

So deeply rooted is this distaste for the idea of external unperceived control (particularly in a culture which sets the goal of personal freedom above all else) that it is understandable that there should have been so many attempts to cast doubts on the validity of this intriguing phenomenon which has continued to confront, and in some cases affront, twentieth century psychologists.

(Dixon 1971: 322)

Among the older studies of this domain one of the most striking is the Poetzl experiment. Poetzl noticed that patients suffering from a particular form of brain damage would 'release' perceptions into consciousness only some time after a visual stimulus had been presented. Thus, a patient who was presented with a stick of asparagus surrounded by roses and who was unable to perceive this at the moment of presentation because of a lesion in the visual area of his brain later selectively perceived a green tie pin on the collar insignia of a uniform. Poetzl concluded that similar delayed-release phenomena would be found among normal subjects in a neurological state resembling the state created by this type of lesion. The delayed release of perception seemed linked to the absence of what Poetzl called the 'abstracting process', and this 'abstracting process' is inhibited during sleep, so Poetzl chose twenty-four experimental subjects and exposed a subliminal image to each of them (exposed for one-hundredth of a second), asking them to report any dreams occurring after this experience. Poetzl found that those features of the stimulus which were not consciously perceived found their way into the subjects' dreams. Poetzl believed that the elements of the stimulus picture that were excluded from consciousness were linked with the subjects' unconscious preoccupations. These elements are, as it were, negatively selected because of the linkage with unconscious concerns and then used to create a dream expressing those concerns. Poetzl thus extended Freud's theory of the role of 'day residues' in the formation of dreams (Poetzl 1917; Freud 1900). The 'Poetzl effect' has been replicated many times (Dixon 1971). Among the most interesting of these subsequent studies is that carried out by Fisher (1954) who reached the conclusion that the unconscious meaning of the *experimental situation* was a powerful factor determining which aspects of the stimulus were to be excluded from consciousness and how these elements were deployed to create a dream.

Silverman (1983) used a technique which he called the Drive Activation Method to demonstrate the effects of unconsciously perceived stimuli on selected groups of subjects. He found that he could aggravate or reduce symptomatic behavior through the use of subliminal stimuli targeting specific unconscious conflicts. For example, a subliminal presentation of the message 'Mommy and I are one' produced a calming of symptoms among groups of male schizophrenics, while the presentation of subliminal oral-aggressive stimuli aggravated symptoms. Male homosexuals reacted to 'fuck Mommy' with increased homosexual behavior (Silverman and Weinberger 1985; Silverman *et al*. 1973). Like Poetzl, Silverman came to the conclusion that the effects of subliminal perception depend on an interaction between the content of the stimulus and the unconscious preoccupations of the subject.

Using a Scandinavian method of studying perception, the percept-genetic approach, some interesting studies have been carried out investigating perceptual defences (Sjoback 1967; Westerlundh 1976; Kragh and Smith 1970). For example, a picture may be defensively transformed by subjects when presented at low levels of intensity. Kragh (1969) found that when a picture of a 'hero' and one of a 'threat figure' were presented in this way some subjects perceived the two figures as inhuman, other saw them as separated from one another, some denied the threat, others turned the threat into its opposite, and so on.

Dixon has developed a sophisticated method for demonstrating that emotionally charged subliminal stimuli affect perceptual thresholds by measuring the threshold for the perception of light in one eye while presenting an emotionally significant stimulus word (such as 'cancer') subliminally to the other eye (Dixon 1981). His results seem to provide watertight evidence for the existence of unconscious perception.

These studies and many others like them appear at first glance to provide impressive corroboration for Freudian ideas about the unconscious mind. On closer inspection, however, they prove to be something of an embarrassment, because the hypothesis of unconscious *perception* is incompatible with the Freudian model of the mind as both the original topography of 1900 and the later structural model retain the intimate linkage between perception and consciousness. Thus, although the experimental work on perceptual defense provides support for the Freudian notion of defense in a general way, it also demands that the Freudian model be expanded to encompass unconscious preceptual processes (Erdelyi 1985). When Freud remarked in a 1919 footnote to *The Interpretation of Dreams* that Poetzl's work was an 'important contribution' which 'carries a wealth of implications' (Freud 1900: 181) he perhaps did not realize himself just how far reaching those implications were.

One expression of the fertility of Freud's genius was his capacity for expressing views which seemed clinically warranted to him and yet contradicted other parts of his theory of the human mind. Such contradictions, which can be located at many points in Freud's work, have created tensions within psychoanalysis which to this day have been neither resolved nor spent. Freud was explicit about his disinclination to create an all-encompassing, seamless explanatory system. He was fond of quoting the final couplet of Heine's *Die Heimkehr* lampooning Kant's architectonic efforts: 'With his bathrobe rags and long nightcaps He mends the world and plugs all the gaps.' We should not therefore be surprised to discover that in a number of passages in his writings Freud makes remarks which implicitly or even explicitly suggest a theory of direct unconscious perception. Among the general references the following quotation from 'A note on the unconscious in psycho-analysis' (1912c: 264) is typical:

A rough but not inadequate analogy to this supposed relation of conscious to unconscious activity might be drawn from the field of ordinary photography. The first stage of the photograph is the 'negative'; every photographic picture has to pass through the 'negative process', and some of these negatives which have held good in examination are admitted to the 'positive process', ending in the picture.

The first of Freud's specific, explicit references to unconscious perception to appear after 1899 is found in 'Recommendations to physicians practicing psycho-analysis' (1912b). He is describing the psychoanalytic method of listening to patients' free associations, which he summarizes as follows:

> To put it in a formula: he [the analyst] must turn his own uncon-
> scious like a receptive organ towards the transmitting unconscious
> of the patient. He must adjust himself to the patient as a telephone
> receiver is adjusted to the transmitting microphone. Just as the
> receiver converts back into sound waves the electric oscillations in
> the telephone line which were set up by sound waves, so the doctor's
> unconscious is able, from the derivatives of the unconscious which
> are transmitted to him, to reconstruct that unconscious, which has
> determined the patient's free-associations.
>
> (ibid.: 115–16)

Here Freud sees unconscious perception as a technical skill which can be consciously brought to bear on the listening process: the analyst is advised to actively 'turn' his unconscious toward that of the patient. Is Freud only speaking metaphorically? It is difficult to understand how so malleable and accessible an unconscious could be reconciled to his notion of the unconscious part of the mind as neither easily influenced nor directly accessible to the conscious part of the mind. In any case we find Freud taking a more consistent stance in 1913: 'I have had good reason for asserting that everyone possesses in his own uncon-scious an instrument with which he can interpret the utterances of the unconscious in other people' (Freud 1913a: 320).

A second passage also published in 1913 makes the same fundamen-tal point:

> Even the most ruthless suppression [of mental impulses] must leave
> room for distorted surrogate impulses and for reactions resulting
> from them. If so, however, we may safely assume that no genera-
> tion is able to conceal any of its more important mental processes
> from its successor.[4] For psychoanalysis has shown us that everyone
> possesses in his unconscious mental activity an apparatus which
> enables him to interpret other people's reactions, that is, to undo
> the distortions which other people have imposed upon the expression
> of their feelings.
>
> (Freud 1913b: 159)

These remarks show a broadened conception of unconscious percep-tion as compared to the 1912 passage quoted above. Unconscious perception is no longer a consciously deployed professional skill. It is seen as a part of the psychological endowment of all humanity. Although this process may be used by the psychoanalyst as a tool of understanding, unconscious perception is not the property of a professional elite. It arises spontaneously in human beings and performs the important function of ensuring the psychological continuity of culture.

Two years later Freud reiterated his position on unconscious perception.

> It is a very remarkable thing that the *Ucs.* of one human being can react upon that of another, without passing through the *Cs.* This deserves closer investigation, especially with a view to finding out whether preconscious activity can be excluded as playing a part in it; but descriptively speaking, the fact is incontestable.
>
> (Freud 1915b: 194)

There are several properties which Freud attributes to unconscious perception in these passages which are of enormous theoretical significance and are therefore worthy of focused attention. Freud sees unconscious perception as a faculty concerned with the interpersonal realm. He does not, for example, talk about the unconscious perception of houses or trees. For Freud, unconscious perception is the perception of emotional reality. Freud emphasizes that this form of perception enables us, without realizing it, to comprehend the psychological realities concealed behind defensive façades. The unconscious mind is able to undo the distortions which conceal raw emotional reality. As the unravelling of such distortions is precisely what psychoanalysis is supposed to be all about, it follows from Freud's hypotheses that we are all, unconsciously, natural psychoanalysts. Perhaps this is why Freud suggested that the psychoanalysts should attempt to turn their unconscious mind toward the unconscious mind of the patient: he wanted practitioners to tap this natural capacity for psychological insight. Freud is quite precise about which aspects of emotional reality are targeted by the unconscious perceptual system. The unconscious mind perceives the unconscious motives, affects, wishes, and so on of *others*. He is talking about *the unconscious perception of unconscious mental contents*. The unconscious part of the mind is not only seen as having direct access to the external world, but is considered to possess sophisticated cognitive abilities. The unconscious mind *analyzes* incoming information; it 'interprets' information and 'undoes' distortion, i.e. it draws valid and accurate inferences about the inner life of others.

All of this means that the unconscious mental system can be seen at least to some extent as adaptive: as in touch with external reality and therefore in principle as enhancing an individual's ability to cope

effectively with the real world. This view of the human psyche is remarkable not only because of its implications for the understanding of the subtle dynamics of human interaction, but also because it is in blatant contradiction to the great bulk of Freud's theorizing about the nature of the unconscious part of the mind. The idea of adaptive, perceptive, cognitively sophisticated unconscious abilities is a minor but persistent theme in Freud's work. It first emerges in the screen-memory theory of 1897–9, is mentioned in *Totem and Taboo* in 1913, in the papers on technique from the pre-First World War period, in the metapsychological paper on 'Repression' in 1915, and is alluded to in Freud's cryptic reference to Poetzl's work being 'rich in implications' in 1919. These references are so scattered and so at odds with the 'official' Freudian system that the majority of Freud scholars and psychoanalytic theorists have completely ignored them. In the 'official' Freudian theory the unconscious part of the mind has no direct access to perceptual information. All that it 'knows' about external reality has been obtained 'second-hand' from the conscious part of the mind.

The unconscious part of the mind is also supposed to operate under the domination of the pleasure principle. The pleasure principle regulates the course of unconscious mental processes. Freud developed his concept of the pleasure principle from the 'principle of constancy' proposed by the German psychophysicist Gustav Fechner (1873) (who derived the idea from the law of the conservation of energy developed by Mayer and Helmholz in the 1840s). The pleasure principle states that the 'mental apparatus' strives to keep its own level of excitation as low as possible, and thus seeks to immediately discharge tension above a certain threshold. In more psychological language this means that the human mind tends to seek pleasure (and banish unpleasure) by the most immediate and direct means possible. The quickest route to the fulfillment of the pleasure principle is hallucination. Under the sway of the pleasure principle the mind is inclined to magically conjure up those experiences which promise pleasure (the relief from internal tension) and to magically annihilate any obstacle to pleasure. It is plain from this account that the pleasure principle is extremely maladaptive, for no organism could survive for long that was capable only of wishing, dreaming, and hallucinating gratifications while simply denying hinderances and dangers. This is why, in Freud's view, the human mind come to be regulated by the reality principle. The reality principle, which makes perception of the external world possible, is simply the ability to adapt one's pleasure-seeking project to the exigencies of reality and thereby become able to substitute real understanding of the external world for infantile fantasies. The pleasure principle is obviously a childish mode of operation and is closely associated with psychopathology (mechanisms of defense, for instance, which 'magic away' threatening ideas, operate according to the pleasure principle), while the reality principle is seen as mature and sane.

Freud initially believed that the unconscious system of the mind was completely dominated by the pleasure principle. In other words, he believed that the unconscious part of the mind was basically childish, pleasure-seeking, wish-fulfilling, and incapable of accurate perception of the external world. The domination of the unconscious part of the mind by the pleasure principle in Freud's metapsychology renders it an *austistic* system in touch only with its hedonistic projects and utterly disabled *vis-à-vis* adaptation to the external environment. To follow the unconscious is to follow the pleasure principle, which is to be misled. A real understanding of the world and other people in it must come from the reality principle which governs the conscious portion of the mind. Later, in 1919, Freud added that a second principle, the repetition compulsion, also dominated unconscious mental life. The repetition compulsion is even blinder and less adaptive than the pleasure principle, seeking to mindlessly repeat experiences regardless of the consequent yield of unpleasure.

A great deal of practical importance hangs on this standard psychoanalytic view of the unconscious part of the mind. The concept of transference, so central to psychoanalytic technique and epistemologically fundamental to psychoanalytic theory, is predicated upon the assumption that the unconscious part of the mind is remote from perception and ruled by irrational forces. Because the unconscious mind is regarded, a priori, as incapable of perception, any unconscious preoccupation with the person of the analyst is assumed to be an expression of factors purely internal to the patient such as phantasy, memory, and desire. Perceptions of the analyst can, of course, be obtained through the conscious mind and then used by the unconscious mind, but because the latter is assumed to be ruled by irrational energies the perceptions will be used for gratification rather than knowledge. The unconscious mental system is seen as a sort of psychological black hole that swallows up everything that comes within its sphere of influence. Everything that the unconscious touches, so the theory goes, is subverted to its own hedonistic and blindly repetitive aims.

The autistic conception of the unconscious mind is also a basis for the psychoanalytic theory of madness and cure. (Following Langs, I use the term 'madness' instead of 'illness' or 'psychopathology' with their inappropriately medical overtones.) In classical psychoanalytic theory madness is seen as an expression of a battle between parts of the mind. The ego, which is the seat of consciousness, but is not itself totally conscious, wars against the instinctually seething id, which is totally unconscious. The chief aim psychoanalytic treatment is to bring this conflict into the open – into the conscious sphere of the ego – which undermines neurotic symptoms and allows fresh learning to be brought to bear upon the anachronistic commitments of the unconscious mind. It follows from all that has been said that the target for therapeutic interventions is the patient's conscious ego, for this is the only portion of the patient's mind that is directly in touch with external reality. The psychoanalyst attempts to enlist the patient's conscious ego as an ally in order to therapeutically explore the murkier unconscious regions. Consequently, no therapeutic maneuver can be understood as having a direct, unmediated impact on the unconscious mental system.

Freud's tentative theory of unconscious perception flies in the face of his more standard theorizing. It depicts the unconscious mental functions as capable of making incisive psychological observations and of drawing sophisticated inferences from them. In short, it offers a portrait of the unconscious mind as *adaptive*. Although Freud does not spell this out, this entails a number of profound implications for psychoanalytic theory and technique. We will return to these implications in the final section of the present chapter.

In our brief survey of Freud's thinking we have explored how the theoretical linkage between perception and consciousness introduced incoherencies in his first topographical model. In his monumental *Being and Nothingness*, Sartre shows, albeit without fully realizing it, how this feature of Freud's thinking generates a different sort of inner contradiction (Sartre 1956). Sartre is interested in the question of whether self-deception (which he calls *mauvaise foi* – 'bad faith') is possible. The concept of self-deception seems modeled on the interpersonal situation in which one person deceives another. Sartre points out that in order to deceive another person successfully it is helpful to be entirely lucid about what one is doing. If one is not quite self-aware when trying to pull the wool over someone's eyes it is very easy to put a foot wrong and spoil the intended effect. Now, if this feature of deception is shifted to the internal stage it produces a paradox. Because in this scenario the deceiver and the deceived are the same person, it would seem that self-deception must by its very nature be a rather self-defeating process, for if to know that you are deceiving someone is intrinsic to deception, then to know that you are deceiving yourself is intrinsic to self-deception. However, if subjects know that they are deceiving themselves the self-deception cannot 'come off' because its victim is never successfully duped. The self-deceiving agent has 'a comprehension of bad faith as such' (205). The coincidence of liar and victim means that 'I must know in my capacity of deceiver the truth which is hidden from me in my capacity as the one deceived' (ibid.). In order to execute this argument Sartre must accept the Cartesian premise of 'the total translucency of consciousness' (ibid.) – that is, Sartre believes that if one perceives something then one *must* simultaneously be conscious of perceiving it. Thus, 'That which affects itself with bad faith must be conscious (of) its bad faith' (ibid.). Sartre describes the paradox that this argument generates as follows:

> It appears then that I must be in good faith, at least to the extent that I am conscious of my bad faith. But then this whole psychic system is annihilated. We must agree in fact that if I deliberately and cynically lie to myself, I fail completely in this undertaking; the lie falls back and collapses beneath my look; it is ruined *from behind* by the very consciousness of lying to myself which pitilessly constitutes itself well within my project as its very condition.
>
> (ibid.: 206)

Sartre has now cleared the way for an existential critique of the psychoanalytic conception of the structure of the mind. He points out that people seize upon the notion of an unconscious mind in order to dispose of this awkward state of affairs. Freud 'has cut the psychic whole in two' (207) with his hypothesis of separate, mutually antagonistic psychic structures. At first sight this seems to solve the paradox because if they are, in fact, two mental agencies we might imagine them relating to one another along interpersonal lines. One mental agency could be imagined as deceiving the other non-paradoxically. The conception of the unconscious part of the mind as similar to a separate mind is canonically sound. Although he does not give his source, Sartre seems to be drawing on a paper entitled 'The unconscious' published by Freud in 1915. In this paper Freud argues that human beings are *directly* acquainted with nothing except their own conscious mental states and that all knowledge of the external world is to some extent inferential. It follows that the notion that other people are also conscious beings is, strictly speaking, an inference based on observations of their behavior and 'cannot share the immediate certainty which we have of our own consciousness' (Freud 1915b: 169).

Psychoanalysis demands nothing more than that we should apply the process of inference to ourselves also. . . . All the acts and manifestations which I notice in myself and do not know how to link up with the rest of my mental life must be judged as if they belonged to someone else: they are to be explained by a mental life ascribed to this other person.

(ibid.)

The question now arises: Where within the Freudian model of the mind can the deceiver–deceived relationship be localized? The deceiver cannot be the conscious part of the mind (Sartre actually switches to speaking about the ego and the id, which are components of a different Freudian model, at this point in the discussion: as this is rather confusing and totally unnecessary I will refer to the conscious and unconscious parts of the mind instead). The conscious part of the mind is the one which has been duped by some other part of the mind. The deceiver cannot be identified with the unconscious mental contents either, because these are continually trying to find a means of expression to announce their presence. Sartre highlights the difficulty by considering the concept of resistance. Who is it that does the resisting in a psychoanalytic session? The conscious portion of the mind is not the resister, for it is totally ignorant of what it is that is being resisted. The unconscious mental contents are not doing the resisting either for they are, as it were, allies of the analyst's uncovering operations. Considered in light of Freud's first topographical model it must be the *censor* who resists and deceives: 'It [the censor] alone can comprehend the questions or the revelations of the psychoanalyst as approaching more or less near to the real drives which it strives to repress – it alone because it alone *knows* what it is repressing' (ibid.: 208–9).

The censor must be able to perceive the offending mental contents in order to perform the task of repression. It must be able to 'target' these. But Sartre then falls back on the dubious Cartesian premise that 'All knowing is consciousness of knowing' (209) to assert that the censor must be *conscious* of that which it represses. It follows that in the Freudian system it is the censor who is in bad faith. This merely defers the problem rather than solving it. The notion that it is the censor rather than the whole person who is in bad faith encounters the same paradox as the original considerations; how can the censor be *conscious* of repressed ideas and continue to keep them *unconscious*? For Sartre proponents of the psychoanalytic explanation of self-deception 'have hypostatized and "reified" bad faith; they have not escaped it' (210). According to Sartre the theory of a divided mind merely gives an illusion of having resolved the paradox of self-deception. In fact, it just deposits us back at our point of departure. Freud was certainly aware of this difficulty, which was one of his motives for revising the topography in *The Ego and the Id* (Freud 1923). To oversimplify somewhat, the antagonism between the conscious and unconscious parts of the mind was replaced by the antagonism between the partially conscious ego and the totally unconscious id. The mechanisms of defense, which are the equivalent of the 'censor' of the first topography, emanate from the unconscious region of the ego and keep the id separate from the ego. Although these defense mechanisms are unconscious, they are not repressed (this would involve an infinite regress of defense mechanisms). The defense mechanisms are unconscious in a *systemic* sense: they are unconscious because that is how the mind is constructed. There is no motive or force keeping the defense mechanisms unconscious just as there is no motive determining why people have two eyes. This formulation allows Freud to explain how it is that unconscious ideas can be defensively targeted and yet remain unconscious. But this explanatory advantage extracts a price. It would appear that the 1923 structural model commits Freud to the idea that the ego is able unconsciously to perceive the contents of the id, and yet Freud retains the view in *The Ego and the Id*, and in all subsequent writings on the subject, that perception is bound up with consciousness. The price that Freud pays for his advance, then, is a contradiction in his theory.

The obvious remedy for both Sartre's paradox and Freud's theoretical contradiction is to jettison the Cartesian premise equating perception with consciousness.[5] If perception is understood to be an essentially non-conscious function which obtains information and relays it to either the conscious or unconscious mental systems, then the notion of a perceptive censor which is at the same time unconscious of the objects which it perceives poses no philosophical dilemma. The distinction between perception and consciousness means that one can perceive something and bar that something from conscious awareness without having to be conscious that one is engaged in this activity. As well as refuting Sartre, this theoretical adjustment heals the lesion in Freud's later structural model because it gives an explanation of how it is that the ego unconsciously perceives the contents of the id in order to keep them repressed. A final advantage of the acceptance of the process of unconscious perception is that it provides a theoretical rationale for the neo-Kleinian theory of countertransference. Heimann's theory presupposes the notion of unconscious perception. She writes, for example, that 'his [the analyst's] *unconscious perception* of the patient's unconscious is more accurate and in advance of his conscious perception of the situation' (Heimann 1950: 82, emphasis added). Heimann makes explicit something which Freud expresses implicitly: not only does the unconscious part of the mind possess perceptual abilities, but these abilities are, within their special sphere of operation, actually *superior* to conscious abilities. The unconscious part of the mind is able to spontaneously interpret the unconscious concerns of other people while the conscious mind is able to make comparable inferences only laboriously and with the benefit of specialized training. There is no reason why the one-sidedness and limited nature of Heimann's theory should prevent us from exploiting its advantages.

As it stands, Heimann's theory of countertransference encourages abuse. Even mainstream psychoanalysts who employ this approach have expressed some concern about its widespread invocation (for example, Kohon 1986). Heimann's theory has the advantage of recognizing the existence and clinical significance of unconscious perception, but it also possesses major disadvantages. First of all, the theory is one-sided. If unconscious to unconscious perception exists it must surely be an ability shared by all humanity. Heimann, and those who follow her, tend to stress the analyst's capacity for unconscious perception of the patient, but pay little or no attention to the patient's ability to unconsciously comprehend the hidden inner life of the analyst. Unconscious perception is therefore treated very much in the spirit of Freud's original 1912 discussion of the subject as a special technical skill of the analyst. To say that the patient has such access to the hidden recesses of the analyst's mind would involve some discussion of what Trombi (1987) call the *patient's* countertransference. The one-sided emphasis of this theory, its description of the flow of unconscious information from patient to the analyst but not vice versa, gives it an elitist and self-serving flavor. Racker takes a step in the right direction when he states that

> Just as countertransference is a 'creation' of the patient . . . and an integral part of his inner and outer world, so also, in some measure, is transference the analyst's creation and an integral part of his inner and outer world.
>
> (Racker 1974: 178)

Racker recognizes that psychoanalytic phenomena have an interactional basis and that attitudes 'in' the patient may be induced by the analyst, but he stops short of affirming that this may reflect patients' sensitivity.

A second difficulty with this perspective is that it encourages an idealised conception of psychoanalysts' unconscious abilities. Analysts' reactions to their patients are taken to be *nothing but* unconscious perceptions. This is not just an abuse of Heimann's position: it is an orientation which she explicitly licensed. In her groundbreaking paper she went so far as to call the analysts' counter-transference the patient's *creation*. Implicitly, the analyst's uncon-scious mind is conceived of as some sort of *tabula rasa* just waiting to be inscribed with the patient's preoccupations. Any countertrans-ference arising in the analyst can then be confidently ascribed to the patient who is in no position to argue because, of course, the 'counter-transferred' elements are supposed to be unconscious. There is little appreciation of the idea that even if all interpersonal responses contain a significant element of unconscious perception, these percep-tions could not possibly – according to psychoanalytic theory – emerge directly into consciousness. Unconscious ideas emerge indirectly as derivatives. Their 'cathexis' is transferred on to preconscious ideas, as I have described in Chapter 2. Racker (1974) has criticized the tendency of psychoanalysts to treat their countertransference responses as direct expressions of their patients' unconscious issues.

Thus, the theory of unconscious perception can encompass Heimann's notion of countertransference, but only if the latter is modified. The perceptual process must be seen as mutual – the possession of both analyst and patient – and also as emerging into consciousness in an indirect, derivative form that requires interpreta-tion. If, as Heimann asserts, the analyst's countertransference is an instrument of research into the patient's unconscious, it must follow that the patient's 'countertransference' is an instrument of research into his or her analyst's unconscious as well.

Given all of the considerations in the foregoing discussion, and bearing in mind the poverty of the rival concept of transference, the theory of unconscious perception emerges as a truly formidable idea capable of resolving contradictions within Freudian theory, estab-lishing powerful experimental support for psychoanalytic hypotheses, refuting philosophical objections to the theory of the unconscious mind, and drawing together diverse strands within the broad spectrum of psychoanalytic thought. In light of these clear advantages bestowed by the theory, it seems puzzling that there has not been a veritable stampede to embrace, integrate, and develop it as a welcome addition to psychoanalytic theory. There would be nothing 'anti-Freudian' about incorporating unconscious perception. Freud was always adamant that the unconscious part of the mind was a theoretical entity which by definition could never be apprehended directly. He described it as an 'unimaginable substratum' (Freud 1933: 90), unknowable in itself. Empirical observation leads us to infer the existence of an unconscious part of the mind, which we represent by means of models. As a scientist, Freud believed that these models are always provisional and should be discarded as they become obsolete. It is curious, then, that the issue of unconscious perception is not even widely debated within the profession. Perhaps this reluctance will not be so difficult to comprehend if we consider the *costs* that would be incurred.

The theory of transference – and the theory of an autistic, infantile unconscious mind upon which it is based – as well as the one-sided theories of countertransference, all conspire to place the analyst in an extremely privileged position *vis-à-vis* the patient. In spite of the fine rhetoric about psychoanalysts' ability to remain in doubt, their non-directive approach, and their concern with patients' inner truth, psychoanalysts work both sides of the street, presenting themselves as knowing their patients better than they know themselves while characterizing patients' views of their analysts as heavily distorted by transference. This skewed conception of the therapeutic interaction is inevitable in so far as one operates within the standard psychoanalytic paradigms: it is built into the theory itself. What I have presented as regrettable aspects of psychoanalytic technique do not stem from the personal attitudes of practitioners. It is not the case that only 'rigid' or doctrinaire analysts fall into this way of seeing things. No matter how humble, open-minded, or flexible one is as a person, one must, by virtue of buying into the theory of the mind propounded by psychoanalysis (and the theory of technique stemming from it), exhalt oneself and denigrate the patient. No amount of good intentions can alter this. Liberal psychoanalysts' talk of 'not knowing', tolerating uncertainty, and so on is wonderful as ideology, but these sentiments run aground upon the realities of psychoanalytic practice. The Bion who wrote that analysts 'must have a great capacity for tolerating their analyzands' statements without rushing to the conclusion that they know the interpretations' (Bion 1974: 72) is the same man who informed his hapless schizophrenic patient that by pulling a small piece of skin off his face he was castrating himself and his analyst, causing all of their insides to pour out of the wounds!

To replace the theory of transference with the theory of unconscious perception would be to eschew the belief that one is, as an analyst, epistemically privileged. Both patient and analyst would be seen as evolutionarily equipped with the ability to unconsciously understand one another. We are wired to comprehend one another, unconscious to unconscious. We transmit and receive psychological information without being in the least consciously aware that this is going on. The analyst has no monopoly on the understanding of unconscious mental content. The theory of unconscious perception would demand of psychoanalysts that they learn from patients about their own unconscious mental life; that they receive insight as well as give it. This means, of course, that the condescending view of patients as unenlightened and uninsightful would have to be discarded in favor of a concept of all people as possessing very penetrating and adaptive psychological resources. The romantic image of the psychoanalyst leading his benighted patients out of the web of transferential illusion would have to yield to an altogether more humbling alternative.

The theory of unconscious perception also entails the idea that psychoanalysis is a deeply interactional process. It would no longer be legitimate to regard the contents of the unconscious mind as things purely 'within' the patient. The emergence of unconscious concerns would no longer be seen as merely *facilitated* by the psychoanalyst; they would be regarded as being to a significant extent *determined* by him. The leading unconscious concerns of a patient, at any given time, would be seen as evoked by his analyst and would be assumed to contain a disguised expression of the patient's valid, accurate unconscious inferences about the unconscious meaning of his analyst's behavior. The paradigm shift from transference to unconscious perception would rule out notions of 'the patient's resistance', 'the patient's transference' and 'the patient's phantasies'. All of these unconscious factors would be regarded as jointly created by the patient and analyst, and it would be absurd for one party to the interaction to absolve him- or herself of responsibility for events within the therapeutic encounter. The idea of a patient's unconscious attitude toward an analyst being 'inappropriate' is rendered a priori impossible, because the analyst him- or herself would be implicated in the formation of that attitude. Thus, the interactional emphasis involves a shift from the standard psychoanalytic stress on phantasy to a new concern with interpersonal reality, and with this comes a concern with the unconscious impact of the here-and-now situation over and above the patient's remembered and reconstructed past. Instead of being a process centrally occupied with the unraveling of a repressed life history, psychoanalysis would of necessity become an exploration of how patients unconsciously process perceptions of the immediate psychoanalytic situation. Of course, here-and-now perceptions are not indiscriminately kept out of awareness. It is reasonable to assume that there must be some reason why certain inferences about the psyche of another person are processed unconsciously, while other percep-tions and inferences are processed consciously. It is consistent with both psychoanalytic theory and common sense to assume that the type of interpersonal perception handled by the unconscious part of the mind must possess particularly intense emotional significance.[6] The unconscious mental system, as Freud said somewhere, does not deal with trivialities. I believe this to be the real reason why the psycho-analytic profession has given unconscious perception a wide berth. Freud himself had the courage to advance to the verge of making unconscious perception a central explanatory concept for psycho-analysis before drawing back to take refuge in the altogether more reassuring theory of transference. Freud discovered screen memories to be disguised, unconscious readings of the implications of here-and-now situations. He used this insight to good effect in his self-analysis. Although Freud believed that the 'reproductions' of his hysterical patients served the same function, he never once wrote an analysis of a psychoanalytic session using this theory. Freud was committed to the notion that the circumstances in which such derivative material emerges provides the context in terms of which the material is to be understood. To apply these powerful ideas to his clinical work would have committed Freud to the proposition that his patients' violent and perverse images suggesting the themes of incest and abuse had some-thing to do with the implications of his own behavior and his own unconscious motives. He would have had to accept and to announce to the world that his patients perceived him, with good reason, as a perverse sexual abuser himself.

I have shown in Chapter 1 that this is quite a plausible interpreta-tion of Freud's technique during this period. D.M. Thomas has noted the erotic quality of much of Freud's writing on his early hysterical patients, conveying the impression of 'mildly sadistic pornography' (Thomas 1982: 3). This is skillfully brought out by means of some strategic deletions. Take, for example, Thomas's rendering of a segment of the case of Fräuline Elizabeth von R.

> [The truth] . . . now forced itself irresistibly upon her once more, like a flash of lightning in the dark . . . the analyst's labours were richly rewarded . . . fending off . . . excitations . . . resistance . . . a shattering effect on the poor girl . . . the most frightful pains . . . one last desperate effort to reject . . . we probed . . . I was able to relieve her once more.
>
> (Freud and Breuer 1895: 156–8)

Freud's case provides an example of the profound impact that the theory of unconscious perception would have on the practice of psychoanalysis. His patients unconsciously told him that by placing them on the couch, massaging their foreheads, pressing them for information, and forcing his interpretations on them, he was behaving in a seductive, perverse, and assaultive manner. They told him, implicitly, that he should not do psychotherapy in that way. To take unconscious perception seriously means to seriously open oneself to such criticisms from one's patients without the convenient distancing device of the concept of transference.

The radical impact of this approach will become even more apparent if we consider another, more contemporary example of the case by Khan referred to briefly in Chapter 2. In 1963 Khan, who at the time was a respected member of the 'independent' group of British psychoanalysts, published a short account of the psychoanalytic treatment of a schizoid adolescent named Peter. Peter had initially been referred to a psychiatrist by his parents because of his gradual withdrawal from social and academic life, which culminated in a refusal to take his exams seriously and go on to university. Peter's upper-class professional parents feared that he would have a psychotic breakdown as his mother had done some years previously. The psychiatrist passed Peter on to Khan, along with this background information. In the initial interview Peter informed Khan that he had come along because of his parents' distress rather than his own. He felt that undergoing psychoanalysis would be a stupid waste of time. After explaining that he did not consider himself to be ill, Peter asked Khan what he wanted him to do. Khan suggested once-a-week psychoanalytic psychotherapy (Khan 1963).

During the first four sessions Peter 'found it hard to speak' (34). After the fourth session Peter fell completely silent and remained in silence for the next six sessions. During these hours of silence Khan spent his time studying his own inner responses to the situation: attempting to understand Peter through analyzing his own countertransference. Khan noticed that he felt impatient with Peter's seemingly apathetic attitude and that he had impulses to shake Peter out of it. He also noted that he was inclined to withdraw into his own world in response to these long, silent, and fruitless hours. Khan inferred that he was being placed in the role of 'child Peter' while Peter himself played the role of his own mother. Khan felt that the two of them were enacting a relationship which Peter had had with his mother during infancy. He, Peter, had been full of childhood liveliness but was confronted with a psychotically depressed mother. He could not provoke warm responses from her and so he became withdrawn and antisocial. Khan expressed these views to Peter in the form of a lengthy interpretation during the eleventh session. Khan presented the idea of the mother's depression to Peter as an inference, but of course he had actually obtained this information from the referring psychiatrist prior to the first consultation. Peter remarked that he remembered his mother's depression and, after discussing this a while, spontaneously reported a dream: 'The dream was: "I am in my grandmother's house by the seaside. A crab is trying to come through the glass window. I feel very threatened and frightened and wake up screaming" ' (ibid.: 39). Khan quickly interpreted, apparently without the benefit of any free associations, that the crab represented Peter's 'aggressive aliveness and excitement which he had repressed and could experience only as a threat' (39–40). Peter then recalled that his mother had had the next child after him at around the time of the depression, and he thought that he might have been sent away when she was due to give birth.

In standard analytic fashion Khan describes Peter's silence, his reaction to the interpretation, his dream, and his associations to Khan's intervention solely in terms of Peter's inner world of desires, phantasies, and memories. There is, naturally, no suggestion that any of this could be determined by Khan's conduct as an analyst and the implications of the psychoanalytic situation which he had established. Khan saw the analytic situation as something which facilitated the emergence of Peter's inner world. Although Peter's inner world is described as having a profound impact on what went on inside Khan, Peter's behavior is implicitly portrayed as untouched by the actualities of the analytic encounter. It is seen as being completely under the sway of his historically rooted intrapsychic conflicts. Khan's silence in response to Peter, for example, is understood as the outcome of carefully considered conscious decisions about what would be the correct psychoanalytic procedure in these circumstances. Peter's silence, on the other hand, is seen as (a) a defensive defiance of the therapeutic process, (b) a typical adolescent flight from intrapsychic conflict, (c) an attempt to establish magical-symbiotic fusion with the analyst, and (d) the communication of a disturbed early object-relationship with his mother. In short, there is little that is adaptive or appropriate about Peter's silence in his analyst's eyes.

Let us consider Peter's silence from the perspective of unconscious perception. Let us ask ourselves the question 'Is there anything about Khan's conduct in this case that would warrant his patient's silence?' I submit that the following facts are essential for any attempt to comprehend the meaning of Peter's silence.

1 Peter was referred to Khan by a third party, the psychiatrist, who also passed on to Khan, without Peter's express permission, details of Peter's personal and family history.
2 Peter did not believe himself to be in need of psychoanalytic help. He was referred to the psychiatrist by his parents, and agreed to speak to Khan because he felt that it would ease his parents' distress.
3 When Peter asked Khan what he should do, Khan suggested that he begin psychotherapy. Khan thereby renounced any pretence of neutrality and implicitly allied himself with Peter's parents who wanted to 'cure' him of the disinclination to attend university.

The reality of the situation is, then, that Peter was in therapy as an act of conformity to the wishes of others. He had evidence to indicate that Khan was in sympathy with his parents over the university issue (later in the case Khan describes his relief when Peter decides to sit his examinations. Peter then remarks to him 'Don't get too hopeful. I have not promised to go to the university' – p. 40). He also may or may not have known at the beginning of therapy that Khan had obtained information about him from the psychiatrist. Like Freud's case of Dora, Peter's analytic experience is riddled with third parties. It is a thinly disguised exercise in coercion. Is it really so surprising, then, that Peter was not inclined to speak? To my mind it would have been infinitely more remarkable, considering the circumstances of his treatment, if Peter had begun to pour his heart out to Khan. From the beginning, Khan understands Peter's taciturn behavior as a problem, remarking that he found it 'hard' to talk (i.e. seeing Peter's silence as reflecting a disability). By doing this he pathologized his patient. Khan took a piece of behavior as a symptom which might equally – or more plausibly – be understood as Peter's effort to retain a measure of integrity in an oppressive situation. I do not offer this interpretation as definitively or self-evidently true. I offer it as a hypothesis. There is some obvious sense in understanding Peter's silence in this way. This does not contradict the existence of other causally relevant factors – Peter's personality, his history, his defenses, and so on, but *it places them in the context of the contemporary material reality of this therapeutic situation*. It is striking that Khan does not mention these factors as relevant to Peter's silence even once in his account of the treatment. Khan was not a psychoanalytic extremist. Like his mentor Winnicott he stressed the importance of the 'real relationship' in psychoanalysis. Despite this, he did not seem to have an inkling that there was something about this analytic set-up that could rationally explain Peter's silence.

When Khan finally comes to make his interpretation of Peter's silence he implicitly announces that he has obtained information from the psychiatrist – who had, in turn, apparently obtained it from Peter's parents. Although Khan claims to have pieced the interpretation together entirely on the basis of his countertransference to Peter, he had already been given the information about the mother's depression by the psychiatrist. Thus, if Peter had not been aware of the passage of information from the psychiatrist to Khan, he would have been alerted to the fact at this point. Although he gives no conscious indication, one can easily imagine how Khan's unwitting confession might have been distressing to Peter. It would have shown him that his analyst was prepared to make interpretations about him based on information obtained ultimately from his parents, thus reinforcing the conspiratorial quality of the psychotherapy. Also, it would imply that his analyst had little regard for confidentiality. The fact that Khan was open to receiving and exploiting information about Peter obtained from others might suggest that he would likewise be prepared to divulge information about Peter to others (later on, just prior to Peter suffering a 'breakdown', Khan does in fact discuss Peter with his parents).

Peter responds to the interpretation in two distinct ways. First, he responds consciously with the statement that he remembers his mother's depression. Second, he reports a dream. It is this second response which would be assumed by any psychoanalyst to convey Peter's *unconscious* response to the interpretation. Some rather speculative interpreting allows Khan to take the dream as a confirmation of his hypothesis. In standard psychoanalytic fashion, Khan sees the dream purely as a reflection of the patient's inner world, jumping to the conclusion that the threatening crab symbolizes Peter's repressed vitality. Once again, the interpretation of the dream does not relate its content in any way to the emotionally fraught realities of this analytic setting. Khan makes no effort to relate this dream to the here-and-now. He hangs it, as it were, in a contextless intrapsychic limbo. What happens if we take the dream as an expression of Peter's unconscious perception of the real implications of that psychoanalytic moment? Phenomenologically, the dream makes no reference to Khan's rather benign central notion of 'aliveness'. It is a terrifying dream of intrusion. Something – a crab – is trying to get somewhere where it doesn't belong. Let us ask ourselves if there is anything about this therapeutic situation which might plausibly be understood as a frightening intrusion? The answer is so obvious that it hardly seems worth specifying. Intrusion is the leitmotif of Peter's analysis: intrusion by his parents, intrusion by the psychiatrist, and intrusion by Khan. These are real intrusions, not mere phantasies and transferences. They are not intrusions of 'aliveness': they are intrusions of real, flesh-and-blood people.

After Khan's interpretation of the dream, Peter remembers that his mother's depression coincided with the birth of another child, and wonders if he had been sent away (to his grandmother?) when the baby was expected. Once again Khan seems to offer this as a confirmation of his hypothesis (because psychoanalysts have no objective criteria for evaluating interpretations, they approach this subjectively), and once again he does not see any connections between Peter's memory and the realities of his immediate situation. If we take this memory as a screen memory, in Freud's pristine sense of the term, it can be understood as a poignant comment on the analysis. In this view Peter likens himself to a child who is displaced by a new baby, whose mother no longer regards him as central and who is actually put aside, sent away, distanced. I submit that this is a highly plausible reading of Peter's contemporary predicament. Peter had communicated to Khan, through the dream, something of his sense of violation. Khan took no notice of the message, relating the dream images rather abstractedly to Peter's inner world with no recognition of the interactional dimension of the way that he, Khan, was impacting upon Peter. The dream contained a desperate, urgent message which was perhaps a message to Khan that Peter felt that he had been dismissed and rejected by Khan. This is not a *transference* interpretation: I am not suggesting that Peter *imagined* these things about Khan. I am suggesting that Khan's neglect of the real analytic situation, with its qualities of pressure, intrusion, exposure, and violation, was unconsciously but accurately perceived by Peter as having qualities in common with the experience of being sent away from home at the time of his sibling's birth.

This brief analysis of a fragment of a case history demonstrates something of the self-critical demands that the theory of unconscious perception makes of psychoanalysts. The theory allows patients to have their say. It grants them the power to perceive the implications of their analysts' behavior rather than theoretically imprisoning them in a web of illusion. The theory also blocks any attempt to dismiss patients' perceptions as mere transference, the inappropriate and infantile imagining of an infantile mind, checking the almost unlimited power of the analyst to determine what is real and what is unreal for the patient. It puts analysts in the firing line, requiring them to take patients' criticisms seriously and respectfully and to question themselves and their techniques accordingly. Psychoanalysts would be compelled by virtue of accepting the theory of unconscious perception to see a great deal of the 'progress' of psychoanalysis since the late 1890s as an evasion of the actual nature of deep unconscious reality. Freud himself was unable to come to grips with this domain and quickly buried his concept of screen memories beneath a massive theoretical edifice emphasizing phantasy over reality, the past over the present, and transference over accurate perception. Psychoanalysis has, in the main, ignored unconscious perception for ninety years. Contemporary practitioners have much more to lose than Freud did in 1900, and steadfastly ignore this explosive domain. In spite of all this, however, over the decades a small number of psychoanalysts have come to grapple, in partial and restricted ways, with the spectre of unconscious perception.

4   Some pioneers

One for the mouse,
One for the crow,
One to rot,
One to grow,
            Traditional

We have seen how Freud now and again expressed an interest in the issue of unconscious perception without ever developing this theory in a sustained or consistent manner and without integrating it into mainstream psychoanalytic theory. Of course, Freud was not the only analyst to take up this much neglected concept. In the present chapter we will have a look at the work of those psychoanalytic theorists who have considered unconscious perception after Freud. This will provide a backdrop to the second half of the book, which will explore the contributions of Robert Langs, the only psychoanalyst who has made the theory of unconscious perception the basis of a major paradigm-shift for psychoanalysis.

None of the analysts before Langs were able to fully tap the radical potential of the theory of unconscious perception. With the possible exception of Ferenczi, whose untimely death truncated his work on this subject, all of these explorers attempted to reconcile unconscious perception with the dominant tradition in which they worked, be it Freudianism, Kleinianism, or existential phenomenology. Despite the ultimate triumph of the standard theories in their work, the contributions of these pioneers is deserving of the highest respect. Working against the tide of a hostile intellectual climate, institutional politics, and their own personal resistance, they all managed to grasp and clinically deploy a theory which, as I have shown in the analysis of Khan's case presentation in Chapter 3, can prove to have emotionally explosive implications. It is therefore not surprising that those concerned with this issue have been some of the most original, creative, and fearless minds in the history of psychoanalysis. Nor is it surprising that, given the previous history of psychoanalysis, each of these men and women applied the theory in a limited and lopsided way.

I will limit myself to a discussion of those authors whose work on unconscious perception preceded that of Langs. Several of these authors have been important influences on Langs's thought. There have been other mainstream analysts who have touched on unconscious perception in recent years (for example, Joseph 1978; Casement 1985; Hinshelwood 1985; Rosenfeld 1987), but these writers have said little or nothing that is original and appear to offer only diluted versions of the insights of Langs and his theoretical forbears.

Finally, I will consider, when possible, the reception of these ideas by the psychoanalytic Establishment. This will serve as a measure of their threatening force, the degree to which they resist assimilation by the dominant paradigms, and will be a prelude to a study of the reception accorded to Langs's work later in the book.

SANDOR FERENCZI

Ferenczi was the father of the Budapest School of psychoanalysis. For many years one of Freud's closest colleagues, he was regarded by many as second only to 'the professor' as a psychoanalytic theorist. Ferenczi's work has had a huge impact on the development of psychoanalysis, and he is nowadays widely regarded as having been well in advance of his time with regard to a variety of theoretical and clinical issues. Toward the latter part of his career Ferenczi fell out of favor with Freud and the senior figures in the movement. This was in part due to his interest in unconscious perception and his attempts to unravel its implications for technique.

As early as 1913 Ferenczi showed a keen interest in the interactional dimension of psychoanalysis. He published an influential paper entitled 'Stages in the development of the sense of reality' (Ferenczi 1913) in that year which provided an alternative to Freud's purely intrapsychic theory of omnipotence. Freud believed that omnipotence was a consequence of narcissism; that is, he believed that in falling in love with its own self-image the infant was led to idealize itself (because idealization is intrinsic to being in love) and that the belief in its own omnipotence was simply an expression of the idealization (Freud 1914a). Ferenczi argued, instead, that omnipotence is an interactional product, a shared creation of mother and infant, and elaborated a theory virtually identical to what has become known as Winnicott's theory of omnipotence (Smith 1986).

As Ferenczi grew older he came to focus more and more intensively on the phenomenology and problems of psychoanalytic technique. Unfortunately, he contracted pernicious anemia which was responsible for his premature death in 1933. Ferenczi appears to have reached his most important insights into the clinical significance of unconscious perception only shortly before his death. Certainly by 1932 he had reached the conclusion that patients are able to accurately perceive their analysts' psychological problems, and had come to understand that these perceptions are expressed indirectly through disguised narratives. He mentioned in his clinical journal of 1932, for instance, that a patient understood that he, Ferenczi, suffered from anxieties about the size of his penis. The patient conveyed this hidden awareness through the medium of a dream involving a powerful man with a tiny penis. Ferenczi made the discovery that patients analyze their analysts – which had only been distantly hinted at by Freud. He also discovered that patients unconsciously attempt to 'cure' their analysts, an insight which was to lay dormant until Little rediscovered it in 1951. This awareness eventuated in his clumsy and misguided technique of 'mutual analysis' which was based on periodic role reversal between analyst and patient (Dupont 1989).

In 1932 Ferenczi wrote down some of the ideas that had been germinating within him with the intention of delivering them to the 12th congress of the International Psychoanalytical Association at Wiesbaden. The paper, which was entitled 'Confusion of tongues between adults and the child', was very badly received. It was published in German in 1933. Jones reluctantly accepted the paper for publication in the *International Journal of Psycho-Analysis* but took advantage of Ferenczi's death in 1933 to withdraw the paper and destroy the proofs. The paper, which was Ferenczi's last, was not published in English until 1949 when Michael Balint, who had been a student of Ferenczi, took steps to get it into print. 'Confusion of tongues' bears the imprint of the considerable strengths and weaknesses of its author. It is filled with bold and highly original conjectures which, however, are developed in a rather naive and unsystematic way. He recounts at the outset of the paper how he had come to consider real, exogenous infantile traumata to be much more important than psychoanalytic theory had allowed. Ferenczi experimented with a cathartic technique in the hope of helping his patients abreact painful memories and emotions stemming from the repressed traumas. Although this approach had some positive impact on his patients' neurotic symptoms it also had side-effects. Ferenczi's patients began to suffer from the new symptom of terrible anxiety states which would eventuate in terrifying nightmares and hysterical attacks during psychoanalytic sessions. Ferenczi attempted to 'analyze' these attacks but this did nothing to resolve them.

Ferenczi's position was therefore very much like Freud's had been forty years previously. He used an abreactive technique resembling Freud and Breuer's 'cathartic method', he held to a theory of the traumatic causation of the psychoneuroses similar to Freud's 'seduction theory', and his patients were having hysterical attacks in their analytic sessions similar to the 'reproductions' that Freud's patients produced. But Ferenczi took a step which Freud never took and which, in fact, he explicitly repudiated. Ferenczi came to regard the hysterical attacks as an *iatrogenic syndrome*, as a neurosis caused by therapy itself. Of course, this was an implication of Freud's 'screen memory' theory as well, but, as I have already described, Freud was unable or unwilling to say this explicitly (perhaps even to himself).[1] It is as though psychoanalysis had, in Ferenczi's hands, gone back to a point of theoretical fixation, a point where its development had gone awry, and was rediscovering its true path. Ferenczi could find the words that Freud had not found: he could venture the hypothesis that the events in therapy that were supposed to be only distorted expressions of repressed memories were, in fact, artefacts of the psychoanalytic situation.

Ferenczi goes on to say that during the attacks his patients would reproach him as cruel, brutal, unfeeling, selfish, and so on. They would also cry out expressions of distress such as 'For God's sake help me! Quick! Don't let me perish without help!', which did not seem to be overtly directed toward him (Ferenczi 1933: 192). Ferenczi initially attributed all of this to 'resistance' but, as careful analysis produced no amelioration, came to regard his invocation of 'resistance' as an expression of his own resistance and began to 'give free rein to self-criticism', examining his own behavior 'to see if in spite of my best conscious intention there was not some truth to these accusations' (ibid.). Although it seems common sense to question oneself in such circumstances, for a psychoanalyst to consider the situation in this way instead of accusing the patients of transference, resistance, defense, or 'unanalyzability' was nothing short of momentous.

> Gradually I came to the conviction that patients have an extremely refined feeling for the wishes, tendencies, moods and dislikes of the analyst, even should these feelings remain totally unconscious to the

analyst himself. Instead of contradicting the analyst, instead of accusing him of certain misdemeanours or blunders, patients *identify with him*. . . . Generally they permit themselves no criticism of us; such criticism does not even occur to them unless we expressly give them permission to do so. . . . Therefore we must, from the associations of patients, discern the existence not only of unpleasant things from their past; we must also, more than we have done until now, look for the existence of repressed or suppressed criticism of us.

(ibid.: 293)

Thus, Ferenczi does not simply assert that patients are capable of valid unconscious perception of their analysts. He says that patients communicate these perceptions and their implications in a disguised manner in the psychoanalytic sessions themselves, and expands the analyst's role to that of recognizing and interpreting patients' valid unconscious perceptions of their analysts' conduct. He states that these criticisms merit serious attention. He also states that such an approach goes counter to psychoanalysts' own defensive emotional needs. Analysts, he writes, 'come up against not inconsiderable resistances, and this time resistances in us, not in our patients' (ibid.).

Ferenczi emphasizes that patients' unconscious perceptions are uncannily accurate. They penetrate the analyst's professional façade, and respond appropriately to the real underlying attitudes of the psychoanalyst toward his patient.

I do not know whether they can tell the difference [between genuine and false empathy] by the sound of our voice, by the choice of our words, or in some other way. In any event they display a strange, almost clairvoyant knowledge of the thoughts and emotions of the analyst. In this situation it seems hardly possible to deceive the patient and if such deceit is attempted, it can only lead to bad consequences.

(296)

'Confusion of tongues' is rich, dense, and obviously written under profound emotional pressure. It contains not only material on patients' perception but also discussion of the relative merits of theories of infantile fantasy and real infantile trauma, as well as discussions of technique. It concludes with a particularly haunting and oracular passage, written by a dying, misunderstood man with an urgent message.

It would please me if you would take the trouble to examine, in practice and in theory, what I have communicated here, and especially if you would follow my advice to pay closer attention than you have in the past to the strange, much veiled, yet critical manner of thinking and speaking of your children, patients and students, and, so to speak, loosen their tongues. You will hear much that is instructive.

(302)

It is equally instructive to observe how the psychoanalytic profession responded to these ideas. In a letter to Jones, Joan Riviere – a prominent Kleinian analyst – presents what appears to have been the official viewpoint. She describes the paper in the following terms: 'Its scientific contentions and its statements about analytic practice are just a tissue of delusions' (Riviere, quoted in Masson 1984: 152). Riviere opposed the publication of the paper on the grounds that it is critical of psychoanalysis and would give ammunition to its opponents. Freud had urged Ferenczi not to publish the paper on precisely these grounds (ibid.). In a letter to Freud dated 9 September 1932 Jones refers to Ferenczi's 'ideas of persecution' and that the paper contains 'pathological ideas' (ibid.: 174). Freud concurred with these views. Jones wrote to Freud on 3 June 1933 that Ferenczi's 'paranoia' was obvious to all of the analysts at the Wiesbaden congress and described him as suffering from an organic paranoia in his biography of Freud.[2] Jones's views on Ferenczi's mental condition have in fact been refuted by psychoanalysts who were with him during the final weeks and months of his life. The whole sordid story of Ferenczi's 'illness' can be found in Masson (1984).

Masson believes that Ferenczi was unjustly labeled as psychotic because of his belief in the reality of infantile trauma. In light of Jones's mention of 'ideas of persecution', however, it seems more likely that it was the ideas about patients' criticisms of their analysts which suggested paranoia. One of the symptoms of paranoia is a proneness to 'ideas of reference', the delusional belief that people are talking about one. A paranoiac might, for example, have an unshakeable belief that a television newsreader is addressing encoded messages specifically to him. It seems probable that Freud and Jones *et al.* regarded Ferenczi's belief that his patients were offering disguised comments to him about his own psychoanalytic behavior as an 'idea of reference'. In construing him in this way Freud and his followers were doing to Ferenczi precisely what Ferenczi accused psychoanalysis of doing to its patients: rejecting a valid but unflattering observation by pathologizing its bearer. History will decide which of the two positions was the more paranoid.

KLEIN AND THE POST-KLEINIANS

The psychoanalytic world had, as it were, been traumatized by the 'Ferenczi episode' (Haynal 1988). Hitler's rise to power followed close on its heels, eventuating in persecution, war, and the diaspora of European psychoanalysts. Gradually, as the smoke cleared away, Great Britain and the Americas emerged as the world centers of psychoanalytic activity. Klein's career spanned this tumultuous period. Trained in Budapest and Berlin in the 1920s, she emigrated to England just prior to Hitler's rise to power, where she flourished and became the dominant figure in British psychoanalysis.

Although the work of Klein and especially of her followers has many points of contact with the theory of unconscious perception, the Kleinian attitude toward this issue has always been ambivalent and ultimately quite conservative. For the Kleinian school unconscious perception undergoes a theoretical transformation which renders it a less threatening concept than Ferenczi's (or even Freud's) theory would entail.

In the work of Klein herself the notion of unconscious perception enters only implicitly in connection with her concept of psychoanalytic drive. Although Klein continually explains mental life in terms of phantasies deriving from discharge-seeking drives, her notion of cure seems incomprehensible without the concept of unconscious perception. Freud's theory of psychoanalytic cure was almost entirely cognitive. The purpose of psychoanalytic treatment was defined as bringing the unconscious 'id' into the sphere of the conscious ego, a process brought about by psychoanalytic interpretation which brings to light unconscious contents and defenses. Freud conceded that cure could come about in other ways as well, for example by the manipulation of the transference ('suggestion'), but maintained that insight into one's unconscious mental life was the distinctively and appropriately psychoanalytic mode.

In Klein's view the human mind is populated by imaginary figures called 'internal objects'. These have been assimilated ('introjected') into the mind during the course of development. The more ill or immature a person is, the more his internal objects will be polarized between very good 'ideal objects' and very savage 'persecutory objects'. In Klein's view the purpose of psychoanalysis is to moderate the extreme 'splitting' between internal objects, leading to greater internal coherence and an improved capacity to relate realistically to oneself and others.

Klein believed that this process was brought about partly by means of cognitive insight, as Freud argued, and partly by the introjection of the analyst as a realistically benign 'object'. The analyst is unconsciously set up as a good-enough internal object within the patient's mind. This helps along the integration of opposites. The inner neighbourhood improves when the analyst moves in. The classical Kleinian concept of cure as introjection was most explicitly and systematically described by Strachey (1934).

It is important to bear in mind that for Klein and her followers introjection is seen as an extremely fundamental unconscious process. Introjection *constitutes* the mind, and is therefore as basic to psychological existence as eating and breathing are to physical existence. Introjection cannot be consciously willed: it just 'happens' as a consequence of one's emotional and instinctual commitments. Thus, the introjection of the analyst as a realistically good internal object is a spontaneous and unconscious occurrence. One is not directly aware of the process taking place. It is also vital to understand that the curative form of introjection that Klein describes entails that the analyst really *merit* his or her benign status. The process could not work in the way Klein describes if the analyst is merely *imagined* to be a helpful person. The analyst who is successfully introjected in this manner must establish her goodness realistically through her interactions with her patient. Taken together these points seem to imply that the analyst must be *unconsciously perceived* to be a truly helpful figure in order to be introjected in a way that positively alters the patient's psychic structure.

The first Kleinian writer to explicitly mention unconscious perception seems to have been Heinrich Racker. Racker gave a paper at the Argentine Psychoanalytic Association in 1948, which was published in 1953 under the title 'The counter-transference neurosis', which refers to the relationship between unconscious perception and countertransference. In terms reminiscent of Ferenczi,[3] Racker wrote that:

> The countertransference affects his [the analyst's] manner and his behavior which in turn influence the image that the analysand forms of him. Through the analyst's interpretations, the form he gives them, his voice, through every attitude he adopts towards the patient, the latter perceives (consciously or unconsciously) the psychological state he happens to be in – not to speak of the debatable question of telepathic perception.
>
> (Racker 1953: 105)

Both in this and subsequent papers, Racker notes the psychological similarities between patient and analyst: both have infantile and mature aspects to their personalities. He also emphasizes that psychoanalysts have attempted to disavow their own infantile, neurotic sides by means of a denial of the prevalence and importance of countertransference.

> The first distortion of truth . . . is that analysis is an interaction between a sick person and a healthy one. The truth that it is an interaction between two personalities, in both of which the ego is under pressure from the id, the superego and the external world; each personality has its internal and external dependences, anxieties and pathological defences; and each of these whole personalities . . . responds to every event of the analytic situation.
>
> (Racker 1957: 132)

For Racker, the failure to bear this in mind contaminates the psychoanalytic situation with the values of 'the patriarchal order'. The lack of attention given to countertransference is seen as an expression of the 'social inequality' of analyst and patient and points to the need for 'reform'. The micro-politics of the psychoanalytic situation are described as potentially harmful to patients.

> For as long as we repress, for instance, our wish to dominate the analyzand neurotically (and we do wish this in one part of our personality), we cannot free him from his neurotic dependence, and as long as we repress our neurotic dependence upon him (and we do in part depend on him), we cannot free him from the need to dominate us neurotically.
>
> (ibid.: 132)

Although Racker's call for moral reform within psychoanalysis was laudable, as was his appreciation of the interactional dimension of analysis and the call for more study of countertransference, his work on unconscious perception was much less radical than that of Ferenczi. Racker more or less limited himself to a discussion of how unconscious awareness influences the way that patients come to form their transferences. There is nothing about patients trying to communicate valid insights about their analysts' problems, and attempting to cure them. The transference dimension remains most important.

In 1950 Heimann published her paper 'On countertransference', which was described in Chapter 2. Eschewing the issue of patients' unconscious perceptiveness, she concentrated on how analysts' countertransference reactions may be responses to their own unconscious perception of their patients' unconscious concerns. Racker, true to his egalitarian ideals, criticized the one-sidedness of Heimann's contribution:

> The transference is . . . an unconscious creation of the analyst. . . . That one's fate is, in some respects, the expression of one's unconscious tendencies and defenses holds good for the analyst and his work. Just as countertransference is a 'creation' of the patient (Heimann 1950) and an integral part of his inner and outer world, so also, in some measure, is transference the analyst's creation and an integral part of his inner and outer world.
>
> (Racker 1958: 178)

Ironically, it was just as Heimann's ideas began to gain popularity among Kleinian analysts that she began to dissociate herself from the Kleinian group and, recanting her earlier beliefs, became one of the Independent group, whose members were aligned with neither the Kleinians nor with the Anna Freudians. In 1952 Herbert Rosenfeld, one of the most important of the rising generation of Kleinian analysts, concurred with Heimann's theory of countertransference (Rosenfeld 1952). Bion (1955) also expressed agreement with Heimann, but gave her theory a distinctive twist which would prove to be fateful for the future history of the concept of unconscious perception within Kleinian thought. Bion spoke of the analyst's unconscious sensitivity to the patient's unconscious issues as the effect of the patient's projective identification. 'Projective identification' was and is a much used if rather obscure term for a defensive mental process. Bion used the term to designate the induction of mental states in another person. By evoking unwanted experiences in another person one can, so to speak, put them 'into' him. So Bion saw countertransference as stemming from the *patient's* unconscious initiative. The patient projects unwanted experiences into the analyst who then experiences them in terms of countertransference.

> How exactly a patient does succeed in imposing a phantasy and its corresponding affect upon his analyst in order to deny it in himself is a most interesting problem. I do not think that we need to assume some form of extrasensory communication; but the communication can be of a pre-verbal and archaic kind − similar perhaps to that used by gregarious animals in which the posture or call of a single member will arouse a corresponding affect in the rest. In the analytic situation a peculiarity of communications of this kind is that, at first sight, they do not seem as if they had been made by the patient at all.

The analyst experiences the affect as being his own response to something.

(Bion cited in Money-Kyrle 1956: 366)

Thus, not only is the patient responsible for the analyst's counter-transferences (in so far as they do not stem from his own psycho-pathology), but the process of transmission itself is of a very primitive nature. It is infantile, pre-verbal, pre-symbolic, and perhaps (given Bion's analogy) even pre-human. It is *'affects'* that are unconsciously received, not cognitions. This is a very different approach to that hinted at by Freud and elaborated by Ferenczi. These authors invoked sophisticated unconscious cognitive processes which are able to draw incisive psychological inferences. The refined receptivity to uncon-scious information has begun to be replaced by the primitive trans-mission of unconscious information.

In 1956 Money-Kyrle followed suit, linking the analyst's uncon-scious perceptions with the patient's projective identifications and dis-tinguishing between 'normal' and 'abnormal' countertransference. In 1959 Bion distinguished between 'normal' and 'abnormal' forms of projective identification, seeing the former as a primitive means of communication.

Although Heimann herself never regarded projective identification as a valid psychoanalytic concept (Hinshelwood 1989) virtually all of the later Kleinian theorists developed her theory along these lines. The idea that it is feelings that are unconsciously perceived and/or trans-mitted had its origin in Heimann, but later theorists came to emphasize the primitive quality of the process.

The Kleinian writers seem to have tamed the revolutionary power of unconscious perception, linking it closely with patients' defensive needs and moving away from the idea of patients being capable of penetrating unconscious inferences about analysts' problems. Despite superficial similarities, Ferenczi's example of the patient who dreamed about a powerful man with a tiny penis is a long way from this sort of thinking.

Kleinian writers have made more positive contributions to this area but these have been more theoretically than clinically orientated. Bion, for example, expressed disagreement with Freud's (1917a) theory of the 'epistemophilic instinct' (the drive to know) which saw it as a mere derivative of scopophilia (erotic pleasure in looking, voyeurism). Bion held that the desire for knowledge was just as fundamental as love and hate as an irreducible human motive and believed in innate 'pre-conceptions' (cognitive pre-adaptations to reality) (Bion 1962a, b).

These ideas would tend to support a theory describing the unconscious mind as a knowledge-seeking mental system that is adapted to the discovery of external reality.

A significant exception to the rather conservative and non-egalitarian tone of most Kleinian writing touching on unconscious perception was a highly original paper by Baranger and Baranger, two South American Kleinians, entitled 'Insight in the psychoanalytic situation' (Baranger and Baranger 1966). The authors take a stand against the essentially 'individualistic' slant of virtually all psychoanalytic theory. Psychoanalysts largely see the psychoanalytic encounter as something taking place between fundamentally separate and differentiated entities: the patient and the analyst. Instead, Baranger and Baranger situate psychoanalytic interaction within what they term a 'bipersonal field', a metaphorical field of force generated by the two participants as well as encompassing them. The bipersonal field is a sort of corporate personality based on the psychoanalytic 'contract' (the ground rules of treatment), the manifest communications by the patient, and the unconscious phantasies of both participants. These three factors cohere to generate a field which then crucially influences everything that happens in the analysis. Because the bipersonal field is always a joint creation, it follows that everything that happens in the analytic situation is an expression of both the analyst's and the patient's internal world, and that nothing can simply and unequivocally be attributed to just the patient or just the analyst. In essence, the Barangers treat the psychoanalytic situation as a unitary system, and pave the way for an appreciation of the exquisite interplay between patient and analyst on an unconscious level, although inevitably they regard projective identification as the main mechanism structuring the bipersonal field.

MARGARET LITTLE

Margaret Little began to develop her original ideas about the psychoanalytic interaction at roughly the same time as Paula Heimann. Little's pioneering paper on the subject, 'Countertransference and the patient's response to it', was read in 1951 (Little 1951). Little had not been aware of Heimann's work on countertransference when she composed the paper (Little and Langs 1981). There may have been some influence from Ferenczi's ideas, as Little worked closely with Ferenczi's protégé and literary executor Michael Balint, assisting him in the preparation of the third volume of Ferenczi's collected papers for publication (ibid.), and although Ferenczi is not directly cited in the countertransference paper, she does refer to him approvingly as a 'revolutionary' (ibid.: 282).

Little's 1951 paper is concerned with the prevalence of countertransference, its destructive impact, and the necessity for admitting countertransference to the patient. The issue of unconscious communication is generally implicit rather than explicit. Little's paper therefore goes against the Kleinian trend, which was beginning to gather momentum in the early 1950s, of understanding countertransference in terms of what the patient projectively identifies 'into' the analyst. Little reconnects with original Freudian tradition of understanding countertransference as basically the analyst's problem, but moves beyond the classical position in exploring the effects of countertransference on the patient and considering how the analyst should intervene in the face of countertransference-induced errors.

Little is in no doubt about the destructive potential of countertransference, and is keen to call into question the idealized image of the mature, helpful, and insightful analyst. She argues that the psychoanalytic calling springs from deep unconscious reparative needs. The analyst *needs* some ill person to treat. Because of the need for an ill person, many analysts will try to keep their patients ill. 'Unconsciously', she writes, 'we may exploit a patient's illness for our own purposes . . . and he will respond to this' (1951: 37). She speaks of the 'paranoid' attitude of analysts toward their countertransferences. Although analysts are likely to have 'the greatest resistance' (45) to acknowledging their own countertransference, it is essential to admit such errors to patients as well as spelling out to them the countertransferential nature of the error. 'Not to refer to countertransference is tantamount to denying its existence or forbidding the patient to know or speak about it' (ibid.). Thus, to ignore countertransference in one's interpretations will cause 'only harm' (44).

Little feels that patients already know, unconsciously, about their analysts' countertransference problems:

> So much emphasis is laid on the unconscious phantasies of patients about their analysts that it is often ignored that they really come to know a great deal of truth about them – both actual and psychic. Such knowledge could not be prevented in any case, even if desirable, *but patients do not know they have it, and part of the analyst's tasks is to bring it into consciousness.*
>
> (ibid.: 45, emphasis added)

Like Racker, Little sees both transference and countertransference as joint creations of both patient and analyst, and like Ferenczi, she recognizes that the patient strives to heal and instruct the analyst. In one of the most memorable passages in the psychoanalytic literature on technique, Little writes that:

> We often hear of the mirror which the analyst holds up to the patient, but the patient holds one up to the analyst too, and there is a whole series of reflections in each, repetitive in kind and subject to continual modification. The mirror in each case should become progressively clearer as the analysis goes on, for patient and analyst respond to each other in a reverberative kind of way, and increasing clearness in one mirror will bring the need for a corresponding clearing in the other.
>
> (ibid.: 43)

HAROLD SEARLES

Harold Searles is an American psychoanalyst perhaps most well known for his work with chronic schizophrenics at Chestnut Lodge. Although Searles was influenced by the interactional approach of Harry Stack Sullivan, his ideas on unconscious perception in the psychoanalytic situation seem to stem mainly from his own clinical observations and theoretical originality. Searles touches on the issue of patients' unconscious perceptions of their analysts in a number of pages, and references to the process in his writing can be found at least as far back as 1948 (Searles 1948). Searles can be seen as carrying forward the ideas mooted by Little in 1951.[4] He emphasizes the role of the analyst's own unconscious conflicts, their effect upon the patient's psychopathology and behavior in psychoanalysis, and most of all the idea of the patient attempting to cure the analyst. The notion of the patient as therapist to his analyst was implicit in the work of Ferenczi and Little, ignored by the Kleinian writers on countertransference, and finally recognized and mentioned explicitly by Searles. Searles traces the idea of the patient as therapist and supervisor back to Groddeck's *Book of the It* (1923). Groddeck writes of a patient that:

> His childlike attitude towards me – indeed, as I understood it later, it was that of a child of three – compelled me to assume the mother's role. Certain slumbering mother-virtues were awakened in me by the patient, and these directed my procedure. . . . And now I was confronted by the strange fact that I was not treating the patient, but that the patient was treating me. . . . Even to get this amount of insight was difficult, for you will understand that it absolutely reversed my position in regard to a patient. It was no

longer important to give *him* instructions, to prescribe for *him* what I considered right, but to change in such a way that *he* could use me.

(ibid.: 252–3)

Searles believes that all people possess an innate need to heal or cure others and that the frustration of this need in childhood is the single most important etiological factor for emotional disorder. The neurotic is a person who has not had the opportunity to heal his or her parents. This factor is taken to be even more important for the understanding of psychosis. The psychotic person has never achieved a stable, autonomous self: 'Instead, life consisted basically in his postponement, as it were, of his individuation, in the service of his functioning symbiotically as therapist to one or another of his family members, or to all collectively in a family symbiosis' (Searles 1975: 98). It follows from this that if a neurotic – and still more a psychotic patient – is to get well in psychoanalysis they must have the opportunity to truly be, and be implicitly acknowledged to be, therapist to their own analyst. The patient must be permitted to function as a therapist or analyst even though he has not been designated as such:

The analyst must dare to know that . . . the patient is functioning, and has been functioning, as his mother-therapist. . . . It becomes mutually and implicitly understood that the patient has been helping him to confront areas of himself with which he had been previously largely unacquainted.

(Searles 1973: 260)

Searles makes it quite clear that this process can only operate because of patients' ability to unconsciously make valid and accurate inferences about their analysts' unconscious preoccupations. Searles traced some of these processes out in his 1972 paper on 'The function of the patient's realistic perceptions of the analyst in delusional transference':

In a recent paper (1972) concerning my work . . . with a deeply ego-fragmented and delusional woman, I described my discovery of the awesome extent to which her highly delusional world was actually flowing from, and thus was based upon, her responding to various real but predominantly unconscious components of my personality – that is, heretofore largely unconscious ways of my functioning with her during the sessions.

(Searles 1973: 260)

In the 1972 paper Searles goes into some detail about how patients' unconscious perceptions are expressed. He takes the Freud/Ferenczi line that the patient's perceptions of the psychoanalyst are expressed in disguised, derivative form. Patients may, for example, *identify* with the unconscious percept of the analyst, attributing the characteristics of the analyst to themselves. These identifications are described as involving 'gigantic irony, on the scale of Jonathan Swift or Rabelais, expressed in leg-pulling satires' (1972: 8). He writes of a patient that:

> I have felt appalled at the thought that her . . . [delusional] endeavour to reach her mother (who in actuality had died some five years before our work began) is a caricaturing of my own small-child seeking to find an ideal mother in her. Her so frequent immersion in large-scale psychotic plans is clearly based in part upon her view of me as a man, typical for her of all men with their heads-in-the clouds, grandiose, intellectual planning, and denying, meanwhile, their infantile dependency upon the women round about them, women of whom they are so oblivious.
>
> (1972: 8)

On other occasions, Searles relates, patients express their perceptions unconsciously by referring to their analysts in a heavily disguised, metaphorical way. He describes, for example, how the same psychotic patient saw two people in his two eyes at war with one another: 'This not uncommon perception presumably is attributable not only to projection but also to the intense state of emotional conflict, revealed in my eyes, which I often experience in these stressful sessions' (ibid.: 12). At other times patients offer their comments more indirectly through remarks which are manifestly about other people entirely but on an unconscious level refer to the analyst. For example, Searles suggests that a psychotic patient's perception of the malevolent, sadistic, vindictive, and omnipotent aspects of his attitude towards her is expressed in the following segment of a session:

> God comes in at odd intervals and, uh, uh, is quite perturbed, and *why* he has to make himself look like *Tiny Tim*, and, uh, walk around with a *limp* is beyond me. And *I* don't want him to be *hurt*, anyway. If he's hurt there would be no sense in anyone ever going to a hospital, 'cause he's the last healthy person we have, absolutely, and all hospitals are attached to him, and it doesn't seem to faze him in the slightest. But we've got to be *very* careful of him, and he *cannot* be a *horse*, 'cause that's the way to kill the one and only doctor.
>
> (1972: 9)

Searles takes 'God' here as an image representing the patient, who makes herself resemble Tiny Tim, a crippled child. She feels that she is 'the one and only doctor' but that Searles wants to kill her by running her as a racehorse. Searles stresses that this is not just an extravagant, primitive transference phantasy, but that it 'is based, upon bits, at least, of what I experience as being, indeed, my intrapsychic reality – in the light, for example, of the sadism I find aroused in me by her during the sessions' (ibid.: 9).

Searles feels that the most important strategy used by patients *vis-à-vis* their analysts is to 'introject' – to absorb and take on the burden of – their analysts' psychopathology while projecting the healthier parts of their personality on to the analyst to strengthen him or her. 'By introjection the patient attempts to take the analyst's illness into himself and treat the "ill analyst" so that a healthier analyst can eventually be born out of the patient' (1975: 126–7). To take this seriously calls for a 'metamorphosis' (1975: 98) or paradigm shift in the psychoanalytic theory of 'cure'. For Searles it is essential to true psychoanalytic cure that the patient's curative efforts be implicitly recognized and constructively used by the analyst:

The more comfortably I can accept these strivings as inherent to the treatment process, the more, I feel certain, does my whole demeanor convey an implicit acknowledgement that the therapeutic process involves both of us. Certainly, I make transference interpretations which implicitly convey my acknowledgement that the patient's endeavor to be therapeutically helpful . . . to the mother is at the same time an endeavor to be similarly helpful to me as the personification of the mother.

(ibid.: 127)

Finally, Searles goes so far as to toy with the metaphysical pluralism which can only describe unconscious perception as an incredibly sophisticated means by which two separate individuals process information about one another. Perhaps the situation can be reinterpreted in terms of an essential unity or connectedness between only *apparently* separate human beings:

The analyst's surprised, recurrent, and deepening realization and acceptance of the fact that these two seemingly so separate worlds, his world and that of the patient, are but separate outcroppings of the unconscious ground joining the two of them. This principle is commonly manifested in the analyst's finding during, for example, one of the frequent periods of silence with a boringly schizoid patient, that his self-examination of his preoccupying and sup-posedly quite free associations, as he is managing to get through this workday time by dint of such inner 'freedom', yields, as he begins to examine these associations, new and highly informative clues to what is going on between himself and the patient, and within the patient. The analyst's own 'private' or 'autistic' world is not nearly so far apart from the patient as he, the analyst, assumed it to be.

(1973: 261)

MICHAEL BALINT

Michael Balint was a Hungarian emigré, a student, and eventually the literary executor of Sandor Ferenczi, who became associated with the so-called 'Independent' group of British analysts. Balint devoted a good deal of his energies to expanding and developing some of Ferenczi's ideas on psychoanalytic technique. His most important work on this subject was unquestionably *The Basic Fault* (1968). Balint writes in this slim volume about an astounding variety of issues surrounding the psychoanalytic treatment of persons suffering from primitive pre-oedipal fixations. He refers to the schizoid, deeply regressed part of the mind as the area of the 'basic fault'. When psychoanalytic treatment begins to approach the area of the basic fault there is a change of atmosphere in the sessions. Verbal interpre-tations are experienced concretely as expressions of love or hate instead of as statements with a cognitive content. Everything that the analyst does 'may assume an importance far beyond anything that could be realistically intended' (Balint 1968: 18). Patients in this regressed condition are frequently, says Balint, capable of penetrating insights into the analyst's mental life.

Moreover – and this is not so easy to admit – the patient somehow seems to be able to get under the analyst's skin. He begins to know much too much about his analyst. This increase in knowledge does not originate from any outside source of information but apparently from an uncanny talent that enables the patient to 'understand' the analyst's motives and to 'interpret' his behaviour. This uncanny talent may occasionally give the impression of, or perhaps even amount to telepathy or clairvoyance. . . . The analyst experiences this phenomenon as if the patient could see inside him, could find things out about him. The things thus found out are always highly personal and in some ways always concerned with the patient, are in a way always correct and true, and at the same time utterly out of proportion, and thus untrue – at least this is how the analyst feels them.

(ibid.: 19)

This is the only passage in the book that deals with unconscious perception. The influence of Ferenczi is obvious, but the protégé has ultimately taken a more conservative line than the mentor: unconscious interpersonal perception is taken to be a symptom of a particular kind of regression rather than as a general human capacity.

In the text, Balint refers the reader to his brief paper entitled 'Notes on parapsychology and parapsychological healing' (Balint 1955). Balint is concerned in this paper with understanding how one is to explain instances of 'apparent telepathy' in the psychoanalytic situation. 'Apparent telepathy' refers to instances of a patient becoming aware of an analyst's inner preoccupations which cannot be explained by any 'normal' communicative process. Balint found that this process typically occurs in a 'particular emotional situation between the analyst and his patient' (32). Apparent telepathy occurs when (a) a patient is in an intensely dependent relationship with the analyst, and (b) the analyst is greatly preoccupied with some personal matter of no concern to the patient and does not recognize the extent of the patient's dependence. The subtle accessing of the analyst's mind by the patient is an attempt to 'get through' to him.

> The result was always a surprise, almost a shock, to the analyst, and had the effect of bringing him round, as he could not help giving more attention . . . to a patient who was producing such highly interesting and puzzling phenomena.

(ibid.)

Balint implicitly relates these observations to Ferenczi's discussion in the 'Confusion of tongues' paper by using his term 'professional hypocrisy'. For Ferenczi, the patient's efforts at unconscious perception and communication are designed to pierce the armor of the psychoanalyst's professional hypocrisy. Following the earlier work of Hollós (1933) and Servadio (1955), Balint believes that 'telepathic' productions are directed to the aim of 'unmasking' the analyst. It is as if the patient were saying ' "I know it anyhow; do not deceive me", i.e. "Do not care for other people, do really what you are pretending to do, i.e. care for me" ' (33). The patient tries to cure the psychoanalyst of his countertransference problem by 'administering a therapeutic shock'. Unfortunately, Balint offers no data for us to examine, so it is unclear if this information is conveyed directly or in disguised, derivative form by patients. He is aware that, technically, these matters are related to how one handles countertransference, 'especially how much and which side of this counter-transference should be openly admitted, communicated or "interpreted" to the patient', but he offers no concrete suggestions.

Thus, in his paper on parapsychology Balint gives a broader, more generally applicable theory of unconscious perception than the *Basic Fault* account, which depends on a particular mode of regression. The idea of the patient's therapeutic intent anticipates Searles's (1975) work but is absent from the 1968 version of the theory. In both the 1955 and the 1968 accounts the phenomenon of unconscious perception is an extraordinary, sporadic occurrence. Like so many psychoanalysts who have touched upon these issues, Balint manages to subordinate unconscious perception to the dominant psychoanalytic paradigm, and is therefore prevented from exploring it in a consistent and systematic manner.

R.D. LAING

R.D. Laing was, of course, a renegade in the psychiatric community. Laing was trained as a psychoanalyst during the 1950s, when ideas about unconscious interactions were being voiced and explored by both Kleinian and Independent analysts. He was familiar with at least some of Searles's work (Laing 1959) and was strongly influenced – like Searles – by the interactional psychiatry of Harry Stack Sullivan (Friedenberg 1973). Laing's philosophical commitment to existential phenomenology, with its Cartesian presuppositions (see my discussion of Sartre in Chapter 3), seems to have hamstrung Laing in much the same way that Freud's residual Cartesianism made it virtually impossible for his successors to entertain the hypothesis of unconscious perception. In spite of this, and his avoidance of references to the unconscious part of the mind, Laing's writings contain numerous references to what can plausibly be understood as unconscious communications.

In Laing's first book, *The Divided Self*, he sets the stage by decrying the individualistic and intrapsychic focus of much psychiatric theory. The very language of such theories blinds us to the formative role of human interaction:

The words of the current technical vocabulary either refer to man in isolation from the other and the world, that is, as an entity not *essentially* 'in relation to' the other and in a world, or they refer to falsely substantialized aspects of this isolated entity.

(1959: 19)

This tendency produces very misleading theories of schizophrenia, because it ignores the causal role of the psychiatric environment in shaping the very phenomena that are being studied.

> The standard texts contain . . . descriptions of the behavior of people in a behavioral field that includes the psychiatrist. The behavior of the patient is to some extent a function of the behavior of the psychiatrist in the same behavioral field. The standard psychotic patient is a function of the standard psychiatrist and the standard mental hospital.
>
> (ibid.: 28)

This is a striking anticipation of the concept of the 'bipersonal field' developed by Baranger and Baranger (1966) some seven years later. The behavior of the patient must be seen in terms of the causal nexus of his or her immediate situation. Laing goes on to illustrate this contention by means of a truly memorable reinterpretation of a clinical illustration given by Kraepelin, the father of modern psychiatry, in 1905. Kraepelin writes that:

> The patient I will show you today has almost to be carried into the room, as he walks in a straddling fashion on the outside of his feet. On coming in, he throws off his slippers, sings a hymn loudly, and then cries twice (in English), 'My father, my real father!' He is eighteen years old, and a pupil of the Oberrealschule (higher-grade modern-side school), tall, and rather strongly built, but with a pale complexion, on which there is very often a transient flush. The patient sits with his eyes shut, and pays no attention to his surroundings. He does not look up even when he is spoken to, but he answers beginning in a low voice, and gradually screaming louder and louder. When asked where he is, he says 'You want to know that too? I tell you who is being measured and is measured and shall be measured. I know all that and could tell you, but I do not want to.' When asked his name, he screams, 'What is your name? What does he shut? He shuts his eyes. What does he hear? He does not understand: he understands not. How? Who? Where? When? What does he mean? When I tell him to look he does not look properly. You there, just look! What is it? What is the matter? Attend: he attends not. I say, what is it, then? Why do you give me no answer? Are you getting impudent again? How can you be so

impudent? I'm coming! I'll show you! You don't whore for me.
You mustn't be smart either; you're an impudent, lousey fellow,
such an impudent, lousey fellow I've never met with. Is he beginning again? You understand nothing at all, nothing at all; nothing
at all does he understand. If you follow now, he won't follow, will
not follow. Are you getting still more impudent? Are you getting
impudent still more? How they attend, they do attend', and so on.
At the end, he scolds in quite inarticulate sounds. . . . Although he
undoubtedly understood all the questions, he has not given us a
single piece of useful information. His talk was . . . only a series of
disconnected sentences having no relation whatever to the general
situation.

(Kraepelin 1905: 79–80)

It is precisely Kraepelin's contention that his catatonic patient has
provided no useful information, that his discourse is unrelated to 'the
general situation', that Laing wishes to contest. 'Surely', writes Laing,
'he is carrying on a dialogue between his own parodied version of
Kraepelin and his own defiant and rebelling self' (Laing 1959: 30).
The patient's responses are intelligible as reactions to the environment
(a demonstration of 'madness' for the benefit of an audience of
psychiatry students) and Kraepelin's interviewing style.

Kraepelin asks him his name. The patient replies by an exasperated
outburst in which he is now saying what he feels is the attitude
implicit in Kraepelin's approach to him: What is your name? What
does he shut? He shuts his eyes. . . . Why do you give me no
answer? Are you getting impudent again? You don't whore for me?
(i.e. he feels that Kraepelin is objecting because he is not prepared
to prostitute himself before the whole classroom of students), and
so on . . . such an impudent, shameless, miserable, lousey fellow
I've never met with, etc.

(ibid.)

In the context of the immediate situation this boy's communications
are not particularly bizarre in content.

What is the boy's experience of Kraepelin? He seems to be
tormented and desperate. What is he 'about' in speaking and acting
in this way? He is objecting to being measured and tested. He wants
to be heard.

(ibid.: 31)

Laing's interest in and awareness of such communicative processes are not confined to his earliest 'anti-psychiatric' publications. I have already mentioned Laing's critique of Bion's treatment of the schizophrenic patient who pulled a small piece of skin from his own face (p. 46 above) in *The Voice of Experience* (1983). Bion goes on to report in the paper that his patient told him that he had tears coming from his ears, which Bion took as an expression of confused schizophrenic thinking. Laing understands the patient's remark to be a rather poetic comment of Bion's approach to psychotherapy:

If someone I had been 'seeing' five times a week for five years were to say to me that tears were coming from his ears, I can imagine a sigh. I might be caught by his talent to say so much in so little. I might be glad that there were no tears in my ears or eyes. I could not help but feel that the tears in his ears betoken a sense on his part, which I could not help but share, of something sad, maybe even pathetic, about our relationship.

(Laing 1983: 52)

This is fine in theory, but in fact there seems to be no evidence that Laing understood his patients' statements in therapy as reflecting on his own behavior in the way that the communications made by Bion's and Kraepelin's patients obviously reflects on them. In the case of Peter, for example, given in Chapter 8 of *The Divided Self*, Laing casually mentions that the psychotherapy sessions were tape-recorded and that he obtained information about the patient from his uncle. It is difficult to see why the presence of a tape-recorder should be less exposing and denigrating than Kraepelin's group of observers, but Laing does not see this as having some causal significance to the way that the therapy unfolds. He does not relate what Peter says to the 'behavioral field' of which he is a component.

At secondary school his feelings about himself were becoming more definitely crystallized. . . . He was beginning to have a growing sense that he was being put by everyone in a false position. He felt under an obligation . . . to be somebody and to make something of himself, whereas all the time he felt that this was on the one hand impossible and on the other hand unfair. He felt that he had to spend all of his time and energy being a credit to his father, his mother, his uncle or his teacher. However, he was convinced in himself that he was nobody and worthless, that all his effort to be somebody was a deception and a pretense. His teacher, for instance, wanted him to 'speak properly' and to wear 'middle class clothes'. . . . She had him, the secret masturbator, reading Bible lessons to the other children at school and held him up as a paragon. When people said how good he must be to read the Bible so well he laughed sardonically to himself. 'It just showed what a good actor I was.' . . . He deeply resented what he felt were everybody's efforts . . . which were ' "more or less just for credit to themselves" '.

(Laing 1959: 123)

Surely it is plausible to make sense of these statements as a reflection of the implications of the presence of the tape-recorder and the therapist's involvement with third parties. This leads Peter to feel that he is put in a false position. Something 'impossible' and 'unfair' is expected of him, i.e. he is expected to engage in an intensive psychotherapy in which there is little confidentiality and privacy (Peter's remarks ended up published in Laing's widely read book). He feels exploited by the people around him (a disguised reference to the exploitative implications of tape-recording psychotherapy sessions), and this reinforces his inner feelings of worthlessness. The teacher who wanted Peter to 'speak properly' seems a parody of Laing and his tape-recorder, and the Bible reading story is plausibly a reference to the sheer hypocrisy of the situation: Laing preaches against those very sins which he himself obliviously commits. Like Freud, Laing seems to have been unable to apply his insights into unconscious perception to an analysis of his own psychotherapeutic work.

SUMMARY AND ANALYSIS

In this chapter we have scrutinized the contributions of numerous psychoanalytic writers to the problem of unconscious perception. Of these, the Kleinian tradition has emerged as the least radical, and has come to ignore the critical potential of patients' unconscious insights into the implications of their analysts' behavior, opting instead for a theory stressing the idea that patients project mental contents (affective states) into analysts. Leaving the Kleinian writers aside, therefore, I will now look at the work of Ferenczi, Little, Balint, Searles, and Laing on unconscious perception to discover what, if anything, these five approaches have in common, and begin to develop on that basis a psychoanalytic theory of unconscious perception.

To begin with, all five authors agree that patients are acutely responsive to difficulties in the psychoanalyst, be it 'professional hypocrisy' (Ferenczi, Balint), 'countertransference' (Little), his or her abusive, exploitative manner (Laing), or the analyst's 'illness' (Searles). All writers describe instances of unconscious perception occurring when things are going wrong in the analysis. Of these Balint, on one end of the spectrum, makes it a necessary condition for unconscious perception that the analyst is not in touch with the analyzand's dependent needs. For him, unconscious perception is an episodic response to analytic crisis. At the other end of the spectrum lies Laing, who seems to hold that what I am calling 'unconscious perception' is an ongoing expression of a patient's 'existence'.

As regards the expression of unconscious perceptions, Ferenczi, Searles, and Laing all state that these are offered in a disguised, indirect, or derivative form, while Little and Balint do not commit themselves to any specific position. Ferenczi and Searles specify the introjection of the analyst as an important mechanism: the patient talks about the analyst indirectly by talking about him or herself. In addition to this Searles mentions displacement as another important process: patients talk about their analysts indirectly by talking about other people. Laing does not talk about specific modes of representation.

All five writers also agree on the immediacy of unconscious perception. Unconscious perceptions are of something in the here-and-now behavioral field. Thus, all five writers discuss the perception of the analyst by the patient in the psychoanalytic situation. Of the five, Ferenczi, Balint, Searles, and Laing mention explicitly that the process can occur in other relationships (parent/child, researcher/subject) as well. Little says nothing about this one way or the other.

Ferenczi, Balint, Little, and Searles explicitly state that the recognition of patients' unconscious perceptions is met with analysts' own 'resistances', and I think it fair to say that Laing implicitly concurs with this view. Thus, there is consensus that psychoanalysts find the content of these communications personally threatening and respond to them defensively.

Ferenczi, Little, Searles, and Laing comment on how the unconscious perception of therapists' difficulties can lead to iatrogenic disorders. Laing and Searles, in particular, argue that the content of psychotic delusions and hallucinations may be meaningfully related to the real implications of their therapists' behavior and attitude.

The idea that these perceptions are uncannily accurate is stressed by Ferenczi, Balint, Searles, and, perhaps, Laing. This strange precision has led some writers (Ferenczi, Balint, and also Bion and Racker) to wonder whether some form of extra-sensory perception is involved. Searles takes the route of challenging the dualist metaphysics which sharply separates 'self' from 'other'. This view is also approached by Little:

I'm not a 'dualist', I'm very firmly monistic. Essentially, everything
is one, but paradoxically that would mean nothing if there were not
also duality or diversity . . . but the monism is important as being
primary. . . . If you and I were not in fact unconsciously one *somewhere*, we couldn't understand each other.

(Little and Langs 1981: 283–4)

Balint, too, I think implicitly approximates the monistic metaphysical
position although he does not really admit it. In *The Basic Fault* Balint
repeatedly asserts that the patient who has regressed to the level of the
'basic fault' resides in a world devoid of sharply demarcated objects.
He or she lives in 'harmonious mix-up' with primary substances rather
than in a world of relations with discrete, unitary objects. Comparing
this condition to the metaphor of a fish in the sea, Balint queries
whether the water flowing through a fish's gills is part of the fish or
part of the sea, and concludes that this sort of distinction is not applicable. In the same way, the relationship between the infant, or the
regressed patient, to its primary 'objects' cannot be understood within
a dualistic framework. Balint continually judges this state of affairs
from the perspective of a putatively 'mature', differentiated ego, stig-
matizing it as an infantile, regressive, and fundamentally illusory
mode of relatedness. This is a recurring theme within psychoanalysis:
the mature, well-functioning individual is supposed to have separated
out from delusions of fusion with others, and to have come to accept
that persons are basically separate existential units. However, Balint
goes on to say that the regressed patient *actually does* succeed in
getting under the analyst's skin and mysteriously gaining access to his
or her ostensibly private mental universe. Balint does not go a step
further and question the belief that the idea of fusion must be an
illusion. Although his thoughts clearly lead in this direction, Balint
does not consider the possibility that 'regressed' patients have access
to an awareness of a real unconscious unity between manifestly
separate individuals which is beyond the grasp of people in 'normal'
states of mind.

Searles, Balint, and Laing see a quality of exaggeration, satire, or
parody in the patient's unconscious portrayals of his or her analyst.
Searles speaks of 'leg-pulling satire', while Laing mentions 'parody'.
Balint speaks of patients' reactions as true but 'utterly out of proportion', but, interestingly, he qualifies this judgement by the remark that
'at least, this is how the analyst feels them'. It seems that Balint is
leaving room for the possibility that conscious judgements about
unconscious perceptions are somewhat biased. It may be that, as in

the case of basic unity, it is misleading to judge these things according to normal conscious standards. This tendency has been largely overcome in the anthropological domain. Anthropologists do not visit an alien culture and condemn its customs as 'out of proportion' because they differ in some respects from American or West European norms. This would involve the fallacy of assuming that one's own culture is the touchstone of appropriateness. Psychoanalysis, I submit, lags beyond anthropology in retaining more or less unquestioningly a sort of ethnocentricity of the mind which condemns unconscious mentation as in some sense unrealistic, infantile, or 'exaggerated' whenever it does not conform to conscious standards. Even those analysts who take an independent and respectful stance toward unconscious perception fall victim to this prejudice.

Finally, all of the five authors agree that the communication of unconscious perceptions by patients to analysts is essentially benign, rooted in a concern for truth and a caring attitude toward the analyst (to be fair, Laing is not really explicit about the latter point). All agree that unconscious perception is not primarily in the service of the discharge of instinctual drives. Searles, in fact, goes so far as to say that inappropriate or perverse sexual and aggressive urges may be a result of the *frustration* of the inherent therapeutic aspirations of patients and therapists alike.

> During moments or even long phases of particularly intense anxiety in his work, the analyst undergoes regression such that his analytic orientation becomes primitivized to the level of relatively raw aggressive and sexual urges. This regression is a manifestation of the analyst's frustrated therapeutic strivings as well as those of the patient. In my work . . . [with a male hebephrenic patient] . . . it was only after some years of four hourly sessions per week, sessions filled with apathy and unrelatedness, punctuated only by moments of murderous rage, violent sexual urges, and acute fear, that I finally realized that it was possible to relate to him in some fashion other than the only two potential means hitherto available . . . fucking him or killing him. To my enormous relief I realized that I could now be related to him without having either to kill him or fuck him.
>
> (Searles 1975: 129)

This brief survey of psychoanalytic views on unconscious perception reveals, and pulls together, the scanty information on the subject in the (relatively) mainstream literature that has been offered since Freud's last statement on the subject in 1915. From these, it has been possible to abstract the elements of a psychoanalytic theory of unconscious perception. It has been observed that none of these writers has been able to apply their insights in a consistent and systematic manner (Searles has come closest to this), and all have, to some extent, subordinated the revolutionary potential of this approach to the dominant psychoanalytic paradigm.

In the following chapters we will consider the work of Robert Langs, the psychoanalyst who, building on both the work of predecessors and his own original research, has effected a scientific revolution within psychoanalysis: a basic paradigm shift which *rebuilds* psychoanalytic theory and technique *around* the powerful and immensely disturbing insights of the unconscious part of the mind.

Part II

The communicative paradigm

5   Psychotherapy exposed

Most true it is, that I have lookt on truth
Asconce and strangely. . . .

                                                    Shakespeare

Robert Joseph Langs, the founder of the communicative aproach to
psychoanalysis, was born on 30 June 1928 in New York City. The son
of a doctor, Langs studied medicine at the Chicago Medical School,
obtaining his MD in 1953, and went on to study psychiatry at the
Albert Einstein College of Medicine, starting a career in psychiatric
research in 1958. In 1959 Langs began training as a psychoanalyst at
the Downstate Psychoanalytic Institute in Brooklyn: a conservative,
classically orientated institute from which he obtained a psychoanalytic qualification in 1969. Langs's publications between 1959 and
1968 were mainly empirical studies of early memories, dreams, and
the psychological effects of LSD (Langs 1959; Langs *et al.* 1960;
Langs and Linton 1962a, b; Langs and Linton 1964; Langs *et al.* 1964;
Langs 1965a, b; Langs *et al.* 1965; Langs 1966; Langs 1967a, b; Langs
and Linton Barr 1968; Langs 1969).

After qualifying as a psychoanalyst, Langs began to turn his scientific sensibilities to the problems of analytic theory and technique.
Although by no means a rigid or dogmatic Freudian, Langs took for
granted the essential correctness of many basic Freudian tenets.

These ideas offered me considerable protection, though I was not
aware of that particular function . . . I could hold the patient
accountable for the regressions, disruptions, and the madness
that would then unfold. . . . I was protected . . . however inadvertently . . . from understanding the complexities of my actual
inputs into the patient's treatment experience and into the vicissitudes of his madness. The patient was always accountable for

what happened in treatment, and I was accountable only on occasion.

(Langs 1982c: 1)

Langs's earliest psychoanalytic research focused on day-residues and recall-residues of dreams. (I will describe the concept of day-residues below; recall residues are events which trigger the recollection of dreams.) This line of investigation naturally led him to pay close attention to the relationship between phantasy and reality (Langs 1971). From very early on, Langs was struck by the absence of any disciplined scientific methodology in psychoanalytic research. Psychoanalysts '. . . relied on subjective impressions rather than on the development of definitive or, at the very least, specific data. . . . This approach was characteristic of almost all psychoanalytic writings: the use of single cases and unvalidated examples prevails' (Langs 1978b: 9).

While studying the contents of a sample of psychotherapy sessions, Langs hit upon what what was to become the single most important component of his theory: the *adaptive context*. An adaptive or adaptation-evoking context is an event occurring in external reality which produces an intrapsychic response. Langs found that the material contained in the fifty psychotherapy sessions that he was studying could not be well understood unless such stimuli from the patients' external reality were taken into account.

Langs's approach to making sense of patients' behavior in psychotherapy was, in fact, inspired by Freud's theory of dream formation. Freud (1900) believed that dreams are 'instigated' by unconscious wishes seeking discharge. Because these wishes are unable to penetrate the barrier imposed by the endopsychic 'censor', they are condemned to finding only indirect expression. They therefore transfer their 'cathexis' on to innocuous pre-conscious ideas, as I have described in Chapter 2. Freud called the unconsciously reinforced pre-conscious ideas the 'latent dream thoughts'. These are worked into the content of dreams through the use of what Freud called 'day-residues' – associated memories from the previous day. In Freud's view, the successful interpretation of a dream – the discovery of its meaningful intrapsychic causes – requires the analyst to trace this whole process backwards to its source in the original unconscious wish. His analytic method consequently contained two steps. First, one must identify the day-residues and the pre-conscious issues linked with them, establishing the relevance of the dream to the dreamer's everyday life. Second, one must attempt to infer the nature of the unconscious wishes displaced on to the pre-conscious contents.

The day-residues and latent dream thoughts link the dream to the context of the dreamer's current experiences. Langs used the concept of the adaptive context in a strictly analogous way to link unconscious material in psychotherapy sessions to the actualities of the dreamer's outer life. Later, in 1988, Langs replaced the term 'adaptive context' with 'trigger', a less unwieldy term highlighting the causal role of the stimulus. Triggers from the external world both bring about intrapsychic responses and reveal their meaning.

Langs's dogged search for triggers for the material which patients brought to psychotherapy led to a discovery which was so revolutionary and unexpected that it not only took Langs himself several years to assimilate it but also, in the end, brought down upon him the wrath of the psychoanalytic Establishment.

Langs found that the unconscious concerns of patients in psychotherapy virtually always center on the behavior of their therapists. Stated in so general a way, this is hardly novel. As early as 1900 Freud wrote that:

> When I instruct a patient to abandon reflection of any kind and to tell me whatever comes into his head, I am relying firmly on the presumption that he will not be able to abandon the purposive ideas inherent in the treatment and I feel justified in inferring that what seem to be the most innocent and arbitrary things which he tells me are in fact related to his illness. *There is another purposive idea of which the patient has no suspicion   one relating to myself.*
>
> (Freud 1900: 531−2)

The same idea is stated more explicitly twenty-five years later in Freud's 'Autobiographical study':

> We must . . . bear in mind that free association is not really free. The patient remains under the influence of the analytic situation even though he is not directing his mental activities on to a particular subject. We shall be justified in assuming that nothing will occur to him that has not some reference to that situation.
>
> (Freud 1925: 40−1)

It is tempting to suppose that Freud is referring to transference in these two passages, as this would make them quite consistent with the overall thrust of his thinking. However, there is no overt mention of transference in either passage, and the context of the 1925 quotation makes it extremely unlikely that Freud had transference in mind when he wrote it (the subject of transference is discussed later in the same paper and in totally different terms). Given the rather general character of these two passages, it would appear that Freud believed that patients respond to the analytical situation in a manner inclusive of but not limited to the transference, and that these responses are reflected in their spontaneous free associations. In other words, the analyst's behavior and the analytic situation have a causal impact on the patient's unconscious mental processes and the derivative manifestations of those unconscious processes have some semantic link with these causes.

It was Klein (1952) who linked this thesis with the theory of transference and developed the distinctively Kleinian concept of transference out of the synthesis:

> For many years – and up to a point this is still true today – transference was understood in terms of direct references to the analyst in the patient's material. My conception of transference . . . entails a technique by which from the material presented the *unconscious elements* of the transference are deduced. For instance, reports of patients about their everyday life, relations and activities . . . reveal . . . the defenses against the anxieties stirred up in the transference situation.
>
> (55)

Klein's view is subtly yet fundamentally different from Freud's. For Freud it is the analytic situation *per se* that unconsciously impacts upon the patient's associations, whereas for Klein the reason that the analytic situation can play such a causal role is because the patient has first unconsciously projected infantile phantasies on to it.

In more classical vein we find Greenson (1967) offering the concept of the 'transference trigger' to explain how it is that transference can interact with the immediate reality of the psychoanalytic encounter. He presents clinical material which '. . . indicates that the analyst's personal qualities and traits and also certain characteristics of his office setting may serve as triggering stimuli for transference reactions' (308). This formulation is a development of Freud's idea, presented in the case of Dora (1950b), that the transference can 'take advantage' of some real peculiarity of the analyst to find expression. Unlike Klein, he feels that the analytic situation triggers *manifest* transference reactions (for example, the analyst's moustache might remind the patient of his or her father's moustache and thus precipitate a 'father transference'), while for Klein the patient's associations to outside persons and situations ostensibly unrelated to the analytic situation refer latently to the patient's transference on to the analyst. For Klein, this relationship is ubiquitous: everything that the patient says has a transferential dimension, while in Greenson's view the transference triggers do not influence all of a patient's transference reactions, much less all of his or her free associations.

In Langs's view patients' behavior in therapy is a disguised expression of their unconscious *perceptions* of the analyst's behavior. It is interesting to note that Freud's remarks of 1900 and 1925 (quoted above) at least leave room for this possibility, whereas the phantasy/transference emphasis of both Greenson and Klein foreclose it.

This finding was a surprise for Langs. As a classically trained analyst he had no reason to anticipate that realistic perception would prove to be a more important variable than phantasy for understanding what patients say and do in analysis. He had, through empirical enquiry, stumbled upon the very theory with which Freud, Ferenczi, Little, and others had grappled unsuccessfully before him. Langs was not familiar with very much of the earlier literature on unconscious perception at this point in his career. He would have read Freud's paper on screen memories during the course of his training, but he could not have known that this was the culmination of several years' theorizing because two of the three references to the development of the screen-memory theory were omitted from the selections from the Fliess correspondence published in the *Standard Edition* of Freud's works. He would have come across Freud's later remarks on unconscious perception, but he was completely unaware of the contributions of Ferenczi, who most strikingly anticipated his ideas. Langs was ignorant of the British contributions to this literature, with the single exception of Balint's *The Basic Fault* (1968).[1] Nor was he familiar with Searles's groundbreaking work on this subject. Thus, although Langs's work had been anticipated by earlier psychoanalytic writers it was not derived from this tradition. It emerged from a consideration of psychoanalytic data and was only subsequently linked with and enriched by the insights of other theorists.

By 1973 Langs had come to the conclusion that patients offer their therapists valid unconscious commentaries on the harmful and helpful implications of their interventions. These were not phantasy-laden infantile narratives. When properly decoded they proved to be frighteningly incisive observations.

> Once I started to listen to patients I heard material I never imagined existed. My Rosetta stone was the concept that a patient adaptively responded to the interventions of the therapist. I found the interventions which included not only interpretations but also silences and any behaviour that reflected the relationship to the patient

in the slightest degree, were loaded with the errors and pathology of the therapist.

(Langs in Freeman 1984: 35)

It was listening to patients' communications as encoded feedback to their therapists that enabled Langs to enter an unrecognized and profoundly unsettling psychotherapeutic realm. Langs found patients to be, in the main, almost unbelievably sensitive to the implications of their therapists' actions. When therapists err, patients respond by telling stories or recounting memories which in a disguised way spell out the nature and significance of the error. Langs argued that patients' commentaries are revealed by the *themes* woven into their narratives.

> Included are the themes of blindness, failure to be helpful, sensitive or understanding, and of being mistreated, frightened, seduced or attacked. . . . Among the displacements commonly used by patients to express such feelings . . . parental figures and persons who are in the healing professions are commonly used, as are teachers or other authorities. . . . It is also extremely common for patients to become self critical and self attacking over failings and disturbances which they have discussed in the therapist.
>
> (Langs 1973: 248)

Thus, Langs found that if a patient were, for example, to complain about her possessive mother, it was likely that the therapist had just done something which had the quality of possessiveness. Similarly, a patient who reproaches himself saying meaningless, empty things may be unconsciously saying that his therapist's interventions were nothing better than vacuous clichés. This approach to unconscious meaning was recognized as having quite radical ramifications for psycho-analytic technique: 'The therapist should recognize that *the analysis of the patient's reaction to the error must take precedence over all other therapeutic work, since it is essential to the restoration of a proper therapeutic alliance*' (Langs 1973: 249). At this point it would appear that Langs had merely added a new dimension to classical psycho-analytic technique. When analysts err it is possible to understand the error through listening to the patient's encoded commentaries and to analyze its impact upon the patient. One can then rectify the error and get down to the real business of analyzing transferences, resistances, and phantasies.

Langs's thesis, however, could not easily be marginalized in this way because the consistent application of the new approach to listening to patients revealed that *patients are unconsciously opposed to and feel violated by the great majority of techniques employed by psychotherapists and psychoanalysts.* Decoding unconscious messages in light of their triggers opened up a can of worms. 'What I mean', wrote Langs (1985a: 8), '. . . is that the substance and primary issue of most therapeutic ventures is not the patient's madness at all, but the responses evoked in the patient by the therapist's madness – either overt or subtle'. This implies that:

> Our techniques are constructed out of our madness. Things that they, the therapists, don't see as mad, their patients unconsciously see as mad. . . . Patients are unconsciously aware of many mad elements in what we do. They understand how our interventions are self-serving, self-gratifying, seductive, narcissistic and so on.
>
> (Langs in Smith 1989: 119)[2]

Langs originally viewed these disguised comments as attempts by patients to supervise their therapists – to put them on the right track – but after reading Searles's 'The patient as therapist to his analyst' (1975) he came to believe that patients are attempting to *heal* their therapists as well.[3] If this is true, it obviously implies that there is something very false about the great majority of psychotherapeutic relationships. In mainstream psychoanalysis (and virtually all forms of psychotherapy) the nature of the therapeutic relationship is highly idealized. It is said to be based on a 'therapeutic alliance' which is only rarely disrupted (usually by the patient, of course). The therapeutic alliance is 'the relatively non-neurotic, rational relationship between patient and analyst which makes it possible for the patient to work purposefully in the analytic situation. . . . The analyst contributes to the working alliance by his consistent emphasis on understanding and insight, by his continual analysis of the resistances, and by his compassionate, empathic, straightforward and nonjudgemental attitudes' (ibid.: 46–7). Greenson continues, 'Under this benign influence the patient tries to understand the analyst's instructions and insights, reviews and mulls over the interpretations and reconstructions, which aids in the integration and assimilation of the insights' (47).

This portrayal clearly bears little resemblance to the picture that emerged from Langs's research. Here we do not find a self-serving fiction of a wise and benevolent analyst dispensing insights to compliant patients. Rather, we have the impression of a world turned upside-down, a world in which rapacious and insensitive therapists are treated by wise and sensitive patients. This cannot be described as a therapeutic alliance. It is, as Langs described it in 1975, a *misalliance*:

> The analyst's inevitable . . . unmastered anxiety and guilt, neurotic and maladaptive defensive needs, his longings for personal and magical closeness and for inappropriate gratifications, his struggles against the severe limits imposed by the analytic relationship, and his own search to repeat and master past pathological interactions prompt him to search for misalliances with his patients.
>
> (Langs 1975a: 183)

Langs's first full-scale presentation of his theory was in *The Bipersonal Field* (1976a), the title of which, drawn from the work of Baranger and Baranger (1966), indicated that Langs had by this time familiarized himself with the psychoanalytic literature on unconscious perception. In the years to follow, Langs advanced his theory in ever more uncompromising ways. He came to speak of the 'psychotherapeutic conspiracy', a term used to denote the fallacy, promulgated by patients and therapists alike, that therapists are in the business of insightfully resolving their patients' difficulties. Although this myth is ultimately damaging both for consumers of psychotherapy and the development of the profession, it is maintained because patients and therapists both seek refuge from the 'catastrophic truths' registered and expressed by the unconscious part of the mind. So although patients *unconsciously* protest against the treatments meted out to them, they usually remain consciously oblivious to, and indeed consciously come to praise, the psychical violence inflicted upon them.

> It is one of the great misfortunes of psychotherapy – and yet one of its great attractions – to have a client or customer who wishes as much for poor service or treatment as for good. Imagine being in a business where your customer clamours for a damaged product. How likely is it that you will give him or her a sound item (especially when it is easier and cheaper to produce the lesser piece)? The situation is virtually hopeless without careful scrutiny, especially when it is both more profitable and self-serving to offer the lesser product. . . . If patients want damaged services, damaged services they will get.
>
> (Langs 1982c: 11)

This tragic and bizarre situation can be delineated further in terms of the designated and functional roles of therapist and patient (Langs 1980). The designated therapist is the person who is *supposed* to be the therapist, the person who claims to be offering therapy to others. The counterpart of the designated therapist is the designated patient, who manifestly seeks help from the designated therapist. If we are not to be fobbed off by mere labels, however, we can approach the question of who is patient and who is therapist more naturalistically on the basis of their actual causal roles. Through a careful assessment of the therapeutic interaction we can try and determine who, at any given moment, is actually functioning as the patient and who is actually functioning as the therapist. That is, we can identify which person is introducing the most confusion, conflict, and defensiveness into the relationship and which person has the most insightful grasp of the other's predicament. As it turns out, it is usually the designated therapist who is the functional patient and the designated patient who is the functional therapist. In psychotherapy things are seldom what they seem. If one wishes to understand what psychotherapy is really all about it is essential to avoid being taken in by the propaganda of its proponents. Einstein remarked that: 'If you want to find out anything from theoretical physicists about the methods they use, I advise you to stick closely to one principle. Don't listen to their words, fix your attention on their deeds' (Einstein, quoted in Szasz 1958: 2). This principle is probably even more apropos of psychotherapists than it is of physicists. In the field of psychotherapy very powerful unconscious motivations and defensive needs come into play. Therapists are partially insulated from an awareness of these forces by the belief that they are almost by definition more sane than the people whom they treat by virtue of having undergone a lengthy and thorough training analysis.

It is a remarkable fact that psychotherapists of sharply conflicting schools of thought suddenly seem to speak as with a single voice when it comes to the issue of the 'necessity' of personal therapy or analysis for the trainee. Pedder (1989: 212), for example, writes that the case for a compulsory period of psychotherapy for the student psychotherapist is 'established'. Pedder quotes Casement (1984) who holds that analysts and therapists 'have to be analyzed' (mere psychotherapy evidently does not suffice) so as to avoid 'being overwhelmed by a patient's pathology' and in order to be capable of understanding patients' unconscious communications (216–17). Pedder also finds support in a quotation from Crown (1988: 268) who writes that: 'In dynamic therapy, where the therapist–patient relationship may be intense, the need for personal therapy inevitably arises, to avoid the therapist projecting personal problems and conflicts upon the patient'.

The first premise of these arguments is to my mind certainly correct. In a mode of therapy based on the search for unconscious truth it is important for therapists to be open to the discovery of their own unconscious issues and to be capable of holding their own madness in check instead of offloading it on to patients. As for the second premise, I have shown in Chapter 2 how analysts rely on having undergone a training analysis to justify a claim to superior insightfulness. This gives them license to make statements to their patients – as in interpretations of 'transference' – that seem quite grotesque if one does not subscribe to the dictum of therapist superiority. Langs's research, which reveals a very large area of unchallenged madness in the field, makes a mockery of such claims. The real function of the training analysis is, I think, revealed in the fact that virtually every truly creative and independent thinker in the history of psychoanalysis who has refused to meekly follow the party line has, at one time or another, been branded as having been inadequately analyzed. Training analysis has a *political* function. Its role is perhaps more about ensuring conformity and obedience to authority than it is about fostering mental freedom and creativity. Psychoanalytic and psycho-therapeutic training functions, in large measure, to mould students into loyal, conformist, true believers who will unthinkingly close ranks against the critic or innovator.

> All that a training analysis does is give you a new form of madness. It's never going to resolve the one you have. . . . Most people who enter therapeutic training, who become part of a movement, refrain from *gross* expressions of their madness because that's part of the code of behaviour. . . . When I finished my [training] analysis I thought 'Hey, we're the elite: we've been analysed.' But if anything, we are really in worse shape than anybody. We've gone in the other direction.
>
> (Langs in Smith 1989: 119)

Such sentiments, especially when stated publicly, have not endeared Langs to the profession. It is true that many practitioners are critical or even cynical about the state of psychotherapy. Anyone who has been in practice for even a few years will be well aware of the damage that is frequently wrought. He or she will have had the experience of patients seeking therapy because of abuse or damage suffered at the hands of a previous therapist. It is common knowledge in the field that many people enter therapy to recover from a prior 'therapeutic' experience. Therapists talk about this among themselves but shy away from making any public statement. They fear the retaliation of professional organizations who regulate the flow of patient referrals, supervisees, and teaching appointments as well as controlling the journals. Therapists and analysts often present the façade of a united front, and are terrified of transgressing the unwritten taboos of the profession. The pressure is particularly great on students (who not having been fully indoctrinated, are most likely to be capable of independent thought), but it permeates the field. I have spoken with individuals in quite senior positions (for example, training analysts) who have shared their doubts about analysis with me and confessed their fear of being extruded from the institutions if they were to make their feelings public.

There can be no doubt that Langs's reception has been predominantly hostile,[4] and the background to this is important to consider. First of all, we must consider the notorious failure of psychoanalysis as a putative science. From its beginnings – and not withstanding those like Habermas (1971), George Klein (1976), and Bettelheim (1983) who favor a 'hermaneutic' construal of the discipline – Freud wanted psychoanalysis to be a natural science of the human soul. Unfortunately, psychoanalysis does not seem to operate in a way which is remotely scientific. As I will describe in Chapter 10, psychoanalysts generally have scant understanding of the nature of scientific reasoning and give little attention to the need for empirical evidence. This is coupled with an exaggerated deference to authority; thus, for example, it is commonplace to read through a psychoanalytic paper purporting to reveal some new psychological discovery and to find that there are only two or three supporting instances and that even these are merely summarized with no detailed presentation of raw data, no attempt at falsification or consideration of falsifiability, and numerous invocations of other psychoanalytic works for support which, upon inspection, turn out to merely express the opinions of so-called 'authorities' instead of factual evidence. The institutionalized self-criticism which is the hallmark of science is almost completely lacking in psychoanalysis:

> It [psychoanalysis] is not *a* hypothesis, located in a wider world, whose fate and applicability is to be decided by the higher court of evidence. On the contrary, it sits in judgement on facts and decrees how they are to be interpreted (and only other interpretations of its own can sit in judgement on interpretations). Its truth, if it be such, does not modify a bit of the world, it pervades and defines it. It is not attained through evidence but by a deep inner experience, an inner revelation which is also a moral regeneration.
>
> (Gellner 1985: 214)

In other words, psychoanalysis takes itself as its own limiting principle. It is a sort of intellectual desperado beholden to no higher authority.

Science embraces what is known as a 'correspondence' theory of truth. That is, science regards a proposition as true to the extent that the proposition matches some feature of the real world. Although psychoanalysis advertises itself as the pre-eminent science of the human psyche, it makes little real use of the correspondence theory. Rather, psychoanalysis tends to use its own version of the 'coherence' theory of truth. The coherence theory, which was popular among rationalistic metaphysicians, states that a proposition is true in so far as it fits in or coheres with other propositions. Psychoanalytic theorists, with rare exceptions, evaluate hypotheses on the basis of their compatibility with 'established theory' rather than through an appeal to states of affairs in the world. Novel psychoanalytic hypotheses are therefore often branded as 'deviant' rather than praised as 'creative'. I do not wish to imply that closed, dogmatic thinking is absent from the more highly developed sciences, but do want to emphasize that in analysis this is the rule rather than the exception. Some analysts seek solace in the notion that psychoanalysis is in fact a higher form of science than such run-of-the-mill disciplines as astrophysics or organic chemistry. Meltzer (1981), for one, writes that: 'The transformation to a Platonic view is implicit in Mrs. Klein's earliest work and it transformed her psychoanalysis . . . from a Baconian science, aiming at explanations and hoping to arrive at absolute truths, to a descriptive science' (178).

Thus, Klein has transcended inductive reasoning! This seems to be an attempt to turn a failing into a virtue; to legitimize as a 'science' a spurious system based on deductions from unsupported foundational myths about psychic reality. This circular and unfalsifiable system, oblivious to the canons of inductive reasoning, is dignified as a 'Platonic', 'descriptive' science. Other writers, like Flax (1981), argue that the criteria of scientificity proper to disciplines such as physics (which is often treated as a sort of ur-science) are inappropriate for psychoanalysis. Psychoanalysis, so these arguments go, should be judged according to its own scientific lights rather than being forced into the Procrustian mold of positivism. Eagle's (1983) objection to this proposal cuts to the heart of the matter.

My point is simply this: to a certain extent, complex discussions regarding the nature of science distract from one attending to and recognizing the simple and stark fact that even from a most informal and common-sense point of view and even employing the most liberal and relaxed criteria, many [psychoanalytic] . . . claims and formulations . . . are either incoherent or without any evidential support. . . . The proper question is not 'are they scientific?' (*whatever* one's conception of science), but do they have *any* coherent meaning?

(Eagle 1983: 49)

The second background factor to Langs's rejection by the psychoanalytic Establishment is sociological. Since the Second World War, the scientific poverty of what I will call 'normal' psychoanalysis has been accompanied by popular acclaim and social prestige (perhaps the latter has brought about the former. As Neitzsche said, 'Power makes stupid'!). During its youth, psychoanalysis was a radical, even revolutionary, approach to the human soul. To become a member of the 'savage hoard' – as Freud called the psychoanalytic movement – was to court profesional and financial oblivion in the service of a great idea. Psychoanalysis recruited the intellectually adventurous. To publicly espouse psychoanalytic beliefs was at that time an act of intellectual daring. With the rise of National Socialism came a diaspora. The analysts fled mainly to the United States and, in lesser numbers, to Britain. In America the refugees encountered a conservative and highly medicalized indigenous psychoanalytic culture. The *emigrés* were faced with the options of conformity or exclusion:

The refugee analysts settled in the United States in the 1930s. However, it was not until the 1950s, after the depression and the Second World War, that the public at large could turn its attention to psychoanalysis. Then psychoanalysis seemed very much in tune with the conservative and conformist times. It had become a respectable medical activity with prosperous practitioners and prosperous clients. As a theory or activity it did not offer any particularly challenging social or political judgements. Rather, it appeared to be a fashionable treatment for fashionable ailments.

(Jacoby 1983: 5)

This 'sleek American psychoanalysis', as Jacoby calls it, was at its apogee during the period of Langs's training and early psychoanalytic work. Psychoanalytic writing was then (and continues to be) notable for its intellectual provincialism, complacency, and self-satisfaction. Then Langs began to question publicly the value of the theories and practices that the profession had come to take for granted. He did this through the application of genuinely scientific reasoning, producing genuinely testable hypotheses rather than appeals to 'authority' and statements inspired by insubstantial and quasi-metaphysical systems of explanation. He rekindled the fiery critical enthusiasm which psychoanalysis, in more comfortable circumstances, had betrayed. Langs emerged as an inconoclast, gadfly, and consumer advocate. Inevitably, the profession began to take up arms against him. Langs described this in a 1988 interview with Laura Botha as follows:

> I wouldn't say that they stoned me. They didn't do that. . . . They ignored me. They pretended that I didn't exist. They treated me as if I were dead and tried to deaden me. . . . I'll say this in their defense, that this turns out to be a very human reaction to the things that threaten us. If you say to an analyst 'Hey, your patients aren't *imagining* that you are doing crazy things to them. They are really *perceiving* that you have been trained in a crazy way.' Nobody wants to hear that. It's a very human thing not to want to give up your basic beliefs. If they're your way of earning money, and your way of protecting yourself, then it's almost impossible.

Langs was placed under considerable pressure, both personal and professional, to attenuate or revoke his position.

> Not one of my public or private critics had seriously considered the extensive clinical material I had presented; nor did they attempt to refute my theoretical derivations and clinical techniques through either different interpretations of my own data or the presentation of contradictory data of their own. I was quickly learning, as had others before me . . . that there is an intense resistance among psychoanalysts and psychotherapists to new ideas and concepts, especially those affecting psychoanalytic and psychotherapeutic technique. . . . This is . . . a barrier against chaotic, underlying truths.
>
> (Langs 1978c: xv)

These reactions reveal

> . . . a remarkable paradox, which, stated in its essentials, is as follows: on the one hand, impingements on the therapeutic environment . . . evoke intense but highly predictable responses in patients, while on the other hand the delineation of this dimension of treatment generates strikingly chaotic and emotional responses in therapists and analysts.
>
> (Langs 1979: i)

The more Langs persisted in his research, the more the guardians of normal psychoanalysis[5] drew away from him. Referral sources dried up – the death-knell for a private practitioner – and teaching contracts were not renewed. Langs was stigmatized as 'paranoid' and 'psychotic', just as Ferenczi had been forty years earlier. 'In this case', writes Lothane (1985: 195), 'the establishment chose silence. Obliteration is a fate worse than excommunication'. Langs's response to this offensive was threefold. While continuing, unsuccessfully, to attempt to influence the profession, Langs simultaneously began to organize a therapeutic movement based on his own research, to forge alliances with scientists working within other disciplines (such as applied mathematics), and to publish works for the general public. Like Freud, who took as his motto Virgil's *'Flectere si nequeo superos, Acheronta movebo'* – 'If I cannot bend the upper gods, I shall move the underworld' – Langs was unable to move the 'upper gods' of the analytic Establishment.

> I had to keep asking myself, Am I trying to be a martyr? Am I inviting all of this condemnation? And I've absolutely decided this is not martyrdom or masochism, but a love of truth. . . . You see, I think this is where a lot of opposition comes from: new ideas frighten many analysts and impinge upon . . . areas that they find too difficult to confront and modify – resolve. . . . There is a kind of massive sharing; it's like the Emperor's new clothes: there is a great need to confirm even when one senses that something is awry. And only babes dare speak the truth – no one else dares to do so.
> (Langs and Searles 1980: 87)

By 1982 Langs had ceased describing his approach as a development within the classical Freudian paradigm. He had become disillusioned with normal psychoanalysis. Langs states in the unpublished interview with Botha that: 'I always believed that the psychotherapist and psychoanalyst were committed to the truth, no matter how painful. . . . I became disillusioned when I found this was not so.' Had Langs been content with merely delivering a critique of psychoanalysis, the reactions of the analysts would seem less extraordinary. There have been many trenchant criticisms leveled against analysis from both inside and outside the profession. Analysis is vulnerable on many fronts and has been attacked many times on therapeutic (for example, Eysenck 1985), moral (for example, Miller 1986), and epistemological (for example, Grünbaum 1982) grounds. To all such attacks psychoanalysts can, I think, quite reasonably respond that even if we grant that psychoanalysis is therapeutically unreliable, ethically ambiguous, or epistemologically shaky, there is still a need for a searching, insight-based form of treatment and that psychoanalysis is the best that anyone has been able to develop along these lines. A purely destructive critique is less of a challenge than a critique which also offers a positive alternative. In Langs's case, the profession was offered an alternative theory to evaluate. This of course is a risky business because an unprejudiced investigation can lead to the refutation of the old paradigm. The ability of an investigator to respond to such a challenge in an open and objective manner, allowing the commitment to truth override the inevitable narcissistic attachment to beloved theories, is a measure of his or her scientific integrity.

From the outset, Langs's project was one of reform rather than demolition.[6] His criticisms of psychoanalytic theory and practice were aimed ultimately toward the development of new and improved forms of psychoanalytic treatment. Once he had come to differentiate his approach from that of mainstream classical analysis, Langs began to call it the 'interactional approach'. This label, which emphasized the mutual impact of analyst and patient upon one another, was soon changed to the unwieldy 'interactional-adaptational approach' when Langs realized that patients' unconscious reactions to the therapists are primarily adaptive (i.e. based on reality rather than phantasy). By 1980 Langs realized that his view of unconscious processes was basically an information-processing theory using patients verbal communications as basic data-structures. This contrasted sharply with most normal psychoanalytic approaches, which take an alleged empathic resonance with patients' inner mental states as basic data – a view developed most explicitly by Kohut (1959). Langs accordingly rechristened his paradigm the *communicative* approach.

The communicative approach is a method of psychotherapy rooted in the wisdom of what Langs calls the deep unconscious part of the mind. Rather than being based on *therapists'* beliefs about what constitutes sound psychotherapy, the communicative approach is designed around following the unconscious advice provided by the patients themselves. The communicative therapist therefore tailors his or her interventions to the deep unconscious requirements of patients. At each and every step, the therapist is guided by the patient's unconscious recommendations. Communicative therapists do not assume that they have gotten something 'right' until the patient has unconsciously confirmed this. By the same token, if the patient unconsciously tells the therapist, through encoded narratives, that he or she has done something 'wrong', the communicative therapist is required to concur with this judgement and waits for the patient to point out the right track. There is no question of bringing the patient round to one's own way of thinking and then calling this 'insight into the unconscious'. The communicative therapist takes the stance of waiting to be brought round to the truth by the patient.

It is difficult, on the face of it, to understand why such an approach to analysis should evoke such intense reactions. Freud's whole approach, after all, was predicated on the idea that patients unconsciously know what it is that most deeply troubles them. The real problem, I think, lies in the fact that Langs has taken this principle quite seriously instead of merely paying it lip-service. He has made the patient's unconscious 'validation' of the analyst's efforts into a basic requirement. He has acknowledged the patient's ultimate and inviolable authority both in theory and in practice and operationalized this notion as a specific method for listening, formulating, intervening, and evaluating one's work. It is simply not possible to remain loyal to the techniques of normal psychoanalysis when approaching matters from this perspective because patients invariably unconsciously tell us that the established methods are inappropriate, destructive, seductive, self-serving, and so on. Because the communicative approach gives the therapist no room to wriggle out of the implications of all of this, many therapists feel 'restricted' by the approach and oppose it on these grounds. But the intense self-discipline asked of the communicative therapist is not arbitrary: it is rooted in an attitude of moral seriousness.

The communicative therapist must strive to be mindful of the true implications of his or her interventions, and to eschew those that are inconsistent with the analytic ideals of insightful healing and the securing of the patient's autonomy. It is no longer possible to embrace a patronizing 'therapist knows best' attitude. The therapist has to 'take it on the chin'. It is highly paradoxical that while Langs's writings have struck many as arrogant and self-congratulatory – Lomas (1987: 123), for example, speaks of his 'self-indulgent and over-confident style' – the practice of communicative psychotherapy requires a degree of subordination of the therapist's personality to the requirements unconsciously laid down by the patient that is unmatched by any other form of psychotherapy. As Lothane (1980: 259) points out:

> Now the patient is the true arbiter. . . . The patient instead of being indoctrinated by his analyst in psycho-analytic theories, will no longer be expected to prove the truth of the theories that happen to be in vogue. He is in analysis for his own needs, to pursue his own project of the examined life – his biography, for his own benefit.

To practice communicative therapy means to be led, taught, and, when necessary, admonished by one's patients. The therapist will, again and again, have his or her vulnerabilities and inadequacies brought into bold relief by the searching spotlight of patients' unconscious perceptions. There is no refuge from the beautiful, terrible poetry of the deep unconscious part of the mind. Not only must therapists acknowledge their failings to themselves, but they must also acknowledge them in their interpretations to patients, to their supervisors, and to colleagues in clinical presentations. Raney (1984b) suggests that the uniquely exposing nature of communicative psychotherapy has greatly contributed to its irrationally defensive reception by the profession.

> Quite possibly the Langs paradigm cannot be discussed in calm scientific debate. The communicative paradigm is especially and distinctly disturbing to others in the psychotherapy field because it acknowledges that the patient can be acutely aware of the validity or invalidity of the therapist's technical interventions, thus forcing the student to work over his or her personal neurosis as well as therapeutic technique. If the student relentlessly scrutinizes his or her work in the light of communicative principles or permits scrutiny by others with such a perspective, the meanings revealed either become obvious or evoke defensive operations. . . . A new paradigm, such as Langs', organizes and explains data in such a way that the observer must change. . . . The ego of the observer is irrevocably altered by the synthesis of the new meanings and the new observations.
>
> (ibid.: 485)

With very few exceptions (Gill 1984, 1985; Lothane 1985) the propositions of the communicative approach have not been critically addressed in a thoughtful manner. Chessick (1982), for example, defends normal psychoanalysis at the expense of sacrificing empirical data to wishful thinking. Although ready to concede that inexperienced therapists are liable to offer patients countertransference-laden interventions, Chessick pulls back from the idea that 'it is necessary to assume that a similar major pattern takes place as Langs postulates' in the case of 'the well-analysed and well-trained therapist' (619). He goes on to assure us that:

> Countertransference flounderings of the novice or poorly or analysed therapist produce these extreme reactions in patients, but interventions from well-trained therapists which, although they may include minor countertransference manifestations, also include significant appropriate and therapeutic or healthy manifestations, do not produce such extreme responses.
>
> (ibid.: 622)

Chessick accuses Langs of 'assuming' that so-called 'well-analysed' therapists impose their own psychopathology on their patients, and suggests that this 'postulate' is not 'necessary'. This is already a very subtle but nonetheless significant distortion of Langs's position. Langs does not 'assume' this to be the case: he *demonstrates* it using clinical data. It is of course possible to question the way that Langs interprets this data, but if one admits – as Chessick seems to do – that Langs's method of formulating unconscious meaning yields accurate results when applied to the work of inexperienced therapists, it is difficult to understand the rational justification for rejecting the results of the application of the *same* method to the work of experienced therapists. By begging this question, Chessick makes Langs's effort to consider afresh the work of analysts and therapists in a non-defensive, empirical spirit seem like an undisciplined and unjustified extrapolation based on mere assumptions and postulations. For all his objections to Langs's 'assumptions', Chessick proceeds, practically in the same breath, to blithely assert, with no presentation of supporting clinical data, that well-trained and well-analysed therapists' interventions have only 'minor' countertransferential and inappropriate properties, and that these do not have severely disruptive ramifications. It is clear, I think, just who is making the assumptions here.

Chessick's statements are typical of one type of criticism of Langs's work. Patrick Casement's are typical of another. Casement was the main British supporter of Langs's work in the early 1980s. He wrote a long, highly complimentary (and indeed completely uncritical) review of Langs's *The Therapeutic Environment* (1979) for the *International Journal of Psycho-Analysis* (Casement 1980); and when James Raney edited a collection of communicative papers published under the title of *Listening and Interpreting: The Challenge of the Work of Robert Langs* (1984a), Casement contributed a chapter on 'The reflective potential of the patient as mirror to the therapist'. A year later, he expanded this into two chapters of his book *On Learning from the Patient* (1985). In 1987 Casement offered the following criticism of Langs's position in a paper published in the *British Journal of Psychotherapy*:

> For a while I tried . . . to apply his [Langs's] way of thinking to my own clinical work. . . . But I began to feel uncomfortable about the incisiveness with which he evaluates the clinical work of others. This comes across from his writings as if there were only one right way of working analytically. Ironically I am now sure that it was precisely this dogmatic certainty that had first attracted me to Langs.
>
> (91)[7]

It seems to me that these thoughts are based, in part, on some confusion about the nature of dogmatism. Dogmatism has nothing to do
with the specific content of a scientist's beliefs. It is a measure, rather,
of scientists' reluctance to open their positions to falsification.
Scientific conscience precludes a comfortable pluralism – Einstein's
'rotten compromises' – without necessarily becoming dogmatic.
Galileo, for example, was not behaving dogmatically in rejecting the
hypothesis that the sun revolves around the earth. His assertion would
have been dogmatic only if he had failed to consider seriously the
opposing point of view. As I will describe in Chapter 10, scientists
demarcate a specific domain and attempt to adjudicate mutually
exclusive hypotheses about processes and entities within that domain
(Edelson 1984). To eliminate one hypothesis in favor of another is not
an example of dogmatism: it is the essence of scientific reasoning and
is based on the hard-won right to *question* assertions.

If the domain of psychoanalysis is taken to be the encoded, unconscious dimension of patient's communications within the analytic
setting, it follows that a psychoanalytic scientist should strive to determine the true nature of unconscious communication and that he or she
must do this by evaluating competing hypotheses against the evidence
and eliminating those that do not stand up to the test. This is precisely
what Langs has tried to do. He has evolved a rigorous method for
evaluating clinical hypotheses which is applicable to both communicative and non-communicative modes of psychotherapy. He has asserted
on the strength of repeated clinical tests that the communicative
approach fares much better than its rivals when evaluated in this way.
This is Langs's justification for saying that there appears to be one
valid way of interpreting the unconscious meaning of derivative
communications in psychoanalysis. Casement neither rejects Langs's
data nor disagrees with his mode of inference. He seems simply to
object to the uncomfortable conclusion that if the communicative
view of unconscious processes is right, the normal psychoanalytic view
must be wrong. In the last analysis the reproach of dogmatism is
highly ironic for the simple reason that the communicative approach
is, as far as I am aware, the *only* psychoanalytic orientation that has
worked out a stringent method for falsifying hypotheses, which it consistently deploys against itself.[8] The communicative approach *invites*
refutation. Kaufmann (1980: 81) puts his finger on the essential issues
when he writes:

What is and what is not dogmatic is frequently misunderstood.
What is truly dogmatic is the failure to consider objections and

alternatives, as if one's own point of view were the only one that needed to be taken seriously. Yet those who simply tell their own story, ignoring all that speaks against it as well as rival accounts, make things easy for their readers by making no demands on them; and the readers tend to be grateful for being entertained and told how things are without being called upon to make a strenuous decision. Authors of that kind are apt to seem self-effacing. Since their own views are the only ones they mention, there is no need to speak of themselves or of their rivals. On the other hand, the writer who takes account of objections to his story and indicates how he proposes to meet them, and who discusses rival views and shows why he cannot accept them and why, in effect, his own story is the best he has been able to come up with, is often experienced as egotistical, threatening – and dogmatic.

Langs's work has more and more confirmed him in the role of a consumer advocate and, of course, a thorn in the side of mainstream psychoanalysis. Certainly many patients, though by no means all, experience relief through psychoanalytic treatment. Langs argues that many of these apparently successful outcomes are in reality 'misalliance cures' rather than cures based on genuine insight into the unconscious realm. Confronted with an insensitive, disruptive therapist:

> The deep unconscious system thinks 'Ah, that therapist is as crazy as your mother. He's even crazier than you are. Oh, that's wonderful. Now you're the least insane person in the picture. You're feeling better already!' It is out of some very powerful and I think pathological deep unconscious needs that patients seek out their therapists.
>
> (Langs in Smith 1989: 118)

Unfortunately, these misalliance cures are accompanied by side-effects. When a new drug is introduced into medical use it has been tested extensively to determine what, if any, side-effects it incurs. Although these procedures are by no means foolproof, they are strenuous attempts to monitor a proposed treatment for harmful consequences. This sort of thing does not happen in the world of psychotherapy, where practitioners are only too happy to attribute every improvement in the patient to their own ministrations while blaming stasis or deterioration on patients' 'resistance' or deeply entrenched psychopathology.

> Every form of therapy – no matter what it is – extracts a price. You will get some relief if you're lucky, but it will cost you something.

> You can't cheat nature. . . . If you're not getting at the truth, by
> substituting one symptom for another, one defense for another,
> there is a price. . . . If you investigate this you find that patients and
> therapists deny the price of a therapy unless it is absolutely
> atrocious.
>
> (Langs in Smith 1989: 118)

Although both patients and therapists deny that therapy often has a
pervasive, destructive impact, Langs argues that patients are usually
unconsciously aware of the 'madness' of their therapists: 'I have come
to believe that . . . as soon as you take on the role of "therapist" . . .
you start to behave in crazy destructive ways, even trying to damage
the patient's own self-healing process' (ibid.: 119). The profession as a
whole shrinks back from this and refuses to acknowledge the existence
of those very phenomena which they, in principle if not in practice,
urge their patients to contend with in themselves.

> To this day, countless therapists dread the contents of the uncon-
> scious part of the mind. They fear the highly sensitive perceptions
> patients unconsciously have of them and the way in which their own
> innermost secrets are revealed. . . . They create misalliances
> designed to exclude all such realizations in their communications.
>
> (Langs in Freeman 1984: 116)

Prior to 1982 all of Langs's numerous books and papers were aimed
at a professional audience. Realizing that he was making little impact
on the profession, he began writing books for the consumer as well.
Beginning with *The Psychotherapeutic Conspiracy* (1982b), Langs
went on to publish *Madness and Cure* (1985a), *Decoding Your
Dreams* (1988c), and most recently *Rating Your Psychotherapist*
(1989a). His aim is to create an informed public that will exert
pressure upon the profession for reform. At the same time, Langs has
given up his psychoanalytic practice and returned to his original career
as a researcher. Since 1987 he has worked with a team of applied
mathematicians toward identifying the deep patterns in psychotherapy
sessions which are undetectable through naive observation. Langs and
his co-workers have created a method for scoring transcripts of
sessions line by line in such a manner that over 50,000 data points can
be generated from a single psychotherapeutic session (Langs *et al.*
1987). This yield of information is then subjected to mathematical
operations to reveal previously undetected interactional processes.
Langs hope that this research will enable him to create a genuine
science of psychoanalysis as well as to test communicative hypotheses

in a far more exacting manner than has hitherto been possible and to generate entirely new concepts of the therapeutic interaction, bringing clinical and theoretical psychoanalysis into the world of twentieth-century science by liberating it from the constraints of the outmoded 'Aristotelian' approach in which it remains enmeshed: 'By concentrating on the patient/therapist system as a unique entity, I have fortuitously set up clinical parameters that can serve as a basis for quantitative research into the moment-to-moment transactions between patients and therapists' (Langs 1987: 156–7).

The shift to a modern scientific approach entails a fundamental reorientation away from impressionistic concepts and observations, and toward the detailed scrutiny of interactional patterns:

> In its present state, psychoanalysis tends to be pervaded by 'why' questions and attempts at answers that are qualitative and global. . . . The history of science suggests that we should be asking, rather, 'what' and 'how'. What are the components of the communication from patient to therapist? How are they interacting and how are they influenced by the conditions of treatment? What are the dimensions of these communications, and how do they vary from moment-to-moment – for example, at five- or ten-second intervals? What is the nature of these trajectories and the definition of their underlying lawfulness?
>
> (ibid.: 571)

Having explored how Langs evolved the communicative approach and situated this within the context of the psychoanalytic background to his work, I am now in a position to describe the communicative theory of the human mind and human interaction in fuller detail.

6   Hidden conversations

The doctor is the patient's fate.
                Karl Jaspers

In this chapter I will set out and illustrate the essential components of
the communicative theory of psychoanalysis. This will both show how
Langs has drawn on and gone beyond the theorists mentioned in
Chapter 4 and serve as a prelude to an account of communicative
technique. At the risk of laboring the obvious, I would like to stress
that a theory as sophisticated as the communicative approach cannot
be fully encapsulated in the space of a single chapter, and that the
reader who wishes to obtain more detailed understanding of theory or,
for that matter, technique, should explore the wider communicative
literature itself. I have, in order to facilitate this, included a comprehensive communicative bibliography after the general bibliography at
the end of this volume.

A MODEL OF THE MIND

All psychoanalytic theories employ some model of the mind. But what
is a model? According to McGinn (1989: 176) a model is 'a *simulating
engine* – a device that mimics, copies, replicates, duplicates, imitates,
parallels reality'.[1] A model of the mind is thus a hypothetical device or
system which simulates mental processes. A model does not have to
physically resemble that which it describes. Rising temperature, for
example, can be modeled as an ascending vertical line (along the lines
of the rising column of mercury in a thermometer), but this does not
mean that rising temperature has anything to do with verticality or
lines; it simply means that there is an isomorphism between the rising
line and its calibrations – which corresponds to degrees of temperature
– and the actual increase in temperature. Thus, mental models do not

have to 'look like' the mind: they are just required to reproduce in themselves the vital relationship between mental functions and structures.

Freud employed many models during the course of his career. Beginning with the 'reflex arc' model, Freud also described the topographical model, dividing the mind into unconscious and preconscious systems; the structural model of id, ego, and superego; the dynamic model, which represents mental events in terms of the interplay of hypothetical mental forces and the economic model, which describes the mind in terms of the accumulation and dispersal of quantities of excitement. Other analytic theorists have brought in additional models, such as Klein's part- and whole-object model and Kohut's 'bipolar self'.[2]

The communicative model of the mind is most reminiscent of Freud's topographical model. It postulates that the human mind consists of two basic systems called the *conscious system* and the *deep unconscious system*.

Both of these mental systems process perceptions – they each take in information about the external world and make sense of it – but each does this in a distinct and unique manner. The conscious system processes information according to learned categories and is therefore tremendously affected by such factors as social conditioning. It follows that there is considerable variation, both from individual to individual and from culture to culture, in how the conscious system operates. Another important property of the conscious system is its capacity to report information directly. Under normal circumstances information taken in by the conscious system can be retrieved, identified, and reported as such. For example, if asked what I ate for breakfast this morning I can recall this (conscious system) information and describe it to my interlocutor.

The deep unconscious system functions in a radically different manner. Its cognitive processes appear to be analogous to the instinctual patterns found in animal species: i.e. they are prior and relatively impervious to social learning. The deep unconscious system functions according to a profound biological wisdom that has apparently been naturally selected and reproduced over countless generations. It follows that there is comparatively little variation, from individual to individual and from culture to culture, in how the deep unconscious system operates. The deep unconscious system is incapable of reporting its contents directly. It can only make its influence felt by impacting upon the conscious system in a way which will be described shortly.

One of the most remarkable features of the deep unconscious system is that it is specifically adapted to understanding intersubjective reality. It is finely tuned to identify the most subtle psychological nuances of other people's behavior. It is able to understand emotional reality more completely and with much greater facility than the conscious system. Realizations which are available to the conscious system only after lengthy and laborious processes of reflection (if at all) occur to the deep unconscious system after only seconds, or perhaps milliseconds, of processing. The deep unconscious system is able to make bewilderingly rapid and highly accurate inferences about the unconscious motives, defenses, and implications of peoples' behavior. According to communicative theory, then, each of us carries within us a brilliant psychoanalytic intelligence, and each of us is, unconsciously, a natural psychoanalyst.

The deep unconscious system appears to influence the conscious system in a way analogous to the theory of transference given by Freud in *The Interpretation of Dreams* (1900). It will be recalled that for Freud, too, unconscious ideas are never directly expressed. In order to make its presence known, an unconscious idea must 'transfer' its 'cathexis' on to a pre-conscious idea with which it can be associatively linked. The innocuous pre-conscious idea is thereby reinforced and given greater prominence in the mind. If one is not engaged in some pressing task and can enter a state of reverie, daydreaming, or free association the unconsciously empowered pre-conscious ideas will readily press into consciousness – will 'come to mind' – as *proxies* for the censored, unconscious ones. According to communicative theory deep unconscious ideas make themselves felt in a similar way. The deep unconscious system is able to evoke conscious ideas which can serve as disguised representatives of the latent thoughts. Following Freud's terminology, Langs refers to these indirect expressions of unconscious ideas as encoded ideas, transformed ideas, or derivatives.

According to Freud there must be some associative link between a repressed mental content and its derivatives. Such links can be immensely convoluted and do not necessarily entail thematic affinities (for example, the 'espe' parapraxis in Freud's case of the Wolf Man (1918)). In communicative theory, on the other hand, there must always be a thematic link between a deep unconscious idea and its derivatives. This is well illustrated by an expample of a patient's differing conscious and unconscious responses to an interpretation. A patient in his second session of psychoanalytic therapy was offered a lengthy interpretation which stopped short of linking the patient's material to the here-and-now of the therapeutic situation. After listening to the interpretation the patient remarked that it seemed to make sense. This was his initial *conscious* response. The patient paused, and manifestly changed the subject, saying: 'My wife is a bad public speaker.' This was his derivative commentary on the intervention – he felt that the (female) therapist, who is represented by his wife, did not express herself fully. The patient had unconsciously noticed that the therapist had expressed herself poorly and incompletely. This perception evoked a preconscious idea which embodies the same theme – that of someone who does not express herself well – and this functions as a substitute for the more emotionally potent unconscious observation. It is the thematic structure of the derivative which alerts us to its unconscious significance.

FORMULATING HYPOTHESES

All forms of psychoanalytic practice stress the importance of formulating hypotheses about the unconscious meaning of patients' manifest communications and behavior. From 1913 onwards Freud referred to the act of constructing a hypothesis as '*interpretation*': for Freud, an interpretation (*Deutung*) is a hypothesis about an unconscious mental content (Freud 1913c). In his papers on technique, Freud emphasized how, once a viable hypothesis has been formulated, the analyst must wait for the appropriate moment to communicate it to the patient, a process which Freud called 'voicing an interpretation'. In more modern parlance the term 'interpretation' has taken the place of 'voicing an interpretation' – it has come to refer to a verbal intervention rather than just an inner cognitive act.

Freud had surprisingly little to say about just how one goes about formulating psychoanalytic hypotheses. Looking at the work of Freud and those who have come after him it becomes clear that, in the broadest possible terms, hypotheses, as provisional explanations, involve placing information generated by the patient into a new context to generate new meaning. This suggests two areas which must be explored if we are to understand the nature of psychoanalytic interpretation: we must identify the type of information used for making interpretations and the specific contexts or frames of reference used by analysts to recontextualize it.[3]

Generally speaking, all analysts use information obtained within the psychoanalytic situation itself – the patient's dreams, transferences, and free associations – as primary sources of data, although some make use of information obtained from third parties (doctors, psychiatrists, spouses) to supplement this. The communicative approach is very specific about the data that is used for forming hypotheses about deep unconscious concerns. Communicative psychotherapists stick to patients' derivative verbal communications within the therapeutic situation. They ignore non-derivative statements as having little relevance to the unconscious domain and refrain entirely from obtaining information from outside sources. Not only is data from third parties often extremely untrustworthy, it is also a breach of total confidentiality and privacy to involve third parties in a treatment in any way, and this practice will invariably undermine patients' trust in the therapist.

Derivatives can usually be identified by their formal properties. They are statements which are *specific*, *concrete*, and therefore *easily visualized*. They do not manifestly refer to the therapeutic situation at all: *they describe other people and situations*. Sequences of derivatives are, manifestly, quite discontinuous, involving numerous *jumps* and *changes of subject*. All of this contrasts with non-derivative communication which is linear, logical, and often abstract and general. Periods of rumination, introspection, and self-analysis, as well as manifest references to the therapeutic situation, are invariably non-derivative in nature.

In normal psychoanalysis patients' manifest messages are recontextualized in terms of archaic and often frankly hypothetical infantile scenarios. A patient's account, say, of arguing with his boss might be seen in an Oedipal context as a disguised representation of his rivalry with his father. A Kleinian analyst would choose an 'oral' context and view the argument as perhaps a derivative of the patient's early relationship with a 'persecutory breast' during the first months of life. In all of the normal systems of psychoanalysis, the primary context of unconscious communication is infantile and archaic. The here-and-now therapeutic situation is given secondary importance only as a vehicle for the patient's transferences. The communicative approach, on the other hand, regards the immediate therapeutic environment – including the silences and interventions of the therapist – as the primary context for unconscious communications. *Unconscious communications, expressed in an encoded fashion through derivatives, primarily express the real implications of the therapist's behavior.* The here-and-now stimulus which has evoked a derivative communication serves as a psychoanalytic Rosetta stone, unveiling previously unsuspected unconscious meanings. Allow me to flesh this out with an example.

A female therapist-in-training presented an account of one of her patient's dreams at a clinical seminar attended by psychoanalytic therapists of various theoretical persuasions. The dream went as follows:

> I am in an unfamiliar room, and am trying to reach my sister Jane, who is standing at the other end of the room. There is a scary man dressed all in black who is between us, blocking me. I can't reach Jane and she can't reach me.

The patient, a middle-aged woman referred to this therapist because of recurring anxiety attacks, awoke from this dream in terror.

One of the participants, who was of a generally Freudian orientation, suggested that this was an 'Oedipal' dream with a homosexual caste. The patient was trying to reach her mother – represented by Jane – but is obstructed by her father, the man in black, who is her sexual rival. The black attire of the interloper was explained as a symbol of death (the patient's father had died when she was in her adolescence). For this therapist, the most probable context for the dream was the Oedipal dilemma which the patient experienced at the age of three or four. Implicitly, the dream was seen as having little to do with the patient's contemporary life. Of course, Oedipal conflicts might be described as having 'psychical reality', but this does not affect the point that I am trying to make. In normal psychoanalysis the unconscious referent of a derivative communication, such as a dream, is inevitably and, given the assumptions of these psychoanalytic theories, *necessarily*, thought to be some memory or phantasy, or some contemporary *pretext* for the same (i.e. transference). Normal psychoanalysis takes a strongly internalist stance (cf. McGinn 1989), holding that perception of external reality is shaped by purely internal, unconscious ideas.[4] An important corollary of this perspective is the idea that expressions of unconscious parts of the mind are maladaptive. The unconscious mental system is believed to *impose* inappropriate concepts upon the world rather than respond adaptively to the realities of life. The resurgence of unconscious infantile desires and anxieties is believed by the great majority of psychoanalysts to *disrupt* adaptations. Normal psychoanalysis therefore tries to bring the unruly unconscious mental contents under the dominion of the allegedly superior, adaptive control of the conscious ego. This, I will show, amounts to a sort of imperialism of the mind. The indigenous population of the unconscious domain is not respected. Their language is not even understood by the oppressor. They are subjugated 'for their own good' and assumed to be brutal, childish, and incapable.

For normal psychoanalysis, the unconscious mental system tells us nothing of value about the external world. The communicative approach, on the other hand, does not regard the unconscious part of the mind as maladaptive: it accords it the profoundest respect. The deep unconscious system can generate insights that are far beyond anything that the conscious system is capable of. To extend the political analogy, communicative psychoanalysis counsels us to refrain from colonizing the unexplored unconscious realm. It seeks, rather, to learn the language of the inhabitants and to gratefully receive whatever fragments of their primordial wisdom they are willing to impart. These two attitudes toward the unconscious part of the mind – colonial and anti-colonial – are well illustrated by the reactions by psychotherapists to the dream described above, to which we will now return.

After listening to the comments of several psychotherapists, the trainee therapist supplied some additional information. She mentioned that her own Christian name was Jane, the same name as the patient's sister in the dream. She then went on to describe how a psychiatrist attached to the outpatient department where the treatment was taking place had begun to put pressure on the patient to take medication to relieve her anxiety. After these disclosures were made, a participant at the seminar suggested that the patient's homosexual-incestuous fixation was being 'played out' in the therapeutic situation. The patient was said to be unconsciously 'using' the therapist as a surrogate mother/sister, while the psychiatrist was cast in the role of her father. It was suggested, then, that the 'homosexual' component of the transference was, in actuality, a defense against heterosexual Oedipal yearnings for the father coupled with murderous rage toward the mother. Various permutations of this were considered and the inevitable suggestion was made that 'the breast' was the ultimate protagonist and was accompanied by speculations about 'primitive splitting' and 'projective identification'.

The therapist remarked that since the psychiatrist had made his presence felt, the patient had seemed more 'resistant' to her therapeutic efforts. At this point a communicative therapist spoke up and suggested that the sense of the dream – the theme of the patient and Jane being kept apart by a man in the middle – was an unconscious portrayal of the actualities of this therapeutic situation. There was, in reality, a third party to treatment: the psychiatrist. The patient seemed to be derivatively saying that his involvement was undermining the treatment, blocking the establishment of a totally private one-to-one therapeutic experience. 'What about the black attire?', protested one of the group members, 'Surely that represents the patient's dead father!' 'Oh', said the therapist, 'I didn't mention that the psychiatrist's name was Dr Black.'

According to this interpretation the dream is highly appropriate. It accurately 'fits' with a piece of reality, throwing up previously unrecognized implications. It is *perceptive*, depicting a *real* and *contemporary* situation with which the patient and therapist need to come to grips. Just as the diameter of the pupil of the eye adapts immediately to any variation in the intensity of light striking the retina, the deep unconscious system instantaneously responds to any input from the environment that is relevant to the individual's safety and well-being. To turn Heinz Hartmann's well-known shibboleth on its head: the deep unconscious system is, primarily, an organ of adaptation (Hartmann, 1939). Unconscious derivatives – like the dream described above – are not as Freud, Klein, and others would have it, infantile subversions of reality. They are sophisticated portrayals of real situations. In light of the communicative hypothesis, then, the patient's resistance since the involvement of the psychiatrist is seen as an entirely rational and justified reaction to a disruption of the therapeutic relationship and not, as in normal psychoanalysis, as an expression of the patient's archaic transferences. Using a Freudian model of the mind, the patient's dream would be understood along the following lines. An unconscious incestuous wish, disturbed from its slumber by the weakening of defenses under the impact of therapy, presses toward consciousness. Because of the anxieties associated with this wish, it cannot emerge directly into consciousness. It is therefore disguised: the sexual element is virtually eliminated and the real identities of the characters are concealed. The communicative model begins with the stimulus of the psychiatrist's interventions. The patient unconsciously perceives the involvement of the psychiatrist in her case as obstructive. This is an entirely predictable derivative response to a third-party situation. It is the very predictability of derivative communications involving the theme of obstructive third parties in this circumstance which makes this more than just another *ad hoc* unfalsifiable hypothesis.

Psychoanalytic theory is notoriously lax about specifying the deductions that can be legitimately made from its hypotheses. With most psychoanalytic hypotheses it is difficult to ascertain whether or not any given piece of evidence contradicts the hypothesis in question. There are always ways to tinker with the evidence to make it fit one's theoretical prejudices. Take, for example, the hypothesis that the man in black in the dream represented a primitive internal object stemming from the patient's earliest infancy. How can this hypothesis be critically investigated? What could conceivably count as evidence against it? On what grounds could one say that it was proven or disproven? The hypothesis that the man in black represents a persecutory beast, 'bad penis', Oedipal father, or what not is cognitively *empty*: it cannot be rationally evaluated and thus provides no justification for belief. This aspect of psychoanalytic reasoning has been explicated in a thoroughly devastating way by Cioffi (1970, 1988), who writes of the 'inoculation' of psychoanalytic theory against falsification.

The question of verification and falsification has proven a scientific Achilles' heel for psychoanalysis, which most theorists have dealt with by the inadequate method of averting their gaze. Because psychoanalysis focuses on the *unconscious* mental sphere, psychoanalytic hypotheses cannot be *consciously* verified or falsified by patients. According to the theory the patient *does not consciously know* whether a proffered interpretation is true or false (if the patient *did* know, there would be no need for an interpretation because the material would not be unconscious). It follows that a patient's conscious response is immaterial for an evaluation of its accuracy: a patient's consent or dissent throws no light on the matter whatsoever.

VALIDATION

How can one meaningfully test the truth or falsity of clinical psychoanalytic propositions? This is a vital question. After all, one can go merrily about propounding as many weird and wonderful theories as one likes – unhampered by any objective limitations – so long as there is no way that any of these considerations can be contradicted by evidence.

Although it is utterly inconsistent with their theory of the mind, many psychoanalysts (for example Khan in the case of Peter) employ the criterion of manifest assent, which states that there are grounds for faith in a hypothesis if a patient consciously agrees with it. How can manifest assent have any bearing on the validity of a hypothesis that concerns unconscious contents? The use of this criterion only makes sense if it is presupposed that the interpretation has made an unconscious idea conscious – i.e. that the interpretation concerns an issue which is *no longer* unconscious. But this assumption merely begs the question. How can we know that this has happened? There are powerful rival explanations for manifest assent, such as the patient's need to idealize the analyst as an omniscient being or the patient's defensive needs (Fenichel 1941).

A second truth test invoked by psychoanalysts is the criterion of therapeutic impact. According to this viewpoint interpretations are to be regarded as 'true' in so far as they bring about remission of the patient's psychopathology. This notion rests on the false premise that therapeutic movement can only come about through accurate interpretations. As Grünbaum (1984) has demonstrated, Freud himself relied on this specious argument but in the end was forced to abandon it because he could not eliminate the possibility that therapeutic effects of psychoanalysis were based on suggestion rather than real insight. Considering the noteworthy therapeutic success of behavior therapy in the treatment of some forms of psychopathology it is clearly foolhardy to rely on the principle that only accurate interpretations can bring about therapeutic change.

A third approach to the problem, the argument from coherence, was also a favorite of Freud's. According to this view, an interpretation is to be regarded as correct if it provides a satisfying explanation for otherwise inexplicable phenomena. Now, it is certainly true that a valid psychoanalytic hypothesis must provide a coherent explanation for the behavior which it seeks to explain, but for this to be a satisfactory test for the truth of a psychoanalytic hypothesis that hypothesis must be *uniquely* satisfying. But – as the history of religion (and psychoanalysis) shows – it is always possible to come up with 'explanations' of puzzling phenomena. Coherence is a precondition for the truth of a proposition, but it does not vouchsafe it.

The communicative approach to validation uses an entirely different test: the test of *derivative assent*. This approach to the problem of validation was first mentioned by Freud in 'Constructions in analysis' (1937). In this paper Freud is much concerned with the issue of how the truth or falsity of psychoanalytic hypotheses is to be established. Freud examines and rejects the test of manifest assent as without value: 'It appears, therefore, that the direct utterances of a patient . . . afforded very little evidence upon the question whether we have been right or wrong' (Freud 1937: 263). He goes on to make the point that it is more fruitful for psychoanalysts to look for indirect evidence pertaining to the validity of their interpretative work: 'It is of all the greater interest that there are indirect forms of confirmation which are in every respect trustworthy' (ibid.).

Freud goes to describe four forms of indirect confirmation. The first is when the patient offers a negation ('I shouldn't ever have thought. . . .') in response to an intervention, which Freud takes as a confirmation. A second form of indirect confirmation occurs when a patient responds shortly after an interpretation with a confirming parapraxis. Yet another form of confirmation is supposed to occur in patients prone to the 'negative therapeutic reaction'. Freud perversely asserts that an interpretation can be judged correct when it *exacerbates* the patient's symptoms. The last of Freud's forms of indirect confirmation is by far the most interesting, and has been almost entirely neglected within the psychoanalytic literature. Freud presents it through an account of a 'small extra-analytical experience'.

> It concerned one of my colleagues who – it was long ago – had chosen me as a consultant in his medical practise. One day, however, he brought his young wife to see me, as she was causing him trouble. She refused on all sorts of pretexts to have sexual relations with him, and what he expected of me was evidently that I should lay before her the consequences of her ill-advised behaviour. I went into the matter and explained to her that her refusal would probably have unfortunate results for her husband's health or would lay him open to temptations which might lead to a break-up of their marriage. At this point he suddenly interrupted me with the remark: 'The Englishman you diagnosed as suffering from a cerebral tumour has died too.'
>
> (263–4)

At the time, Freud could not understand the meaning of this remark. The man's mind had evidently been wandering during Freud's lecture to his wife. He has recollected an event pertaining to Freud but which had no manifest relevance to the situation at hand, which he suddenly blurted out. Later Freud realized the unconscious significance of this statement. 'The man was evidently intending to confirm what I had been saying; he was meaning to say: "Yes, you're certainly quite right. Your diagnosis was confirmed in the case of the other patient too"' (ibid.). In other words, Freud believed that this man unconsciously found a way of conveying an agreement with his diagnosis of the situation. This came about indirectly and unconsciously through the evocation of a memory capable of serving as an encoded expression of confirmation. The memory of the diagnosis of the man with a brain tumour was a screen memory in the original sense of the term. In interpreting it Freud took the *theme* of the apparently irrelevant association – 'an accurate diagnosis' – and applied it to the here-and-now situation to produce the formulation that *his patient unconsciously regarded him as having correctly 'diagnosed' his marital situation.* Freud's next comments are extremely suggestive. 'It was', writes Freud, 'an exact parallel to the indirect confirmations that we obtain in analysis from associations' (264). Freud was evidently in the habit, late in his career, of monitoring patients' free associations following an intervention for disguised, derivative indications of confirmation or disconfirmation.[5]

To my knowledge Langs is the only psychoanalytic writer to have consistently employed and refined this approach to the verification of psychoanalytic hypotheses. In the communicative approach the patients' first derivative communications following the offer of an intervention will either validate or falisfy the intervention. Validation occurs when the patient responsively produces positively toned constructive derivative imagery, reflecting an unconscious appreciation of the positive, insightful qualities of the intervention.[6] Falsification, on the other hand, is revealed by patients' negative derivative imagery. With a knowledge of communicative theory, probable validating or falsifying derivative communications can be predicted to a high level of accuracy. A communicative therapist will not regard his or her interpretations as accurate unless they receive this sort of validation. Thus, communicative hypotheses most certainly do not come under the rubric of safe, vacuous, unfalsifiable (or not readily falsifiable) propositions. Communicative psychoanalysis advances exacting criteria for verification and is, in fact, more explicit about this vital issue than any other psychoanalytic orientation.

THE PATIENT/THERAPIST SYSTEM

The communicative approach never conceptualizes the patient in isolation from the 'system' in which he or she is embedded. In the context of psychotherapy this consists of the patient, the therapist, and the factors structuring the therapeutic interaction (the frame – see Chapter 7). 'The basic proposition in communicative therapy', says Langs, 'is so obvious any layman would laugh – it's like rediscovering the wheel!' (Langs in Botha 1988: 1). This laughably obvious contention is that the main focus of any psychotherapy lies in the real interaction between the two participants. According to communicative theory, everything that takes place within the patient's mind while he or she is in the therapeutic situation must be a function of the total 'behavioral field' (Laing), 'bipersonal field' (Baranger and Baranger), or 'patient/therapist system' (Langs). This idea invites comparison with Winnicott, who was fond of saying that there is no such thing as a baby. He meant to emphasize that when we speak of babies we imply mothers, for the baby and its mother are a 'dual unity': they comprise a system. Similarly, from the communicative perspective there is no such thing as a psychotherapy patient – because every patient is one component of a system involving a therapist and a set of conventions or 'boundary conditions' as well.

These views are absolutely central to the communicative conception of mind, which rejects the individualistic metaphysics of normal psychoanalysis. Minds are interdependent, mutually constituting entities. In this connexion, Little's metaphor of patient and analyst holding up mirrors to one another is strikingly prescient. The 'spiraling interaction' of the psychoanalytic process is based on endless mutual reflection, and reflection of reflection. The philosopher, Colin McGinn, expresses this conception quite beautifully: 'Your mind penetrates mine, mine embraces yours. . . . I have mental states which *contain* your mental states, which could not indeed exist without them. Our mental states are . . . *inter*dependent, since you can (of course) make like judgements about me' (McGinn 1989: 52).

Both patient and therapist are exquisitely sensitive to any variation in the behavior of the other or in the boundary conditions of therapy. As information-processing systems, human beings tend to *amplify* input, so that slight, low-energy causes impacting upon them are transformed, through a series of sensitive 'switching' processes, into high-energy, clearly observable effects (Dennett 1984). Dennett points out that:

> Moreover, such a system's input switches – the transducers that form the perceptual organs – are also amplifiers. The 'firing' of a retinal neuron, for instance, may be 'triggered' by the arrival of a single photon on a retinal receptor. Vast amounts of information arrive on the coat-tails of negligible amounts of energy, and then, thanks to the amplification powers of systems of switches, the information begins to do some work – evoking other information that was stored long ago, for instance, transmuting it for the present occasion in a million small ways and leading eventually to an action whose pedigree of efficient (or triggering) causation is so hopelessly inscrutable as to be invisible.
>
> (ibid.: 77)

Thus, although our behavior – for example our verbal communications – may have a cause within the system in which we are enmeshed, the cause may be so subtle, so microscopic by the standards of commonsense and naive observation which demands that cause be commensurate with effect, that the causes remain undetected and the resultant effect appears to be uncaused. 'We see the dramatic effects leaving', writes Dennett (ibid.), 'we don't see the causes entering; we are tempted by the hypothesis that there are no causes' (77).

The immediate here-and-now reality is the all-powerful causal nexus for events taking place within that situation. Past events, such as infantile traumas, or internal forces, such as instinctual drives and motivational systems, are causally relevant in so far as they are activated by that immediate reality.

Although this refined sensitivity is mutual, it emerges asymmetrically in the psychotherapeutic interaction: patients usually display a far higher level of sensitivity to therapists than vice versa. This may be just an appearance produced by the fact that therapists' professional behavior renders their unconscious reactions difficult to detect, while free association is an ideally subtle medium for registering the presence of unconscious influence. Another possibility is that it is the *role* of patient which heightens perceptual sensitivity. The patient is, by definition, one who suffers (the word derives from the Latin 'patior', to suffer). The therapist is someone who is supposed to deliver the afflicted from suffering. This situation immediately places the patient in a dependent and therefore vulnerable position *vis-à-vis* the therapist. For the patient – unlike the therapist – there is a great deal at stake. In addition to this, the patient is exposed more intensively to influences from the therapist than the therapist is to the patient; for not only does the patient absorb the impact of the therapist's behavior – his interventions and silences – he is also confronted with the therapeutic environment which, being established, controlled, and maintained by the therapist, must be seen as an expression of the therapist's psyche. Thus, the therapeutic situation is, as it were, *saturated* by the therapist's presence, and this impacts consciously and especially unconsciously upon the patient, determining aspects of his or her behavior in the sessions and having a deep and decisive influence on how the patient will fare in therapy. Because of the therapist's inevitably overwhelming presence and the powerful role that he or she adopts, it follows that psychotherapy is rich in opportunities for abusing and victimizing patients. Little wonder, then, that patients are unconsciously mobilized to be so preoccupied with the implications of their therapist's behavior and are so miraculously responsive to the faintest breath of emotional threat implied by it. Patients take in, absorb, and are affected by information about their therapists' psyches, which is processed with bewildering accuracy and rapidity (Langs 1988a).

CLINICAL ILLUSTRATIONS

I will now present some examples illustrating the basic components of the communicative perspective: the workings of the deep unconscious system, the presentation of derivatives of unconscious perceptions, validation, non-validation, and the exquisitely refined unconscious sensitivity of patients to therapists. These examples show how patients strip us of our grand pretensions, our professional hypocrisy (Ferenczi). Making no concessions to our narcissism, they confront us with truths which we would all be inclined to sweep under the carpet. They tell us, through derivatives, of our narcissism, our seductiveness, our anxieties, our self-serving exploitations and our blindness. Listening to patients in this way is inescapably painful for therapists, yet patients do not tell us these things *in order to* hurt us. They do it to teach us, guide us, and heal us. They do it to make us better therapists.

Jonathan (1990) records an example of a therapist who attempted to interpret his patient's derivatives in a communicative fashion, but did so incorrectly. Immediately after the intervention, the patient responds as follows: 'That's really interesting. You know, I was saying to Nick that in the flat, or anywhere for that matter, there always seems to be a radio playing and it's either too loud or too soft.' The patient begins with a manifest comment that the interpretation is 'interesting'. But as this is merely his conscious appraisal, the communicative analyst must wait until the patient offers an unconscious comment − by means of disguised and displaced derivatives − before coming to any conclusions about the validity of the preceding intervention. In this instance he does not have to wait long. The patient launches into a story about radios that has no manifest connection with the content of the therapist's intervention. The patient continues: 'It's like that with all media things with me. I use my glasses to watch TV. Yet sometimes even with my glasses on there's a blurred image' (87). A theme emerges of things not sounding right − the wireless is either too loud or too soft − and a 'blurred image'. These images indicate that the patient feels that the earlier intervention was incorrect. It did not seem right. The therapist's image of him was 'blurred'.

Now, the theme changes slightly: 'It's like going to church; you go with a lot of faith and often you're disappointed' (ibid.). This is clearly a non-validation. The patient has unconsciously processed his therapist's interpretation and concluded that it was quite disappointing. He expresses this in a disguised manner through the account of going to church and being disappointed with what happens there. He had hoped for something more fulfilling from the therapist. Realizing that he had erred, the therapist went on to interpret these remarks:

> Steve, this seems to be very much to do with what's going on here between us. You're telling me a lot, but I don't seem to be getting the message quite right, hence your reference to the blurred images

on the TV and the distorted sounds from the radio. Maybe you're disappointed in my interpretation, in my lack of understanding.

(ibid.: 88)

Notice that this interpretation did not put the patient's response down to transference, did not reduce it to an expression of phantasy or infantile psycho-sexual wishes. The therapist implicitly conveyed that he regarded his patient's unconscious observations as pertinent and sound. He merely delineated the themes found in the patient's discourse and organized around the trigger of the incorrect intervention. This effort was validated by the patient, who replied:

> You remember I told you about how I try to go for a swim at least once a week. Well, I didn't tell you that for a long time I couldn't swim. Then one holiday I decided to learn. I went for lessons. I thought it would be pure pleasure, but I was wrong. There was a helluva lot of pain, but actually I recovered quickly afterwards. The instructor did his best and I learned a lot from him. In the end I thought it was worth it. It was worth it in the end.

(ibid.: 88)

This latter passage is full of constructive, validating imagery. The patient represents the therapist mainly through his own person (in normal psychoanalysis this is called 'introjection' or 'identification'). The theme is the difficult process of learning something new, and refers to this therapist's struggle to learn to do sound psychotherapeutic work (the fact – which the patient did not *consciously* know – that this therapist was indeed a trainee gives the imagery an added dimension of poignancy). The patient is aware that the effort is costing his therapist (emotional) pain: this was clear from both the incorrect, countertransference-laden intervention which was not validated, and the second intervention in which the therapist had to grasp the nettle of his own shortcomings. But, says the patient, he 'recovered quickly': the poor intervention was followed by a more competent one. The image of the instructor can be understood both as a portrayal of the patient, who is unconsciously supervising his therapist, or as a representation of the therapist, who is able to offer his patient valuable learning. In either case the patient concludes that this therapy is worth enduring the pain and difficulty which accompanies it. This is a typical unconscious validation of a therapist's interpretation. Such sequences of constructive derivative imagery are very rare in psychotherapy. They virtually always follow a correct communicative intervention and can therefore be predicted at a high level of reliability. As we have found in this example, the derivative imagery is always specifically adapted to represent the specific details of the situation. Had this therapist *not* been greeted by this type of response, but instead had heard negatively toned derivatives, he would have concluded that his efforts had been deeply flawed.

Here is an example of a non-validation which occurred in the psychoanalysis of a primary-school teacher, Mrs J. The analyst, who was an experienced, classically trained practitioner, had offered his patient a prima facie unwarranted interpretation concerning her oral impulses. The patient immediately replied:

> I am having great trouble teaching maths to Neill, even though I give him special attention. I ask him to do a simple sum and he just pulls some number out of the air without giving it any thought. I wonder why he does this. Maybe he wants to hurt me.

The patient clearly conveys that the interpretation was incorrect. She recognizes at once the arbitrary quality of the intervention ('he just pulls a number out of the air without giving it any thought') and feels that he is deaf to her unconscious supervision ('I'm having great trouble teaching maths to Neill'). Mrs J. goes on to offer an encoded *interpretation* of her own: she feels that the analyst may be motivated by a desire to hurt her.

Interventions which have significant appropriate properties as well as being significantly incorrect will evoke a mixed derivative response containing both positively and negatively toned imagery. A therapist in training, Mrs A. was able, for the very first time, to offer a reasonably well composed communicative interpretation to one of her patients. Although repetitive, and over-intellectualized, the intervention nonetheless addressed the meaning of the patient's derivatives in light of a here-and-now trigger. Here is what the patient then said:

> Last week I met Sally. You know, the friend that I spent a lot of time with before. The last time that I saw her, about a year ago, she was really fucked up. She had these symptoms, you know, hand-washing rituals and all, but when I saw her last week she was really a different woman. She was much better, and it was great being with her. It turns out, though, that she still has to check ten times if the door is locked and the gas is off before leaving the house.

In the patient's eyes the therapist has improved quite a bit, and she appreciates this ('she was much better, and it was great being with her'). She thinks that the therapist's earlier problems doing therapy were caused by neurotic problems ('she was really fucked up').

Although she has surmounted some of her difficulties, there remain some residual neurotic problems hampering this therapist's work ('she still has to check ten times if the door is locked and the gas is off').

Here is an extract from a psychotherapy session which concerns a frame-managment issue rather than an intervention. The patient, Ms H., is a middle-aged woman suffering from psychosomatic symptoms, who had been in Kleinian analysis for ten years prior to beginning work with a communicative psychoanalyst. She had been in analysis for eight weeks when the session to be reported took place. Since the beginning of the analysis, this patient had started to lengthen the sessions, which she accomplished by continuing to talk after the analyst announced that their time was up. The patient would persist in this even though the analyst did not actively participate. The analyst was concerned about this situation – which she found awkward – but was unable to find a way to resolve it appropriately. Ms H. began one session in the following way:

> I feel irritated but I don't know why. I think it might have some-
> thing to do with what happened at the business this morning. I hired
> a new assistant a while back. He's very nice and friendly, but he
> spends too much time chatting with the customers. It's not very pro-
> fessional. It's too 'matey'. When I'm with customers who hang
> around without buying anything I snatch the items away and put
> them back on the rack. You know, it might seem abrupt and nasty,
> but with my attitude I get the sales while he doesn't. It isn't good for
> the business. Anyway, I confronted him about it this morning, and
> I'll see if he changes his style.

Here the patient is giving the analyst a chance to rectify the pattern of letting her extend the hours. The analyst is compared with an un-businesslike shop assistant who wastes time chatting to customers. The patient feels that this is destructive and should not go on. Although a more professional attitude may seem 'abrupt and nasty' it is ultimately more beneficial. The patient is curious to see if the analyst will take her advice to heart.

If one takes patients' unconscious evaluations of one's work seriously, and applies the principles of communicative listening consistently, it soon becomes obvious that patients object to *most* of what therapists do, considering such interventions invalid, inappropriate, incorrect, and quite mad. A bizarre scene emerges, rather reminiscent of Poe's 'The strange case of Dr Tarr and Professor Fether', in which crazy therapists, with deluded beliefs that they are insightfully treating patients, are in actuality being treated by patients who behave, unconsciously, as wise therapists. Looking at the average psycho-therapy session through Langsian spectacles discloses a strange inter-change. When the patient's derivatives are decoded we usually find a scene identical in all essentials to Sartre's account of 'The man with the tape-recorder' (quoted in Charlesworth 1980–1). A man enters his analytic hour, produces a tape-recorder, and informs Dr X, his analyst, that he intends to tape-record the session. Clearly shaken by his patient's proposal, Dr X first responds by telling his patient that if he insists on taping the session he will terminate the analysis. The patient challenges him and the analyst, obviously at a loss when deprived of his guru-like mystique, becomes more and more fright-ened, but cannot admit this either to himself or to his patient.

> *A*: But you're frightened. And your libido, what are you doing about that? Do you think that I want to cut off your little willie? Of course I don't! I'm here to give you a real. . . . But it's fantastic! You've had this little occasion coming to you for a long time. Listen, admit that you're getting out of it very nicely. Doctor!!! Doctor, I've got nothing against you, but you obviously have . . . you've got something . . . you've got something against yourself.

> *Dr X*: At this moment you're. . . .

> *A*: I've got nothing against you, but . . . I feel you abuse your position. You have abused me. I would even go so far as to say that you've defrauded me, if we're going to use legal jargon: you haven't met your obligations. You don't know how to cure people – you only know how to make them worse. That's a fact – all we need to do is ask your other patients . . . people who come to you for help and get nothing, who get nothing but one long wait. Come on, sit down! Let's be reasonable! There. Are you a man or a mouse? Are you a man?

> *Dr X*: For the last time, you've got a tape-recorder there and I won't put up with it.

The interaction goes on in this vein for some time. It concludes in this way:

> *Dr X*: . . . Now let me go; this is a highly dangerous situation.

> *A*: Dangerous?

> *Dr X*: Yes, you're dangerous.

A: I'm not dangerous at all; you're only saying that. You never stop trying to make me believe I'm dangerous, but I'm not in the least bit dangerous.

Dr X: You're dangerous because you don't have a grasp on reality.

A: That's not true.

Dr X: You don't have a grasp on reality!

A: I'm a little lamb. I've always been as gentle as a lamb.

Dr X: You don't have a grasp on reality!

(Charlesworth 1980–1: 37–8)

Is this comparison actually well founded, or is it more hyperbole than truth? Let us move on to an actual example of a psychoanalytic session so that readers can decide for themselves.

Dominique by Françoise Dolto (Dolto 1974), is a remarkable, virtually verbatim account of the psychoanalytic treatment of a psychotic adolescent boy. In her introduction to the text Dolto rightly notes that the vast majority of psychoanalytic case accounts are so incomplete and selective that they are quite worthless for research purposes. Any reader can verify this by picking up a copy of a psychoanalytic journal or book at random. Thumb through the pages and ask yourself the question 'Where is the data?' Psychoanalytic is top heavy, containing an overwhelmingly massive and convoluted theory, a small and incompletely presented database, and only the vaguest rules of inference connecting the two. When reading most psychoanalytic case histories one is placed in a position of having so little concrete information about what has gone on that it is impossible to intelligently question the author's conclusions. These case accounts are, as Gill (1987) nicely puts it, editorials rather than news reports. This sort of control over the flow of information is of course essential for the maintenance of an intellectually totalitarian regime. Freudian censorship is not just in the mind: it is in the Freudian literature as well. By withholding information psychoanalytic writers, I think unwittingly, pre-empt rational doubt. This is profoundly anti-scientific. The average psychoanalytic clinical account bristles with evasive locutions such as 'we went on to consider . . .', 'a new issue emerged . . .', 'it became clear that . . .', but this sort of statement tells us worse than nothing. We need to know *how* they went on to consider, *how* a new issue emerged, and *how* it became clear. We need the raw data if we are to make our own inferences instead of just taking the author's inferences on board. The confusion between an explanation and what one is trying to explain, which I have discussed in relation to the theory of transference, appears to pervade the psychoanalytic system.

As if this were not bad enough, the accounts usually tell us little or nothing about the frame. What sort of setting is involved? How does the setting influence the patient? If we read an account of, say, a woman with a (so-called) 'delusional transference' that her analyst is attempting to seduce her, it matters for our understanding of the situation if we find out that the sessions take place in the analyst's home. In any other science it would be unthinkable to be so lax about specifying the conditions under which observations were made. Dolto's book is admirably free from these defects. She gives all of the raw data – describing exactly what was said by both analyst and patient – and spells out the nature of the frame within which these events occurred. In the true scientific spirit Dolto offers the book as a stimulus for 'critical and constructive thinking'.

Dominique, Madame Dolto's young patient, began to fall ill at the age of three. His parents, expecting the arrival of a new baby, sent Dominique away to live with his grandmother at around the time that the baby was expected. When he returned home, he discovered that the baby now occupied the cot in his parents' room where he had previously slept. Dominique was promoted to a bed in his elder brother's room. Dominique became quite anxious when observing his baby sister nursing. He feared that she was eating his mother. Dominique became incontinent, unstable, and aggressive. He was expelled from nursery school. Later, after entering primary school, Dominique decompensated further. Psychoactive medication only exacerbated his condition. Six months of twice-weekly psychoanalytic therapy had little effect. The analyst terminated the treatment, telling Dominique's mother that he would improve little by little.

At the age of fourteen Dominique has experienced little substantial improvement. His mother brings him to Dolto for another attempt at psychoanalytic treatment. The frame in which the treatment will take place involves several departures from the ideal. First of all, there are observers sitting in on the interviews taking notes (this is how Dolto was able to produce verbatim transcripts). This violates the patient's right to total privacy and confidentiality. Next, Dominique does not pay for his own treatment. This is inevitable with a child patient, but it is nevertheless something to which patients – even child patients – unconsciously object. Third-party payment means that someone other than the patient controls the therapy. The patient is in the power of the person who pays for him. The third major factor is the fact that this analysis takes place in a clinical setting where there is a receptionist who books appointments and collects fees. This is, of course, a further erosion of the privacy and confidentiality which patients unconsciously expect from their analysts.

Dominique and his mother arrive for their initial consultation. Dominique is asked to remain in a waiting-room while Dolto interviews his mother, Mrs Bel. After the interview with Mrs Bel, Dolto escorts her patient into the consulting room where she sees him, for the first time, alone. Dolto's interview with Mrs Bel is yet another violation of the ideal frame. Communicative research demonstrates, again and again, that patients unconsciously object to any involvement with third parties. Therapy, they feel, should be a completely private affair.

The scene is now set. Before going into the clinical material, though, it is possible to make some predictions about the session that we are about to examine. To some this might seem outrageously grandiose. How can we presume to predict something like this? The communicative approach says that there is a lawful relationship between stimulus and derivative response in the therapeutic situation. We already know some of the stimuli that will be impinging upon the patient. We know that the third-party involvement, with which this analysis is riddled, will be experienced by the patient as quite disruptive and that he will produce derivatives expressing this through themes of intrusion, violation, and disruption. We can also predict that unless the analyst interprets the patient's negative derivatives of valid concerns and attempts to rectify the situation there will be a total absence of positive 'validating' derivative imagery. These are risky predictions. They are easily falsifiable. Should they fail to 'come off' I cannot rationalize it away. I will be driven to question the foundations of the very theory which I am promoting. An approach that attacks prediction as inappropriate is an approach which evades falsification and is therefore scientifically disreputable. Let's see what happens.

Dominique enters the consulting room. Dolto asks him if he has anything he wants to say to explain his own feelings. Dominique replies 'Well, me, I'm not like everybody else. Sometimes when I wake up I feel like I've lived through a true story.' Let us consider Dominique's rather cryptic opener. He comes into the session pre-occupied both with his own uniqueness and with the theme of stories. We need to ask ourselves the question 'What is there about *this* particular psychoanalytic set-up at *this* particular moment that could account for these two concerns?' Mrs Bel had just been telling the analyst her version of Dominique's 'story'. He is also surrounded by people to whom he has not been introduced, and whose presence has not been explained to him, who are busily writing down everything that is going on. It is hardly surprising that the thought of a story comes to Dominique's mind. But why does Dominique also stress that he is a unique individual? The obvious hypothesis is that Dominique fears, with some justification, that the analyst will rely more on his mother's version of events than on his own. These must be regarded as very tentative hypotheses which await corroboration or disconfirmation.

The analyst responds to Dominique's remark, saying 'A story which made you untrue.' In order to understand events as they will unfold we need to pause with this intervention and identify its implications. Dolto has responded quite quickly and definitively to her patient's obscure remark (she does not even phrase it as a question). This implies that Dolto feels that she is in a position to know what Dominique meant when he spoke of waking up and living through a true story. Now, as she has only seen the patient for a couple of minutes we must consider what grounds Dolto could conceivably have for her intervention. Either she believes herself to be capable of incredible feats of intuition or she is basing the intervention on information gleaned from Dominique's mother. The latter explanation seems the more probable. This, of course, would implicitly convey to Dominique that Dolto intends to interpret what he says in the light of his mother's 'story'. He responds to the intervention saying 'That's it! But how do you know?' (29). Communicatively speaking, 'That's it!' is worthless as a validation. It tells us something of the patient's conscious view but nothing of his unconscious reading of the analyst's efforts. But Dominique goes on to ask her how she knows. This is a very pointed question. Given the frame issue of the discussion with the mother which had been made even more salient by the analyst's previous intervention, it is hardly surprising that Dominique wants her to honestly spell out where he has obtained her information. This is an admirably logical and appropriate question betraying a refined ability for making psychological inferences. Dominique addresses the frame issue head-on.

How will the analyst respond? She tells him, 'I don't really know. That's what I think when I see you' (ibid.). This is without doubt a countertransference-determined response, an expression of the therapist's own madness. The analyst fails to bring in her conversation with the boy's mother as an important issue. Rather, she asks him to believe that her inference came out of the blue when she 'saw' him. Remember Sartre's man with the tape-recorder? Who is really behaving in the more psychotic fashion here, the patient or the analyst? Again we need to pause and consider the implications of this remark carefully. Besides showing that there is something threatening about the situation for the analyst and showing her narcissistic needs, the intervention also tells Dominique in no uncertain terms that the analyst intends to avoid the issue of third parties to treatment. We can predict that Dominique will find this to be extremely distressing. He will feel that the analyst is not interested in those things that are of real, immediate concern to him. He will be confirmed in the impression that the analyst is conspiring with his mother.

Dominique now speaks, offering a highly derivative communication: 'I thought I was in the dining-room as a little boy again, afraid of burglars. They can take money, they can take silverware. Don't you think they could take almost anything?' (ibid.). The imagery is strongly negative, so the intervention has not been validated. Dominique refers to thinking that he was a little boy again. In other words, the here-and-now situation in the analysis reminds Dominique of childhood experiences. Perhaps he feels betrayed, like he did when his sister was born. If so, this is not mere transference, for Dominique has *good reason* to feel betrayed by his analyst. He thinks of being in the dining-room. This is a place where one expects to be fed. Instead of food there is a worry about burglars. Burglars are unwanted intruders who violate privacy and security, taking things away from one. Dominique does not know where all of this burglary will end. This is a superb portrayal of the third-party situation and its destructive consequences. Instead of being nourished by the analysis, the patient feels that he is being depleted. He is being robbed of a sound psychoanalytic experience. The boundaries are violated and there is no safety, security, or privacy.

Dolto responds to this with an interpretation. Not, of course, a communicative interpretation which would spell out how the patient justifiably regards the therapist as someone who is doing violence to his mind. Dolto, in accord with her training and theoretical orientation, serves up standard Freudian fare. She asks 'They might take your little sister?'. Dolto has formulated the material along the lines of Freud's principle that 'every fear betokens a wish'. She feels that Dominique harbors a repressed wish to get rid of his little sister. He projects this desire on to the figure of the burglar while the valuables being stolen stands for the sister. In communicative theory this type of intervention is called a *psychoanalytic cliché*;[7] an interpretation couched in intrapsychic terms which functions as a barrier against more pressing, anxiety-laden, here-and-now realities. Without consciously realizing it, this analyst seems to be attempting to erect a barrier, a psychoanalytic Berlin Wall, against her patient's realistic unconscious concerns. This intervention will convey to him yet again that his analyst wants to stay away from frame issues and refuses to question her own *modus operandi*. The intervention also announces to the patient even more definitively that the analyst is conceptualizing his difficuties in the light of his mother's story, for she has now mentioned his sister, a person that Dominique has not yet mentioned to Dolto himself. It can be safely predicted that this interpretation will not get derivative validation from Dominique. Dominique in fact replies, 'Oh you, how do you know everything?' The mention of the patient's sister has provoked him to give the analyst another chance to 'come clean' about the interview with Mrs Bel. Dolto goes on to say to him:

> I don't know anything at first, but it's because you say things to me in your own words and I listen as well as I can. It's you who knows what has happened to you, not me. Together we might be able to understand.
>
> (29)

This is patently false. The intervention can be understood as an even more strenuous attempt to seal over the third-party issue. The amount of disavowal implied in the statement spills over into unintentional mockery, as Dolto avers that she can understand only because Dominique has said things in his 'own words'. The analyst is, in effect, behaving quite madly here, a fact that will not escape the unconscious notice of her young patient.

Dominique falls silent here (and who could blame him?). There seems little point in him speaking, because that analyst cannot hear his most urgent messages. She lives in a world of her own devising and he, introjecting this, withdraws from her. The silence is, of course, a resistance but the fact that it is a resistance does not mean that it stems from the patient's irrational defensive needs. If we place the boy's resistant silence in the context of the unconscious dialogue, the hidden conversation, up to this point it is quite obvious that we are dealing with an *iatrogenic resistance*:[8] a resistance created by the analyst. Since the outset of the session, I suggest, Dolto has been striving, without realizing it, to *shut her patient down*, to break off the flow of threateningly meaningful unconscious derivatives. Now in Dominique's silence she has obtained what she had all along been pursuing. But this is not good enough either. Dolto interrupts the silence, asking Dominique what he is thinking about. Dominique responds with a truly breathtaking derivative sequence, confronting his analyst with what Langs calls 'the terrible poetry of the unconscious domain':

I'm trying to figure out what's wong in life. I'd like to be like everyone else. For instance, when I read a lesson several times over, I still don't know it the following day. Sometimes I feel I'm dumber than everyone else, or I say to myself that I can't go on like this. Things are going wrong. I'm talking nonsense.

(29–30)

Dominique has introjected his analyst. In the guise of a confession he offers a pointed critique to her. A communicative translation of the passage would run along these lines:

I am trying to figure out what is wrong with this analysis. I want you to function normally but no matter how often you are confronted with reality you are unable to learn. I cannot go on like this. The analysis is going wrong. You are talking nonsense.

Because of Dolto's repeated failure to respond to the question 'how do you know?' and related derivatives the patient feels that she suffers from a severe learning disorder. He is aware that the analysis is not proceeding as it should and tells the analyst that her last intervention was 'nonsense'. Tragically, because the patient has begun to introject the analyst – to encode his unconscious perceptions of her by misattributing them to himself – this process is beginning to reinforce his own psychopathology. Dominique begins to berate himself for being stupid. Dolto now intervenes: 'But it's true, you are talking nonsense. I see you know it: maybe you're pretending to be a nut so as not to be scolded' (30). The temptation to put all of the illness into the patient can be overwhelmingly tempting. Here Dolto uses her patient's remarks to projectively identify her own madness into him. It is a basic communicative principle that when the analyst introduces topics that the patient has not mentioned, introducing her own 'associations', this can often be construed as an unconscious confession. This is particularly true of so-called 'confrontations' in analysis: the very things which we accuse our patients of are things which we ourselves are doing. Here Dolto both confronts Dominique and inserts some of her own preoccupations. She says that he is pretending to be a nut so as not to be scolded. If we take this as applying more, in truth, to the analyst than to the patient, Dolto seems to be saying that her bizarre behavior stems from attempts to evade her own guilt about the conversation with Mrs Bel. She is frightened of Dominique 'scolding' her. Dominique says 'That must be it. But how do you know?' again and Dolto responds, predictably, with 'I don't know. But I see that you've disguised yourself as a nut or an idiot. But you aren't since you notice it and you want to change' (30). The remainder of the session is described rather more impressionistically.

Early in the second session, after a meeting between the analyst and Dominique's father, the patient summed up the whole situation as follows:

> And so the dreams, well, I got lost in a railway station and I met a witch and all she said was crack, crack, crack (with his hands he makes a gesture of cracking something). I was looking for some information and it was getting on my nerves, I didn't want any trouble, especially since I was in a station. Once in a while I managed to help out, but I didn't succeed and nobody needed me. And then, you see, whenever I have five hundred francs, all I have to do is wait until I have 500 francs and then I'll be rich. But you know, it will take a long time. What's needed is patience.
>
> (ibid.: 39)

The reference to getting lost in a railway station is a beautiful metaphor for the confused and rather public (remember the observers) psycho-analytic interaction. The witch is Madame Dolto, who offers meaning-less words in a somewhat menacing manner. Dominique has indeed been looking for some information, and his analyst's responses – her 'crack, crack, crack' – have been getting on his nerves. Dominique feels that his therapeutic-cum-supervisory interventions have been in vain ('nobody needed me'). This remark is particularly poignant in light of both the boy's history and of Searles's idea that psychotic individuals suffer primarily because their own therapeutic potential has been frustrated early in life. Dominique feels that he is super-fluous in the complex choreography of analyst, mother, father, and observers. The phrase '500 francs' refers, of course, to the analyst's fee. The fact that Dominique's father was to pay for his son's analysis was the reason for his interview with Dolto. Dominique is not uncon-sciously telling his analyst that if he were paying his own way he would not have to put up with this sort of thing. The final remarks sound for all the world like the sighs of an analyst who has just taken on a very difficult case – 'It will take a long time. What's needed is patience.'

TRANSFERENCE AND COUNTERTRANSFERENCE

I have mentioned in the previous chapter that Langs began by regard-ing unconscious perception as a form of 'nontransference' which exists side-by-side with transference, and that later he discarded the notion of transference altogether as no longer clinically useful. The concept of transference was important to the early stages of communicative theory.[9] It focused attention on relational issues. In particular, it was the Kleinian notion that *everything* the patient does and says in analysis possesses a transference component, and that consequently transference is not to be identified with merely manifest preoccupations with the analyst, which paved the way for Langs's notion of ongoing encoded commentaries on the analyst's behavior. Even if one approves of the arguments marshalled in Chapter 2, however, the communicative rejection of the concept of transference may appear to be rather more problematic. This has to do with the theoretical role of the concept of transference. In standard psychoanalytic theory the concept of transference is used to explain how it is that past experiences impact upon the present. This is clearly an important datum for explanation, and it is probably plausible to say that any psychoanalytic theory which does not offer an explanation of how it is that early events, stored only in unconscious memory, can influence contemporary cognition and behavior must be regarded as seriously incomplete. If the communicative approach cannot fill this theoretical gap left by the departure of transference it will emerge as an impoverished 'here-and-now' psychology that cannot encompass the developmental dimension or offer convincing causal explanations of psychopathology. Explanations couched in terms of acquired habit patterns (as in behaviorism) or developmental arrest (Boss) do not suffice to explain the highly *specific* phenomena under consideration.

Langs (1988a) replaces transference with unconscious perceptual selectivity. Each trigger experienced by a patient contains a wealth of plausible implications. In their derivative responses, patients will not represent all of the implications: they will select only certain ones. This selection, of course, will not be random: it will be guided by the patient's unconscious sensitivities which are determined, in large measure, by his developmental history. According to this view, therefore, the past comes into the present as a force which organizes perceptual selection. Early experiences do not *override* perception, they guide it. In addition to this, there is a second theory of how the past impinges on the present implicit in Langs's writing. Perception involves the assimilation of information to previously acquired schemes (Neisser 1967). For example, when, as a child, I learn what a horse is I can go on to classify all similar animals, both conceptually and linguistically, to the prototype that has been pointed out to me. If a percept is to be *meaningful* it must be situated within an established network of ideas. This commonplace can be worked into a theory of how a patient's history emerges in the present complementing the hypothesis of perceptual selection. Each perception of a trigger can be imagined as being unconsciously analyzed by the deep unconscious system. Part of this must involve the assimilation, or at least comparison, of the percept with perceptions of important figures and situations stored in the patient's memory. If there is a striking similarity between the here-and-now perception and the there-and-then memory, the memory may be evoked to serve as a derivative of the perception. In other words, it is the here-and-now perception which determines the general thematic content of a derivative and it is the patient's memories of earlier experiences which, in some instances, determine the specific *form* in which the theme is expressed.[10]

Looking back over the account of Dominique and Françoise Dolto, we can use the passage about the fear of burglars to illustrate these points. Dominique thought of being in the dining-room where instead of being fed he was confronted by burglars stealing things. Dolto was aware that Dominique expressed anxiety when at the age of three he saw his little sister 'eating' his mother. Dolto was also aware that Dominique was very jealous of his sister. She therefore saw the 'burglar' derivatives as pertaining directly to these early experiences. The trauma that the patient suffered as a child was seen as the efficient cause of his derivative remarks. Communicatively, we can consider this differently. One possibility is to say that because of his experiences in childhood, Dominique was unconsciously sensitive to the issue of oral deprivation. As a consequence, he selectively but nonetheless validly perceived the orally depriving implications of his analyst's behavior. The other possibility would be that Dominique unconsciously detected a similarity between the analytic situation he was in and the circumstances surrounding his sister's birth, and, consequently, expressed his perception of the contemporary situation using metaphors derived from his earlier, similar experiences. From this perspective Dominique was unconsciously saying to his analyst something like 'In depriving me of a sound analytic setting by letting others come into this space, you are behaving just like my mother did when she favored my baby sister over me'. This is precisely Freud's first screen-memory theory of infantile memories (Freud 1899). In the standard psychoanalytic account the early memory causes the emergence of 'transferred' derivatives, while in the two communicative explanations the cause of the derivatives lies in the here-and-now, and the early experiences only influence their emphasis or form. The early memories compose, as it were, the 'language' by means of which contemporary realities are expressed. *Distortion* is not the only way that the past can influence the present. Without going into full detail,

Balint (1968) says as much when he hypothesizes that Kleinian analysts elicit so much material involving the theme of persecution because Kleinian technique is in reality quite persecutory.

It follows from these considerations that communicative psychoanalysts explain their patients' phantasies about them *not* as inappropriate displacements from a steamy infantile past but as provoked, in some way, by the analysts' own behavior. If Freud's early patcints frequently fell in love with him it was not because they unconsciously mistook him for an incestuously desired father. It was because, as D.M. Thomas (1982: 3) nicely puts it, 'Freud, too, kissed his patients unconsciously.' If, by the same token, a patient mentions some important figure from the past, the communicative analyst does not assume that he has hit some ultimate causal bedrock. Rather, he or she hypothesizes that the patient's memory of a father who seduced her or a mother who deprived her is an unconscious representation of the analyst. The patient is saying, in effect, 'There is something about this situation right now that unconsciously reminds me of my relationship with *x* in childhood.' Freud's words ring out across the decades: 'The mirror-image of the present is seen in the fantasied past, which then prophetically becomes the present' (1887–1904: 320).[11]

It should be emphasized that, as Freud discussed in 'Screen memories', there is no reason to doubt the veracity of the memories which are used to carry unconscious truth. Because a memory is evoked and expressed to convey something about the analyst it does not mean that the content of the memory is unreal. An example occurs to me of a student who was giving therapy on a time-limited basis in a large London hospital. The policy of the hospital, at that time, was that psychotherapy patients were to be seen for no longer than six months at a stretch. From the beginning the patient unconsciously protested at this Procrustean arrangement. Early on, for example, she discussed the issue of abortion ('premature termination') extensively, emphasizing how she believed it to be immoral. During one session close to the termination date the patient began the hour mentioning the upcoming termination and then went on to mention something about her childhood that she had never mentioned to anyone before: the patient had been sexually abused by her uncle. The patient tearfully described how her uncle would force sex on her. She was helpless. There was nothing she could do to fend off his superior strength. The rest of the family turned a blind eye. The therapist thought that the patient had made a real breakthrough in telling him these facts. There was no reason to cast doubt upon their truthfulness. However, from a communicative standpoint we must enquire why did *these* particular memories emerge at *this* particular moment in therapy. In the previous session the therapist had informed the patient that she would have to bring forward the termination date by a couple of days. This seemingly trivial alteration was *consciously* acceptable to the patient, who happily agreed to it. This 'trigger' heightened the already important issue of the forced termination. Derivatively, then, the incestuous uncle appears to be a disguised portrayal of the therapist who is forcing the termination on her against her will. She was helpless, unable to contest the therapist's unilateral decision. She felt violated – psychologically raped – she says that the therapist and the hospital administrators turn a blind eye to the situation (the therapist had consistently avoided interpreting derivatives pertaining to the termination).

Langs also jettisoned the term 'countertransference'. From the beginning, 'countertransference' was a rather ambiguous term. The 'counter' of it was taken to mean that 'countertransference' was a reaction to the patient's transference. According to this interpretation, although countertransference was understood to be an expression of the analyst's emotional conflicts, it was something evoked by the patient's transference rather than brought into the room and imposed upon the patient. I have already described how countertransference became idealized as it was recognizable as inevitable. At present, therefore, there is one notion of countertransference, primarily associated with the British school, which conceives of it as ongoing and primarily non-pathological (in the tradition of Heimann) and another which sees it as episodic and pathological (in the tradition of Freud). Langs needed a third alternative: a notion encompassing the analyst's ongoing 'pathology'. Analysts emphasizing the pathological aspect of countertransference tend to play down its intensity or severity. Analysts' own hang-ups are supposed to have been cleared away, for the most part, by their own (coerced) personal analysis. The analyst's own psychopathology is therefore often distinguished as 'residual' psychopathology (in order to differentiate it from the ordinary, common-or-garden-variety psychopathology). The attitude here is clearly rather defensive and stands in sharp contrast to the communicative findings regarding analysts' actual behavior with their patients. Langs, therefore needed a term which did not imply the systematic understatement of therapists' psychological problems which pervades the normal psychoanalytic literature. The search for a serviceable term led him to choose 'therapist madness' as a replacement for 'countertransference'. Here, at last, was a true democracy of madness with no built-in assumptions about the craziness of the patient and the sanity of the therapist. Communicative psychotherapists must be ready and willing to confront their own madness in every session that they conduct, because patients unconsciously hold up the mirror in which this madness is starkly reflected back to them:

> *Unconsciously, the patient automatically functions as a supervisor to the therapist,* making use of the enormous wisdom of the deep unconscious system to detect expressions of therapist-madness. In addition . . . the patient will also offer general interpretations as to the unconscious factors in the therapist that relate to his or her disturbance.

(Langs 1988a: 191)

Working psychotherapeutically offers therapists many opportunities to unwittingly display their madness. Every missed or incorrect intervention, for example, announces to the patient information about the therapist's inner conflicts, dreads, and defenses. The manifestations of therapist madness are usually missed by practitioners who have defensive needs to idealize themselves or who do not understand how to decode unconscious communication correctly. It is quite usual for the interventions that a therapist is most proud of to be the ones that his or her patients unconsciously consider to be the most mad.

One of the most surprising discoveries of the communicative approach has been that the most significant medium for the expression of a therapist's madness – or sanity – is the way that he or she manages the therapeutic 'frame'. It is this subject that we will explore in the following chapter.

7   The limit situation

No matter which way you cut the pie, 'meanings' just ain't in the head.

Hilary Putnam

One of the most characteristic and distinctive features of communicative psychoanalysis is an intense focus on the frame or 'ground rules' of the psychoanalytic situation. The frame is given great importance both theoretically and technically. This is not because of any preconceived notion about its importance: it is based on innumerable clinical observations. In their derivative communications, patients point again and again to the frame as a vital feature of psychotherapy. These consistent unconscious reactions to the frame indicate that it does not function as a mere backdrop to the real business of psychoanalysis. The structuring of the frame, the management of the ground rules, *is* the real business of psychoanalysis. It is a basic communicative tenet that the management of the frame has a more powerful impact upon the patient, for good or for ill, than any other feature of the psychoanalytic interaction (including the content of the analyst's interventions). The communicative approach asserts that there is a single way of structuring the frame – a single set of ground rules – appropriate for most (although not *all*) psychotherapy patients. This is referred to as the *'secure frame'*. To many this idea has an arbitrary, authoritarian ring. Many analysts baulk at the idea that the frame is so centrally important to the psychotherapeutic process or feel that it should be managed in a far more relaxed and variable manner. I hope to show here why it is that the communicative ideas on the frame are plausible and why an easy eclecticism about the ground rules cannot be readily justified.

The term 'frame' was coined by Milner (1952) who took the metaphor from the world of painting:

The frame [of a picture] marks off the different kind of reality that is within it from that which is outside it; but a temporal spatial frame also marks off the special kind of reality of a psychoanalytic session. And in psychoanalysis, it is the existence of this frame that makes possible the full development of that creative illusion that analysts call transference.

(183)

Although the metaphor of the frame was introduced by Milner, the concept to which this refers goes right back to Freud. Freud's papers on technique (1911b, 1912b, 1912c, 1913c, 1914a, 1915a) are to a great extent concerned with the delineation of the ground rules of analysis. Freud's concern with the frame revolved around several interlocking issues. First, Freud wished to structure the analytic situation so as to create an 'atmosphere of safety' (Schafer 1983) which would encourage his patients to bare their souls to him. Second, he wanted to create a relatively contamination-free environment to foster the growth of an analyzable transference neurosis. Third, he wanted to exclude the presence of those non-cognitive means of influence (which he collectively termed 'suggestion') that are anathema to the psychoanalytic values of autonomy and insight (see Dorpat 1977). Finally, Freud may have wanted to establish the fixed parameters that any scientific enterprise requires to test causal hypotheses. Freud touched on many specific frame issues during the course of his discussions, such as the fee, confidentiality, neutrality, and abstinence. He offered 'recommendations' — arrived at through trial and error — and refrained from drawing hard-and-fast rules.

After Freud, there was little work on the frame *qua* frame until the contributions of Winnicott (1954), who spelled out the elements of the frame implicit in Freud's approach. He argued that in the analytic situation the frame possesses a 'maternal' function. Just as Freud saw the frame as safeguarding the fruition of an analyzable transference, for Winnicott the frame safeguards a therapeutic regression. 'The setting of analysis', he writes, 'reproduces the early and earliest mothering techniques. It invites regression by reason of its reliability' (1954: 286). It follows for Winnicott that the frame increases in importance the more one deals with extremely regressed and profoundly disturbed patients. With psychoneurotic and what Kernberg calls 'higher level character pathology' patients (Kernberg 1976), the influence of the frame is said to be negligible.

Where there is an intact ego and the analyst can take for granted these earliest details of infant care, then the setting of the analysis is unimportant relative to the interpretative work. . . . Even so there is a basic ration of management in ordinary analysis which is more or less accepted by all analysts.

(1955–6: 297)

Winnicott uses the term 'management' to denote the therapeutic structuring and maintenance of the frame. Management is a form of psychoanalytic intervention. In contrast to the analysis of neurotics, where management is not tremendously important, we find in the analysis of deeply regressed patients that 'the setting becomes more important than the interpretation. The emphasis is changed from the one to the other'[1] (ibid.). The therapeutic effect of the appropriate management of the setting is to encourage the schizoid patient to reveal his or her 'true self'.

The behaviour of the analyst, represented by what I have called the setting, by being good enough in the matter of adaptation to need, is gradually perceived by the patient as something that raises a hope that the true self may at last be able to take the risks involved in its starting to experience living.

(ibid.)

Bleger (1967) developed, refined, and in some respects modified Winnicott's position. Like Winnicott, he felt that the frame represents the most primitive maternal relationship. Bleger calls this 'the patient's ghost-world of the non-ego' (514). This refers to the intrapsychic remnants of the infant's most primitive and absolute symbiotic fusion with its mother. This 'ghost-world' is associated with terrifying psychotic anxieties. In analysis, the patient will attempt to alter the frame in order to avoid these anxieties. It is only by maintaining the frame in the face of patients' pressures to yield that it is possible to reach patients' 'psychotic core'. The benign, security-giving aspects of the frame emphasized by Winnicott give way to the frame as a harbinger of primitive anxieties. The logical implication of this conception, which Bleger directly states, is that the state of the frame must have a powerful determining effect on the contents of an analysis.

As a 'constant' which structures the flow of the psychoanalytic process, the frame must possess a logical role in psychoanalytic interpretation. Bleger touches on this, but it is developed much more fully by the Italian psychoanalyst Enzo Codignola. Codignola's views can be found in his book *The True and the False: Essay on the Logical Structure of Psychoanalytic Interpretation* (Codignola 1987), the title of which harks back to the writings of Gottlob Frege, the father of modern logic, who believed that true and false sentences denoted abstract entities which he called 'The True' and 'The False' respectively (Frege 1892). Codignola used 'the true' to designate everything in analysis which is 'not further decomposable by analysis' (ibid.: 372), i.e. the frame, while 'the false' refers to all of those interpretable elements of the analytic interchange. The 'true' elements of the psychoanalytic situation form a relatively stable background context for interpreting the 'false' elements.

> The moment the analyst interprets, he or she places that which is being interpreted into the sphere of the false; but whether the analyst is aware of it or not, this cannot be done without postulating a 'true' element as a mark of cognitive reference.
>
> (ibid.: 374)

Viderman (1974), Modell (1976), and others have also made contributions to the literature on the psychoanalytic frame.[2]

According to communicative theory, an analyst's management of the frame implicity or explicitly shows the type of relationship he or she wishes to establish with patients. This can be understood at the level of common sense. To use an example from education, it is obvious that the way a teacher structures a class – the way that he or she manages space, time, resources, and so on – will reveal the type of relationship that she is attempting to establish, consciously or unconsciously, with her pupils. It will also reveal a great deal about the teacher's inner resources: her strengths, weaknesses, blind spots, biases, and so on. In addition to all of this, the teacher's handling of the educational frame will have a decisive impact upon the behavior of the pupils. A teacher who manages the setting chaotically is likely to have a class which behaves chaotically. The chaotic situation will, in turn, reinforce and exacerbate the inner chaos which led the teacher down this path in the first instance. It seems legitimate to extrapolate from this to consider the role of the frame in psychotherapy. Not only does the management of the frame disclose the 'mode of relatedness' that the therapist adopts toward the patient, it also powerfully influences what the patient says or does in therapy, and how the therapist is able to respond. The frame surrounds, contains, and structures its contents. It is more like a mold than a neutral backdrop or matrix.[3] The impact of the frame can be seen quite clearly in Khan's treatment of Peter, recounted in Chapter 3. Peter was silent – a powerful resistance – for a long time. I demonstrated that Khan's purely intrapsychic explanation of Peter's silence was less plausible than the communicative hypothesis linking it with Khan's poor structuring of the frame – his violations of neutrality and confidentiality. When Peter did speak, the content of his communications also seemed shaped by the frame on a deep level. He spoke of a dream of a crab trying to enter a window and offered associations about the birth of his younger sister. Both of these contained themes of intruders, which seemed linked to the involvement of third parties in his analysis. The third-party issue had an equally powerful impact in the treatment of Dominique, described in Chapter 6, who derivatively represented the involvement of his parents in his treatment by the image of burglars in the dining-room. The specific content of these sessions cannot be understood without reference to the frame. According to communicative theory, the frame is the single most powerful factor in the psychoanalytic situation.

Psychoanalytic practitioners fall along a spectrum with regard to their attitudes toward the frame. On one extreme lie those – mainly 'orthodox' Freudians and Kleinians – who insist on a strict adherence to the classical ground rules. This is somewhat ironic, as both Freud and Klein took a distinctly *laissez-faire* line concerning the frame. Freud analyzed his own daughter Anna, conducted analyses while walking in the park, and in a now famous episode provided one of his patients (the 'Rat Man') with a meal of herrings. Klein analyzed her own children and did not hesitate to persuade her friend and assistant Paula Heimann to embark upon an analysis with her (for more examples see Grosskurth 1985).

Most of the more contemporary schools and subschools of psychoanalytic thought fall nearer to the other end of the spectrum, viewing the frame as quite mutable. Analysts of this persuasion do not normally feel it necessary to substantiate their position by means of clinical evidence. Instead, they tend toward exhortation and appeals to common sense. Consequently, the arguments in favor of a more loosely structured frame are often rather a prioristic and superficial. Lomas (1987) writes that:

> Explanantion and interpretation are means by which we may attempt to control and diminish the full force of being. Just as man cannot live by bread alone, so he cannot live by taking thought alone: interpretation is not enough. . . . Could we really hope that a person will be moved to the degree that is often necessary to emerge from sickness except in the presence of someone who shows feelings?
> (4–5)

Stone appeals to human kindness:

A shy, schizoid girl with tremendous social anxiety who comes from a background where Christmas gifts are a sine qua non of relationships with anybody who is important to the individual suddenly comes in at Christmas time with a box of cookies that she made herself, or a handkerchief that she embroidered herself, or something like that. The question is, you see, whether it is important to put this down, and say 'No, I don't accept gifts in the analytic situation. The real job is for you to talk to me about it in free association and to come to understand why you feel impelled to give me a gift.' First of all, you know darn well why she feels impelled to give me a gift. It's because she gives one to anybody whom she likes or who is important to her. . . . Second, the question is whether you estimate that she can accept your rejection of the gift, however gentle, without being hurt, or maybe so hurt and taken aback that she won't be able to tell you much about it. First, she'll think you're strange and she'll think that the whole damn rule is strange. So what, so she gives you a box of cookies! Now, it may be that you can accept this gift and very gently and gradually impart to her the idea that modest as this gift is, and grateful as you are for her kindness and regard and the very fact that she has this warm inclination, the work usually proceeds better if one abstains even from a very benign impulse of this kind and tries to talk about it. That would be the best procedure in the future. Perhaps something can even come up about this gift now?

(Langs and Stone 1980: 27−8)

Lomas, Stone, and others who argue for a more relaxed attitude toward the frame are moved by the human ideal of preventing cruelty and suffering.[4] Their position is quite convincing *providing that one accepts the implicit premises*. These theorists argue, generally, as follows. Patients respond quite variably to the structure of the frame. Because of their personality, conflicts, and history some patients respond well to a strictly maintained frame while others require a more relaxed atmosphere. Some patients require the modification of selected ground rules, so as to permit physical contact with the analyst, extended or 'extra' sessions, the acceptance of gifts, and so on. As 'the law was made for man, not man for the law' concessions need to be made to human variability. Freud's ground rules should be taken in the spirit that he offered them: as 'recommendations' of a general nature rather than commandments inscribed upon tablets of stone.

The 'flexible' approach to the frame is plausible *only if the reactions*

of patients taken into account are conscious rather than unconscious.
Conscious attitudes to the frame certainly fall within a wide range.
Some patients, for example, abhor any physical contact with their
analysts and are very happy under the classical 'hands off' regime,
while others express the desire to have their hand held or to give their
analyst hugs, threatening to leave analysis if their analysts refuse to
comply. The deep unconscious attitude to frame issues is quite
another matter. As I have mentioned in the last chapter, the deep
unconscious system of human beings is remarkably consistent. This
applies to the frame. Certain ways of structuring the frame are
invariably not validated by patients, while other arrangements are
consistently validated. This has led communicative theorists to a
conception of a single, non-variable *secure frame*.

Communicative psychoanalysts, then, are on the 'strict' end of the
spectrum of attitudes toward the frame. Indeed, they are far more
exacting than the most orthodox of the orthodox, but their convictions stem from a different basis entirely. Conventional analysts who
insist on a strict frame do so because, by and large, they 'believe' that
such an arrangement is 'appropriate'. Their devotion to the ground
rules is somewhat dogmatic and excludes *in principle* the possibility of
adapting the frame to individual needs. The communicative analyst
proceeds differently. When a patient proposes a modification of the
frame the analyst waits for the patient to provide unconscious
guidance in the form of derivatives which, in an encoded way, advise
the analyst what to do. The communicative psychoanalyst says neither
'yes' nor 'no' to the patient. He or she waits for unconscious feedback
about the issue and is fully prepared to conform with the patient's
unconscious recommendations. Unconsciously, patients virtually
always urge analysts to maintain a secure frame with strictly defined
ground rules and clear interpersonal boundaries.

Perhaps an example will clarify this. A patient was working toward
the termination of his therapy. A termination date had been set, but
the patient did not turn up for the penultimate session. The patient
arrived for the final session equipped with a bottle of wine and two
glasses and proposed that he and the therapist have a drink together to
commemorate the final hour. The therapist did not respond directly to
the request. Instead, she suggested that they see what came up. The
patient expressed some disappointment and mild irritation with this
sober response, but then began talking about the missed session of the
previous week. He apologized for not turning up. He had had a
lengthy business meeting with an important client. Afterwards, the
client had invited him out for a drink. The patient remembered being

very angry with himself and thinking 'Here I am wasting my time sitting around and drinking when I could be doing something much more important – going to one of my last therapy sessions.' He then went on to give a detailed account of a meeting with another man whom he had known as an adolescent. They had dinner together and had a lot to drink afterwards. The next morning driving to work the patient noticed that this hands were shaking. He attributed this to having drunk so much wine the night before, and mentioned that drinking excessively was definitely bad for his health. At this point the therapist was able to offer an interpretation. Throughout the session she had been listening for unconscious guidance as to how to respond to the offer of a glass of wine. It was precisely this, now, that she wanted to clarify in her interpretation, which went as follows:

> When you came in you suggested that we have a drink together. I said 'let's see what comes up before making a decision'. You then talked about missing last week's session because you were having a drink with a client. You stressed that this was a waste of time and that you regretted that you were not having therapy instead. Later, you talked about having a lot to drink with a friend and noticing afterwards that it affected you badly: that it was bad for your health. It sounds to me like this is all connected, that you are telling me that if we had a drink together we would be wasting time – like you and your client last week – instead of getting on with the therapy. You also seemed to be telling me that if we had a drink together it would have a bad effect on you and damage your well-being, like the morning after the heavy drinking with your friend. So, although in a way you would like me to have a drink with you it sounds like deep down you are saying that this would really be the wrong thing for us to do, so we shouldn't do it.

This intervention produced a validation. The patient began to talk about his daughter, how well she was doing in school, her many accomplishments, and how proud he was of her. This was his way of unconsciously telling the therapist that she had done something very constructive in making that intervention. The patient then went on to consciously state that he had hoped to keep the last session 'light' but upon refelction he saw that he resented having to terminate and was frightened of no longer having the 'safety net' of therapy.

This example contrasts sharply with another example of a frame intervention that was not validated. A young woman asked her therapist if they could reschedule their therapeutic hour, moving it from a Monday to a Thursday. The therapist agreed to this without having sought out unconscious guidance from the patient. She agreed to the proposed arrangement because she felt it was a kind and humane thing to do. The patient arrived for her next session and began it with the following words:

> Thanks for changing the time of the sessions last week. That was really helpful. My lecturer at college has messed us about. He's cancelled classes again. This time he wants to swap the time around. That guy doesn't know what he's doing. He gets me *so* angry. He should set something up and *stick to it*!

Here the patient is unconsciously telling the therapist that she should not have consented to changing the patient's hour. Note the disparity between the conscious evaluation of the situation – the patient feels grateful and describes the therapist as 'helpful' – and the unconscious evaluation. Unconsciously the patient represents the therapist by means of the image of the lecturer and feels 'messed about' by the change. The patient unconsciously questions her therapist's competence ('That guy doesn't know what he's doing'), says that she feels anger toward the therapist because of her mismanagement of the frame, and suggests that in future the therapist stick to her agreed time.

It is very typical for the conscious and deep unconscious systems to have radically different values and commitments. Why then follow the advice of the deep unconscious system rather than the conscious system? Communicative therapists do this because they feel that the deep unconscious system is more in touch with emotional reality, less caught up in defense and self-deception than the conscious system. If this is indeed true, and the available data would certainly support it, it implies that the deep unconscious system is a more *reliable* guide than the conscious system to achieving a meaningful and thoroughgoing psychoanalytic 'cure'. This, by the way, is diametrically opposed to the conventional wisdom of psychoanalysis, which states that the unconscious mind is totally dominated by the illusions of the pleasure principle and is therefore out of touch with reality, whereas the conscious portions of the ego are said to be less defensive, more rational, and more reliable a guide to reality. Just as the conventional analyst attemps to enlist the aid of the patient's conscious ego in order to forge a 'therapeutic alliance', the communicative therapist seeks assistance from the deep unconscious system. In a sense, the communicative therapist is only there as a translator and hired hand of the patient's deep unconscious system, making use of its amazing storehouse of psychological wisdom.

When the therapist structures the frame according to the deep unconscious requirements of patients, an extremely powerful, creative therapeutic atmosphere is established. Such an environment encourages most patients to bring their deepest unconscious fears and concerns to the light of day and to form strongly constructive introjects of the therapist. It is therefore vital for communicative analysts to possess a knowledge of the fundamental components of the secure frame, as well as some understanding of their specific properties. According to Langs (1988a) the secure frame offers the patient:

1 *A sense of basic trust.* This arises mainly because the therapist is fulfilling the patient's unconscious role expectations for him or her. In substance, the therapist has promised to be a therapist, and by securing the frame, has done exactly that. Trust also stems from other positive attributes of the secure frame.

2 *Clear interpersonal boundaries* between patient and therapist, creating both appropriate distance and intimacy and thus making the relationship safe and secure.

3 Unconscious *support for the patient's contact with reality* and his or her capacity to test reality.

4 The foundation for a relationship that entails *a healthy therapeutic symbiosis* – the ideal treatment relationship (cf. Searles 1973).

5 The basis for a mode of cure that will take place through *genuine insight* and not entail relief through action-discharge.

6 *A situation in which the unfolding dynamics and genetics will center on the patient's madness* rather than the madness of the therapist.

7 *An unconscious image and introject of the therapist as having a sound identity* and an inner state of *healthy narcissistic balances.*

8 *An image of the therapist as sane.*

9 *A powerful sense of being held well and of appropriate containment.*

10 *A situation of appropriate frustration* and *healthy satisfactions.*

(138)

To the extent that any analytic situation departs from this ideal it is *deviant* (i.e. it deviates from patients' deep unconscious expectations). To the extent that a frame is a *deviant frame* it offers patients the opposites of the qualities listed above; for example, the 'deviant' therapist will be seen as mad, as not holding the patient well, as having a confused identity, as undermining the patient's contact with reality, and so on.

The secure frame has approximately eleven components (more may yet come to light as communicative research proceeds). I will describe each of these and, when appropriate, give examples of patient's derivative responses to deviations from them.

COMPONENTS OF THE SECURE FRAME

Component 1: use of the couch

In the secure frame the patient reclines on the couch with the analyst sitting behind and out of sight. This, of course, is the traditional psychoanalytic setup, which originated in the days when Freud practiced hypnosis. In standard forms of psychoanalysis, this arrangement is advocated in order to encourage transference and regression. Communicative analysts have found that the traditional arrangement encourages derivative communication. The couch itself becomes a powerful symbol of the deep unconscious domain, while the fact that the patient reclines with the analyst out of sight discourages superficial social interaction.

Component 2: free association and free-floating attention

In the secure frame the patient is permitted to free associate while the analyst listens with free-floating attention. The purpose of the 'basic rule' of free association was laid down in Freud's *The Interpretation of Dreams* (1900) in relation to what he called the 'two pillars of psychoanalytic technique'. These are (a) 'when conscious purposive ideas are abandoned, concealed purposive ideas assume control of the current of ideas', and (b) 'superficial associations are only substitutes by displacement for suppressed deeper ones' (531). In communicative as opposed to standard forms of psychoanalysis the 'concealed purposive ideas' that the free associations reflect are seen to be mainly valid unconscious perceptions of the analyst rather than memories and phantasies. The patient may be told, in the initial consultation session, that he or she can say everything that comes to mind. The patient will never be directly reminded of this during the subsequent course of the analysis and many communicative therapists never mention this 'rule' overtly at all, but instead convey it implicitly. This is because it is vitally important to allow the patient to orchestrate the analysis as much as is possible within the parameters set by the frame.

In its most absolute form the attitude of 'free-floating attention' would require the analyst, following Bion's advice, to enter a quasi-meditative state by abandoning memory, desire, and understanding

(Bion 1967). This attitude maximizes intuition by relegating the more logical, linear thought processes to the background. Its use in this form is necessary for the practice of standard forms of psychoanalysis which are forced to rely intensively on intuition because of the lack of any clear rules for formulating the meaning of derivative material. Because the communicative therapist does have a definite procedure for decoding unconscious meaning, he or she does not find it necessary – or indeed helpful – to function in such a completely unstructured way. In the context of communicative practice, listening with free-floating attention means opening oneself as fully as possible to the images offered by the patient and therefore gathering as much information as possible to organize into hypotheses. In situations where the analyst is stuck and cannot understand the unconscious import of the patient's discourse, a bit of unstructured free-floating attention may supply clues to what it is that has been missed. The fact that the analyst has been listening in this way is conveyed to the patient through interpretations that draw on the patient's specific derivative images without discounting those which seem manifestly unimportant.

Component 3: the analyst's neutrality

The communicative therapist behaves neutrally toward his or her patients. The term 'neutrality' has been used in the psychoanalytic literature ever since Freud's papers on technique, and has engendered a certain amount of controversy. Some analysts mistakenly associate neutrality with inhuman detachment, and recommend that it be abandoned (for example, Hammet 1954; Lomas 1987; Sterba 1975). One of the most penetrating studies of the meaning of 'neutrality' was by Dorpat (1977). To paraphrase Dorpat slightly, neutrality means acting in accord with the three cardinal professional values of psychoanalysis: the love of truth, the unfailing respect for the patient's autonomy, and a patient-centered orientation.

The love of truth is expressed in the cognitive goal of psychoanalysis: the fostering of genuine insight. The communicative analyst uses interpretation – the sharing of hypotheses (Smith 1987) – as the only mode of actively influencing the patient. All other mechanisms for producing 'change' such as praise, intimidation, advice, confrontation, and so on are renounced. Thus, the love of truth is revealed both in what one does and what one refrains from doing. Schafer writes that:

Analysts do not view their role as one of offering or promising remedies, cures, complete mental health, philosophies of life, rescue, emergency-room intervention, emotional Band-Aids, or self-sacrificing or self-aggrandizing heroics. It is more than likely that each of these alternatives to a primarily interpretive approach manifests countertransference.

(1983: 11)

Respect for the patient's autonomy is closely linked with the love of truth, as is the patient-centered attitude. The interpretative approach to psychotherapy precludes making any attempt to run the patient's life. The analyst cannot presume to know what path is best for the patient and must, as Anna Freud (1936) counseled, remain equidistant from the conflicting forces within the patient. The patient-centered attitude requires the analyst to be primarily concerned with the inner truth and autonomy of the patient, even if this proves to be discomforting for the analyst.

It is probably correct to say that all interventional errors entail a violation of the rule of neutrality. After every intervention the patient will normally unconsciously inform the analyst (a) whether or not the intervention was non-neutral, (b) in what respect the intervention was non-neutral, and (c) what the main psychotherapeutic implications of the intervention are. Here are a few examples of non-neutral interventions and the unconscious responses that they evoked.

A male patient suffering from an obsessional character neurosis had been in Freudian analysis with male analyst. In one session, during the second year of the analysis, the patient seemed to ruminate interminably about matters which seemed inconsequential to the analyst. Toward the end of the session the analyst found himself in a state of considerable frustration with the patient's 'resistant' behavior and decided to 'confront' him. He told the patient, in essence, that he had been talking about trivial matters in order to avoid deeper and more distressing issues. The patient replied as follows:

I don't know. That could be right. When you said that a thought flashed into my mind about my mother. I visited her in hospital. I think that the medication keeps her from feeling much pain. It's strange that what really gets to me is seeing her completely incontinent.

This is a pointed commentary on the analyst's intervention. The analyst's behavior unconsciously reminds him of his elderly mother. He feels that the analyst is disabled, and that the non-neutral intervention was actually an anesthetic for the analyst, designed to block out the emotional pain evoked in him by the patient. The analyst's inability to contain his own distress is compared to incontinence. The confrontation itself is likened to feces: something nasty that the analyst wants to get rid of (in this instance by offloading it on to the patient).

The second example is taken from the work of a psychoanalytic psychotherapist who, during a session in the third year of the therapy of a rather schizoid female patient, interpreted the patient's persistent attitude of withdrawal as a defense against her envy of the breast. This interpretation was offered toward the end of the session. The patient opened the next session with these remarks:

> I visited my father yesterday. He can't walk or eat by himself anymore so I had to push him around in a wheelchair and feed him. I feel guilty about saying it, but I really resent having to do that for him. I need him to be a father for *me* still, not the other way round. I read in the paper this morning about this weird religious group. They've got all sorts of incredible ideas about the end of the world and the afterlife. They have meetings where they think they talk to the spirits of enlightened masters who tell them all sorts of bullshit. It's pathetic, really, because they can't accept that death is inevitable.

Although she never manifestly refers to it, the patient here offers her therapist an incisive analysis of her prior interpretation. The interpretation is compared to the fanciful theories of the religious cult, and the 'bullshit' promulgated by alleged enlightened masters. The patient's verdict is that the interpretation is 'pathetic'. She specifies that the members of the religious cult resort to these bizarre beliefs and practices because of their unacknowledged fear of death – which serves as an unconscious interpretation of the therapist's difficulty (the therapist admitted in supervision that she was frightened that the patient, when withdrawn, would terminate the therapy). The patient's derivatives concerning her ill father refer to further implications of the non-neutral intervention. As the interpretation was based on the therapist's own defensive needs, it was, implicitly, an appeal to the patient for psychotherapeutic help. The patient feels that she must care for the therapist ('push him around in a wheelchair and feed him') and she resents him for this, feeling that *she* should be the one being given psychotherapeutic help ('I need him to be a father for *me* still, not the other way around').

The third example that I will give here involves a woman who had

just begun psychoanalytic therapy with a female therapist. The patient
had only recently emigrated to Britain from New Zealand, and sought
therapy because of a sexual difficulty. In the session prior to the one
to be discussed the therapist, who was attempting to master the communicative approach, had slipped back into her old ways and offered
a fairly standard Freudian type of interpretation devolving upon the
patient's penis-envy. The patient did not respond derivatively to this
intervention until the beginning of the next session, which opened as
follows:

> I was walking around Guildford for a day out last week. I walked
> and walked and worked up quite an appetite. Eventually I came to a
> lovely looking pub. You know, real Old English style. It looked so
> cozy and they served food, the menu looked good, so I went in. I
> ordered lunch. It was pretty expensive. When the food arrived it
> was *dreadful*. The salad was a couple of soggy lettuce leaves, and
> the fish tasted rancid. I didn't complain, but after I left I felt
> poisoned.

The patient unconsciously expresses her disappointment with the
therapist's work in the previous session. She had been looking
forward to being given something good that would satisfy her ('The
menu looked good') and was paying for this ('It was pretty expensive')
but was served up something 'dreadful'. The images of old, rotten
food may reflect the clichéd qualities of the therapist's interpretation.
The patient feels that this intervention was more harmful than helpful
('I didn't complain, but after I left I felt poisoned').

Thus, the communicative approach adheres to the rule of
neutrality, as do standard forms of psychoanalysis. An important distinction, though, lies in the fact that communicative analysts interpret
neutrality much more strictly than other forms of psychoanalysis.
Most analysts feel comfortable using a variety of verbal interventions
such as questions, confrontations, requests for free associations,
educative interventions, and so on. Communicative analysts feel that
interpretation is the only verbal intervention that is consistent with a
rigorous concept of neutrality. Similarly, communicative analysts
reject as non-neutral those types of interventions which avoid the
immediate reality of the analytic encounter in favor of highly speculative and theoretical notions such as oral greed and penis-envy. Such
interpretations are based too much on the theoretical entities which
fascinate the analyst, and are referred to as 'psychoanalytic clichés' in
the communicative literature. Like ordinary clichés the content of
these interpretations is not necessarily *false* in a general sense, but it

fails to grasp the patient's specific and immediate dilemma. Needless to say, non-interpretative verbal interventions and clichéd interpretations do not receive derivative validation.

Component 4: absence of physical contact

In the secure frame there is no physical contact between patient and therapist apart from an initial handshake. Physical contact is ruled out in classical analysis, usually on the grounds that it would 'contaminate the transference', although many analysts have come to advocate touching as an acceptable form of therapeutic intervention (Balint 1968; Little 1966; Mintz 1973; Woodmansey 1988). While the classical aversion to touch may seem phobic in its absoluteness and intensity, the advocacy of touch is usually based on such shaky theoretical grounds as dubious extrapolations from infancy (babies need to be touched therefore patients in therapy who have been deprived during infancy also need to be touched). The term 'touch' in this context covers everything from holding patient's hands to hugs. Although rarely advocated in the literature, a recent survey indicates that as many as 15 per cent of American psychotherapists have had sexual relations with their patients (Bouhoustos 1984). This is undoubtedly a conservative figure, as it is based on the responses of those therapists prepared to admit that they have had sexual contact with patients. The *Report of the Senate Task Force on Psycho-therapists' and Patients' Sexual Rights*, prepared in 1987 for the California Senate Rules Committee, states:

> A very small number of victims ever complain to any authority. Roughly three-quarters to one half of all victims are unaware that sex between therapists and patients is unethical or actionable. However, among those who are aware, only between one and four percent of victims ever take action.
>
> (quoted in Masson 1989: 224)

Many patients who have been sexually used by their therapists and analysts exonerate them and blame themselves instead. Like the child victim of sexual abuse who remains loyal to the incestuous parent, patients often have a powerful need to idealize and remain faithful to their therapists. Unfortunately, there are no figures available on the incidence of therapist/patient sexual relations in Britain.

Almost all therapists are opposed (or at least *say* they are opposed) to sexual 'acting out' with patients. A large number of therapists, however – perhaps the majority – countenance more delimited forms of physical contact. The communicative approach goes against this trend. Communicative therapists refrain from touching their patients because physical contact is invariably unconsciously condemned by patients, who derivatively describe it as highly seductive. Refraining from touch is part and parcel of allowing oneself to be guided by the wisdom of the deep unconscious part of the mind: it is not based on an irrational 'taboo'.

An example given by Langs illustrates a typical derivative response to inappropriate physical contact:

> A young woman was in therapy with a young man in a clinic setting. As she got up to leave at the end of an hour her sweater slipped to the floor. The therapist picked it up and handed it to her. The patient thanked him and left. She arrived late for the next session, and began by telling the therapist how nice it had been when he picked up her sweater. She said that she hadn't realized he could be such a gentleman. She then said 'I dreamed last night that my brother was touching my breast'.
>
> (Langs in Smith 1989: 117)

For the communicative therapist even the picking up of the sweater constitutes inappropriate physical contact. As Langs goes on to explain:

> A communicative therapist would see the dream – that is, the dreamer – as saying something like 'When you touched my sweater you touched my body. When you did that you stopped being my therapist and became an incestuous object like my brother'. . . . So, the communicative therapist would say, in essence, 'When I picked up your sweater I committed an act of incest with you . . . just as your brother did in the past'.
>
> (ibid.: 117–18)

Component 5: the analyst's anonymity

The analyst should remain relatively anonymous to the patient. This requirement goes back to Freud's writings on technique. As is well known, Freud counseled that 'The doctor should be opaque to his patients and, like a mirror, should show them nothing but what is shown to him' (1912b: 118). The reason most frequently given for this stance (for example, Greenson 1967) is that realistic knowledge about the analyst interferes with the formation of transference illusions. The analyst is expected to be a relatively blank 'screen' upon which the patient can freely project his or her infantile fantasies. In the original 1912 discussion, Freud recommends opacity because exposing one's own problems to the patient it likely to make him or her more keen on analyzing the analyst than on being analyzed himself.

Communicative analysts do not uphold the rule of anonymity in order to safeguard the transference for the simple reason that they do not conceptualize their patients' behavior in terms of transference. Although they recognize that self-revelation may often produce the result that Freud mentions, this is not the primary reason for maintaining anonymity either. Communicative therapists refrain from self-revelations for the simple reason that these are invariably derivatively condemned by analyzands. The reason for this appears to be that at the very least self-revelations violate the 'patient-centered' component of neutrality – the non-anonymous analyst 'hogs' the therapeutic space – and at worst involves an implicit role-reversal and appeal for psychotherapeutic help from the patient. This is aptly illustrated by a patient who arranged to see a therapist in a public clinic. Because of grossly inadequate funding the conditions in this London clinic were very poor and the patient – a man with obsessional symptoms – pleaded with his allocated therapist to be seen elsewhere. The therapist agreed, and decided to see the patient in his home, in a room which was not specifically designed as a consulting-room. Because this was a clinic patient, he was not paying a fee. The patient began the first session in the domestic setting as follows:

> I have a lot to say but have trouble talking to you. [*pause*] It's about sex. I think I might be homosexual. When I was a kid a friend and I used to expose our genitals to each other. I'm sure people could see us sometimes. I feel so ashamed. Once my father burst into my room and caught us.

The therapist's agreeing to see the patient in a room at home entailed considerable self-exposure. The patient compares this, unconsciously, to a mutual homosexual exhibition. The remarks about being observed and, eventually, apprehended are derivative references to the fact that there were other people around in the house where the session was taking place.

Component 6: total privacy

The analytic setting should be entirely private. Ideally, sessions should be held in a private office in a professional building. There should be no receptionist present. The consulting room should have a separate entrance and exit, so that patients do not meet one another coming and going. In the example of violated anonymity given above, the derivatives reflected a lack of privacy as well. To the deep unconscious system it is vital that the analysis be restricted to two people – the analyst and the patient – with no third parties present.

George was a thirty-three-year-old schizophrenic who had recently taken up residence in a therapeutic community in Britain. The therapist assigned to George is taken to his room by a psychiatrist who works in the community. The psychiatrist remains in George's room while the therapist conducts his first interview with the patient. For the first half hour of the session there is no derivative communication whatsoever: George gives concise, purely manifest, answers to the therapist's incessant if well-meaning questions about his life-circumstances. During the final fifteen minutes, however, George switches to the derivative mode.

George: There have been strange things going on.

Therapist: What kind of 'strange things'?

George: Psychic stuff. My grandmother's involved.

Therapist: Your grandmother?

George: Yea. I don't like her. She's a bad person. There's been creepy stuff going on in Manchester. My grandmother's in London and my father's in Brighton. They're plotting together, the two of them. I tried to call CID but couldn't get through on the line. What they are doing now is more and more dangerous. The authorities can't handle it, can't straighten them out, which is why I called CID. I couldn't get through so they didn't do anything, but it needs to be stopped before someone gets killed.

In his derivative communication George highlights the persecutory, conspiratorial quality of the presence of the psychiatrist ('They're plotting together'). He condemns the therapist ('I don't like her. She's a bad person') and regrets that there is no higher authority to whom he might complain ('I tried to call CID but couldn't get through on the line'). The therapist is unable to manage the frame adequately ('The authorities can't handle it'). The patient indicates that the situation is harmful ('What they are doing now is more and more dangerous') and hints that he may be driven to suicide or violence ('it needs to be stopped before someone gets killed').

Component 7: total confidentiality

The analysis should be totally confidential. This is linked to privacy, but goes beyond it. Total confidentiality means that information about the patient should not be divulged to others. There should be no note-taking or recording of sessions on audio- or video-tape, because this implies that the material could fall into someone else's hands. Communicative therapists even go so far as to insist that professionals referring patients to them provide no information about the patient being referred. The deleterious consequences of violating confidentiality are clearly illustrated in Khan's case of Peter and Dolto's session with Dominique.

Patient's derivatively condemn modifications of confidentiality even if they have consciously agreed to it. When therapists tape-record sessions, for instance, both clandestine and consented-to tapings are unconsciously disapproved of. I have come across one example of clandestine recording where the patient developed a delusion that her house was haunted. She described to the therapist how she felt that there was a 'mysterious presence' about. She would search for the ghost, but was unable to find it. She was losing sleep, because she was no longer secure in her own environment. Here, of course, the tape-recorder is unconsciously portrayed as a ghost. The patient was not consciously aware of the recorder, but had somehow unconsciously detected its presence immediately. The framework deviation produced, in this patient, an iatrogenic paranoia: the 'delusion' of being watched. Langs has reported to me a strikingly similar example in which the clandestine recording eventuated in the patient developing the 'paranoid' belief that the FBI was tapping her telephone. In a typical response to non-clandestine taping a patient agreed to allow her therapy sessions to be recorded and on the next night dreamed that she was being interviewed by 'J.R.', a character from the soap opera *Dallas* known for his ruthlessness and duplicity. Although the patient willingly gave conscious consent for the taping, she unconsciously felt that her therapist was no longer trustworthy.

It is probably impossible to overestimate the importance that patients unconsciously attach to confidentiality issues. This was driven home to me by a supervisory experience in which the therapist brought me material from one of his patients which consistently pointed to the involvement of some third party in the treatment. When I pointed this out, the therapist could find no reason why such concerns could be justified. As I had come to learn that communicative decoding is highly reliable, I was very puzzled by the anomaly. I reviewed the material mentally to check if I had misunderstood its meaning, but this was to no avail. Two weeks later the therapist entered my office for his next supervision session with an astounded expression on his face, saying 'You were *so* right last time'. He then described how it had come to light that *ten years previously* the patient's boyfriend had worked for the same organization and in the same building as the therapist. Although therapist and the boyfriend were not closely associated, the patient retained this memory unconsciously and regarded it as a threat to the confidentiality of the treatment.

Component 8: consistency of the setting

The analysis should take place in a single setting. Consistency and reliability are centrally important deep unconscious values. These qualities − or their opposites − are strongly expressed through the therapist's management of the physical setting.

A female psychotherapist worked in a psychiatric outpatient department of a London hospital which was run along psychoanalytic lines. In this setting therapists could not always rely on seeing the patient in the same room from week to week. In ongoing therapy with an alcoholic woman she was obliged to change rooms several times. The first time that they were forced to use a different room from the usual one the patient opened with this derivative sequence:

> This room is nicer than the other one. I like it better. [*pause*] Have you ever seen the people sleeping rough under Waterloo Bridge? I wonder how they live and who feeds them. I gave one everything I had in my purse but it was just about enough for a cup of coffee. [*pause*] My friend S entertained the vicar during the week and invited me as well. He preaches the Christian virtues when it suits him and he ends up doing whatever the hell he wants. What a hypocrite.

The patient's first remark about the setting is a purely manifest approval of the shift. She then switches into the derivative mode and berates the therapist for altering the frame. She likens her situation in therapy to that of a homeless person. She feels that she is not being given enough ('It was just about enough for a cup of coffee'). The reference to money may relate to the fact that the patient does not pay a fee. This may lead her to feel like a beggar who must be greateful for every pittance that he receives. The patient knows that the therapist understands derivative messages about the importance of the frame, and feels that this is incompatible with working in such a deviant frame ('He preaches the Christian virtues when it suits him and . . . ends up doing whatever the hell he wants'). The patient feels this to be sheer hypocrisy.

Component 9: the fee

There should be a single, fixed fee paid by the patient. If at all possible, the therapist should not unilaterally alter the fee once it is set. Patients should be financially responsible for the sessions that they miss. The fee should be paid by the patient and not by third parties. Patients should have the responsibility of calculating their own monthly accounts rather than being handed a bill by the analyst.

There is a burgeoning literature on the role of the fee in psychoanalysis. Many writers feel that free treatment or treatment with a reduced fee has no deleterious effects on the analysis (Lorand and Console 1958) while others – probably the majority – disagree (Goldensohn and Haar 1974; Nash and Cavenar 1976). The importance of the fee has been consistently confirmed by communicative research. James Raney, a communicative psychoanalyst, provides examples of several types of fee deviations and describes patients' derivative responses to these (Raney 1986). The following vignette is from Raney's paper:

A patient was not charged for missed appointments. After he cancelled an appointment, he alluded to images of betrayal, to his mother who once remarried in his absence, and to other disturbances. After a second cancellation, he alluded to clients who wasted his time. He had decided to bill one of them for the time spent. He missed having an appointment last time. He mentioned a spoiled colleague who kept everyone waiting at meetings and who finally was told to keep the schedule because he was interfering with the work of others. A dream of a pile of Christmas presents awakened him in a cold sweat. He spoke of spoiling his children with gifts and 'buying them off'. When the therapist linked these images with the cancellation without charge, the patient recalled worrying at the time of the first cancellation that his time would be filled. [Hence his remark about his mother remarrying in his absence – DLS]. A firm contract and not getting just monetary gifts was important. Gifts made especially for him were the most valuable (a reference, perhaps, to the interpretation). The patient then suggested that he be charged for cancelled sessions.

(91)

This patient's derivatives make it clear that the failure to charge for a missed session is tantamount to the therapist offering a gift. Patients do not (unconsciously) approve of exchanges of gifts in therapy. They expect an appropriate fee to be charged for services rendered and require that this be the only transaction between patient and therapist. The offer of a gift to the therapist, or the acceptance of a gift by the therapist, is unconsciously viewed as being contrary to the aims of psychoanalysis.

The following is an extract from a session from the beginning phase of a psychotherapy conducted at the psychiatric outpatient department of a large London hospital. The therapy was obtained on the National Health Service, and there was consequently no charge to the patient.

> I had a row with my mother last night. Well it's not that, it's just that because I'm doing this party on Thursday, actually she is helping me really. I said I wanted some garden furniture and she's got enough to sort of seat 500 people. I only wanted a couple of chairs and it seemed silly to go out and buy them. . . . She's been looking after Jonathan [the patient's son] and she sent me a beautiful card from Italy, and bought Jonathan a really nice Italian game that he really liked. She's been giving her time, helping me get things ready for the party. But it's a tricky situation, you know, because she suddenly turns on me and is very hurtful. I should just tell her to 'fuck off' but I feel helpless. It's a sort of Snow White thing with her at the door with a poisoned apple.

The patient feels taken over by the therapist's apparent generosity. She feels that she must be grateful for what she is given, but unconsciously would prefer not to be dependent on free therapy ('I should just tell her to "fuck off" but I feel helpless'). The absence of a fee makes it difficult for the patient to express her negative feelings toward the therapist. In the end, the patient regards the gift of free therapy as harmful ('her at the door with a poisoned apple').

Component 10: set frequency and duration of sessions

Sessions should be at a set time and each session should have a set duration. Most communicative therapists retain the psychoanalytic convention of the 'fifty-minute hour'. There is nothing sacrosanct about this. What is important from the patient's point of view is that sessions take place at the same time each week and that they are always the same length. Lengthening or shortening sessions always gets a damning derivative reception from the patient.

The following account from Langs is quite typical. An analyst, Dr Baker, inadvertently extended his patient's session by ten minutes: she had been given sixty rather than the agreed fifty minutes for her hour. The patient – Mrs Able – began the next session by reporting a dream:

> I had a dream. It was frightening. A man with a moustache was chasing me. He cornered me in a motel room and wanted to rape me. I was ready to surrender, but then felt furious. Suddenly I was outside and a huge tree was swaying in the wind. I was afraid it would fall on me and crush me.
>
> (Langs 1982c: 198)

Mrs Able then associated to the dream. She mentioned that her father had a moustache and that at the age of eleven she once shared a bed in a motel with him. She had been frightened when she saw his naked body. Mrs Able went on to describe how, a few nights previously, a neighbor and his wife visited: 'Now that I think of it', she remarked, 'he also had a moustache. She kept wanting to leave, but he insisted on staying on. He seemed attracted to me' (ibid.).

Almost any analyst would interpret this dream as provoked by the patient's infantile incestuous longings for her father. The scene of attempted rape would be understood as a wish fulfillment, while the falling tree (a phallic symbol) would be viewed as a more heavily disguised portrayal of sexual intercourse. The association of the patient getting into bed with her father would be used to support this hypothesis. One might then go on to suggest that Mrs Able's attitude to her male neighbor, whom she thought was attracted to her, was based on his resemblance to her father. Some analysts might go on to conclude that all of this points to the patient's unconscious transference on to Dr Baker, for whom the neighbor might serve as a surrogate.

Over and against this normal Freudian analysis, a communicative analyst would suggest that the dream – and the associations prompted by it – point to Mrs Able's unconscious perceptions of her analyst's framework deviation. She says, in effect, that Dr Baker was unconsciously motivated by sexual urges to extend the hour. This is an unconscious interpretation of the basis for the therapist's lapse. It is clear from the imagery that Mrs Able found this situation very dangerous, experiencing it as tantamount to a physical assault. In her associations she tells her analyst that in keeping her over time he was behaving in a manner reminiscent of her father. It was like going to bed together. The analyst had, by virtue of his lapse, exposed himself to his patient. Like the neighbor, the analyst wanted to stay with the patient because he was attracted to her.

A corollary of the insistence on keeping strictly and reliably to the time boundaries originally agreed between therapist and patient is that there should be no 'make up' sessions for those that the patient misses. Patients unconsciously experience attempts to schedule extra sessions to compensate for those missed as highly seductive and defensive and often relating to the therapist's need to deny loss and death.

Mr N was in his fourth year of psychoanalysis, a treatment which he had undertaken because of sexual problems. He was forced to cancel a session because of illness and, when he met with his analyst again, asked if they could squeeze in a session later in the week to make up for the absence. The analyst had hours available and readily agreed. Mr N then proceeded to report a dream:

> I was in a large ship, a ferry, and it had capsized. I was trapped inside and it was pure devastation. Everywhere there were dying and wounded people. I wanted to help them. Suddenly you came along, took me by the hand, and helped me escape.

This dream focused on the defensive aspect of the analyst's facile agreement to an extra session. The patient sees him as encouraging Mr N to turn away from a disturbing situation ('Suddenly you came along . . . and helped me escape') which the patient unconsciously felt required some *therapeutic* attention ('I wanted to help them').

Ms L, in the final year of her analysis, wished to attend a meeting which conflicted with her psychoanalytic hour. She asked if, exceptionally, an alternative time could be arranged. The analyst said 'Let's see what comes to mind before making any decisions.' Ms L began to talk about a meeting she had arranged with a man she had recently met. He wanted her to travel to Brighton to be with him and she had agreed to this but had later realized that she was not happy with the situation. She felt that they should have talked together about who would travel to whom, and reach a *mutual* agreement. Ms L then spoke about an irritating meeting that she had had with a client. He had cut their interview short to make a lengthy telephone call, and then returned when the alotted time was spent. Ms L insisted that it would have been inappropriate to cut into extra time for the sake of this man. He had chosen to use the time for telephone calls and should therefore take the consequences.

Component 11: patient's responsibility on termination

Finally, the patient should be the one to decide when and how the therapy is to be terminated. The common practice of attempting to 'block' terminations which are, in the therapist's view, 'premature' is a gross violation of the ethical imperative of neutrality. By the same token, any attempt by a therapist to unilaterally set a date for the therapy to terminate is a violation of the secure frame and generates tremendous unconscious distress.

To the extent that a therapeutic frame approximates the secure ideal, it will produce both a sense of security and reliability and an experience of profound dread. The security-giving aspects of the frame, its function as a 'holding environment', have already been discussed. The secure frame gives the patient an experience of a sane therapist who is able to establish clear interpersonal boundaries, refrains from exploiting the patient, and so on. It was a surprising discovery to find that the secure frame also generates it own special anxieties. Many patients seem to unconsciously feel that the secure frame will *destroy* them. The powerful form of unconscious existential dread that emerges in the face of a secure analytic frame has been termed 'secure frame anxiety' or 'death anxiety'. Although this phenomenon is not yet well understood, a plausible explanation seems to be that the secure frame universally symbolizes the limitations of human existence, the inexorable constraints of time and death imposed by nature which throw us back on an awareness of our own fragile mortality. In Jaspers's (1986) terminology the secure frame provides a 'limit situation', an experience of finality which, if accepted honestly rather than denied, can have a tremendously constructive existential impact.[5] Communicative research does seem to support the contention that the dread of annihilation – death anxiety – is a powerful unconscious factor implicated in a great deal of psychopathology and human distress. This idea harmonizes well with evolutionary thinking, which points out that the prime 'motive' of all life forms is the perpetuation of their own genes – to live and to produce offspring that will live. It would follow from these premises that every deviation from the secure frame is tantamount to a manic denial of death, a hypothesis that is often borne out by an analysis of the derivatives following on from such deviations. Patients regularly experience deviant therapists unconsciously as attempting to seduce them, to draw them in to participating in strongly defensive maneuvers. Deviations are also quite regularly unconsciously understood as expressions of perverse, often incestuous sexuality. This 'oedipal' dimension of framework deviations may relate to the fact that the incest taboo is one of the most powerful personalizing limits imposed upon a growing child, defining him or her as separate from, and in crucial respects unable to participate in, aspects of the parental world. In this view the child must accept its (metaphorical) 'castration' in order to grow into a psychologically healthy adult. If, as the paradigmatic limit situation, the secure frame subsumes the incest taboo it is hardly surprising that deviant therapists are unconsciously perceived as committing acts of incest and pervasion.[6] The other side of this picture, of course, is that the magical banishment of mortality and limitation, and the possibility of gratifying taboo incestuous urges, renders deviant frame therapy immensely attractive to the conscious mental system. Patients clamor for forms of psychotherapy which they *unconsciously* know to be extremely damaging because of the bastions that they establish against our most profound existential terrors. The fact that communicative psychotherapy strives to maintain a secure frame as an essential, indispensible component of the psychotherapeutic situation places limitations on the type of patient who can benefit from the approach. Patients must be able to tolerate the existential anxieties evoked by the secure frame if the approach is to be of help to them. Certain 'frame-sensitive' patients who are very vulnerable to such anxieties (who often have a history of severe traumatization) will not tolerate the communicative setting for long. One of the reasons that Langs decided to give up his private psychoanalytic practice in favor of full-time formal research was to work toward creating new and benign forms of psychotherapy appropriate for the treatment of frame-sensitive patients.

So far I have confined myself to a discussion of how *patients* respond to secure- and deviant-frame psychotherapy, but of course the identical considerations apply to therapists. Unconsciously therapists too gravitate toward a secure frame which permits the confrontation with death within a secure and reliable setting. However, therapists also dread this and have powerful needs to deny it. They are attracted to forms of psychotherapy which advocate modifications of the frame which seal these issues off from awareness. The inner forces propelling a therapist in this direction can be very powerful indeed. Even communicative therapists, who believe in maintaining a secure frame, experience almost irresistible temptation to deviate in order to attenuate the highly charged therapeutic atmosphere that the secure frame brings in its wake.

The contrast drawn between secure and deviant modes of therapy is not meant to imply that only psychotherapy conducted within a totally secure frame is of value. Deviations introduce insurmountable constraints upon how penetrating a psychotherapeutic experience is possible, but this does not preclude the possibility that very meaningful work can be accomplished within those constraints. For many therapists – especially those working within the public sector – the establishment of a secure frame is a physical impossibility. Patients seen on the National Health Service, for example, cannot be charged fees. In many hospitals and clinics it is not possible to count on the availability of the same room from week to week. Receptionists may be present, therapists may be required to take notes, and time limits may have to be set by the therapist restricting the duration of therapy (see Cheifetz 1984; Vlosky 1984; Hoag 1989; Jonathan 1990). However, there is always scope for some securing of the frame. Even in the most deviant environment there are points when a ground rule can be upheld or established. These are called *secure frame moments*, and will have constructive effects despite the presence or even preponderance of contradictory factors.

The technique of communicative therapy is based on an understanding of the process of unconscious perception, the nature of unconscious communication, and the formative role of the frame. In chapter 8 the nature of communicative technique will be described.

8 The technique of communicative psychotherapy

Freud was a hero. He descended to the 'Underworld' and there met stark terrors. He carried with him his theory as a medusa's head which turned these terrors to stone. We who follow Freud have the benefit of the knowledge he brought back with him and conveyed to us. He survived. We must see if we now can survive without using a theory which is in some measure an instrument of defence.

R.D. Laing

In the last two chapters I have outlined the general theoretical and philosophical underpinnings of the communicative approach. In the present chapter I will describe how these ideas are applied concretely and practically to the practice of psychotherapy.

The communicative approach is fundamentally concerned with the accurate interpretation of derivative messages consisting of transformed, encoded unconscious information comparable, in at least some respects, to a text written in an unknown script.[1] To understand the meaning of such a text a disciplined, consistent and systematic translation procedure is required. Rather than 'translating' the script capriciously or in a purely 'intuitive' manner – a procedure which would yield misleading results – it is necessary to discover the underlying rules, the law-like conventions governing the syntax and semantics of the language and script. Only then is it possible to determine its real meaning. This analogy holds true for understanding the meaning of derivative communications. 'Intuition' will not serve. A set of translation rules is required. In the case of derivative messages, however, the *content* of the text itself discourages us from making an accurate translation because, as Freud first pointed out, the content of derivative messages is usually highly threatening. In order to understand these encoded meanings we must, as Langs puts it, commit an 'un-natural act'. We must defy our own defenses and stare in the face of those things which we are most disposed to ignore. It is therefore necessary to have a reliable method of translation that can overcome both cognitive and emotional limitations of the therapist. He or she must overcome inner resistances to a significant degree and find the means to decode patients' unconscious messages as accurately as possible.

IDENTIFYING DERIVATIVE MATERIAL

Because of the crucial importance of derivative meaning, it is essential to be able to distinguish derivative from non-derivative material. Functionally, the distinctive characteristic of derivative communication is its multicontextual quality. In contrast to such phenomena as puns, metaphors, and innuendos, which are also multicontexual, derivative messages are meaningful in at least two contexts *at least one of which must be unconscious*. I have already listed the main formal characteristics of derivative communications in Chapter 6. To briefly recapitulate: derivative messages are *concrete* and *specific* (and therefore easily *visualized*). They portray people, situations, and events *outside of the therapeutic situation* (although latently pertaining to it) and are usually manifestly *discontinuous* (although latently fully coherent). The discontinuity of derivative content may sometimes appear to be chaotic, but this chaos conceals an intricate hidden order. Derivative communications normally possess a narrative structure, appearing as *stories*.

The absence of any of these qualities suggests, at most, a weakly derivative message. If two or more of these properties are lacking, the communication should be considered non-derivative and be treated at a purely manifest level. Although there are now objective measures of 'derivativeness' used in formal psychotherapy research (Langs *et al*. 1988) these are not useful to the practicing therapist at work in the clinical situation. By no means foolproof, the indices listed above are highly reliable and entirely serviceable for practical therapeutic work.

BRIDGING THEMES

The most therapeutically meaningful dimension of derivative discourse is its relationship to the therapeutic situation itself. The stories a patient tells may be apparently about something else entirely – a film, a childhood experience, or a conversation with a friend – but the underlying themes expressed will invariably be highly appropriate to the here-and-now context. The themes which are a common denominator of both the patient's manifest message and his or her unconscious perception of the therapist and frame are called *bridging themes*. They are so called because they form a bridge or link between the conscious and unconscious realms, and between the patient's stories and the therapeutic situation. Bridging themes are the poetry of psychotherapy.

In her psychotherapeutic hour, Ms L discussed a number of apparently unrelated topics. Her therapist made no active interventions during the first thirty minutes, but offered an interpretation toward the end of the hour that took no account of Ms L's unconscious perceptions. Instead, the interpretation was an effort to explain the unconscious phantasies underlying her problems relating to other women. The patient agreed that the interpretation was probably correct, and then went on to describe how a friend had once said to her that despite his overtly sincere behavior – he seemed very open and willing to talk about intimate matters – he was actually the most cut-off, self-centered person she had ever met. In this example the patient initially responds to the intervention with manifest agreement. Because this is based on a purely conscious assessment of the interpretation, it is of little use for a communicative analysis of the interchange. Ms L's unconscious response can be determined by finding the themes in the derivative comments following on from this. The two bridging themes revealed in this short account are:

1 Two people talking together.
2 A person who appears to be sincere, open, and willing to discuss intimate issues, but who is actually quite self-centered and out of touch with others.

How can these two themes be related to the therapeutic interaction? As the therapy is based on a one-to-one verbal transaction, we might take the reference to two people talking together as a derivative portrait of the patient and the therapist. The next image, of someone emotionally remote who masks this with an appearance of emotional openness, might be an unconscious perception of the therapist. We must ask ourselves what recent interaction between therapist and patient could have been plausibly interpreted as an indication of this incongruity. I have already noted that the therapist had, after being silent throughout the first part of the session, offered an interpretation which had no direct bearing on the here-and-now therapeutic situation. If we take this as the stimulus for the derivatives, the patient seems to be saying that through silently listening, the therapist had given the appearance of being receptive to Ms L's concerns, but that the content of the intervention contradicted this. The interpretation was a hypocritical act, an attempt to *appear* 'in touch' which, in actuality, was quite 'cut-off'. The therapist's failure to be sensitive to his patient's real needs is experienced as a manifestation of self-centeredness. The intervention is therefore not validated.

The process of decoding the unconscious meaning of Ms L's remarks involved identifying the stimulus or *trigger* for the derivatives and finding the *themes* that connect this material to the trigger. This placed her comments in a new context: the context of the immediate situation. A dimension of depth is suddenly introduced. Her remarks now seem alive and pregnant with meaning. Let us consider a second example.

> While working with Mr H, a depressed, apathetic patient, Dr D persuaded himself against his better judgement that this patient required a more active, directive therapeutic approach. He therefore adopted a style, for two sessions running, of asking Mr H numerous questions and frequently offering highly confrontative comments. The patient consciously expressed approval of the new technique, but his symptoms and resistances remained unmodified. After the two 'active' sessions, on the day the patient was due to pay his therapist for the preceding months' work, the patient opened the hour saying that the last two sessions had been 'great'. He then described how he had taken his car to a garage to have what he hoped was a minor malfunction repaired. The problem turned out to be much more serious than he had anticipated, and he was told by the mechanic that it would be more than the car was worth to have it repaired. Mr H then said, forlornly, that he had been throwing his money away on this car and should have scrapped it long ago. He then mentioned that he was unhappy at home: his wife did not pay him sufficient attention. He could not mention this directly to her because it would hurt her feelings. Next he spoke of a joke that he had heard on the radio the night before concerning a psychoanalyst who fell asleep during sessions.

At the very beginning of this session Mr H consciously referred to the therapist's new style of working. This statement picks out the stimulus – or trigger – for the mode. The bridging themes implicit in this material are:

1 Something not functioning.
2 Attempting to have it repaired.

3 A serious malfunction.
4 An uneconomical repair job.
5 Throwing away money on something.
6 Someone giving insufficient attention.
7 An analyst sleeping on the job.

With the exception, perhaps, of number two, these are all negatively toned themes. Taking the change of technique as the trigger – as the patient has specified – we can formulate the latent meaning of this material as a commentary on the implications of the change. A paraphrase would run something like this:

> This therapy is not working, and repairing it does not seem feasible. I have been throwing my money away working with you, and to continue to try and rectify things is not worth the cost. I should have given it up a long time ago. You, therapist, are inattentive to me. I cannot tell you this directly because it would hurt you too much. You have been asleep on the job.

This example illustrates how a thorough decoding of derivative messages can cast an entirely new light on psychotherapeutic interchanges. On the surface, this patient is rather pleased with his therapist. Only by taking the unconscious meaning of his stories into account can we realize that he is very distressed by his therapist's behavior and is on the verge of terminating the treatment.

PORTRAYALS OF TRIGGERS

In the example of Mr H and Dr D the unconscious meaning of the derivatives was very easy to divine because of the sequence in which the patient chose to present his material. Mr H began the session by manifestly specifying the trigger and only after having done this went on to provide unconscious messages about the implications of the trigger. Because the trigger was unambiguously represented at the outset, the therapist was prepared for the messages to follow. It was as though the patient said 'What you are about to hear will be a disguised commentary on the implications of your change of technique'. This simple pattern, unfortunately, is only one of several more complex permutations.

Sometimes, a patient will provide a sequence of rich derivatives and only mention the trigger afterwards. This pattern is more difficult for therapists to handle because the derivatives cannot be 'slotted into place' as they appear. The therapist can register the emergent themes, but may not know what they pertain to until later in the session.

At the end of the hour prior to the one to be described an analyst, Mr C had announced to his patient, Mr G, that they would have to change the time of their normal weekly appointments. Together they decided that the best plan was to make the sessions one hour earlier than the original time. Mr C felt awkward about the changes and vaguely explained to Mr G why they were necessary. The patient began the next hour by mentioning an event that had 'tainted' his day. He reported that a client had tried to avoid paying an account. This man was a real con-man, a smooth-talker who tried to take advantage of others while trying to appear 'nice'. Mr G had foolishly allowed himself to be swayed by this man and, as a result, had been cheated out of what was owed to him. This particularly angered the patient because the terms of their agreement had been clearly set out beforehand. He despised his devious client and despised himself for yielding to him. After a period of silence Mr G mentioned that the change in the times of his appointments was not really very convenient, but he felt that it would be OK.

Here the bridging themes are:

1 An upsetting event.
2 Someone who tries to avoid giving someone what is owed to him.
3 A con-man who takes advantage of people while pretending to be 'nice'.
4 Yielding to someone to one's own disadvantage.
5 The violation of an agreement.
6 People who are despised.

Understood in the light of the trigger of the change of appointment times mentioned at the end of the derivative sequence, the unconscious meaning of these communications can be paraphrased as follows:

> When you changed our schedule last week you 'tainted' this therapy. You are trying to avoid giving me what you owe me. You are a con-man, a smooth-talker who pretends to be 'nice' while taking advantage of me. You have violated our original agreement and I despise you for this.

Triggers are not manifestly represented. They may be portrayed only in a disguised, symbolic, derivative form. Derivative representations of triggers may be so thinly disguised as to be quite transparent or so heavily disguised as to be virtually unrecognizable. Here is an example of a thinly disguised portrayal of a trigger followed by several clear derivatives:

The session to be described took place in a psychiatric clinic which was being redecorated. Workmen were obviously present in the building and had, in fact, obstructed the entrance to the waiting room with equipment and debris. The patient, Ms L, who had begun her therapy several weeks before, began this session talking about her new flat. She was unhappy with it because she had discovered, just after moving in, that there was a builder's yard next door which was very noisy and disturbed her peace of mind. She was no longer able to get fully absorbed in anything because of the interference from outside which was disruptive.

The builder's yard is obviously a representation of the presence of the workmen. The patient feels that they are an intrusion which prevents her from getting fully absorbed in the therapeutic process. Although the trigger is disguised, it is not difficult to decypher. A communicative therapist hearing this material would be likely to identify the trigger and would then be in a position to understand the unconscious meaning of the derivative images as they are presented.

The next example of a session in which a heavily disguised portrayal of the trigger is offered at the end of a session is much more difficult.

A therapist in private practice, Mr J, had decided to set a termination date for Mr M, a long-standing patient who had been in once-a-week psychotherapy for some seven years with little apparent improvement in his condition. Mr M concurred with Dr L about terminating and the date was agreed. The session to be described occurred approximately one month prior to termination. Mr M began by remarking that he was feeling quite depressed because he had not gotten a post that he had applied for. Next there was a lengthy series of negative derivative images centering on two events: his emotional betrayal at the hands of a trusted friend and an accident suffered by a friend at work because the management had instituted very inadequate safety precautions. He then spoke tearfully about how his mother had tried to abort him when she discovered that she was pregnant. He described abortion as a 'sick' thing to do. In the past he had felt bad about himself because his mother didn't want him, but now he realized that his mother must have been a sick, unhappy person to do such a thing.

The reference to the abortion attempt near the end of the session appears to be a disguised portrayal of the termination, as does the earlier remark about not getting a job. Although he consciously accepts the idea that termination is appropriate, Mr M unconsciously regards it as a betrayal and a consequence of inadequate management. In his concluding comments it seems clear that the patient has decided that his therapist is a sick, unhappy person.

Just considering the relationship between manifest and disguised presentations of triggers and their related derivatives four patterns can be discerned:

1 Sessions in which a manifest portrayal of a trigger is followed by a sequence of related derivatives.
2 Sessions which a derivative portrayal of a trigger is followed by a sequence of related derivatives.
3 Sessions in which a sequence of derivatives is followed by a manifest portrayal of their trigger.
4 Sessions in which a sequence of derivatives is followed by the derivative portrayal of their trigger.

It is possible to analyze sessions of each of these types to determine the unconscious forces at play and, in principle, to offer sound communicative interpretations within them. There are three further types of session, however, which do not permit a clear recognition of unconscious dynamics and during which meaningful verbal interventions are ruled out. These are:

5 Sessions in which there is a sequence of derivatives but no portrayal of their trigger.
6 Sessions in which there is a portrayal of a trigger but no related derivatives.
7 Sessions in which neither trigger nor derivatives are mentioned.

TYPES OF DERIVATIVE THEME

Derivative themes are the key for unlocking the deeper implications of therapist's behavior. By means of these themes patients are able to communicate their uncannily accurate and incisive perceptions and inferences. Because of the differing values and commitments of the conscious and deep unconscious sectors of the mind, derivative messages may seem tremendously overstated once they have been translated (recall how both Searles and Laing referred to them as 'parody'). As the conscious system naturally tries to down-play if not obliterate entirely most deep unconscious concerns, it is hardly surprising that the raw meaning of derivatives is often experienced as extreme or bizarre.

In order to use the communicative method it is essential to be able to identify and decode derivatives. A useful way to begin is to acquire some knowledge about the types of derivative theme most frequently encountered in practice. There are three basic categories of derivative theme: themes of *relationship*, themes of *function*, and themes of *environment*.[2]

Relationship themes

Relationship themes are present whenever a patient offers derivatives manifestly portraying the interactions between two or more people. When patients tell stories about arguments, childhood relationships, making love, conversations, lies, partnerships breaking down or being repaired, kind deeds, and so on, they are presenting relationship themes. Relationship themes are used to convey unconscious perceptions of the quality of the relationship between patient and therapist. Through these derivatives patients tell their therapists about their abusiveness, seductiveness, deceitfulness and, destructiveness as well as their constructiveness, creativity, and contactfulness. Here is an example of how raw unconscious perceptions of the therapeutic relationship are 'transferred' on to manifestly unrelated material.

> Mr G, a French psychotherapist working in London, was referred a French patient, Ms B, because of their common national origin. From the beginning the two of them spoke French rather than English in the therapy sessions. It became clear in supervision that Ms B unconsciously objected to this situation. Her derivatives indicated that she felt the therapist was speaking French to her because he needed companionship from her and that this was quite seductive. On one occasion the patient gave the therapist every possible opportunity to interpretatively address the language issue, but it was not taken up. Toward the end of the hour she remarked that she was beginning to experience attacks of anxiety again, as she had several years previously. She then said that she had spent a 'heavy' day with her boyfriend and had been very nervous. She had asked the boyfriend to stay with her, but he had to go away. The next day he was fine. Ms B could not reconcile her lover's distant, abandoning behavior with his more loving, intimate behavior.

The trigger for this material, as later became evident, was the therapist's failure to intervene around the language issue. Ms B felt this as an abandonment: for although she wanted him to 'stay with' her – to be in touch with her unconscious concerns – he, the therapist, was distancing himself. Ms B could not reconcile Mr G's inability to address the language derivatives with his sound, insightful therapeutic work around other unconscious issues.

Here is another example involving relationship themes.

A therapist in training, Mrs K, described to her communicative supervisor the first segment of a session with Mr S, a long-term patient. Mr S began the hour complaining bitterly about how an associate at work was taking too many days off and even when at the office wasted a great deal of time. This basic theme continued, with small variations, for approximately fifteen minutes. The therapist had no idea what to make of it. The supervisor noted the theme 'Someone is angry with someone else with whom he works for being wasteful and taking more than he is entitled to'. The therapist found this interesting, but could not take it any further. Finally, the supervisor focused on the reference to *time* and enquired if there had been any difficulties with time (cancellations, schedule changes, late starts, and so on). Mrs K looked startled and confessed that she had announced to the patient at the beginning of the session under consideration that she would have to shorten it by ten minutes.

Here, of course, the patient represents the therapist as someone who greedily and wastefully does what she wants without considering those with whom she works. In light of the shortening of the hour, the patient views his therapist as establishing a selfish, exploitative relationship with him.

Function themes

Themes of function and dysfunction involve references to how things work. When patients tell stories of broken vacuum cleaners, clogged drains, leaky pipes, efficient airlines, healthy bodies, fine athletic performance, and so on, they are offering themes of function and dysfunction. Themes of function and dysfunction usually express patients' unconscious awareness of how well or how poorly their therapists are functioning.

In his first meeting with Mr W, a student therapist, Mr M described his symptom of mood swings. He offered the example of what happens when he has to do a repair job and worried if he has the right tools and fixtures, if he will be able to repair what he has been asked to repair and if he will be faced with unseen difficulties. Then he starts to wish that he hadn't taken the job on, because all of the worry was not worth the money.

The trigger for this material is evidently the patient's unconscious perception of the therapist's inexperience (it was, in fact, this therapist's very first attempt to conduct a psychotherapy session). By describing himself, this patient finds a method for describing the therapist. He accurately perceives that the therapist is very worried about being able to complete the 'repair job' of therapy without botching it. He knows that the therapist is fearful and would like to withdraw from the situation. The final statement points to a more specific trigger. Because this therapy took place on the National Health Service, the patient did not pay the therapist a fee. The patient evidently feels that the absence of a fee is ominous in that the therapist is not adequately compensated for struggling with the difficulties confronting him.

Here is a second example of a dysfunction theme:

> A patient working toward termination began his hour discussing problems he was currently having with his car. He had retained the car for some years because of its reliability, but now parts were wearing out and it was beginning to cost the patient a great deal of money. The patient thought that he should finally make up his mind to get rid of it.

This patient set his own termination date later in the same session.

Environment themes

Environment themes, the third crucial thematic type, refer to places and their properties. When patients speak derivatively of peaceful rural scenes, tiny claustrophobic rooms, flats which are chaotic, the destruction of the ozone layer, a busy train station, and so on, they are offering environment themes. Environment themes almost always unconsciously depict the state of the therapeutic frame.

> Mr M described to his trainee therapist, Mr W, who was seeing him in a home office and not charging a fee, how he had been befriended by a male teacher in university. This relationship soon became sexual. The teacher offered him a job in a company he had formed, but Mr M found the situation quite awkward, quit, and left the country.

The triggers for this material are the home office and absence of a fee. The theme is of someone leaving one environment which inappropriately mixes business and sexuality in favour of another. It is clear that Mr M perceives the framework deviations of this therapy as homosexually seductive and wishes to terminate.

Here is another example of a session taking place in the therapist's home:

> A patient, referred to a trainee therapist for treatment, could not be seen at the local psychiatric outpatients' department because of a shortage of space. The therapist, who was not paid a fee, decided to see the patient in a room in his own home. During the first interview the patient reported having met a man whom she liked. She visited his home, which was outwardly very impressive but was a real mess inside. There was rubbish everywhere, and he paid no attention to her requests to get it in order. After several such meetings she was so disturbed by the chaotic quality of his home that she decided that future meetings should be on more 'neutral ground'.

Taking the trigger as the domestic setting of the therapy, the patient can be seen to describe the destructive ramifications of this framework deviation through the image of the chaotic home. She unconsciously wants the therapist to set this aspect of the frame right, and stipulates that the therapeutic environment should be on a more 'neutral' territory.

MAJOR COMPONENTS OF DERIVATIVE COMMUNICATIONS

Having considered the main thematic types, we can now move on to characterize those elements of derivative messages which cut across these categorizations. All derivative messages will possess at least one of these components. Generally speaking, the more full and complex a derivative sequence is, the more of these factors will be represented in it.[3]

Implications for the patient's well-being

Patients derivatively convey the extent to which therapists' efforts have a constructive or destructive impact on them. It is surprising how frequently the conscious and deep unconscious systems are at odds on this matter. A patient may *consciously* state that an intervention has been helpful for a variety of reasons. The intervention may be felt to be agreeable because of its defensive qualities or because of the patient's masochistic need to suffer. A patient may concur with virtually everything a therapist says because of a need to idealize the therapist (which, I hasten to add, is usually induced by the therapist). Deep unconscious responses are not hampered by these constraints. They offer a true reading of the therapeutic or anti-therapeutic properties of an intervention. This is probably the most fundamental function of derivative communication. Virtually all derivatives touch on the implications of the trigger for the patient's well-being.

Genetic links

Derivative communications not infrequently contain references to significant people from the patient's past such as father, mother, sister, or brother. Conventional therapists generally take this to indicate that important buried conflicts concerning these figures are beginning to come to light. Often links to past relationships are used as a basis for making transference interpretations – i.e. statements to the effect that the patient is treating the therapist as though he or she were mother, father, and so on. More fanciful transference interpretations, which may or may not draw on patients' remarks about past figures, may postulate elaborate 'unconscious phantasies' active in the patient's mind. The patient, of course, is in no position to refute such allegations precisely because the phantasies are supposed to be unconscious. This kind of interpretation is invariably refuted unconsciously by patients.

As I remarked in Chapter 7, communicative psychotherapists do not regard transference as a major causal influence on patients' communication and behavior. They therefore construe manifest references to early figures in a radically different way than mainstream psychoanalysts. When patients mention figures from their childhood these are usually treated as disguised representations of the therapist. A patient might, for example, bring up the memory of her father beating her *because her father's past behavior is analogous to the therapist's present behavior.* It is not that the patient has formed an illusion about the therapist under the pressure of unconscious forces, but rather that the patient has accurately, albeit unconsciously, identified a real resemblance between past and present.

> A therapist seeing a new patient for the first time asked her question after question about the origins of her symptom of social anxiety, allowing no periods of silence or sustained free association. After about forty minutes of this the patient suddenly described a dream that she had experienced at the age of ten. Her father was trying to lock her in a coffin. Whenever she would struggle to get free he would slam down the lid.

The therapist described in this vignette believed that she had begun to recover the repressed historical basis for the patient's chronic anxiety in her hostile relationship with her father. Although this may contain some element of truth, the main significance of the patient's recollection, as seen from a communicative standpoint, is the patient's perception of the therapist as attempting to trap her, push her, shut her up, and kill her. It seems reasonable to infer that the patient unconsciously felt that in her violent persecutory interventions the therapist resembled her violent, persecutory father.

Models of rectification

Models of rectification are derivative communications unconsciously intended as corrective guidance for the therapist. They are images which convey what the therapist *should* be doing, and are therefore positively toned. Models of rectification are the prime expression of the patient's constructive effort to supervise the therapist.

Models of rectification are offered when the therapist has committed major errors. When they are heeded patients almost always respond with positive, confirmatory derivative material. Because they emerge in situations of error, these models are characteristically offered as a conclusion to a sequence of negative derivative images spelling out the destructive implications of the therapist's behavior. When derivative material has a negative valence, then, it is quite important to be prepared for the offer of a model of rectification and to respond appropriately.

There are two principle means by which models of rectification can be recognized. Perhaps the most common is the *should-statement*, a statement from a patient that something 'should' be organized in some way, that someone 'should' behave in a certain manner, and so on (or the converse that something 'should not' occur in some way). The word 'should' should alert the therapist to the possibility that a model of rectification is on offer.

Mr M, a psychotherapist, was forced to make several changes in his working schedule which directly affected his work with a patient, Mrs B. Mr M canceled two consecutive sessions and negotiated mutually acceptable alternative times with Mrs B. In the next hour Mrs B spoke of workmen from the Electricity Board who had arranged to visit her home to give her an estimate for some re-wiring. They did not show up at the time arranged, but telephoned her later in the afternoon to arrange a visit on the following day. This was very inconvenient for Mrs B, who went on to describe the workmen as careless and in all probability incompetent. She stated emphatically that a service should not be run in such a sloppy way. Workmen should be more reliable so the customer knows where she stands. Once something is professionally agreed, it should be adhered to.

Here the therapist's rescheduling of the patient is unconsciously regarded as careless, incompetent, and sloppy. The patient states, through her derivative model of rectification, that the therapist should be more reliable, sticking to his original agreement.

Models of rectification may also be conveyed through sharply contrasting derivative images: a representation of the therapist's inappropriate behavior is juxtaposed with a portrayal of the more desirable option. Any derivative mention of contrasts between good and poor workmanship, responsible and irresponsible behavior, honesty and dishonesty, and so forth, would alert the therapist to a possible model of rectification.

After a sequence of incorrect and highly non-neutral interventions a psychotherapy patient opened the following session by describing the upcoming American elections. She had witnessed a debate between the two vice-presidential candidates, Quayle and Bentsen, on the television and considered it to be 'horrible'. Quayle, she said, was an incompetent fool, a complete idiot. She could not imagine how the American people could choose him for such a position of power. Bentson, on the other hand, appeared to be a much better and more honest man.

In this sequence Quayle represents the incompetent, foolish side of the therapist which is incompatible with his role. She counsels that the therapist take a more honest stance, like she perceives in Bentson.

Attempts to heal the therapist

As I described in Chapter 4, the notion that patients attempt to heal their therapists goes back to the work of Ferenczi, was touched upon by Balint and Little, and was explicitly developed by Searles. Unconscious curative efforts are expressed by patients in a variety of ways. In response to a therapist who is expressively troubled by derivative meaning, for example, a patient may cease producing derivatives in an effort to 'stabilize' (as Langs puts it) his or her therapist. Efforts to cure the therapist are frequently expressed in derivative fashion.

All therapist errors are unconsciously perceived by patients as expressions of madness or emotional instability. This creates a highly charged therapeutic field saturated with a quality of psychological danger to the patient. Many patients strive, under such circumstances, to heal the therapist in order to restore a secure, benign therapeutic atmosphere. As Searles (1975) wrote, if the patient can restore the therapist's sanity, he or she then becomes capable of truly helping the patient.

Unconscious therapeutic strivings usually take the form of encoded *unconscious interpretations* which convey important insights into the defenses, conflicts, and motives of the therapist.

> Ms S, a trainee therapist working in a psychiatric clinic, was assigned Mr P, a young man suffering from depression, for treatment. Prior to the onset of the therapy this patient had been interviewed by a psychiatrist with students present as observers and then, after a long delay, was informed by post that he would receive psychotherapy from Ms S. The patient did not pay a fee. At the start of the first session Ms S introduced herself and mentioned that she was in training before going on to describe her way of working. After a few interchanges Mr P described how his mother had been quite depressed when she was young. She had married early and had never had the opportunity to develop an independent life for herself. Mr P's mother had just qualified as a counselor, and knew from experience what depression was like.

The patient uses the image of his mother here as a representation of the therapist. The patient inferred, quite accurately, that his therapist had strong depressive propensities (this may have been deduced, in part, from her choice of confessing to the patient that she was still in training). The patient also offered unconsciously the very plausible hypothesis that this therapist had never developed a strong sense of her own autonomy. Mr P's final comment shows that he felt that there was some common ground between them by virtue of these features of her personality.

COMMUNICATIVE INTERVENTIONS

In normal psychoanalysis the criteria for intervening and the form and content of acceptable interventions are loosely defined, intuitive, and impressionistic. Although lip-service is paid to the centrality of the interpretation of unconscious contents and processes, psychoanalytic interventions are very often manifest-content orientated and non-interpretative. Communicative psychoanalytic practice contrasts sharply with this. Acceptable interventions always address, in one way or another, the unconscious domain, and there are clearly defined rules for intervening. There are, in fact, only a small number of interventions that are consistent with communicative practice: these are *frame management, interpretation, silence,* and, under very special cirumstances, *soliciting free associations.*[4] All of the other types of intervention used quite freely in other modes of psychoanalysis and psychotherapy such as confrontation, reflecting back, questioning, and offering educational interventions are ruled out. The restricted interventional repertoire of the communicative psychotherapist is not an expression of obsessional rigidity, nor does it betoken a mistrust of intuition or an impoverishment of imagination. It is based on the observation that there are only very few kinds of intervention which, when used at the appropriate time, will receive derivative validation. It is a hard saying, and may strike the reader as flagrantly dogmatic, that consistent attention to the derivative sequelae of intervention reveals that other types of intervention are unconsciously felt by patients as seductive, assaultive, and defensive rather than genuinely therapeutic.

Frame management is an ongoing activity from the beginning of therapy until its termination. The ground rules are set out in the initial consultation and, in so far as they approximate the optimal secure frame, are maintained throughout the treatment. Frame management becomes a salient aspect of therapy at those moments when the patient responds to a deviant aspect of the frame or attempts to modify the secure frame in some way. The basic rule for the management of the frame in such situations is that the frame is to be structured according to the patient's unconscious behest. If the patient unconsciously addresses a deviation and derivatively informs the therapist that this should be rectified, the therapist should interpret this material and, if possible, alter the frame accordingly. Patients often try to unilaterally modify the secure frame because of the powerful existential anxieties that it evokes. A proposed alteration – such as a request for physical contact, a change of schedule, an offer of a gift – should neither be refused nor concurred with. The communicative therapist listens for the patient's unconscious guidance as to how he or she should handle the situation. The therapist waits for the patient to derivatively indicate the correct path to take, and must be fully prepared to follow the patient's unconscious recommendations. Strangely, patients virtually always unconsciously recommend to therapists that they should maintain the secure frame and refrain from any deviation.

A therapist had allowed his patient to defer payment of his account for several weeks. The payment, as usual, was to be provided by the patient's mother as she herself was in dire financial need. At the beginning of the session to be described the patient, whom I will call Ms K, handed the therapist a cheque signed by her mother and began immediately to talk about a colleague at work who was extremely unreliable, unprofessional, and 'a real creep'. Ms K next went on to recount how a friend had offered to buy her an expensive meal. Although this seemed attractive, Ms K refused, feeling that it would in some way be inappropriate. Another friend, who was living with a man, had recently had a clandestine affair, and spoke in a derogatory way to the new man about her partner. Ms K felt that there was something perverted about this arrangement.

The patient responds here to the therapist's tolerance of delayed payment and the third-party involvement of her mother. Although consciously very grateful to him, she unconsciously regards him as behaving in an unreliable and unprofessional manner. She compares the delayed and third-party payment situation to the free offer of a lavish meal, and offers a model of rectification: the therapist should reject this as inappropriate. The involvement of Ms K's mother reminds her of a perverse triangular relationship, and she feels that the therapist and her mother are engaged in a hostile alliance against her.

Here is another example of a patient attempting to correct a therapist who has conceded to a request for a frame deviation.

A rather schizoid patient requested her therapist to alter the time of one of their sessions. The therapist was guided by the belief that it was important to be 'flexible' with this patient, even though it caused him considerable inconvenience. In the session after this had been agreed, this patient thanked and complied with her request (stressing how helpful it had been). She went on to reflect upon how different her therapist was from the analyst whom she had been seeing before, who would never agree to change the set routine. Then, seemingly changing the subject, she complained about the unreasonable demands made upon her at work. She gave in to these demands and allowed herself to be exploited. This, she thought, must stem from some powerful need for approval. It was this that led her to yield, even though the situation was destructive both to her and to the organization as a whole. People should know where to draw the line.

Again, typically, the therapist is consciously praised but unconsciously damned for going along with the deviation. The image of a therapist who goes along with the demands made on him and allows himself to be exploited is introjected by the patient and reinforces her own lack of autonomy. The patient offers the unconscious interpretation that the therapist agreed to the requested schedule change because of his powerful need for approval. The deviation, she argues, is destructive. The therapist should know where to draw the line.

In normal psychoanalysis interpretations refer basically to the intrapsychic realm, attempting to explain patients' behavior in terms of archaic drives, phantasies, defenses, and object relations. The therapist is taken into account merely as a transference object, a pretext for the reliving of infantile experiences. The basic structure of normal psychoanalytic interpretations therefore runs something like this: 'You (the patient) are behaving in such and such a way because you are frightened of the emergence of some terrifying memory/phantasy/ desire within you.' Communicative interpretations, on the other hand, are fully interactional. They trace out how the patient is unconsciously responding to some trigger arising in the therapeutic situation. The skeletal form of a communicative interpretation is: 'I (the therapist) have done a, you (the patient) have perceived this to imply x, y, and z, which is why you are behaving in such and such a way.'

In order to formulate such an explanation one must be able to identify the efficient cause of the behavior to be explained (the trigger), the way that the patient has unconsciously construed this stimulus (the derivatives), and the behavior to be explained, which is called an 'indicator'. Indicators are direct or indirect manifestations of emotional pain in the patient. There are two types of indicator: symptoms and resistances. 'Symptoms' in this context include both relatively minor emotionally founded phenomena such as nightmares, tension headaches, and anxiety states, and the more extreme conversions, obsessive thoughts, delusions, and so on. Symptoms can occur either inside or outside of the therapeutic environment. Resistances, on the other hand, always occur in psychotherapy sessions. According to classical theory:

> All those forces within the patient which oppose the procedures and processes of analysis, i.e. which hinder the patient's free association, which interfere with the patient's attempts to remember and to gain and assimilate insight, which operate against the patient's reasonable ego and his wish to change; all of these forces are to be considered resistance.
>
> (Greenson 1967: 60)

Greenson goes on to list numerous manifestations of resistance such as silence, absence of affect, inappropriateness of affect, forms of posture, fixation of associations in the past, present or future, discussion of trivia or external events, the avoidance of certain topics, rigidity of behavior, evasive language, lateness, missing hours, failure to pay, the absence of dreams, and so on and so on. He emphasizes that this is by no means exhaustive for 'resistances may occur in a variety of subtle and complex ways' (ibid.) and, in fact, 'There is no activity that cannot be misused for the purposes of resistance' (ibid.: 61). It follows from all of this that anything that a patient does or refrains from doing can be considered as an expression of resistance in so far as an analyst regards it as operating in opposition to the analysis. Apart from this rather subjective judgement there are no clear rules for determining what is and what is not resistance in normal psychoanalytic practice.

In communicative psychotherapy the concept of resistance is operationalized. It is no longer seen as a mysterious force or confluence of forces inside the patient's head: it is seen as a form of behavior. There are two ways in which resistance is expressed: one of these is a manifest statement by the patient that he or she feels stuck or blocked in the therapy; the other is the violation of the agreed ground rules of therapy. The latter includes protracted silences (which break the rule of free association), failure to attend sessions, late arrivals, attempts to engage the therapist in conversation, and so on. This explicit definition of resistance leaves little scope for ambiguity and arbitrary judgement.

So long as the patient has not provided a representation of a trigger, a rich sequence of derivatives and an indicator interpretation are not warranted. By the same token, as soon as this 'recipe for interpretation' (Langs 1985f) has been fulfilled it is opportune to offer an interpretation.

Because of transport difficulties, a therapist, Mr S, arrived ten minutes late for his session with Mr D, his patient. Mr S immediately apologized, explaining why he had been held up, and offered to extend the patient's hour ten minutes by way of compensation. The patient readily agreed to this and seemed reassured. Mr D then began to recount an experience that had been troubling him for several days. In some business dealings with a firm of solicitors Mr D had been unable to reach a particular person with whom he needed to speak. The man was out of the office when Mr D 'phoned, but a secretary informed him that the solicitor would soon be back and would return the call in about an hour. Mr D waited for an entire afternoon but received no telephone call. Finally, he 'phoned the solicitor's office again and managed to get through to the right person, who apologized profusely and offered an elaborate explanation as to why he had been unable to return the call. The patient was secretly very suspicious of this explanation and decided to himself to transfer his business to a different solicitor. All too often in life, the patient reflected, one ends up depending upon people who are basically dishonest and are only interested in getting away with as much as they can. Mr D then complained of a headache that had been coming on since the beginning of the session.

All three ingredients for an interpretation appear in this vignette. The trigger for the material is the therapist's lateness, his apology and explanation. It is best under such circumstances to begin the session in the normal fashion and interpret the patient's reaction to the lateness as it emerges naturally. Apologies and explanations indicate strong defensive needs and suggest that the therapist is attempting to preempt and truncate the patient's expression of disapproval and disappointment. The account of the solicitor provides a derivative commentary on the trigger. The themes concern a meeting that did not take place at the appropriate time, a person who apologizes and explains himself in a way that evokes suspicion, the decision to take one's business elsewhere, and the dilemma of being dependent upon dishonest and greedy people. The solicitor is, of course, a representation of the therapist. Finally, the mention of the headache is a symptom indicator. A correct interpretation of this material must conform to a certain structure if the intervention is to be successful. The rules for the construction of a communicative interpretation are as follows.

The therapist should begin with the best representation of the trigger. If the patient has manifestly referred to a trigger, this is the best place to start. If there has been no manifest mention of a trigger, it is possible to use thinly disguised portrayals if the patient has, in some general way, mentioned the therapeutic situation (for instance, the patient might say 'it's nice being here'). The general reference to therapy in such cases provides what is called a 'bridge to therapy' which provides some justification for linking derivative imagery to the here-and-now situation and without which any interpretation, however accurate, will possess an arbitrary, hollow ring. In the present example there is no need to worry about bridges to therapy because there is a manifest mention of the trigger at the beginning of the session. The start of our interpretation will therefore run like this: 'At the beginning of this session we talked about my late arrival. You said it was OK after I apologized. You said that you understood how difficult public transport can sometimes be. . . .'

Next one must select the derivative images that seem linked with the known triggers. It is essential to stay as close as possible to the shades of meaning intended by the patient. At the same time, though, one must be selective in picking out the level of meaning most relevant to the triggers at hand. These derivatives are listed sequentially before any attempt is made to explain them to the patient.

> . . . After that you talked about your efforts to speak to the solicitor. He was not there when you wanted to discuss something with him and treated you inconsiderately in not returning your call. When you finally reached him you were most suspicious of his apology and explanation and you decided to take your business elsewhere. You talked about how one is often dependent upon dishonest and greedy people, like your solicitor.

Having listed all of the relevant derivatives, one then goes on to interpret their unconscious meaning in light of the triggers.

> . . . It seems to me that all this is connected. I, like the solicitor, was not here when you wanted to speak to me, and you feel that this was very inconsiderate. Also, like the solicitor, I offered you explanations and apologies, and it seems that you see this as suspicious. As a result of my lateness today and the way that I handled the issue once the session began you feel that in being in therapy with me you are dependent on a dishonest and self-interested person. From what you said about finding a new solicitor it sounds like you may be considering finding a new therapist because of all this. . . .

Finally, one links the derivatives and trigger to the indicator: '. . . Perhaps these concerns have produced the headache that has been coming on since the session began.'

This is a fairly typical example of a communicative interpretation. Although it may seem a daunting task to remember to link the trigger, derivatives, and indicator together appropriately, the essential principle is very simple and logical. If we view the patient's mind as an information-processing system, the *input* of information is the trigger, the *unconscious processing* of the information is reflected in the derivatives, and the behavior *output* is the indicator. Communicative interpretations attempt to capture the entire sequence from input through to processing and output.

As long as the recipe for intervening has not been fulfilled the appropriate intervention is silence. In communicative psychotherapy silence is understood to be an active intervention rather than a mere lack or absence. A Japanese riddle poses the question 'What is the most important part of a rice bowl?' The answer is 'the space inside'. Silence is such a space. It gives the patient a chance to speak and the therapist a chance to listen. So long as the patient has not provided the therapist with enough material for an interpretation, silence is warranted. If, however, a therapist remains silent after a patient has supplied the elements for an intervention – a representation of a trigger, derivatives, and indicator – this silence becomes inappropriate. Patients respond to inappropriate silence in various ways. Some patients tend to renew their efforts at derivative communication, often offering unconscious messages to the effect that an interpretation has been missed. These *missed intervention derivatives* allude to the therapist's inappropriate silence through themes of people not getting in touch, overlooking important things, being blind, and so on. Another common response to a missed intervention is for the patient to ask the therapist directly to say something. When asked by a patient who does not use it habitually, this question almost always occurs at the moment when a silence has become inappropriate. Even psychotherapists who are not familiar with the communicative criteria for interpreting often feel intuitively that an intervention is warranted at just that point when the last element of the recipe for interpreting has been supplied by the patient.

What does a communicative psychotherapist do in response to a direct question from a patient, or a sudden proposal to modify the frame? Because the golden rule of the approach is to be guided by the patient's unconscious wisdom, there is little point in responding directly on a manifest level. In these circumstances a communicative therapist may choose to be silent, as silence implicitly conveys that the therapist is waiting for derivative material. A second option is to say 'Let's see what comes to mind' or some equivalent statement. By soliciting free associations in this manner it is usually possible to identify the unconscious issues prompting the patient's question and to understand the patient's unconscious recommendations about how to handle the situation.

Each time the communicative therapist offers an interpretation or secures the frame, he or she listens carefully to the subsequent derivatives to determine whether or not the intervention has been validated. A validated intervention is followed by highly constructive derivative themes, which indicate that the patient unconsciously regards the intervention as truly therapeutic. *A communicative intervention is considered appropriate only if it is followed by constructive derivative imagery.*[5] If the patient responds with negative imagery after the intervention, the communicative therapist concludes that his efforts were seriously flawed.

To set out upon the communicative path requires an attitude of humility. There is no opportunity to play the part of an all-knowing 'guru' in this approach, for one must be willing to be led every step of the way by the deep unconscious recommendations from the patient. One must also be prepared to be confronted with all of the weaknesses, defenses, and psychological problems which would normally be swept under the carpet. These inner factors are highlighted in an unbelievably incisive manner and although it can be extremely painful, it is encumbent upon the communicative psychotherapist to consciously come to terms with patients' perceptive unconscious insights and to spell these out in his or her interpretations. It is not a nice thing to be told that one is perverse, self-serving, parasitic, mentally ill, and so on. To embrace this dimension of reality goes against all of our natural defensive tendencies, and yet it only amounts to us doing precisely that which we expect of our patients. We are required to struggle with the deep and frightening unconscious side of our nature, and to confront the existential terrors that lie therein. In working as a communicative therapist one must come to accept one's own limitations and faults and, in accepting these, to change. To work as a communicative therapist means to be 'in therapy' every working hour of the day. The deep unconscious mind of the patient is the therapist's therapist. No psychotherapist can hope to consciously match the psychological sensitivity of the deep unconscious system. One is perpetually 'outclassed', trotting, as it were, behind the patient trying to keep up. Because of this one could not hope to find a better therapist than one encounters in the deep unconscious system of one's patients.

By its very nature, communicative psychotherapy makes tremendous emotional demands upon its practitioners. One's psyche is continually 'on the line'. Learning the approach can be a shattering experience both for the newcomer to the world of psychotherapy and to the established practitioner who is trying to expand his or her repertoire. Friedman (1987) graphically recounts the trials and tribulations of the novice. The first stage of learning the technique involves coming face to face with one's own destructiveness. As a therapist begins to acquire some facility in decoding patients' unconscious messages as valid commentaries on the therapeutic process, his or her idealized self-image as a healer is challenged. Many therapists respond to this discovery in a way that is primarily defensive.

One therapist attempted to deny his errors by deleting material for supervision that might show him in a negative light. . . . Other therapists attempted to deny outright that the derivative material contained encoded perceptions of them. They also resorted to blaming the problems of therapy on the patient's resistances, lack of motivation, hostility or primitive character structure.

(ibid.: 165)

Another common reaction at this stage is to round on the communicative approach itself in an effort to conceal a sense of personal inadequacy.

At times Langs was blamed for adhering so rigidly to the concept of the frame and the patient's derivatives. This was probably so because he was the bearer of bad tidings . . . and therefore aroused the impulse to 'kill the messenger' just as the ancient Greeks did.

(ibid.)

A large percentage of people flee from the approach at this juncture as they realize the deep psychological transformation that is required. Others, leaving behind their former narcissistic attitude, enter a depressive period.

For most therapists . . . these flimsy defenses inevitably broke down and psychological symptoms were experienced. Depression seemed to be the most commonplace. This included self-doubt, tremendous feelings of inadequacy, and self-deprecating thoughts that became ruminative and obsessional. One therapist seriously wondered whether he possessed the intellectual capacity to learn the approach. Another was convinced that he could not continue practicing the communicative approach without massive doses of personal psychotherapy. A third therapist did return to therapy when her self-worth took a dramatic plunge.

(ibid.)

Friedman goes on to quote some remarks made to her by an experienced psychoanalytic psychotherapist who was striving to learn the approach:

This has been difficult work. It means, in essence, taking everything I have known how to do, everything I have perfected in the sphere where I feel most confident, and tossing it aside. . . . It is as though I have built a house that I believed to be beautiful, and yet when I looked at the foundation with Langs, I see that there are all sorts of flaws and termites, and that the foundation is not at all substantial.

(165–6)

Any communicative therapist will be able to confirm the painful, humiliating qualities of the learning process. Yet, in persevering the learner comes eventually to realize that he or she can make positive, constructive therapeutic contributions. As soon as one starts to get it right – to make sound communicative interpretations – patients begin to respond with expressions of profound appreciation and gratitude and make real therapeutic progress. It is only at that point that one sets foot on the other shore: one has become a communicative psychotherapist.

How does communicative therapy cure? The approach clearly does not rely on making the unconscious conscious, as does classical psychoanalysis: it does not rest upon *conscious* insight. Invoking vague and hypothetical processes like 'holding' and 'introjecting the therapist as a good object' do not avail, for they merely explain the obscure through the even more obscure. Suggestion, placebo effects, conditioning, and so on are not the operative factors either.

It is difficult to know just how it is that communicative therapy cures. The processes involved are deeply private and hard to access. One thing is certain: *the deep unconscious experience of being truly understood sets off the curative process.* The experience of receiving an accurate communicative interpretation is probably a unique experience. In no other situation are derivative presentations of threatening unconscious perceptions met with understanding and respect. There seems to be something about this experience which has a profound impact on the basic unconscious cognitive schemata through which the patient organizes his or her experiences of the world. Phenomenologically, it is is clear that the world becomes a 'different place' for the patients after a good communicative interpretation has been offered. Initially, of course, the patient experiences a spontaneous upsurge of positively toned, constructive mental imagery, but this, it seems is part of a larger process of cognitive reorientation. For reasons that are not yet clearly understood, patients become more sensitive to the nurturing, creative, and constructive dimensions of life in the aftermath of a sound communicative interpretation. I recall an example of a patient who received an extremely skillful communicative interpretation toward the end of a session. The intervention was given striking and unequivocal derivative validation – the patient spoke of having had an experience of enlightenment when visiting a Buddhist temple – and this in turn was followed, in the ensuing week, by a transformation of the relationship between the patient and her elderly father. The patient, who had hitherto been hostile toward the old man, suddenly began to see him differently. She realized that she really cared for him deeply and this led to a moving *rapprochement* between the two of them. It is as though the caring attitude implicit in a good communicative intervention is contagious: it progressively 'infects' the patient's whole orientation to herself and to the world around.

In the next chapter we will examine this process *in vivo* through the work of two British psychotherapists who were courageous enough to move through the disheartening early stages of learning the approach to arrive at the point of being capable of deep and sensitive communicative work.

9   Two communicative sessions

Physician, help yourself: thus you help your patient too. Let this be the best help that he may behold with his eyes the man who heals himself.

Nietzsche

One criticism leveled against communicative psychotherapists is that they do not present samples of their own work for public scrutiny. Gill, for one, complains that:

> To some extent Langs is able to maintain the illusion that the good analyst will behave essentially appropriately by using the work of relatively inexperienced trainees for his clinical demonstrations. He is not willing to submit his own work for examination, on the grounds that to do so would violate the rule of privacy.
>
> (Gill 1984: 400)

Although there is much with which to take issue in Gill's remarks, they do possess a certain validity in that the vast bulk of the clinical communicative literature deals with examples of poor, non-communicative therapeutic work. There are comparatively few detailed presentations of sound communicative analytic work presented by Langs (see Langs 1981, 1985c). The paucity of published examples of good communicative work is no doubt partially due to therapists' sensitivity to the deleterious effects of violations of patients' privacy and disruptions of confidentiality, but there can be little doubt that this seriously weakens the communicative case. With little detailed data from correctly conducted psychotherapeutic sessions to draw on, readers have little reason to believe that the communicative approach has anything truly constructive to offer. Why, for example, should a reader believe the communicative claim that correctly constructed interpretations consistently receive derivative validation? There are precious few published transcripts of communicative sessions containing appropriate interventions. It could be said that in keeping their confirmatory data close to their chests, communicative therapists commit the very sin that they reproach in others: the failure to report psychotherapy sessions fully, unambiguously, and in a manner not skewed by therapists' own assumptions.

The present chapter is a contribution to the small literature giving examples of communicative psychotherapy in action. It is devoted to two detailed accounts of communicative sessions conducted by British practitioners who have generously made transcripts of their work available to me. The fact that these therapists have allowed me to use their work does not bespeak any blunting of ethical sensibilities on their part, but arises from their appreciation of the need for published examples of communicative work.

Both of these sessions are fairly typical examples. It is common for therapists who have delved into the communicative literature without any experience of applying the method to assume that communicative practitioners hold themselves up as paragons of correct technique. This is not at all the case, as I hope the two transcripts will decisively demonstrate. Characteristically, the first portions of a communicative session center upon some error that the therapist has committed. In a 'good' communicative hour the therapist is able to comprehend the meaning of the patient's derivatives pertaining to the error, interpret the derivatives, possibly rectify the situation, and receive derivative validation for the effort. There is no pretence of being above and beyond error — far from it.

Some of the details of the two accounts have been altered in order to protect the identity of the participants. These modifications are in all instances trivial, and do not affect the sense of the reported interchanges. Both transcripts were transcribed by the therapists from memory and written down immediately after the sessions ended. Communicative therapists object to the use of electronic recording as a violation of the secure frame, so there will inevitably be some sacrifice of complete accuracy in spite of the fact that the sessions were recorded as faithfully as possible.

FIRST EXAMPLE

The session to be described involves a female therapist, who is skillful but not yet very experienced in the use of the communicative approach, and a thirteen-year-old female patient. The patient had been referred to the therapist — at her mother's insistence — because of difficulties in school. She was seen in a clinical setting where the mother was also in treatment. A week prior to the present session the patient's mother had telephoned the therapist to enquire about her daughter's progress and the therapist had, against her better judgement, allowed herself to be drawn into a discussion: a major violation of privacy and confidentiality.

The present session begins with a long silence. The patient then speaks.

> *Patient*: Jessica is still playing up. She has now got her mother to ring up the school so that the headteacher could speak to Julia and me. She wants us to be nice to Jessica. I don't think she should have done this behind our backs. [*pause*] No wonder we can't be best friends. I thought I could trust her.

The patient begins the hour in a derivative mode: she tells stories about people outside of therapy. The first theme to be introduced is that of a mother who makes a clandestine telephone call which pertains to the patient. This is a very thinly disguised representation of the trigger of the therapist's telephone conversation with the patient's mother. The first component of the recipe for interpreting − the trigger − has therefore been supplied. Because it is so very thinly disguised it might be possible to use this portrayal without the support of a general bridge to therapy, if need be.

As the narrative unfolds it turns out that Jessica's mother got the headteacher to try and get the two other girls to be 'nice' to Jessica. The theme is one person pressuring someone else to do her bidding and, as such, appears to be a representation of the conspiratorial quality of the telephone conversation. The patient feels that her therapist has become her mother's 'lackey'. Next comes an implicit model of rectification: the patient thinks that the therapist should not have done this behind her back. Two more derivatives follow which convey that this situation makes it impossible for the patient to be close with the therapist and to trust her.

This young patient emerges as a powerful derivative communicator. She goes directly to the acute break in the frame and addresses it by means of bold, unambiguous derivatives. This will, inescapably, place the therapist in a difficult situation. Under the impact of these strong images of her undermining behavior the therapist has two basic emotional options: to react defensively or to move toward a valid communicative interpretation. The second course of action will require further silent holding. Although the protracted silence at the beginning of the session *could* be used as an indicator, it would be

better to have something more definitive. A deep and thorough interpretation would also require more derivatives. Let us see how the
therapist responds.

Therapist: You sound very disappointed with Jessica, as though she
betrayed you.

This intervention is predominantly defensive. The therapist merely
picks out a rather obvious implication of the patient's manifest
material. There is no reference to the therapeutic situation at all. The
appropriate communicative intervention at this juncture would have
been silence. There is not yet any justification for a verbal intervention.

Because of this therapist's lapse into a non-communicative mode,
the situation at once becomes more complex. By intervening, in a
manifest-content orientated way this therapist *implicitly* says that she
cannot handle the unconscious message that the patient wants to get
across. It is as if she says, 'I don't want to know about the implications of my own actions. Let's talk about you and Jessica instead'.
This defensive move cannot fail to become an additional trigger for
the material to follow. It can be safely predicted that the patient's next
derivative communication will be negatively toned and portray the
defensive implications of this intervention.

Patient: I just think she is very weak. She should have told me how
she felt rather than doing this behind my back. Now she has
involved her mother and the whole school in this. [*silence*] I am
angry with her. Last Saturday after I had been to see you, Julia and
I went to the cinema. We had made arrangements for this in class
and we knew Jessica had overheard us. And who should be there
but Jessica! She pretended not to see us and when we asked what
she was doing there it was all an accident, that she didn't know we
were going to be there. But I knew she knew. I knew I was right but
she would never admit to this.

The patient's immediate unconscious commentary on the preceding
intervention is that it shows the therapist to be very weak. Then comes
a model of rectification (marked off by a should-statement) to the
effect that the therapist should speak directly with her patient rather
than going behind her back. The patient then alludes to the deviation
involving numerous other people in what is essentially a private matter.
This most probably pertains to a related background deviation: the
fact that she and her mother attend the same clinic for treatment. This

factor exacerbates the impact of the telephone conversation because the patient is probably well aware that her mother speaks about her in her own therapy sessions and that the two therapists speak to one another about mother and daughter. This creates a dangerously boundaryless situation. The patient is angry with the therapist about these things.

She next offers a general bridge to therapy, mentioning 'after I had been to see you'. A derivative theme of an unwanted third party (the mother) intruding on a one-to-one arrangement (patient and therapist) is brought forward. Jessica makes excuses, pretending not to be aware of what is really going on. The patient can see through this, but knows that Jessica will not own up. This is certainly a commentary on the therapist's defensiveness. Like Jessica, she will not own up to the telephone conversation and pretends that nothing untoward has happened. The patient, however, can see through this. Here we have a good example of the patient attempting to cure the therapist through the offer of an unconscious interpretation of resistance. It is as if the patient were saying 'You intervened in the way that you did because you are trying to pretend that the telephone conversation with my mother never happened.'

The pressure is clearly building up for the therapist. The patient not only refuses to join her in the pretense that the conversation with her mother was unimportant, she offers increasingly trenchant unconscious commentaries and even tries to interpret the therapist's behavior to her.

> *Therapist*: What seems to have upset you about this incident is that your perception of what had happened was not confirmed. Instead, Jessica pretended it was all a coincidence but you knew she had overheard you. This reminds me of how you described feeling in relation to your parents. They both give you different versions of events. Even though you tell me you know what was happening at the time, you sometimes start doubting.

Things are beginning to look bleak indeed. Oblivious to the absence of validation, the therapist presses on with a second inappropriate intervention. It is a rather half-hearted effort at a genetic interpretation. Once again the patient's material is not interpreted in light of the therapeutic situation. The therapist has reinforced her ostrich-like stance, and this will not escape the patient's notice. Once again the theory predicts non-validation and a derivative preoccupation with the therapist's attitude of denial.

Patient: I do get confused but I remember what happened. I just wish my mother would accept that even though I was young at the time of their divorce I was still aware of what was happening. [*silence*] She always uses the excuse that because I was young I don't know what I'm talking about . . . that I can't remember correctly. Then she goes on and on and tells me her version. But I remember she was drunk, and that she is the one that can't remember.

Once again the patient unconsciously responds to her therapist's failure to come to grips with the prevailing trigger, criticizing the therapist for treating her as though she were unaware of what had occurred. The patient feels that the therapist is infantilizing her, assuming that just because she is a child she is unaware of the framework deviation and its implications. The patient sees this as an excuse. In avoiding the issue of the telephone conversation and pressing the purely manifest dimension of the patient's discourse the therapist 'goes on and on', swamping the patient with 'her version' of what is important.

Images of alcoholic or chemical intoxication usually mean that the therapist is seen to resort to non-insightful methods of relieving anxiety. The patient has unconsciously concluded that this is precisely what is implied by the nature of the interventions that have been offered to her thus far. She goes on that it is the *therapist* who 'can't remember' (i.e. who is repressing the memory of the telephone conversation) and not she.

It would certainly be possible to give an interpretation at this point in the session. As noted before, the silence at the beginning of the session can serve as a resistance indicator. The patient has portrayed the main trigger in a thinly disguised manner and offered a general bridge to therapy. There are numerous powerful and explicit derivatives as well. A sound communicative intervention would have to spell out the implications of the frame violation and, secondarily, the therapist's interventional errors using the patients own derivative imagery and, in the end, use this material to explain why the patient was silent at the start of the session. Although this is possible, the task would be far easier if the patient were to *manifestly* allude to the trigger and produce a stronger indicator.

The therapist is in a rather poor position for doing the right thing. Her interventions betray considerable resistance to the patient's unconscious concerns. When a therapist has gone this far astray for this long (the session is now approaching its end) it is practically impossible to salvage the situation. A very strong effort at silent self-analysis will be required for this therapist to amend her attitude and contribute a truly insightful intervention.

Therapist: How does it feel when she tells you such things?

The therapist asks a question and continues to ignore the latent issues. Questions are never unconsciously validated by patients. They are experienced as attempts to shut down derivative communication by encouraging conscious rumination. This question, then, will confirm the patient's diagnosis of her therapist's difficulties.

Patient: I lose confidence in myself and I get angry. I often go and hide in the toilet just to get away from her. When I was little I used to go up to my room and lie on my bed talking to my teddy bears. I liked talking to them because I knew I could trust them. I could talk to them and they would not tell anyone what I had said because they could not speak. I could cry with them. [*long silence*]

The patient has begun to clearly show that she is in a state of distress. Her voice is full of suppressed weeping, she alludes to the loss of self-confidence and the feeling of anger, and describes her withdrawal into solitude. This is crowned by a long silence. At this point the indicators have become quite strong.

Derivatively, this material can be understood in two distinct ways: as alluding primarily to the therapist or as alluding primarily to the patient. According to one reading the patient is saying that the therapist is undermining her self-confidence and exacerbating feelings of anger. The patient tells the therapist that she is being driven into isolation and a regressive reliance on transitional objects because the therapist has once again confirmed that other people are not to be trusted with her deepest emotional issues. A second communicative analysis sees the first portion of this material as focused on the therapist. The patient says that the therapist is driven to her non-insightful measures because she lacks self-confidence and is angry with the patient. The therapist has autistically sealed herself off from her patient. Both hypotheses are plausible. The two can be reconciled on a higher level if we assume that the patient is now *introjecting* her unconscious perception of a withdrawn, angry psychotherapist.

The intensity of the indicators and the continued power of the derivative imagery show that a communicative interpretation is definitely warranted. The therapist, almost miracuously, rises to the challenge and offers a communicative interpretation.

Therapist: You started off your session today expressing your disappointment and anger with Jessica. You describe her as being weak. Instead of telling you up front what was wrong she got her mother to call the school. By doing this she brought other people into something which concerned just you and her. Also, last week when you met at the cinema she pretended that your meeting was a chance meeting even though you knew that she had overheard your arrangements with Julia. You felt she was unwilling to admit to this and it seems important to you that people are honest.

You also describe how you could only talk to your teddy bears as they were the only ones with whom you could have a unique, safe relationship without bringing anyone else in. I think you might feel betrayed by me because not only have I had some contact with your mother when she called me but I have not mentioned this to you. You seem to be stressing that your mother, or anyone else, should not be involved in this relationship. It should be like the relationship you had with your teddy bears or else you feel betrayed.

Let us have a detailed look at this interpretation, evaluating its assets and liabilities.

On the positive side it complies with the general formula for communicative interpretations. The therapist attempts to explain an indicator – the patient's state of distress – through unconscious responses to the two triggers of the telephone conversation and her subsequent dishonesty about the issue. On the whole, this was done in a satisfactory way.

In spite of this the interpretation does possess some major flaws. The therapist does not make use of the patient's bridge to therapy. She also does not make use of all of the derivatives (for instance, she does not mention the allusions to undermining the patient's self-confidence and driving her into isolated withdrawal – the derivatives that the therapist involuntarily omits are invariably those that he or she finds most threatening). Finally, and less importantly, the therapist does not make use of the patient's silences as indicators. It would be unreasonable, considering the circumstances, to criticize the therapist too sharply for these flaws. She was in a position of having to cobble together an interpretation under the pressure of time (the session was about to finish) and her own defensive needs. Given this context, the interpretation is remarkably well constructed.

Because of the mixed properties of the interpretation one would logically predict that the derivative response will also be mixed, containing some constructive validating imagery and also some negative derivatives in response to the intervention's defensive properties.

Patient: [*silence*] After my first session Mum asked me how it went. I just said I liked it. I needed someone to talk to but there are some things I just can't tell her. Dad also asked me why I came to see you. [*silence*]. I can talk to Julia. She really understands. We really get on. She really is my best friend. It's not that we don't argue but she seems to know when I'm upset. When I go all quiet she will eventually come up to me and asks what is wrong so that we can talk about it.

Therapist: It's time to finish now.

The patient begins by revealing that her mother and father have been asking her for information about the therapy. This provides further background context for the deviation. The statement that the patient can't talk about everything to her mother may be derivative response to her therapist's omissions (i.e. that the therapist can't handle certain of the patient's issues). Finally there comes a sequence of validating derivatives. The therapist 'really understands', patient and therapist 'really get on' like best friends. The final remarks allude to the indicator of the patient's silence. The therapist's final intervention was offered after a long period of silence by the patient. Although the silence is not mentioned at all in the interpretation, the patient is aware that it was this that prompted the therapist, expressing this through the beautiful image of a caring friend who asks what is the matter when the patient goes all quiet.

SECOND EXAMPLE

The patient in this example is as male Fine Arts student at a British polytechnic, who sought out therapy because of moderately severe neurotic depression. He had been in a relationship with two girls, one after the other, over a five-year period, and had just ended a third relationship fairly recently. His parents were divorced some six years previously.

The therapist, who was in the process of learning the communicative approach, saw this patient under the aegis of the polytechnic's student counseling service. This entailed a number of framework deviations. Therapists were forbidden to charge a fee for their work. The room in which patient and therapist met was situated in a busy building frequented by dozens of people each day. To obtain therapy through the counseling service the patient had to visit the Medical Center and speak to a receptionist, who was one of three people simultaneously in the office, and was asked to fill out a form. On the basis of information given in the form, the patient was assigned to a therapist.

A consultation session was arranged in which the patient described his difficulties and the therapist set out the ground rules of treatment. They agreed to meet once a week for six weeks initially, after which they would review the situation (this practice was required by the counseling service).

The patient arrived on time for the next session and sat in silence for approximately five minutes.

> *Patient*: I've been feeling quite happy for two or three days, which is strange for me. [*pause*] Oh, I've been depressed a bit a couple of times during the week, but not too badly.

Unlike the patient in our first example, this young man opens with non-derivative discourse. The therapist's silence implicitly invites the patient to delve more deeply.

> It's odd, but I've felt different since coming here last week, even though it was the first time; even spending just that short time with you. I find myself looking at people quite differently. Even just sitting in the park or in the refectory, I find myself looking at people and wondering what's going on in their minds.

The patient continues in a basically non-derivative vein, which does, however, contain a general reference to therapy which might serve as a 'bridge to therapy' in a later interpretation. The last sentence has a slightly derivative quality: the patient is wondering what is going on in the therapist's mind.

> *Patient*: You know, in a place like this it is difficult to know who you can talk to. You don't know who you can trust. I was having a chat in the refectory with someone from my class the other day, when I noticed that two people I don't even know who were sitting at the next table were actually listening in to our conversation.

The patient begins to recount an experience: the material begins to definitely take on derivative characteristics. The theme of third parties listening in on a private conversation between two people is an apt representation of the gross violations of the rules of privacy and confidentiality riddling this treatment setting. The refectory – a public, impersonal place where the same basic fare is dished up to hundreds of people – is a marvelous representation of the counseling service. At this point, therefore, there is a general bridge to therapy and a derivative portrayal of a set of triggers. The initial silence might be construed as an indicator. The reference to depression in the intervening week is a good symptom-indicator. In theory, then it would be possible for the therapist to offer an interpretation at this early point in the session. This, however, would not be advisable because the patient has not yet presented a very full, complex derivative picture. As he has only just begun communicating unconsciously in this session, it is probable that more derivatives will be forthcoming.

Patient: My first reaction was to tell them something like 'Why the hell don't you mind your own business?' but then I thought 'what the hell'.

The patient offers a model of rectification: third parties should not be involved in the therapy. He continues:

Patient: When I got back to the flat, I told my flat-mate Bill about it. He knows what I'm going through at the moment. We were discussing the business of talking to other people. I told him that I'd been wondering whether it's possible for me to just get on with it and try to get my life together on my own or whether it's better to talk to other people. Bill is the one who told me about counseling in college. He'd been for a year and found it very helpful.

The patient now presents some faintly positive imagery. The patient describes talking to someone who understands his dilemma and someone who found counseling helpful. These are probably responses to the therapist's appropriate silence, which gives the patient the impression of being listened to with understanding. He also offers a further indicator: the thought of sorting out his problems by himself rather than with the aid of a therapist. Now that the derivatives are more complete and another indicator has been brought in the time is ripe for an interpretation. The therapist's task is to explain the indicators – the initial silence, the depression, and, most importantly, the thoughts about leaving therapy – through the implications of the trigger. The therapist has to find a way of conveying to the patient the hypothesis that the violations of privacy and confidentiality are unconsciously causing distress.

Therapist: You've been talking about looking at people differently, wondering about what they're thinking and what's going on in their minds. You've also said something about trust: not being sure who could be trusted. There was also something about people listening in to your private conversations. You mentioned something about wondering whether it was possible for you to sort out your life by yourself, or whether it was necessary to talk to other people. . . .

This is not a very promising beginning. The therapist has neglected the rule of starting with the clearest representation of the trigger. It would have been better to begin with the bridges to therapy, move on to the derivative portrayal of the trigger and then specify the model of rectification. This would run something like this:

> You've mentioned coming here a couple of times in what you've been saying – so this situation here must be on your mind. You went on to talk about something that seemed on the surface to be quite unrelated. You were having a private conversation with a friend when you noticed some people listening in. Your first impulse was to tell them to mind their own business. You also mentioned not being sure who you can trust around here.

The therapist continued with the interpretative portion of the intervention.

> *Therapist*: Well, it seems to me that you've been making reference to our situation right here and now. From what you told me before, you had to speak to a receptionist in the Medical Center about wanting counseling. There were other people in the office and you must have been aware that there was no privacy or confidentiality there. They could all listen in and hear what you were saying. You must be wondering who you can trust. This includes me. You're perhaps wondering whether I can be trusted. All this has also set you wondering whether it's really necessary for you to come and talk to someone like me, or whether you could just sort out your life by yourself.

This intervention has some difficulties. First, the therapist forces a link between the derivatives and the therapeutic situation. This would have been avoided had he begun with the bridge to therapy as illustrated above. Second, the therapist makes use of information from the previous consultation session to make his point. This goes against the rules of communicative therapy. The therapist should confine himself entirely to the material presented in the session at hand. By resorting to material from a previous session the therapist conveys either that he has insufficient grounds for his interpretation or, as is true in this case, he is unable to make full use of what the patient has just given him. Both of these errors express the therapist's impatience: his need to force the patient's resistances rather than fully respecting them.

The next error comes when the therapist talks about the issue of trust. He says that the patient is wondering whom he can trust, and this includes the therapist. By putting it in this way, the therapist rather defensively implies that he plays a merely secondary role here. The therapist would have done better to say 'You are wondering if you can trust me' or, more accurately, 'You don't know if you can trust me.' This is a common error: one is invariably inclined to play down or forget entirely those derivatives which we as therapists find most threatening. Finally, the therapist ignores the patient's model of rectification. A more technically correct version of the latter part of the interpretation, then, would have gone something like this:

> As you've mentioned being here a couple of times, I think that what you've been saying might be connected with your experience of coming to therapy. You seem to be saying that there's not enough confidentiality here, that you have a sense of other people intruding on what is supposed to be a private interchange. This leads you to feel that you might not be able to really talk to me and trust me. It's clear that you think that it is not right for other people to be involved in this situation – they should 'mind their own business'. Maybe this is why you were wondering about sorting things out on your own instead of coming to see me. It could be that deep down you feel that it may not be appropriate for us to work together unless I can provide complete privacy and confidentiality.

The model intervention that I have offered would almost certainly have received derivative validation. The therapist's actual intervention is marred by the errors enumerated but, nevertheless, does possess some constructive qualities. The therapist does manage to pick out the important trigger, interpret derivatives in light of it, and use this to explain an indicator. By communicative criteria, then, we are obliged to predict a rather mixed response from the patient. There will be some negative, nonvalidating imagery and some positive, validating imagery. In all probability the former will outweigh the latter.

> *Patient*: You know, my life seems to be so mixed up at the moment. I think I really need some help.

Manifestly, of course, this is a response to the issue of whether or not the patient should try to sort things out on his own. Derivatively, it sounds like a commentary on the intervention, portraying the therapist as floundering and confused.

> *Patient*: Just look at me! I want to paint and create things but we're required to produce things to order, almost. Like for the exams.

These remarks depict the quality of pressure on the patient implicit in the therapist's interpretation. There may also be a reference to an additional framework deviation: the six-week trial period. The patient is saying that he cannot work productively within this constraint. As for the reference to exams, we must bear in mind that the patient's progress is going to be 'reviewed' after the trial period has elapsed. This is unconsciously compared to an exam, and the patient feels under pressure to produce the right sort of the material in order to pass. A further possibility is that the patient is unconsciously aware that his therapist is a trainee, and under pressure to perform appropriately for his supervisor. This seems to be hinted at in the patient's next remark.

> *Patient*: And when you've finished the course, you're supposed to produce works of art that people will buy. Whereas all I want to do is to be creative.

As a reference to the therapist's status as a trainee, the patient appears to be saying that the experience of working under these constraints ill prepares the therapist for his future as a worker whose skills people will 'buy' (recall that the patient is not paying a fee). The patient may also be spelling out the implications of the frame deviations for himself. He finds the situation deeply contradictory and is unable to be fully creative under these circumstances. He feels – quite reasonably – that he is forced to conform to the requirements of others in this therapeutic situation, to 'produce works of art that people will buy'.

> *Patient*: It's the same like being short of money. I hate it. Yet I also hate the thought of being forced to go out to ask for work to get some money.

The reference to money may well pertain to the fact that the patient does not pay a fee. On a more unconscious level the patient feels that this, too, poses contradictions. He needs more sound conditions of treatment, but hates the thought of having to go elsewhere to obtain them.

> *Patient*: You know, I went home over the weekend. My mum was alone at home and for the first time ever I managed to talk with her on her own for a long time. I think that it's the first time I've ever spoken to her really seriously and intimately. I really felt close to her.

This is the expected validation for the constructive aspects of the interpretation which the patient says had a quality of seriousness and intimacy. But

Patient: It's so different when I visit my father. I just can't get close to him. He usually enters into a bantering, intellectual type of conversation with me. You know, I can be like that with anyone.

The split between mother and father represents the split that the patient accurately perceives in the therapist's attitudes and behavior. The patient offers an implicit model of rectification in the statement that he could have a distant, defensive conversation with just *anyone*. At this point the therapist attempts a second intervention.

You're talking about things in your life being really mixed up at the moment. On the one hand, you're wanting to paint and be creative, whilst on the other you're required to paint to order, for exams and the like. The question of money also seems to be cropping up. You also talk about ambivalent feelings regarding your mum and dad. You're managing to get close to and talk intimately with your mum, while it's exactly the opposite with your dad.

The therapist begins with derivative representations of three triggers: the trial period, the lack of a fee, and the defensive aspects of the preceding intervention. The situation is a bit awkward, though, in that there has been no bridge to therapy since the last intervention. The therapist should have introduced the bridge to therapy given by the patient earlier in the session to forge a link between the derivative communications and the here-and-now situation. He continues:

Therapist: It seems to me that you're quite mixed up about the situation confronting you here now.

This statement has a defensive quality. It would have been more appropriate for the therapist to say something like: 'It seems that you see me as quite mixed up now.'

Therapist: You're wanting to speak spontaneously and freely and yet you feel pressured to produce something to order that can be looked at, examined, and discussed.

Thus, the therapist implicitly relates these derivatives to the trigger of the trial period.

I think that the business about money has to do with the counseling service being free. Perhaps there's the feeling that it should really be paid for if it's to be any good. And yet the whole notion of paying is distasteful to you.

Now the trigger of the absence of a fee is brought in. This portion of the interpretation is rather confused. The patient has offered no unconscious communications to the effect that he only values therapy if he pays for it. The final sentence contains a distortion: the patient didn't say that *paying* was distasteful to him, he said that he hates the idea of being forced to ask for work.

> *Therapist*: You also have ambivalent feelings about our relationship. On the one hand, you're able to speak to me about quite intimate matters in a serious way and this is when you feel that I'm listening to you. On the other hand you regard what is going on between us as a sort of intellectual exercise, something which you could have with just anyone at all. You may perhaps see my approach as being somewhat bantering – as if I'm not taking what you say seriously. Hence the mixed-up feelings.

This interpretation is basically sound. A minor imperfection is the use of 'also' in the first sentence, which relegates the patient's relationship with the therapist to a secondary position. The patient's sense of being 'mixed-up' is taken as an indicator. Because the interpretation is substantially in accord with communicative criteria, and its constructive aspects far outweigh its problems, it is necessary to predict that the therapist's effort will be given derivative validation. After a long pause the patient says:

> *Patient*: You know, I went to the South of France last summer with Ingrid, my girlfriend at the time. You know, the one I broke up with. Well, we spent some time with this older guy we met – a French guy. I talked to him a helluva lot. He was a good listener. I used to laugh and ask him why it was that I could talk to him whereas I couldn't talk to people back home. He blamed it on the British being so phlegmatic. He used to say 'We French, we're not like the English. We understand emotions and feelings. We know about affairs of the heart!' We got on very well together.

> *Therapist*: We have to end the session now. Time's up. I'll see you next week at the same time.

The patient provides the expected validation, referring to the therapist as a good listener, who understands about emotions, feelings, and affairs of the heart. The one discordant note is the reference to having broken up with Ingrid. This may well be linked with unconscious thoughts about terminating therapy, although there is insufficient evidence to warrant coming to firm conclusions.

DISCUSSION

These examples illustrate the deeply lawful relationship between therapists' behavior and patients' derivative responses. Both therapists made an effort to 'tune in' to their patient's unconscious concerns and, going against the current of their own defenses and resistances, proposed interpretations which were deeply threatening and exposing rather than remain concealed behind an impregnable armor of fanciful theorizing about their patients' intrapsychic world or remaining with homilies about interpersonal relationships. Not only did these therapists lay themselves on the line emotionally through valuing truth more than personal comfort, they also laid themselves on the line by offering interpretations and measuring these against a strict and definite criterion of falsification. They were, in the last analysis, willing to be *taught* by their patient's, listening respectfully rather than discounting and discrediting. Both accordingly received derivative validation of their work. Validation did not take a dramatic form. There was no conscious 'Aha!' experience. Consciously, the validated interpretations passed by apparently unnoticed. Unconsciously, however, powerfully constructive images were brought to the fore, portraying the therapeutic virtues of listening, emotional understanding, and empathy. So unobtrusive were these responses that a therapist ignorant of the communicative concept of validation would not regard them as such (these remarks would probably be seen as an expression of resistance – a simple evasion of the intervention). Communicatively, though, they were predictable and unmistakable.

Both of these patients were given something immensely valuable by their therapists. Not only did they experience a unique and therapeutically potent moment of being understood, they were also given a living model of someone who struggles successfully with his or her own madness and defensiveness. Actions speak louder than words. A therapist may verbally advocate insight, but this will have little impact (beyond providing an illustration of hypocracy) unless he or she provides a living example of the willingness to look into oneself and to change. Furthermore, both of these practitioners implicitly showed their patients that they took their therapeutic responsibilities, and therefore their patient's well-being, so seriously that they were willing to endure considerable discomfort in order to provide a truly curative and insightful moment. Finally, the two therapists supported and honored their patients' own deep reparative urges by taking their unconscious guidance seriously.

We have seen something of the challenges that the communicative approach poses to individual psychotherapists. We will now move on to consider, by way of a conclusion to this book, how these resemble the challenge that the approach poses to the field as a whole.

10 Toward a new science of psychoanalysis

Although the arguing from Experiments and Observations by Induction be no Demonstration of general Conclusions, yet it is the best way of arguing which the Nature of Things admits of.

Sir Isaac Newton

Freud intended psychoanalysis to be a natural science of the human soul. As a candidate for membership in the family of sciences psychoanalysis possesses only the most dubious of qualifications. For many years now there has been an intense debate amongst psychoanalysts, scientists, and philosophers of science as to whether or not Freud's brainchild can be considered a true science. The verdict has not generally been favorable. As Sir Peter Medawar puts it:

> The opinion is gaining ground that doctrinaire psychoanalytic theory is the most stupendous intellectual confidence trick of the twentieth century: and a terminal product as well – something akin to a dinosaur or a zeppelin in the history of ideas, a vast structure of radically unsound design and with no posterity.
>
> (Medawar cited in Farrell 1981)

There is a rather striking resemblance to be found between the history of psychoanalysis since the end of the nineteenth century when Freud made his first, seminal discoveries and the history of European philosophy during the one hundred-odd years between the publication of Kant's *Critique of Pure Reason* in 1781 and the rise of logical positivism.

Kant's monumental *Critique* argued that human beings can never know things as they really are, because the very act of perception was said to impose certain properties upon its objects. According to this view, human beings are condemned to life in a world of mere appearances. Kant's dictum placed constraints upon metaphysics by implying that efforts to work out the ultimate nature of reality were doomed to failure. Unfortunately, these strictures produced a paradoxical effect. The fact that ultimate reality was described as inaccessible to normal forms of enquiry was taken as granting metaphysics license to ignore the cannons of empirical science and common sense. Metaphysics came to regard itself as an autonomous discipline. More and more speculative systems were created, on a more grandiose scale than ever before. However, the abandonment of scientific rationality was a sword that cut in two directions. Metaphysics was now bereft of any reasonable method for adjudicating rival philosophical claims except on the grounds of logical coherence.

> Without shared standards to serve as a basis for arbitrating metaphysical disputes, matters took a predictably subjective turn. Attempts at justifying a . . . system invariably culminated in special appeals to some sort of inexplicable insight, romantic intuition or religious faith. A system was as likely to be embraced for its creative originality, its speculative boldness, or its grandeur and elegance as for any element of truth that it purported to contain.
>
> (Romanos 1986: 6)

At several points in his writings Freud compared his theory of unconscious mental contents to Kant's concept of unknowable things-in-themselves (Freud 1915b, 1940). The Freudian unconscious can never be known directly, a principle which places methodological restrictions upon those who wish to study it. If our knowledge of the unconscious domain can never be more than inferential, it is necessary to tread carefully. The obscurity and remoteness of the object of study from ordinary human experience demands that investigators relate hypothesis to evidence with care and full logical rigor.

Psychoanalysis has not heeded the cautionary note implicit in its own theory. It has approached the unconscious realm in a reckless fashion, taking the remoteness of the unconscious domain from conscious experience as permitting an 'anything goes' attitude. Like the metaphysicians of the last century psychoanalysts have created a proliferation of self-contained 'schools' of theory and practice and, having abandoned the self-correcting methodology of empirical science, have been unable to rationally decide between rival theories. Modern psychoanalysts who take theory seriously find themselves 'isolated from one another within the confines of their idiosyncratic . . . systems, arguing futility and always at cross purposes' (ibid.). The best minds in psychology tend to be repelled by the muddle that psychoanalysis has generated around itself and tend to gravitate toward more rigorous theoretical traditions and research programs in a manner reminiscent of the original logical positivists who, as scientifically trained and orientated thinkers, found traditional metaphysics deeply repugnant.

Philosophers of science have leveled three powerful criticisms against psychoanalysis: the positivist charge of unverifiability proffered by Nagel, the charge of nonfalsifiability offered by Popper and Cioffi, and the charge of epistemic contamination given by Grünbaum.

Logical positivists took the position that for a statement about the world to be meaningful it had to be verifiable. Unverifiable statements were therefore held to be meaningless.[1] It follows from this that the positivists required the theoretical terms of a science to be closely tied to basic observation-statements: theoretical entities had to be linked with observable phenomena by means of a set of 'correspondence rules'. Ernest Nagel (1959) felt that psychoanalytic theory did not measure up to these requirements. The theoretical terms of psychoanalysis are not *'tied down to fairly definite and unambiguously specified* observational materials'. Theory is 'stated in language so vague and metaphorical that almost anything appears to be compatible with it' (40−1). Eagle (1983) gives several examples of the sort of empirically empty psychobabble commonly found in psychoanalytic writings which nicely illustrate Nagel's contention.[2] He provides a quotation from Kohut, who states that:

> The danger against which the ego defends itself by keeping the archaic grandiose self dissociated and/or repression and the dedifferentiating influx of unneutralized narcissistic libido (towards which the threatened ego reacts with anxious excitement) and the intrusion of archaic images of a fragmented body self. . . .
>
> (Kohut 1971: 152)

What could the statements possibly mean? What kind of observations could conceivable lend them credence? Mahler manages to surpass even Kohut in ambiguity when she writes:

> Metapsychologically speaking, this seems to mean that, by the second month, the quasi-solid stimulus barrier (negative, because it is uncathected) − this autistic shell, which kept external stimuli out − begins to crack. Through the aforementioned cathectic shift towards the sensoriperceptive periphery, a protective, but also receptive and selective, positively cathected stimulus shield now begins to form and to envelop the symbiotic orbit of the mother−

child dual unity. . . . This eventually highly selective boundary seems to contain not only the pre-ego self representations, but also the not yet differentiated, libidinally cathected symbiotic part objects, within the mother–infant symbiotic matrix.

(Mahler 1968: 15)

Eagles's crowning example of 'practically incomprehensible jargon' (p. 47) is an extract by Giovaccini, who writes that

what I am emphasizing is that the vicissitudes involved in the formation of this first mental construct have an important bearing on the formation of the postsymbiotic introjects which, in turn, serve as a source of cathexis that can lead to the stabilization of a function as well as the construction of self and object representations.

(Giovaccini 1981: 411–12)

It is one of the tragedies of psychoanalysis that its proponents can say the most blatantly meaningless things with completely unruffled self-assurance!

The lesson that Nagel teaches us is that in order to be scientifically credible, psychoanalytic theory should be firmly anchored in observational reality.

When logical positivism began to blow away the cobwebs from the dusty corridors of European philosophy, it also brought with it new errors. One of these was the verificationist approach to the validation of scientific theories. The positivists believed that the validity of a theory is established by the accumulation of numerous examples of its positive instances. The poverty of this approach can be illustrated by the hypothetical example of a researcher who wishes to test the thesis that all doughnuts are chocolate flavored. Using a naive inductivist strategy, this intrepid gentleman visits every bakery in the United Kingdom and enquires at each if they produce chocolate doughnuts, compiling a vast list of tens of thousands of 'confirmations' (sightings of chocolate-flavored doughnuts). It is obvious, though, that no matter how many positive instances this man accumulates, he will never be able to prove his thesis in this manner. He would have saved considerable time, effort, and expense if he had merely visited the nearest baker and looked for a doughnut which was *not* chocolate flavored.

Although a million positive instances cannot prove a universal generalization, a single non-confirmation can falsify it. This falsificationist approach to scientific methodology was developed by Popper, who believes that we should strive to disprove rather than prove our pet theories.[3] For a theory to be scientifically interesting there must be some way, in principle, of proving it wrong. Thus, after advancing a theory, or a hypothesis deduced from a theory, a conscientious researcher should spell out just what sort of observations would count against its validity and should attempt to make just this kind of observation. Those hypotheses that withstand strenuous efforts at falsification can then be accepted as provisionally true. Popper himself mounted a falsificationist attack upon psychoanalytic theory.

I found that those of my friends who were admirers of Marx, Freud, and Adler, were impressed by a number of points common to these theories and especially by their apparent *explanatory power*. These theories appeared to be able to explain practically everything that happened within the fields to which they referred. The study of any of them seemed to have the effect of an intellectual conversion or revelation. . . . Once your eyes were thus opened you saw confirming instances everywhere: the world was full of *verifications* of the theory. Whatever happened always confirmed it.

(Popper 1963: 35)

It occurred to Popper that this attractive feature was in fact a weakness. Psychoanalysis compared unfavorably with, say, Einstein's theory of gravitation because the latter made predictions which could, in principle, easily be disproven. There is an element of intellectual 'risk' in Einstein's theory which, according to Popper, is almost totally lacking in Freud's.

Now the impressive thing about this case [Einstein's theory] is the *risk* involved in a prediction of this kind. If observation shows that the predicted effect is definitely absent, then the theory is simply refuted. The theory is *incompatible with certain possible results of observation.* . . . This is quite different from the situation I have previously described, when it turned out that the theories in question [psychoanalysis, Adlerian psychology, and Marxism] were compatible with the most divergent human behaviour, so that it was practically impossible to describe any human behaviour that might not be claimed to be a verification of these theories.

(ibid.: 36)

It does not therefore follow that these theories must be false: 'But it does mean that those "clinical observations" which analysts naïvely believe confirm their theory cannot do this any more than the daily confirmations which astrologers find in their practice' (ibid.: 37–8).

Although Grünbaum (1984) has shown that Popper's critique of psychoanalysis is technically incorrect – i.e. that Freudian theory can produce at least some falsifiable hypotheses – Cioffi has pointed out forcefully that the *spirit* of Popper's criticism certainly finds an appropriate mark. The fact is that psychoanalysts desperately try to avoid falsification rather than opening themselves to it in the name of scientific truth. 'A pseudo-science', writes Cioffi, 'is not constituted by formally defective theses but by methodologically defective procedures' (1970: 471).

A glance at any mainstream psychoanalytic journal will confirm the validity of the falsificationist critique. The standard psychoanalytic paper begins with the author advancing some hypothesis or other, and then goes on to scrutinize some clinical material chosen to support the hypothesis being advanced. The paper then concludes with the author stating that the clinical 'evidence' supports the hypothesis. There is typically no effort made to falsify the hypothesis. The dice are loaded: there is no risk. This standard strategy makes reading the latest psychoanalytic publications a rather tedious exercise. One knows beforehand that the evidence presented will inevitably support the author's pet idea.

A piece by Boschán, an Argentinian psychoanalyst, which I have chosen at random from the *International Journal of Psycho-Analysis*, illustrates this nicely. Boschán sets out to: 'postulate that the interpretive resolution of a narcissistic resistance is often followed by the appearance of material centered on the denial of dependence and/or catastrophic consequences of accepting it' (Boschán 1987: 109). If this hypothesis is to be assigned definite empirical content it needs to be clarified in several respects. The author would need to specify what, in observational terms, constitutes a 'narcissistic resistance', likewise 'interpretive resolution'. The author would need to present more specific characterizations of the predicted outcome and the term 'often' would need to be tightened up into a more definite probabilistic commitment. Such clarification would yield a falsifiable hypothesis. However, Boschán does not offer such clarification nor does he follow the path of falsificationism. He merely presents four clinical examples 'in support' (116) of his hypothesis.

Popper and Cioffi teach us that scientifically interesting psychoanalytic hypotheses must be falsifiable, and that analysts should specify what sort of evidence would falsify their hypotheses and attempt to gather such falsifying evidence.

Popperian falsificationism has left a profound mark upon the philosophy of science. Since Popper, other philosophers have identified weaknesses in his approach and have attempted to modify it accordingly (see Chalmers 1982). Contemporary sophisticated falsificationists no longer adhere in all respects to the classical falsificationist program. In particular, attention is paid to the need for verification as well as falsification, but the logical asymmetry between these two principles, which grants falsification its distinctive significance, is retained. As Chalmers sums up, 'Theory acceptance is always tentative. Theory rejection can be decisive' (Chalmers 1982: 60).

Platt (1964) proposes that a modern post-Popperian inductivist approach of *'strong inference'* is the most potent methodological tool available for scientific research. The strategy of strong inference seeks to falsify some hypothesis not absolutely, but in relation to some *rival* hypothesis, pitting competing hypotheses against one another in an attempt to eliminate all but one from the running. The surviving hypothesis is then pitted against new contenders. The hypothesis which consistently beats all challengers is then accepted provisionally as true. The status of 'true' can never be granted absolutely, because a more powerful hypothesis may yet arrive to defeat the champion. The strategy of strong inference is rather like an accelerated intellectual Darwinism. Only the fittest hypothesis will survive. The fittest hypothesis is that most adapted to the reality of its proper domain and is, consequently, regarded as true. According to Platt the rapid development of a scientific discipline can usually be attributed to the systematic use of strong inference. The moral for psychoanalysis is obvious:

> The clinical investigator whose habit of mind leads him to seek out positive instances in an effort to garner support for his hypothesis, rather than to subject it to rigorous test in competition with other hypotheses, does run the risk of committing himself to a weak hypothesis. He is more likely to produce ideology, mythology, or politically motivated position papers than science.
>
> (Edelson 1984: 22)

The most profound, rigorous, and detailed philosophical critique of the scientific claims of psychoanalysis is undoubtedly Adolf Grünbaum's monumental *The Foundations of Psychoanalysis: A Philosophical Critique* (1984). Grünbaum shows that Freud took the challenge that suggestion, rather than true insight, was the therapeutic force in psychoanalytic treatment very seriously. Freud tried to eliminate the rival hypothesis of suggestion by the use of what Grünbaum has christened the 'Tally Argument'. The Tally Argument states that an interpretation will have a curative effect if and only if it 'tallies' with something that is real inside the patient. Freud predicated the truth of his theories upon the therapeutic effectiveness of interpretations deduced from them. Unfortunately, he was unable to provide any empirical justification for the Tally Argument, and was in consequence never able to rule out 'placebo effects' in psychoanlytic treatment.

> Freud . . . was keenly aware that unless the methodologically damaging import of the patient's compliance with his doctor's expectations can somehow be neutralized, the doctor is on thin ice when purporting to mediate veridical insights to his client rather than only fanciful *pseudo*insights persuasively endowed with the ring of verisimilitude. Indeed, if the probative value of the analysand's responses is thus negated by brainwashing, the Freudian therapy might reasonably be held to function as an emotional corrective *not* because it enables the analysand to acquire bona fide self-knowledge, but instead because he or she succumbs to proselytizing *suggestion* which operates the more insiduously under the pretense that analysis is *non*directive.
>
> (ibid.: 130)

A classic study of the psychotherapeutic work of Carl Rogers conducted by Truax brings home the plausibility of Grünbaum's argument. Although not a psychoanalyst, Rogers also eschewed any attempt to 'suggest' to patients that they conform to the expectations of their therapist. Indeed, the Rogerian therapist is advised to focus on his client's desires rather than his own. Rogers advocated that if patients are consistently treated in a warm and empathic manner they will make psychotherapeutic progress. Truax found, in an intensive study of Rogers's interaction with one of his clients, that Rogers responded – without realizing it – in a highly selective fashion. Certain behavior on the part of his patient would be rewarded by warm, emphic responses while other forms of behavior would receive no such reward. For example, Truax found that Rogers consistently behaved warmly toward his client in so far as he expressed himself in a manner similar to Rogers's own style of expression and was given little or no empathy when he departed from this norm. Rogers's rewards acted as positive reinforcers which increased the frequency of the forms of behavior that Rogers evidently approved of. Rogers unwittingly 'suggested' certain forms of expression and behavior to his unconsciously compliant patient!

Freud himself believed that suggestibility stemmed from 'positive' transference and freely admitted to cultivating positive transference in his patients to induce them to endure the hardships attendant upon psychoanalytic treatment. 'It is used . . .', writes Freud, 'to induce the patient to perform a piece of psychical work. . . .' (1925: 43). After the positive transference has served its purpose it too is subjected to analysis and is interpretatively eliminated. Freud offered the alleged destruction of the positive transference by analysis as an argument against explaining the therapeutic effects of psychoanalysis as due to suggestion. This defense rests upon unstable logical and empirical foundations. First, it relies on the thesis that the suggestion is a manifestation of transference, which is never substantiated. Second, it presupposes that the analyst is in a position to reliably distinguish transferences from nontransference, a presumption that I have undermined in Chapter 2 of this book. Third, if prior to the analysis of the positive transference psychoanalytic interpretations have been accepted in order to satisfy the analyst's expectations, there is no reason to suppose that the interpretations of the positive transference are not accepted for the very same reason, thus rendering the whole argument 'logically a viciously circular bootstrap operation' (Grünbaum 1984: 144).

There is tremendous insidious pressure on the patient in the normal psychoanalytic situation to conform to his or her analyst's expectations. By definition, analytic cure can only come about if the patient consciously embraces some account of the origins of his or her psychological disorder that is consistent with the analyst's theoretical orientation. The analyst attempts, to put it bluntly, to bring the patient round to accepting his or her point of view. The patient whose perspective is incompatible with that of the analyst is 'resistant'. The patient who concurs is 'insightful'. It seems plausible to assume that *any form of therapy which makes 'cure' contingent upon the patient's conscious acceptance of the therapist's hypotheses must necessarily be suggestion-ridden and full of artefacts.* These considerations led Grünbaum to the conclusion that psychoanalytic theories cannot be evaluated against data taken from psychoanalytic sessions because such data is bound to be 'epistemically contaminated': chock-full of spurious 'confirmations' and other by-products of analysts' theoretical commitments. He therefore states that psychoanalytic theories can only be tested against non-clinical (experimental or epidemiological) data if such tests are to have any real probative value.

It would be foolish of me to assert that the communicative literature satisfies the exacting criteria set down by Popper, Grünbaum, and others. I do believe, however, that the communicative literature comes closer to this idea than the literature on normal psychoanalysis and, more importantly, that the communicative approach is capable of satisfying these strictures much more fully than it does at present. Indeed, the structure of communicative theory is such that it lends itself to scientific investigation.

The communicative approach fares exceptionally well against Nagel's verificationist critique. Virtually all of its theoretical terms are operationalized. Theoretical entities are consistently linked with observable behaviors by means of clear correspondence rules.

Likewise, the communicative theory is eminently falsifiable. Clear predictions are deduced from the theory about derivative responses to interpretations and frame events. The theory predicts that formally correct communicative interpretations will elicit encoded, derivative validations while incorrect or non-communicative interventions will evoke derivative non-validation. Although there are sometimes anomalies (in response to *extremely* disruptive interventions *some* patients paradoxically produce very positively toned derivatives), communicative therapists expect this relationship between intervention and response to hold quite reliably. Should this pattern be shown *not* to hold consistently it would certainly count, according to communicative canons, as a falsification of the theory. Thus, communicative hypotheses are readily falsifiable, and Langs has set out just what sort of observations would falsify them. To my knowledge communicative therapists have not yet attempted to seek out data to attempt to falsify the theory in any systematic manner, but the potential is certainly there. Because of its predictive power and openness to falsification, the communicative approach also lends itself to the strategy of strong inference. Given an accurate description of initial conditions a communicative analyst can use his or her theory to deduce the tone and general thematic content of the ensuing derivatives. These could, in principle, be tested against predictions deduced by means of a competing psychological theory to see which of the two stands up best to the evidence. Although communicative therapists often use this strategy in an informal manner, it has, to my knowledge, never been applied in a rigorously controlled way conforming to the six canons of eliminative inductivism outlined by Edelson (1984).

This issue brings us face to face with Grünbaum's contention that psychoanalytic hypotheses cannot be tested in the clinical setting. This argument is made credible by the fact that normal psychoanalysis limits its clinical predictions to predictions about psychoanalytic cure: that is, normal psychoanalysis predicts that *if* an analyst makes a correct interpretation about a symptom or resistance *and* the patient consciously accepts the truth of this interpretation *then* the symptom or resistance will disappear. This statement is not biconditional:

analysts do not any longer believe that analysis is the only way to remove symptoms. Thus, we are left with the possibility of studying accounts of psychoanalytic sessions to determine if this allegedly lawful relationship is falsified; but because of the pressure on the patient to accept psychoanalytic doctrines, it is not possible to exclude the possibility that positive instances are due to suggestion rather than insight, in which case the accuracy of the proffered interpretation is entirely beside the point. (Given the woeful paucity of evidence that psychoanalytic interpretations possess any curative effect whatsoever, these niceties seem rather academic!) The communicative approach is freed from this dilemma by virtue of not confining its predictions to therapeutic outcome. As a general theory of psychotherapeutic inter-action, the communicative approach does not need to rest its case on the issue of cure. The theory can therefore be used to make predictions and retrodictions about *non-communicative* therapeutic interactions. My analysis of the sessions by Khan and Dolto, neither of whom operated with communicative sympathies, illustrates how the theory can be extended beyond the domain of the technique. Now, if the communicative theory can be tested against non-communicative clinical data – on data taken from the work of therapists whose beliefs are actually *incompatible* with communicative theory – then the charge of epistemic contamination can be effectively neutralized.[4]

One difficulty remains. Communicative theory states that non-communicative therapists will not obtain (or obtain only occasionally and fortuitously) derivative validation for their efforts. As derivative validation is taken to be the unique response to appropriate therapeutic work, and derivative validations are said to occur only rarely, it follows that these validations are of strong probative value for the assessment of the theory (if an improbable event can be reliably predicted this gives the theory upon which the predictions are based considerable credence). In order to study the incidence of derivative validation in response to accurate communicative interpre-tations it is necessary, therefore, to rely on communicative data. Here the spectre of contamination raises its head. If there is indeed a relatively high incidence of derivative validation in communicative psychotherapeutic sessions, how can one eliminate the possibility that this is due to the effects of suggestion?

This important charge can be met in three ways. First, it is important to note that in comparison to Freudian psychoanalysis (or even Rogerian psychotherapy) there is no expectation that the patient will achieve conscious insight. The conscious acceptance of an intervention is regarded as having no bearing upon its therapeutic efficacy. Thus, the level of suggestive pressure must be quantitatively less, rendering suggestion less probable although not ruling it out entirely.

Second, there is no obvious reward or reinforcement offered in response to patients' derivative validations. In fact, the rules of communicative technique require the therapist to be *silent* in response to derivative validations which should, if anything, tend to *extinguish* rather than perpetuate it. It is difficult to understand how derivative validation can reasonably be attributed to suggestion unless some process *transmitting* the suggestive influence can be identified.

Finally, and most importantly, the *independent characterization* of the correctness of a communicative interpretation and the validating quality of derivative responses strongly militates against the objection based on the charge of epistemic contamination. If derivative validations do occur with greater frequency in communicative psychoanalysis than, for example, in classical psychoanalysis and if this heightened frequency is caused by some suggestive influence flowing from therapist to patient, it would follow that patients would *indiscriminately* validate their therapists' interventions. According to communicative theory, however, this should not occur. The theory states that only those interpretations conforming to a particular set of objective criteria for formal correctness will be rewarded with derivative validations. Those interpretations which a therapist merely believes to be correct, but which do not in fact comply with these criteria for correct communicative interventions, will not, according to the theory, obtain such validation. If research can demonstrate that patients' derivative validations (which, remember, have been operationally defined) follow only those interventions which are independently judged to be in accord with the criteria for correct interpretations, then the possibility that suggestion plays an important role in the positive instances of the theory seems to be virtually ruled out.

In recent years the real scientific potential of the communicative approach has begun to be made a reality. In 1987, after a long detour through clinical psychoanalysis, Langs abandoned his practice to resume his career as a researcher. His goal was to attempt to make a credible science out of psychoanalysis. In Langs's view psychoanalysis is an anachronistic 'Aristotelian' science which is: 'based on common sense observation and the statistical norm, concerned with the 'essential nature' of the psyche's presumed elements, and intent on classifying those elements in terms of their apparent attributes and predetermined course of development' (Langs 1987: 555). This has had deleterious effects upon the discipline.

This static, global, impressionistic . . . approach characteristic of classical psychoanalytic thinking and therapy creates serious limits at the level of both research and practice. It hampers the generation of abstractions, such as models, integrated theories, and extractions from data, and it keeps interpretation from moving beyond the concrete and self-evident.

(ibid.: 567)

As an Aristotelian science, psychoanalysis is: 'essentially incapable of producing a modern-day science characterized by measurement, quantification, effective prediction and universal laws' (ibid.: 556).

Langs recognized that the key for transforming psychoanalysis into a fully fledged 'Galileian' science lay in the use of quantification. Between 1986 and 1988 he made contact with four mathematicians – Ralph Abraham, Paul Rapp, Richard Albanese, and Anthony Badalamenti – who were interested in mathematically modeling psychotherapeutic interactions. These four men were expert in the new mathematical discipline of 'chaos theory' (non-linear dynamical systems theory), which is a branch of mathematics that is able to demonstrate the presence of an underlying order and coherence in apparently random, chaotic behavior. It has been successfully applied to domains as diverse as weather forecasting, fluid dynamics, economics, and the functioning of the human heart (Gleick 1987). Gradually a research team assembled who were interested in discovering the order underlying the chaotic dynamics of psychotherapy. A research scoring manual was devised consisting of sixty items used to evaluate patient and therapist communications at five-second intervals and generating tens of thousands of data points for each psychotherapeutic session studied. This work is still in its infancy. Little of it has been published in any detail, although a great deal is poised for publication.[5] Much of it is highly technical, using sophisticated mathematical methods to reveal striking communicative interchanges between patients and therapists. Measures for monitoring the level of unconscious communication in psychotherapy sessions have been developed and these have been used to show the tremendous impact of therapists' behavior upon patients' communicative propensities.

One thing is certain: by exposing itself to the full glare of the cold light of scientific scrutiny, the communicative approach will either vindicate itself as a uniquely powerful psychoanalytic theory or else be exposed as a false hope – yet another intellectual 'dinosaur' which must be hastened to its grave.

Notes

1 Seduction

1 See also Schimek (1975), Cioffi (1975), and Steele (1982).
2 According to Masson (1984) this paper has suffered from mistranslation. Masson avers that in the original German Freud says that it was he himself who linked the symptoms with the hypothesized seductions, not his patients.
3 See also Rubenstein (1983).
4 The Löwenfeld quotation was located by Masson (1982).
5 The theory of memory elaborated in this paper was remarkably prescient. See Loftus (1980).
6 Freud clearly uses the term 'phantasy' in this context to denote any unconscious representation(s). The term is not meant by him to imply that such mental contents are necessarily out of touch with reality.
7 Quoted in Masson (1984).
8 Langs (1976b) provides an interesting analysis of Freud's treatment of Dora and her responses to it.
9 This hypothesis was initially advanced by Langs (1982b). See also Langs (1984).

2 The distorting mirror

1 For a good discussion of this issue see Eagle (1982).
2 It is for this reason that Kleinian and Klein-influenced analysts sometimes described valid unconscious perception as a form of transference. It should be noted, though, that the umbrella concept of transference allows these analysts to construe patients' associations as expressions of unconscious perception just when it suits them. The concept of unconscious perception, then, does not *discipline* the listening process: it is invoked on an *ad hoc* basis.
3 See Chertok (1968).

3 An unimaginable substratum

1 I am indebted here to Lyons's (1986) study of the rise and fall of introspectionism in psychology.

2 See Eagle (1982).

3 Ironically, it was Freud's intellectual hero Herman von Helmholz who pioneered the notion that visual perception involves unconscious inferences.

4 This passage has been ignored by most, if not all, commentators on *Totem and Taboo* who have assumed that Freud's argument rests entirely on the discredited Lamarkian notion of the inheritance of acquired characteristics (cf. Wallace 1983).

5 The invocation of unconscious perception also provides a solution for Davidson's (1982, 1986) paradoxes of motivated irrationality.

6 The usual explanation, inherited from Freud, is that mental contents are unconscious *because* they are emotionally threatening (for example, Langs 1988a). But cognitive scientists such as David Marr (1982) have shown conclusively that some unconscious items are naturally and intrinsically unconscious. There are, in fact, compelling reasons for rejecting the Freudian view in favor of the theory that the unconscious mind deals with emotionally charged perceptions because it is selectively sensitive to such perceptions.

4 Some pioneers

1 There is reason to believe that Freud was *unconsciously* aware of his abusiveness. See Langs (1984).

2 Langs (personal communication) was criticized on precisely the same grounds as Ferenczi by his Freudian colleagues, including the charge of paranoia.

3 It is not clear if Racker was familiar with Ferenczi's 'Confusion of tongues' paper. It does not appear in his list of references.

4 Searles was apparently unaware of Little's (1951) contribution, which does not appear in his list of references.

5 Psychotherapy exposed

1 Langs had been trained in the strict, classical approach to psychoanalysis and therefore had only the vaguest conception of an interactional dimension. While in training he had once heard Winnicott speak, but this had little conscious impact. After graduating from his institute in 1968 a colleague, Harriet Barr, gave him a copy of Balint's *The Basic Fault* which, as Langs put it to me, 'blew me away' (personal communication). It was after reading Balint that Langs began to explore the British psychoanalytic literature with its appreciation of the interactional dimension. On the more classical side Greenson (1968, 1971) and Arlow (1969a, b) were major influences. On the more personal level Langs had always been somewhat sceptical of the role assigned to phantasy in psychoanalytic theory because of his awareness of the significance of real traumas in his own psychological development. The communicative approach itself originated as a form of self-analysis. Langs emerged from his training analysis with new, iatrogenic symptoms. He developed the communicative approach as a (successful) attempt to resolve the pathology that his previous analysis had engendered.

2 This finding goes dead against the psychoanalytic dogma that the analyst is by definition 'healthier' than the patient and thus serves as a more integrated object for identification. See Loewald (1960) and Dewald (1976).

3 It was Peter Giovaccini who introduced Langs to Searles's thesis.

4 See, for example, Calef (1979). On one occasion Langs submitted a paper on his approach to the *International Journal of Psycho-Analysis* which was rejected on the grounds that he was 'asking too much of the analyst'!

5 This is a special case of Kuhn's (1962) concept of 'normal science'. Normal science is the activity of using an established paradigm – a way of understanding things – to deal with the scientific problems at hand. In contrast to this, revolutionary science, of which I take the communicative approach to be an example, happens when a vigorous new vision enters the scene to challenge the hegemony of the established order.

6 Lothane (1980) seems to have been the first commentator to recognize the consistently methodological thrust of Langs's project.

7 Casement includes a slightly modified version of this paper in his second book (Casement 1990).

8 By communicative standards Casement decodes unconscious communications capriciously and confuses the implications of manifest contents with genuine, encoded meaning. In particular, he seems to rely on patients' conscious assent to interpretations and does not use derivative validation consistently. For example, he recounts (1985: 117) telling a patient that she saw him as her 'needy mother', remarking in the text that the patient nodded her head in agreement while the interpretation was being made. The patient then went on to describe how she had eaten too much of a rich, sweet dessert and how this had made her ill. Casement takes the patients' nodding her head as a validation of his hypothesis. If he had been operating communicatively, however, he would have been constrained to regard his hypothesis as falsified. Readers anxious to understand the encoded meaning of this patient's remarks should return to the example after reading Chapter 8 of the present volume.

6 Hidden conversations

1 Johnson-Laird (1983) is the classic text on mental models. McGinn (1989) argues persuasively that all mental representations are models.

2 See Gedo and Goldberg (1973) for a comprehensive account of the main psychoanalytic models of the mind.

3 See Smith (1987).

4 Epistemologically, normal psychoanalysis takes an idealist view of the relationship between the unconscious part of the mind and the external world, whereas the communicative approach is uncompromisingly *realist*. See Trigg (1989).

5 Sara Young has called my attention to the fact that at one point Freud uses this strategy in the case of Dora as well (Freud 1905b).

6 Langs describes two forms of derivative validation. Interpersonal validation, the type that I have been describing, takes the form of constructively toned derivative imagery (strictly speaking, the term 'interpersonal' is too limiting, as derivative portrayals do not have to make use of representations of human beings). The second type is called 'cognitive validation'. Cognitive validation is indicated by: 'the emergence in the patient's

material of a displaced and disguised . . . narrative or image that reveals an entirely new dimension of the patient's madness, a dimension that clearly extends the therapist's interpretation' (Langs 1988a: 82). As things stand, these criteria are far too subjective to be of use as a reliable validating device. Langs needs to spell out what is meant by 'an entirely new dimension of the patient's madness' and to clarify the relationship between this and the interpersonal variety of validation. Because of the ambiguity of the concept of cognitive validation I have chosen not to emphasize it in the present exposition.

7 See Langs (1981).

8 See Langs (1974).

9 In 1984 Gill (1984) criticized Langs for making a sharp conceptual distinction between transference and non-transference. By 1988 Langs had abandoned the concept of transference altogether, in favor of various forms of non-transference (unconscious perception).

10 The standard communicative model of unconscious information processing conforms, in essence, with orthodox computationalist thinking. In recent years there has been a movement in the field of artificial intelligence toward the theory of parallel distributed processing – also called the new connectionism – which provides an alternative to the orthodox approach (see Rumelhart, McClelland, and the PDP research group 1986). The connectionist strategy can be exploited by the communicative approach to explain how genetic influences can effect derivative processes without having to invoke the problematic notion of transference. Briefly, if infantile experiences are thought of as effecting the strength of the connections between processing units it is possible to specify just how genetic material enters the scene. The genetic influences would be present as inexplicit content (Cummins 1989), as features of the cognitive architecture rather than explicit data structures. In other words genetic factors influence the 'transformation rules' guiding the expression of unconscious ideas as derivatives: they are not incorporated as unconscious mental *contents*.

11 There is a convergence of communicative and existential thought on this issue. See van Deurzen-Smith (1988).

7 The limit situation

1 In spite of his emphasis on the importance of a secure frame, Winnicott's attitude toward the frame in his own analytic practice seems to have been rather haphazard (see Little 1951; Winnicott 1986).

2 Some major contributors have been Arlow and Brenner (1966), Eissler (1953, 1958, 1974), Halpert (1972), Lipton (1977), Rodgers (1965), and Stone (1961).

3 The system constituted by patient and therapist is an example of an *auto-poetic* system. Autopoetic systems are those which create their own boundaries which then become central to the metabolism of the system (Maturana and Varela 1987).

4 See Strupp (1978) and Langs's (1978e) response.

5 The concept of death anxiety forges links between the communicative and existential modes of analysis (Yalom 1980; van Deurzen-Smith 1988; Ogilvie 1989).

6 Chasseguet-Smirgel (1985) has developed this line of enquiry considerably, but without linking it to the issue of the frame.

8 The technique of communicative psychotherapy

1 This is intended metaphorically and is not supposed to suggest a semiotic understanding of derivative expression. Grünbaum (1985) provides an excellent critique of this exegetical and theoretical trend.
2 This categorization is my own and does not appear in any of Langs's accounts.
3 For a more fine-grained account see Langs (1982a, 1985b, 1988a).
4 This last type of intervention is, for some reason, never included in lists of acceptable communicative interventions although it is consistently recommended as an appropriate response to patients' efforts to modify the frame. I have therefore taken the initiative of promoting this Cinderella to a more prominent position in the theory of technique. I have subsumed under interpretation Langs's concept of the playback of selected derivatives in accord with current thinking on communicative technique.
5 See Chapter 6, note 5.

10 Toward a new science of psychoanalysis

1 See Ayer (1950).
2 Leites (1971) develops this theme.
3 Popper's approach is rooted in Hume's discovery that inductive reasoning is logically unsound. No matter how many times one observes a sun rise this does not logically establish that the sun will continue to rise. It occurred to Popper that there is a strange logical asymmetry between confirmation and falsification. No amount of positive instantiation can prove a universal generalization, but a single negative instance can disprove it.
4 It was Paul Kline (1972, 1988a) who first suggested this general research strategy.
5 See Albanese (1988), Langs (1988, 1989a), Langs and Badalamenti (1990a, b, c).

Bibliography

Albanese, R. (1988) 'An increased role for mathematics in research and practice in psychotherapy', *British Journal of Psychotherapy* 5(2): 213–18.
—— (1969b) 'Fantasy, memory and reality testing', *Psychoanalytic Quarterly* 38(1): 28–51.
Arlow, C. and Brenner, C. (1966) 'The psychoanalytic situation', in P. Litman (ed.) *Psychoanalysis in the Americas*, New York: International Universities Press.
Arlow, J. (1969a) 'Unconscious fantasy and disturbances of conscious experience', *Psychoanalytic Quarterly* 38(1): 1–27.
Ayer, F. (1950) *Language, Truth and Logic*, New York: Dover.
Balint, M. (1955) 'Notes on parapsychology and parapsychological healing', *International Journal of Psycho-Analysis* 36(1): 31–5).
—— (1968) *The Basic Fault*, London: Tavistock.
Balint, M. and Balint, A. (1939) 'On transference and countertransference', in M. Balint *Primary and Psycho-Analytic Technique*, New York: Liveright, 1965.
Baranger, M. and Baranger, W. (1966) 'Insight and the analytic situation', in R. Litman (ed.) *Psychoanalysis in the Americas*, New York: International Universities Press.
Bettelheim, B. (1983) *Freud and Man's Soul*, London: Chatto and Windus.
Bion, W. (1955) 'Language and the schizophrenic', in M. Klein, P. Heimann, and R.E. Money-Kyrle (eds) *New Directions in Psycho-Analysis*, London: H. Karnac Books, 1985.
—— (1962a) 'A theory of thinking', *International Journal of Psycho-Analysis* 43: 306–10.
—— (1962b) *Learning from Experience*, London: Heinemann.
—— (1967) 'Notes on memory and desire', in E.B. Spillius (ed.) (1988) *Melanie Klein Today: Developments in Theory and Practice* vol 2, London: Routledge.
—— (1974) *Brazilian Lectures, 1*, Rio de Janero: Imago Editora.
Blamary, M (1978) *Psychoanalyzing Psychoanalysis*, Baltimore: Johns Hopkins University Press.
Bleger, J. (1967) 'Psycho-analysis of the psycho-analytic frame', *International Journal of Psycho-Analysis* 48: 511–19.
Boschán, P.J. (1987) 'Dependence and narcissistic resistances in the psycho-analytic process', *International Journal of Psycho-Analysis* 68(1): 109–19.

Botha, L.I. (1988) Interview with Robert Langs, unpublished.
—— (1989) *The Role of 'Psychic Structure' in the Communicative Approach*, unpublished.
Bouhoustos, J. (1984) 'Sexual intimacy between psychotherapists and clients: policy implications for the future', in *Women and Mental Health Policy*, Beverly Hills: Sage.
Brenner, C. (1955) 'The validation of psychoanalytic interpretations'. Reported by J. Marmor, *Journal of the American Psychoanalytic Association* 3: 496–7.
Brentano, F. (1874) *Psychology from an Empirical Standpoint*, London: Routledge and Kegan Paul, 1973.
Calef, C. (1979) Review of *The Bipersonal Field*, *Journal of the American Psychoanalytic Association* 27: 702–5.
Casement, P. (1980) Review of *The Therapeutic Environment*, *International Journal of Psycho-Analysis* 7: 525–8.
—— (1984) 'The reflective potential of the patient as mirror to the therapist', in J. Raney (ed.) *Listening and Interpreting: The Challenge of the Work of Robert Langs*, New York: Jason Aronson.
—— (1985) *On Learning from the Patient*, London: Tavistock.
—— (1987) 'Between the lines – *On Learning from the Patient* – before and after', *British Journal of Psychotherapy* 4: 86–93.
—— (1990) *Further Learning from the Patient*, London: Routledge.
Chalmers, A.F. (1982) *What is This Thing Called Science?*, 2nd edition, Milton Keynes: Open University Press.
Charlesworth, M. (1980–1) 'Sartre, Laing and Freud', *Review of Existential Psychology and Psychiatry* 17(1): 23–41.
Chasseguet-Smirgel, J. (1985) *Creativity and Perversion*, New York: Norton.
Chertok, L. (1968) 'The discovery of the transference: toward an epistemological interpretation', *International Journal of Psycho-Analysis* 49: 560–76.
Chessick, R. (1982) 'Psychoanalytic listening: with special reference to the views of Langs', *Contemporary Psychoanalysis* 18(4): 613–34.
Chiefetz, L.G. (1984) 'Framework violations in the psychotherapy of clinic patients', in J. Raney (ed.) (1984) *Listening and Interpreting: The Challenge of the Work of Robert Langs*, New York: Jason Aronson.
Cioffi, F. (1970) 'Freud and the idea of a pseudo-science', in R. Borger and F. Cioffi (eds) *Explanation in the Behavioural Sciences*, Cambridge: Cambridge University Press.
—— (1975) 'Was Freud a liar?', *The Listener*, 7 February: 172–4; repr. *Journal of Orthomolecular Psychiatry* 5: 275–80.
—— (1988) ' "Exigetical myth-making" in Grünbaum's indictment of Popper and exoneration of Freud', in P. Clark and C. Wright (eds) *Mind, Psychoanalysis and Science*, Oxford: Basil Blackwell.
Codignola, E. (1987) 'The true and the false: Essay on the logical structure of psychoanalytic interpretation', *Yearbook of Psychoanalysis and Psychotherapy* 2.
Comte, A. (1830–42) *Cours de Philosophie Positive*, 6 vols, Paris: Bachelier.
Crown, S. (1988) 'Supportive psychotherapy: a contradiction in terms', *British Journal of Psychiatry* 152: 226–69.
Cummins, R. (1989) *Meaning and Mental Representation*, Cambridge, Mass.: MIT Press.

Davidson, D. (1982) 'Paradoxes of irrationality', in R. Wolheim and J. Hopkins (eds) *Philosophical Essays on Freud*, Cambridge: Cambridge University Press.

——— (1986) 'Deception and division', in J. Elster (ed.) *The Multiple Self*, Cambridge: Cambridge University Press.

Dennett, D. (1984) *Elbow Room: The Varieties of Free Will Worth Wanting*, Oxford: Clarendon Press.

——— (1988) 'Quining qualia', in A.U. Marcel and E. Bisiach (eds) *Consciousness in Contemporary Science*, Oxford: Clarendon Press.

Deurzen-Smith, E. van (1988) *Existential Counselling in Practice*, London: Sage.

Dewald, P. (1976) 'Transference regression and real experiences in the psychoanalytic process', *Psychoanalytic Quarterly* 45: 213–30.

Dixon, N.F. (1971) *Subliminal Perception: The Nature of a Controversy*, London: McGraw-Hill.

——— (1981) *Preconscious Processing*, Chichester, Sussex: John Wiley.

Dolto, F. (1974) *Dominique*, London: Souvenir Press.

Dorpat, T. (1977) 'On neutrality', *International Journal of Psychoanalytic Psychotherapy* 6: 39–65.

——— (1987) 'Unconscious perception – day residue and dreaming', *Yearbook of Psychoanalysis and Psychotherapy* 2: 34–7.

Dupont, J. (ed.) (1989) *The Clinical Diary of Sandor Ferenczi*, Cambridge: Harvard University Press.

Eagle, M. (1982) 'Privileged access and the status of self-knowledge in Cartesian and Freudian conceptions of the mental', *Philosophy of the Social Sciences* 12: 349–73.

——— (1983) 'The epistemological status of recent developments in psychoanalytic theory', in R.S. Cohen and L. Laudan (eds) *Physics, Philosophy and Psychoanalysis*, Dordrecht and Boston: D. Reidel.

Edelson, M. (1984) *Hypothesis and Evidence in Psychoanalysis*, Chicago: University of Chicago Press.

——— (1988) *Psychoanalysis: A Theory in Crisis*, Chicago: University of Chicago Press.

Eissler, K. (1953) 'The effect of the structure of the ego on psychoanalytic technique', *Journal of the American Psychoanalytic Association* 1: 104–43.

——— (1958) 'Remarks on some variations in psychoanalytic technique', *International Journal of Psycho-Analysis*, 39: 222–39.

——— (1974) 'On some theoretical and technical problems regarding the payment of fees for psychoanalytic treatment', *International Review of Psycho-Analysis* 1: 73–101.

Erdelyi, M.H. (1974) 'A new look at the new look: perceptual defense and vigilance', *Psychological Review* 81: 1–25.

——— (1985) *Psychoanalysis: Freud's Cognitive Psychology*, New York: W.H. Freeman.

Eysenck, H. (1985) *Decline and Fall of the Freudian Empire*, Harmondsworth: Viking.

Farrell, B.A. (1982) *The Standing of Psycho-Analysis*, Oxford: Oxford University Press.

Fechner, G.T. (1873) *Einige Ideen sur Schöpfungs – und Entwickelungsgeschichte der Organismen*, Leipzig: Breitkopf.

Fenichel, O. (1941) *Problems of Psychoanalytic Technique*, Albany, New York: The Psychoanalytic Quarterly, Inc.

Ferenczi, S. (1913) 'Stages in the development of the sense of reality', in *Selected Papers of Sandor Ferenczi*, Vol. 1, New York: Basic Books.

—— (1919) 'On the technique of psycho-analysis', in *Further Contributions to the Theory and Technique of Psychoanalysis*, London: Hogarth Press.

—— (1933) 'Confusion of tongues between adults and the child', in *Final Contributions to the Problems and Methods of Psycho-Analysis*, London: Hogarth Press; newly translated by J.M. Masson in Masson, J.M., 1984.

Fisher, C. (1954) 'Dreams and perception: the role of preconscious and primary modes of perception in dream formation', *Journal of the American Psychoanalytic Association* 2(3): 289–445.

Flax, J. (1981) 'Psychoanalysis and the philosophy of science: critique or resistance?', *Journal of Philosophy* 78: 561–9.

Freeman, L. (1984) *Listening to the Inner Self*, New York: Jason Aronson.

Frege, G. (1892) 'Sense and reference', in P.T. Geach and M. Black (eds) *Translations from the Philosophical Writings of Gottlob Frege*, Oxford: Basil Blackwell.

Freud, S. (1887–1904) *The Complete Letters of Sigmund Freud to Wilhelm Fliess 1887–1904*, Cambridge, Mass.: Harvard University Press, 1985.

—— (1894) 'The neuro-psychoses of defence', 3. *The Standard Edition of the Complete Psychological Works of Sigmund Freud*, translated and edited by James Strachey, London: Hogarth Press and the Institute of Psycho-Analysis, 1953–1974.

—— (1896a) 'Heredity and the aetiology of the neuroses', *S.E.* 3.

—— (1896b) 'Further remarks on the neuro-psychoses of defense', *S.E.* 3.

—— (1896c) 'The aetiology of hysteria', *S.E.* 3.

—— (1899) 'Screen memories', *S.E.* 3.

—— (1900) 'The interpretation of dreams', *S.E.* 4, 5.

—— (1905a) 'Three essays on the theory of sexuality', *S.E.* 7.

—— (1905b) 'Fragment of an analysis of a case of hysteria', *S.E.* 7.

—— (1906) 'My views on the part played by sexuality in the aetiology of the neurosis', *S.E.* 7.

—— (1909) 'Notes upon a case of obsessional neurosis', *S.E.* 10.

—— (1910) 'Five lectures on psycho-analysis', *S.E.* 11.

—— (1911a) 'Formulations on the two principles of mental functioning', *S.E.* 12.

—— (1911b) 'The handling of dream interpretation in psycho-analysis', *S.E.* 12.

—— (1912a) 'The dynamics of the transference', *S.E.* 12.

—— (1912b) 'Recommendations to physicians practising psycho-analysis', *S.E.* 12.

—— (1912c) 'A note on the unconscious in psycho-analysis', *S.E.* 12.

—— (1913a) 'The disposition to obsessional neurosis', *S.E.* 13.

—— (1913b) 'Totem and taboo', *S.E.* 13.

—— (1913c) 'On beginning the treatment (further recommendations on the technique of psycho-analysis I)', *S.E.* 12.

—— (1914a) 'On narcissism: an introduction', *S.E.* 14.

—— (1914b) 'On the history of the psycho-analytic movement', *S.E.* 14.

—— (1914c) 'Remembering, repeating and working through', *S.E.* 12.

—— (1915a) 'Observations on transference-love (further recommendations on the technique of psycho-analysis, II), *S.E.* 12.

—— (1915b) 'The unconscious', *S.E.* 14.

—— (1915c) 'Repression', *S.E.* 14.

—— (1917a) 'On the transformation of instinct as exemplified in anal erotism', *S.E.* 17.

—— (1917b) 'A metapsychological supplement to the theory of dreams', *S.E.* 14.

—— (1917c) 'Introductory lectures on psycho-analysis', *S.E.* 15, 16.

—— (1918) 'From the history of an infantile neurosis', *S.E.* 17.

—— (1923) 'The ego and the id', *S.E.* 19.

—— (1925) 'An autobiographical study', *S.E.* 20.

—— (1933) 'New introductory lectures on psycho-analysis', *S.E.* 22.

—— (1937) 'Constructions in analysis', *S.E.* 23.

—— (1940) 'An outline of psycho-analysis', *S.E.* 23.

—— (1950) 'The origins of psycho-analysis', *S.E.* 1.

Freud, S. and Breuer, J. (1895) 'Studies on hysteria', *S.E.* 2.

Friedenberg, E.Z. (1973) *Laing*, London: Fontana.

Freidman, P.T. (1987) 'The making of a communicative psychoanalytic psychotherapist', *Yearbook of Psychoanalysis and Psychotherapy* 2: 158–86.

Gedo, J. (1988) *Conceptual Issues in Psychoanalysis*, Emerson, NJ: The Analytic Press.

Gedo, J. and Goldberg, A. (1973) *Models of the Mind*, Chicago: University of Chicago Press.

Gellner, E. (1985) *The Psychoanalytic Movement*, London: Paladin.

Gill, M.M. (1984) 'Robert Langs on technique: a critique', in J. Raney (ed.) *Listening and Interpreting*, New York. Jason Aronson.

—— (1985) 'A critique of Robert Langs' conceptions of transference, evidence by indirection and the role of the frame', *Yearbook of Psychoanalysis and Psychotherapy* 1: 177–89.

—— (1987) 'The analyst as participant', *Psychoanalytic Inquiry* 7(2): 249–61.

Giovaccini, P.L. (ed.) (1975) *Tactics and Techniques in Psychoanalytic Therapy, Vol. 2: Countertransference*, New York: Jason Aronson.

—— (1981) 'Object relations, deficiency states, and the acquisition of psychic structure', in S. Tottman *et al.* (eds) *Object and Self: A Developmental Approach*, New York: International Universities Press.

Gleick, J. (1987) *Chaos*, London: Heinemann.

Glover, E. (1955) *The Technique of Psycho-Analysis*, New York: International Universities Press.

Goldensohn, S.S. and Haar, E. (1974) 'Transferences and countertransferences in a third party payment system (HMO)', *American Journal of Psychiatry* 131: 256–60.

Greenson, R. (1967) *The Technique and Practice of Psychoanalysis*, London: Hogarth Press.

—— (1968) 'The use of dream sequences in detecting errors of technique', in R. Greenson (1978) *Explorations in Psychoanalysis*, New York: International Universities Press.

—— (1971) 'The "real" relationship between the patient and the psychoanalyst', in M. Kanzer (ed.) *The Unconscious Today*, New York: International Universities Press.

Groddeck, G. (1923) *The Book of the It*, London: Vision Press, 1950.

Grosskurth, P. (1985) *Melanie Klein: Her World and Her Work*, London: H. Karnac Books.

Grünbaum, A. (1984) *The Foundations of Psychoanalysis: A Philosophical Critique*, Berkeley: University of California Press.

Habermas, J. (1971) *Knowledge and Human Interests*, Boston: Beacon Press.

Halpert, E. (1972) 'The effect of insurance of psychoanalytic treatment', *Journal of the American Psychoanalytic Association* 20: 122–3.

Hammet, V.B.O. (1954) 'A consideration of psychoanalysis in relation to psychiatry generally', *American Journal of Psychiatry* 122: 42–54.

Hartmann, H. (1939) *Ego Psychology and the Problem of Adaptation*, New York: International Universities Press, 1958.

Haynal, A. (1988) *The Technique at Issue*, London: H. Karnac Books.

Heimann, P. (1950) 'On countertransference', *International Journal of Psycho-Analysis* 31: 81–4.

Hinshelwood, R. (1985) 'The patient's defensive analyst', *British Journal of Psychotherapy* 2(1): 30–42.

—— (1989) *A Dictionary of Kleinian Thought*, London: Free Association Books.

Hoag, L. (1989) 'Psychotherapy in the General Practise Surgery: Considerations of the Frame', unpublished MA dissertation, Psychology Department, Regent's College.

Hollós, H. (1933) 'Psychopathologie alltäglicher telepathischer Erscheinungen', *Imago* 19: 529.

Isaacs, S. (1943) 'The nature and function of phantasy', in M. Klein, P. Heimann, S. Isaacs, and J. Riviere (eds) *Developments in Psycho-Analysis*, London: Hogarth Press, 1952.

Jacoby, R. (1983) *The Repression of Psychoanalysis*, Chicago: University of Chicago Press.

James, W. (1890) *Principles of Psychology*, New York: Dover, 1950.

Jaspers, K. (1986) *Basic Philosophical Writings: Selections*, Athens, OH: Ohio University Press.

Johnson-Laird, P. (1983) *Mental Models*, Cambridge: Cambridge University Press.

Jonathan, A. (1990) 'Counselling in a college setting: considerations of the frame', unpublished MA dissertation, Psychology Department, Regent's College.

Jones, E. (1953–7) *The Life and Work of Sigmund Freud*, New York: Basic Books.

Joseph, B. (1978) 'Different types of anxiety and their handling in the analytic situation', *International Journal of Psycho-Analysis* 59: 223–8.

—— (1985) 'Transference: the total situation', in E.B. Spillius (ed.) *Melanie Klein Today, Vol. 2: Mainly Practice*, London: Routledge, 1986.

Kaufmann, W. (1980) *Discovering the Mind, Vol. 3: Freud vs. Adler and Jung*, New York: McGraw-Hill.

Kenny, A. (1970) 'Cartesian privacy', in G. Pitcher (ed.) *Wittgenstein: The Philosophical Investigations*, New York: Doubleday-MacMillan.

Kernberg, O. (1975) *Borderline Conditions and Pathological Narcissism*, New York: Jason Aronson.

—— (1976) *Object Relations Theory and Clinical Psychoanalysis*, New York: Jason Aronson.

—— (1980) *Internal World and External Reality*, New York: Jason Aronson.

Khan, M.M. (1963) 'Silence as communication', *Bulletin of the Menninger Clinic* 27: 300–10.

Klein, G.S. (1976) *Psychoanalytic Theory*, New York: International Universities Press.

Klein, M. (1930) 'The importance of symbol-formation in the development of the ego', in *Love, Guilt and Reparation and Other Works*, London: Hogarth Press, 1975.

—— (1952) 'The origins of transference', *International Journal of Psycho-Analysis* 33: 433–8.

—— (1961) *Narrative of a Child Analysis*, London: Hogarth press.

Kline, P. (1972) *Fact and Fantasy in Freudian Theory*, London: Methuen.

—— (1984) *Psychology and Freudian Theory*, London: Methuen.

—— (1988a) 'Freudian theory and experimental evidence: a reply to Erwin', in P. Clark and C. Wright (eds) *Mind, Psychoanalysis and Science*, Oxford: Basil Blackwell.

—— (1988b) *Psychology Exposed: Or the Emperor's New Clothes*, London: Routledge.

Kohon, G. (1986) 'Introduction to G. Kohon (ed.) *The British School of Psychoanalysis: The Independent Tradition*, London: Free Association Books.

Kohut, H. (1959) 'Introspection, empathy and psychoanalysis', *Journal of the American Psychoanalytic Association* 7: 459–83.

—— (1971) *The Analysis of the Self*, New York: International Universities Press.

Kraepelin, E. (1905) *Lectures on Clinical Psychiatry*, 2nd revised edition, London: Balliere, Tindall, and Cox.

Kragh, U. (1969) *The Defense Mechanism Test*, Stockholm: Testforlaget.

Kragh, U. and Smith, G. (1970) *Percept-Genetic Analysis*, Lund: Gleerups.

Krüll, M. (1986) *Freud und sein Vater: Die Entstehung der Psychoanalyse und Freuds ungeloeste Vaterbindung*, Munich: C.H. Beck.

Kuhn, T. (1962) *The Structure of Scientific Revolutions*, Chicago: University of Chicago Press.

Laing, R.D. (1959) *The Divided Self*, Harmondsworth: Penguin, 1965.

—— (1983) *The Voice of Experience*, Harmondsworth: Penguin.

Langs, R.J. (1959) 'A pilot study of aspects of the earliest memory', *Archives for Neurology and Psychiatry* 81: 709.

—— (1965a) 'Earliest memories and personality: a predictive study', *Archives of General Psychiatry* 12: 375–90.

—— (1965b) 'First memories and characterologic diagnosis', *Journal of Nervous and Mental Diseases* 141: 318–20.

—— (1966) 'Manifest dreams from three clinical groups', *Archives of General Psychiatry* 14: 634–43.

—— (1967a) 'Stability of earliest memories under LSD-25 and placebo', *Journal of Nervous and Mental Diseases* 144: 171–84.

—— (1967b) 'Manifest dreams in adolescents: a controlled pilot study', *Journal of nervous and Mental Diseases* 145: 43–52.

—— (1969) 'Discussion of "Dream content in psychopathological states" by Milton Kramer', in M. Kramer (ed.) *Dream Psychology and the New Biology of Dreaming*, Springfield, Ill.: Charles C. Thomas.

—— (1971) 'Day residues, recall residues and dreams: reality and the psyche', *Journal of the American Psychoanalytic Association* 19: 499–523.

—— (1973) 'The patient's view of the therapist: reality or fantasy?', *International Journal of Psychoanalytic Psychotherapy* 2: 411–31.

—— (1974) *The Technique of Psychoanalytic Psychotherapy, Vol. 2*, New York: Jason Aronson.

—— (1975) 'The patient's unconscious perceptions of the therapist's errors', in P.L. Giovaccini (ed.) *Tactics and Techniques in Psychoanalytic Therapy, Vol. 2: Countertransference*, New York: Jason Aronson.

—— (1976a) *The Bipersonal Field*, New York: Jason Aronson.

—— (1976b) 'The misalliance dimension in Freud's case histories: I. The case of Dora', *International Journal of Psychoanalytic Psychotherapy* 5: 301–18.

—— (1978a) *The Listening Process*, New York: Jason Aronson.

—— (1978b) *Technique in Transition*, New York: Jason Aronson.

—— (1978e) 'Validation and the framework of the therapeutic situation', *Contemporary Psychoanalysis* 14: 98–104.

—— (1979) *The Therapeutic Environment*, New York: Jason Aronson.

—— (1980) *Interactions: The Realm of Transference and Countertransference*, New York: Jason Aronson.

—— (1981) *Resistances and Interventions: The Nature of Therapeutic Work*, New York: Jason Aronson.

—— (1982a) *Psychotherapy: A Basic Text*, New York: Jason Aronson.

—— (1982b) *The Psychotherapeutic Conspiracy*, New York: Jason Aronson.

—— (1982c) 'On becoming a communicative psychoanalyst', published in Italian as: Diventare uno psicoanalista comunicativo, *Psicoterapia e Scienze Umane* 3 (1986): 273–7.

—— (1984) 'The Irma dream and the origins of psychoanalysis', *Psychoanalytic Review* 71: 591–617.

—— (1985a) *Madness and Cure*, Emerson, NJ: Newconcept.

—— (1985b) *Workbooks for Psychotherapists, Vol. 2: Listening and Formulating*, Emerson, NJ: Newconcept.

—— (1985c) *Workbooks for Psychotherapists, Vol. 3: Intervening and Validating*, Emerson, NJ: Newconcept.

—— (1987) 'Psychoanalysis as an Aristotelian science: pathways to Copernicus and a modern-day approach', *Contemporary Psychoanalysis* 24: 555–76.

—— (1988a) *A Primer of psychotherapy*, New York: Gardner Press.

—— (1988b) 'Mathematics for psychoanalysis', *British Journal of Psychotherapy* 5: 204–12.

—— (1988c) *Decoding Your Dreams*, New York: Henry Holt and Company.

—— (1989a) *Rating Your Psychotherapist*, New York: Henry Holt and Company.

—— (1989b) 'Models, theory and research strategies: towards the evolution of a new paradigm', *Psychoanalytic Inquiry* 9: 309–11.

Langs, R.J. and Badalamenti, A.F. (1990a) 'Stochastic analysis of the duration of the speaker role in psychotherapy', *Perceptual and Motor Skills* 70: 675–89.

—— (1990b) 'The thermodynamics of psychotherapeutic communication', unpublished.

—— (1990c) 'Some dimensions of power and cyclicity in psychotherapy consultations', unpublished.

Langs, R.J. and Linton Barr, H. (1962a) 'Placebo reactions in a study of lysergic acid diethylamide (LSD-25)', *Archives of General Psychiatry* 6: 369–83.

—— (1962b) 'Subjective reactions to lysergic acid diethylamide (LSD-25)', *Archives of General Psychiatry* 6: 352–68.

—— (1964) 'Empirical dimensions of the LSD-25 experience', *Archives of General Psychiatry* 10: 469–85.

—— (1968) 'Lysergic acid diethylamide (LSD-25) and schizophrenic reactions', *Journal of Mental and Nervous Diseases* 147: 163–72.

Langs, R.J. and Searles, H. (1980) *Intrapsychic and Interpersonal Dimensions of Treatment*, New York: Jason Aronson.

Langs, R.J. and Stone, L. (1980) *The Therapeutic Experience and its Setting*, New York: Jason Aronson.

Langs, R.J., Fox, M., and Abraham, R. (1987) 'A scoring manual for psychotherapy sessions', unpublished.

Langs, R.J., Linton Barr, H., and Paul, I.H. (1965) 'Individual differences in the recall of a drug experience', *Journal of Nervous and Mental Diseases* 140: 132–45.

—— (1964) 'Retrospective alteration of the LSD-25 experience', *Journal of Nervous and Mental Diseases* 138: 403–23.

Langs, R.J., Rothenberg, M., Fishman, J., and Reizer, M. (1960) 'A method for the clinical and theoretical study of the earliest memory', *Archives of General Psychiatry* 3: 523–34.

Langs, R.J., Bucci, W., Bryant, B., Ferguson, R. and Thompson, L. (1988) 'Two methods of quantitatively assessing unconscious communication in psychotherapy', unpublished.

Leites, A. (1971) *The New Ego*, New York: Science House.

Levinson, E. (1981) 'Facts or fantasies: the nature of psychoanalytic data', *Contemporary Psychoanalysis* 17: 486–500.

Lipton, S. (1977) 'The advantages of Freud's technique as shown in his analysis of the Rat Man', *International Journal of Psycho-Analysis* 58: 255–74.

Little, M. (1951) 'Countertransference and the patient's response to it', *International Journal of Psycho-Analysis* 32: 32–4.

—— (1960) 'On basic unity', *International Journal of Psycho-Analysis* 41: 377–84.

—— (1966) 'Transference in borderline states', *International Journal of Psycho-Analysis* 47: 476–85.

—— (1985) 'Winnicott working in areas where psychotic anxieties predominate – a personal record', *Free Associations* 3: 9–42.

Little, M. and Langs, R.J. (1981) 'Dialogue', in R.J. Langs (ed.) *Transference Neurosis and Transference Psychosis*, New York: Jason Aronson.

Leowald, H. (1960) 'The therapeutic action of psycho-analysis', *International Journal of Psycho-Analysis* 41: 16–33.

Loftus, E. (1980) *Memory,* Reading, Mass.: Addison-Wesley.

Lomas, P. (1987) *The Limits of Interpretation*, Harmondsworth: Penguin.

Lorand, S. and Console, W.A. (1958) 'Therapeutic results in psychoanalytic treatment without fee', *International Journal of Psycho-Analysis* 39: 59–64.

Lothane, Z. (1980) 'The art of listening: a critique of Robert Langs' (Review of *The Listening Process*), *Psychoanalytic Review* 67: 353–64.

—— (1985) 'Robert Langs', in J. Reppen (ed.) *Beyond Freud: A Study of Modern Psychoanalytic Theories*, Hillsdale, NJ: The Analytic Press.

Löwenfeld, L. (1899) *Sexualleben und Nervenleiden: Die Nervosen Storungen Sexuellen Ursprungs*, Wiesbaden: J.F. Bergmann.

—— (1903) *Die Psychischen Zwandsursch-einungen*, Wiesbaden: J.F. Bergmann.

Lyons, W. (1986) *The Disappearance of Introspection*, London: MIT Press.

McGinn, C. (1989) *Mental Content*, Oxford: Basil Blackwell.

Mahler, M.S. (1968) *On Human Symbiosis and the Vicissitudes of Individuation*, Vol. 1, *Infantile Psychosis*, New York: International Universities Press.

Marcel, A.J. and Bisiach, E. (eds) (1989) *Consciousness in Contemporary Science*, Oxford: Clarendon Press.

Marr, D. (1982) *Vision*, San Francisco: Freeman.

Masson, J.M. (1982) *The Assault on Truth: Freud's Suppression of the Seduction Theory*, Harmondsworth: Penguin.

—— (1989) *Against Therapy*, London: Collins.

Maturana, H. and Varela, F. (1987) *The Tree of Knowledge*, New York: Shambhalla.

Meltzer, D. (1981) 'The Kleinian expansion of Freudian metapsychology', *International Journal of Psycho-Analysis* 62: 177–85.

Miller, A. (1986) *Thou Shalt not be Aware: Society's Betrayal of the Child*, London: Pluto Press.

Millikan, R.G. (1984) *Language, Thought and Other Biological Categories*, London: MIT Press.

Milner, M. (1952) 'Aspects of symbolism and comprehension of the not-self', *International Journal of Psycho-Analysis* 33: 181–5.

Mintz, E. (1973) 'On the rationale of touch in psychotherapy', in H. Ruitenbeek (ed.) *The Analytic Situation*, Chicago: Adline.

Modell, A. (1976) ' "The holding environment" and the therapeutic action of psychoanalysis', *Journal of the American Psychoanalytic Association* 24: 285–308.

Money-Kyrle, R. (1956) 'Normal counter-transference and some of its deviations', *International Journal of Psycho-Analysis* 37: 360–6.

Nagel, E. (1959) 'Methodological issues in psychoanalytic theory', in S. Hook (ed.) *Psychoanalysis, Scientific Method and Philosophy*, New York: New York University Press.

Nash, J.L. and Cavenar, J. (1976) 'Free psychotherapy: an enquiry into resistance', *American Journal of Psychiatry* 133: 1066–7.

Neisser, U. (1967) *Cognitive Psychology*, New York: Appleton-Century-Crofts.

Ogilvie, R. (1989) '*Practical philosophy or emotional science? A comparison of existential psychotherapy and the communicative approach*', unpublished MA dissertation, Psychology Department, Regent's College.

Pedder, J. (1989) 'Courses in psychotherapy: evolution and current trends', *British Journal of Psychotherapy* 6(2): 203–22.

Platt, J. (1964) 'Strong inference', *Science* 146: 347–53.

Poetzl, D. (1917) 'The relationship between experimentally induced dream images and indirect vision', in George S. Klein (ed.) *Preconscious Stimulation in Dreams, Association and Images*, Monograph 7, 2(3): 41–121.

Popper, K. (1963) *Conjectures and Refutations: The Growth of Scientific Knowledge*, New York: Harper and Row.

Racker, H. (1953) 'The counter-transference neurosis', in J.D. Sutherland (ed.) *Transference and Countertransference*, London: Hogarth Press, 1974.

—— (1957) 'The meaning and uses of countertransference', *Psychoanalytic Quarterly* 26: 303–57.

—— (1958) 'Countertransference and interpretation', *Journal of the American Psychoanalytic Association* 6: 215–21.

—— (1974) *Transference and Counter-Transference*, London: Hogarth Press.

Raney, J. (1982) 'The payment of fees for psychotherapy', *International Journal of Psychoanalytic Psychotherapy* 9: 147–81.

—— (1984a) (ed.) *Listening and Interpreting: The Challenge of the Work of Robert Langs*, New York: Jason Aronson.

—— (1984b) 'Narcissistic defensiveness and the communicative approach', in J. Raney (ed.) *Listening and Interpreting*, New York: Jason Aronson.

—— (1986) 'The effect of fees on the course and outcome of psychotherapy and psychoanalysis', in D.W. Krueger (ed.) *The Last Taboo: Money as Symbol and Reality in Psychotherapy*, New York: Bruner Mazel.

Reich, A. (1951) 'On countertransference', *International Journal of Psycho-Analysis*, 32: 25–31.

Reiff, P. (1959) *Freud: The Mind of a Moralist*, Garden City, New York: Doubleday.

Rodgers, T. (1965) 'A specific parameter: concurrent psychotherapy of the spouse of an analysand by the same analyst', *International Journal of Psycho-Analysis*, 3: 238–9.

Romanos, G.D. (1986) *Quine and Analytic Philosophy*, Cambridge, Mass.: MIT Press.

Rosenfeld, H. (1952) 'Transference-phenomena and transference-analysis in an acute catatonic schizophrentic patient', in H. Rosenfeld *Psychotic States: A Psychoanalytical Approach*, London: H. Karnac Books.

—— (1987) *Impasse and Interpretation*, London: Tavistock.

Rubenstein, B. (1983) 'Freud's early theories of hysteria', in R.S. Cohen and L. Laudan (eds) *Physics, Philosophy and Psychoanalysis*, Boston: D. Reidel.

Rumelhart, D.E., McClelland, J.L., and the PDP research group (1986) *Explorations in the Microstructure of Cognition, Volume I: Foundations*, Cambridge, Mass.: MIT Press.

Sandler, J., Holder, A., and Dare, C. (1973) *The Patient and the Analyst*, London: H. Karnac Books.

Sartre, J.P. (1956) *Being and Nothingness*, extracts in R. Wolheim and J. Hopkins (eds) (1982) *Philosophical Essays on Freud*, Cambridge: Cambridge University Press.

Schafer, R. (1983) *The Analytic Attitude*, London: Hogarth Press.

Schimek, J.G. (1975) 'The interpretations of the past: childhood trauma, psychic reality and historical truth', *Journal of the American Psychoanalytic Association* 23: 835–65.

—— (1985) 'Fact and fantasy in the seduction theory: a historical review', *Journal of the American Psychoanalytic Association* 35: 937–65.

Searles, H.F. (1948) 'Concerning transference and countertransference', *International Journal of Psychoanalytic Psychotherapy* 7: 165–88, 1977–8.

—— (1972) 'The function of the patient's realistic perceptions of the analyst in delusional transference', *British Journal of Medical Psychology* 45: 1–18.

—— (1973) 'Concerning therapeutic symbiosis', *The Annual of Psychoanalysis* 1: 247–65.

—— (1975) 'The patient as therapist to his analyst', in P.L. Giovaccini (ed.) *Tactics and Techniques in Psychoanalytic Therapy, Vol. II: Countertransference*, New York: Jason Aronson.

—— (1979) *Countertransference and Related Subjects*, New York: International Universities Press.

Segal, H. (1967) 'Melanie Klein's technique', in B.B. Wolman (ed.) *Psychoanalytic Technique: A Handbook for the Practicing Psychoanalyst*, New York: Basic Books.

Servadio, E. (1955) 'A presumptively telepathic-precognitive dream during analysis', *International Journal of Psycho-Analysis* 36: 27–30.

Sharpe, E. (1947) 'The psycho-analyst', *International Journal of Psycho-Analysis* 28: 1–6.

Silverman, L.H. (1983) 'The drive-activation method', in J. Masling (ed.) *Empirical Studies of Psychoanalytic Theories*, Hillsdale, NJ: The Analytic Press.

Silverman, L.H. and Weinberger, J. (1985) 'MOMMY AND I ARE ONE: Implications for psychotherapy', *American Psychologist* 40: 1296–308.

Silverman, L.H., Kwawer, J.S., Wolitzky, C., and Coron, M. (1973) 'An experimental study of aspects of the psychoanalytic theory of male homosexuality', *Journal of Abnormal Psychology* 82: 178–88.

Sjoback, H. (1967) *The Defense Mechanism Test*, Lund: The Calytographic Foundation.

Smith, D.L. (1986) 'Omnipotence', *British Journal of Psychotherapy* 3(1): 52–60.

—— (1987) 'Formulating and evaluating hypotheses in psychoanalytic psychotherapy', *British Journal of Medical Psychology* 60(4): 313–17.

—— (1989) 'An interview with Robert Langs', *Changes* 5(4): 407–11.

Spillius, E.B. (1988) 'Introduction to E.B. Spillius (ed.) *Melanie Klein Today, Vol. 2: Mainly Practice*, London: Routledge.

Steele, R. with Swinney, S. (consult. ed.) (1982) *Freud and Jung: Conflicts of Interpretation*, London: Routledge and Kegan Paul.

Sterba, R. (1975) 'The formative activity of the analyst', in P. Giovaccini (ed.) *Tactics and Techniques in Psychoanalytic Therapy, Vol. 2: Countertransference*, New York: Jason Aronson.

Stone, L. (1961) *The Psychoanalytic Situation: An Examination of its Development and Essential Nature*, New York: International Universities Press.

Strachey, J. (1934) 'The nature of the therapeutic action of psycho-analysis', *International Journal of Psychoanalysis* 15: 117–26.

Strupp, H. (1978) 'Suffering and psychotherapy', *Contemporary Psychoanalysis* 14: 73–97.

Sulloway, F. (1979) *Freud, Biologist of the Mind: Beyond the Psychoanalytic Legend*, New York: Basic Books.

Szasz, T.S. (1958) 'Psycho-analytic training: a socio-psychological analysis of its history and present status', *International Journal of Psycho-Analysis* 39(6): 1–16.

—— (1963) 'The concept of transference', *International Journal of Psycho-Analysis* 44: 432–43.

Thomas, D.M. (1982) 'A fine romance: review of A. Caretenuto's *A Secret Symmetry*', *New York Review of Books* 13 May.

Trigg, R. (1989) *Reality at Risk*, London: Harvester Wheatsheaf.

Truax, C. (1966) 'Reinforcement and nonreinforcement in Rogerian psychotherapy', *Journal of Abnormal Psychology* 71: 1–9.

Trombi, G. (1987) 'La teoria della tecnica di Robert Langs: l'approccio "communicativo" ', *Psicoterapia e Scienze Umane* 21(3): 55–95.

Viderman, S. (1974) 'Interpretation in the analytic space', *International Review of Psycho-Analysis* 1: 467–80.

Wallace, E.P. (1983) *Freud and Anthropology: A History and Reappraisal*, New York: International Universities Press.

Westerlundh, B. (1976) *Aggression, Anxiety and Defense*, Lund: Gleerups.

Wilkes, K.V. (1978) *Physicalism: Studies in Philosophical Psychology*, London: Routledge and Kegan Paul.

—— (1988) '_____, yishi, duh, um and consciousness', in E.J. Marcel and E. Bisiach (eds) *Consciousness in Contemporary Science*, Oxford: Clarendon Press.

Winnicott, D.W. (1954) 'Metapsychological and clinical aspects of regression in the psycho-analytical set-up', in J.D. Sutherland (ed.) *Through Paediatrics to Psychoanalysis*, London: Hogarth Press, 1982.

—— (1955–6) 'Clinical varieties of transference', in J.D. Sutherland (ed.) *Through Paediatrics to Psycho-Analysis*, London: Hogarth Press, 1982.

—— (1986) *Holding and Interpretation*, London: Hogarth Press.

Woodmansey, C. (1988) 'Are psychotherapists out of touch?' *British Journal of Psychotherapy* 5(1): 57–65.

Yalom, I. (1980) *Existential Psychotherapy*, New York: Basic Books.

Further reading

Albanese, R. (1988) 'An increased role for mathematics in research and practice in psychotherapy', *British Journal of Psychotherapy* 5(2): 213–18.

Anisfield, L.S. (1984) 'The therapist's disability as an adaptive context', in J. Raney (ed.) *Listening and Interpreting*, New York: Jason Aronson.

Beatrice, J. (1984) 'Empathy and the therapeutic interaction', in J. Raney (ed.) *Listening and Interpreting*, New York: Jason Aronson.

Bejerholm, L. and Windahl, G. (1984) 'A comparison of Langs' interactional frame and Schafer's new language for psycho-analysis', in J. Raney (ed.) *Listening and Interpreting*, New York: Jason Aronson.

Berchulski, S., Conforti, M., Guiter-Mazer, I. and Malone, J. (1990) 'Chaotic attractors in the therapeutic system', *Newsletter of the Society for Psychoanalytic Psychotherapy* 4(1): 10–14.

Billow, R.M. and Lovett, J.G. (1984) 'Psycholinguistic phenomena in the bipersonal field', in J. Raney (ed.) *Listening and Interpreting*, New York: Jason Aronson.

Blank, R.J. (1976) 'Response to Dr Langs' discussion', *International Journal of Psychoanalytic Psychotherapy* 4: 281–3.

Brown, R.D. and Krausz, R. (1984) 'The patient's unconscious perceptions of the therapist's disruptions', in J. Raney (ed.) *Listening and Interpreting*, New York: Jason Aronson.

Burland, J.A. (1980–1) 'Discussion paper: Developmental perspective on the bipersonal field', *International Journal of Psychoanalytic Psychotherapy* 8: 35–45.

Calef, V. (1979) Review of *The Bipersonal Field* by R. Langs, *Journal of the American Psychoanalytic Association* 27: 702–5.

Casement, P. (1980) Review of *The Therapeutic Environment* by R. Langs, *International Review of Psycho-Analysis* 7: 525–8.

—— (1984) 'The reflective potential of the patient as mirror to the therapist', in J. Raney (ed.) *Listening and Interpreting*, New York: Jason Aronson.

Chessick, R.D. (1981) 'Critique: the wild supervisor', *American Journal of Psychotherapy* 35(3): 445–8.

—— (1982) 'Psychoanalytic listening: with special reference to the views of Langs', *Contemporary Psychoanalysis* 18(4): 613–34.

Chiefetz, L.G. (1984) 'Framework violations in psychotherapy with clinic patients', in J. Raney (ed.) *Listening and Interpreting*, New York: Jason Aronson.

Coleman, E.Z. and Clements, J. (1989) 'Group process: a developmental view', *British Journal of Guidance and Counselling* 17(2): 138–53.

Detrick, D. (1984) 'Self psychology and the dynamics of the bipersonal field', in J. Raney (ed.) *Listening and Interpreting*, New York: Jason Aronson,

Dorpat, T.L. (1984a) 'The technique of questioning', in J. Raney (ed.) *Listening and Interpreting*, New York: Jason Aronson.

—— (1984b) 'Technical errors in supervised analyses', in J. Raney (ed.) *Listening and Interpreting*, New York: Jason Aronson.

—— (1985) *Denial and Defense in the Therapeutic Situation*, New York: Jason Aronson.

—— (1987a) 'Discussion of Langs' "Clarifying a new model of the mind" ', *Contemporary Psychoanalysis* 23(1): 163–79.

—— (1987b) 'Unconscious perception – day residue and dreaming', *Yearbook of Psychoanalysis and Psychotherapy* 2: 46–68.

Ellis, S. (1988a) 'Time and the fixed frame', *Newsletter of the Society for Psychoanalytic Psychotherapy* 3(1): 4–6.

—— (1988b) 'Response to Thibideau and Friedberg', *Newsletter of the Society for Psychoanalytic Psychotherapy* 3(2): 5.

Erdheim, J.B. (1984) 'The development of communicative modes in the mother–child relationship', in J. Raney (ed.) *Listening and Interpreting*, New York: Jason Aronson.

Fintzy, R.T. (1978) Review of *The Listening Process*, by R. Langs, *Southern California Psychiatric Society News* 25.

—— (1979) Review of *The Therapeutic Interaction: A Synthesis*, by R. Langs, *Southern California Psychiatric Society News* 26: 10.

Freeman, L. (1984) *Listening to the Inner Self*, New York: Jason Aronson.

Frick, E.M. (1985) 'Latent and manifest effects of audiorecording in psychoanalytic psychotherapy', *Yearbook of Psychoanalysis and Psychotherapy* 1: 151–77.

Friedberg, J. (1988) 'Discussion of "Time and the fixed frame" by Susan Ellis', *Newsletter of the Society for Psychoanalytic Psychotherapy* 3(2): 4.

Friedman, P.T. (1987) 'The making of a communicative psychoanalytic psychotherapist', *Yearbook of Psychoanalysis and Psychotherapy* 2: 158–86.

Gill, M. (1981) Review of *The Therapeutic Environment* by R. Langs, *Contemporary Psychology* 26: 36–7.

—— (1984) 'Robert Langs on technique: a critique', in J. Raney (ed.) *Listening and Interpreting*, New York: Jason Aronson.

—— (1985) 'A critique of Robert Langs' conceptions of transference, evidence by indirection and the role of the frame', *Yearbook of Psychoanalysis and Psychotherapy* 1: 177–89.

Goodheart, W.B. (1980) 'Theory of analytic interaction', *San Francisco Jung Institute Library Journal* 1(4): 2–39.

—— (1987a) 'A clinical illustration', *Contemporary Psychoanalysis* 23(1): 145–61.

—— (1987b) 'Towards an understanding of Freud's overlooking unconscious perception', *Yearbook of Psychoanalysis and Psychotherapy* 2: 46–68.

—— (1988a) 'The deviant frame and career success', *Newsletter of the Society for Psychoanalytic Psychotherapy* 3(1): 6–7).

—— (1988b) 'Scientific evidence vs. authoritative opinion: the dilemma posed by the Pollock case', *Newsletter of the Society for Psychoanalytic Psychotherapy* 3(2): 6–8.

—— (1988–9) 'Freud, Jung, Goethe, Langs: *Decoding Your Dreams* and the illusiveness of "human stuff" ', *Newsletter of the Society for Psychoanalytic Psychotherapy* 3(3) and 4(1): 16–20.

—— (1989) 'Crises of revision: phlogistic thinking in the 18th century and psychoanalytic theory in our own', *Newsletter of the Society for Psychoanalytic Psychotherapy* 4(3): 4–9.

Green, M. (1984) 'Psychoanalytic psychotherapy of the non-symbolic communicator', in J. Raney (ed.) *Listening and Interpreting*, New York: Jason Aronson.

Grotstein, J.S. (1984) 'The higher implications of Langs' contributions', in J. Raney (ed.) *Listening and Interpreting*, New York: Jason Aronson.

—— (1990) 'The mirror and the frame', *Bulletin of the Society for Psychoanalytic Psychotherapy* 5(3): 21–33.

Hoag, L. (1989) 'Psychotherapy in the general practise surgery: considerations of the frame', unpublished MA dissertation, Psychology Department, Regent's College.

Hodges, A.J. (1984) 'The Langsian approach to acting out', in J. Raney (ed.) *Listening and Interpreting*, New York: Jason Aronson.

Hoffman, I.Z. (1983) 'The patient as interpreter of the analyst's experience', *Contemporary Psychoanalysis* 19(3): 389–422.

Hopkins, P. (1988–9) 'Multiple layers of decoding', *Newsletter of the Society for Psychoanalytic Psychotherapy* 3(3) and 4(1): 11.

Jackel, M.M. (1978) Review of *The Bipersonal Field*, by R. Langs, *International Journal of Psycho-Analysis* 59: 537–9.

Jiji, V. (1984) 'Pinter's use of language and character interaction compared with Langs' theories of communication', in J. Raney (ed.) *Listening and Interpreting*, New York: Jason Aronson.

Kanefield, L. (1985) 'Feminist values and psychoanalysis: the patient's curative capacities', *Yearbook of Psychoanalysis and Psychotherapy* 1: 3–25.

Keene, C. (1984) 'Framework rectification and transient negative effects', in J. Raney (ed.) *Listening and Interpreting*, New York: Jason Aronson.

Kelleher, D. (1989) 'The GP as counsellor: an examination of counselling by general practitioners', *British Psychological Society Counselling Psychology Section Review* 4(1): 7–14.

Kessler, M. and Brown, R. (1990) 'The identification of adaptive contexts: report from the workshop', *Newsletter of the Society for Psychoanalytic Psychotherapy* 4(1): 5–9.

Khan, M.M.R. (1984) 'Negotiating the impossible', in J. Raney (ed.) *Listening and Interpreting*, New York: Jason Aronson.

Korn, S. and Carmignani, R.P. (1987) 'Process notes as derivative communication about the supervisory field', *Yearbook of Psychoanalysis and Psychotherapy* 2: 68–85.

Langs, R.J. (1971) 'Day residues, recall residues and dreams: reality and the psyche', *Journal of the American Psychoanalytic Association* 19: 499–523 (reprinted in R.J. Langs, 1978l).

—— (1972) 'A psychoanalytic study of material from patients in psychotherapy', *International Journal of Psychoanalytic Psychotherapy* 2: 71–111 (reprinted in R.J. Langs, 1978l).

—— (1973a) 'The patient's view of the therapist: reality or fantasy', *International Journal of the Psychoanalytic Psychotherapy* 2: 411–31 (reprinted in R.J. Langs, 1978l).

—— (1973b) *The Technique of Psychoanalytic Psychotherapy Vol. 1*, New York: Jason Aronson.

—— (1974) *The Technique of Psychoanalytic Psychotherapy Vol. 2*, New York: Jason Aronson.

—— (1975a) 'The patient's unconscious perceptions of the therapist's errors', in P. Giovaccini (ed.) *Tactics and Techniques in Psychoanalytic Psychotherapy, Vol. 2: Countertransference*, New York: Jason Aronson, 1975 (reprinted in R.J. Langs, 1978l).

—— (1975b) 'Therapeutic misalliances', *International Journal of Psychoanalytic Psychotherapy* 4: 77–105 (reprinted in R.J. Langs, 1978l).

—— (1975c) 'The therapeutic relationship and deviations in technique', *International Journal of Psychoanalytic Psychotherapy* 4: 106–41 (reprinted in R.J. Langs, 1978l).

—— (1976a) 'On becoming a psychiatrist: discussion of "Empathy and intuition in becoming a psychiatrist" by Ronald J. Blank', *International Journal of Psychoanalytic Psychotherapy* 5: 255–80 (reprinted in R.J. Langs, 1978l).

—— (1976b) *The Bipersonal Field*, New York: Jason Aronson.

—— (1976c) 'The misalliance dimension in Freud's case histories: 1, the case of Dora', *International Journal of Psychoanalytic Psychotherapy* 5: 301–18 (reprinted in R.J. Langs, 1978l; also reprinted in M. Kanzer and J. Glenn (eds) *Freud and His Patients*, New York: Jason Aronson, 1979).

—— (1976d) *The Therapeutic Interaction: Abstracts of the Psychoanalytic Literature, Vol. 1*, New York: Jason Aronson.

—— (1976e) *The Therapeutic Interaction, Vol. 2: A Critical Overview and Synthesis*, New York: Jason Aronson.

—— (1977a) *The Therapeutic Interaction: A Synthesis*, New York: Jason Aronson.

—— (1977b) 'Psychoanalytic interaction', in B.B. Wolman (ed.) *International Encyclopedia of Psychiatry, Psychology Psychoanalysis and Neurology*, Vol. 9. New York: Aesculapius (reprinted under the title 'Framework, misalliance and interaction: three encylopedia articles' in R.J. Langs, 1978l).

—— (1977c) 'The psychoanalytic situation: the framework', in B.B. Wolman (ed.) *International Encyclopedia of Psychiatry, Psychology, Psychoanalysis and Neurology*, Vol. 9, New York: Aesculapius (reprinted under the title 'Framework, misalliance and interaction: three encyclopedia articles', in R.J. Langs (1978l).

—— (1977d) 'Therapeutic misalliance', in B.B. Wolman (ed.) *International Encyclopedia of Psychiatry, Psychology, Psychoanalysis and Neurology*, Vol. 9, New York: Aesculapius (reprinted under the title 'Framework, misalliance and interaction: three encyclopedia articles' in R.J. Langs 1978l).

—— (1978a) 'The adaptational-interactional dimension of countertransference', *Contemporary Psychoanalysis* 14: 502–33 (reprinted in R.J. Langs 1978l); also reprinted under the title 'The interactional dimension in countertransference', in L.E. Epstein and A.H. Feiner (eds) *Recent Studies in Countertransference*, New York: Jason Aronson, 1979).

—— (1978b) Discussion paper: 'Responses to creativity in psychoanalysts' (Reply to Harold F. Searles, M.D., 'Concerning transference and counter-transference') (reprinted under the title 'Reactions to creativity in psycho-analysts' in R.J. Langs *Technique in Transition*, New York: Jason Aronson.)

—— (1978c) 'Dreams in the bipersonal field', in R.J. Langs *Technique in Transition*, New York: Jason Aronson (reprinted under the title 'The dream in psychotherapy', in J.M. Natterson (ed.) *The Dream in Clinical Practice*, New York: Jason Aronson, 1980).

—— (1978d) 'Interventions in the bipersonal feild', in R.J. Langs *Technique in Transition*, New York: Jason Aronson (reprinted in *Contemporary Psychoanalysis* 15: 1–54, 1979).

—— (1978e) 'Misalliance and framework in the case of the Rat Man', in R.J. Langs *Technique in Transition*, New York: Jason Aronson (reprinted under the title 'The misalliance dimension in the case of the Rat Man', in M. Kanzer and J. Glenn (eds) *Freud and His Patients*, New York: Jason Aronson).

—— (1978f) 'Misalliance and framework in the case of the Wolf Man', in R.J. Langs *Technique in Transition*, New York: Jason Aronson (reprinted under the title 'The misalliance dimension in the case of the Wolf Man', in M. Kanzer and J. Glenn (eds) *Freud and His Patients*, New York: Jason Aronson).

—— (1978g) 'A model of supervision: the patient as unconscious super-visor', in R.J. Langs *Technique in Transition*, New York: Jason Aronson.

—— (1978h) 'Some communicative properties of the bipersonal field', *International Journal of Psychoanalytic Psychotherapy* 7: 87–135 (reprinted in R.J. Langs, 1978l; also reprinted in R.J. Langs, 1978m; also reprinted in J.S. Grotstein (ed.) *Do I Dare Disturb the Universe? A Memorial to Wilfred R. Bion*, Beverly Hills, Calif.: Ceasura Press, 1981).

—— (1978i) 'Technique in transition', in R.J. Langs *Technique in Transition*, New York: Jason Aronson.

—— (1978j) 'Transference beyond Freud', in R.J. Langs *Technique in Transition*, New York: Jason Aronson (reprinted under the title 'Trans-ference beyond Freud: reality and unconscious processes', in L. Chertok (ed.) *The Unconscious*, Col. 2, Tbilissi Symposium, 1978).

—— (1978k) 'Validation and the framework of the therapeutic situation: thoughts prompted by Hans H. Strupp's "Suffering and psychotherapy" ', *Contemporary Psychoanalysis* 14: 98–104 (reprinted under the title 'Validation and the framework of the therapeutic situation', in R.J. Langs 1978l).

—— (1978l) *Technique in Transition*, New York: Jason Aronson.

—— (1978m) *The Listening Process*, New York: Jason Aronson.

—— (1979a) 'On the formulation and timing of interventions', *Journal of the American Academy of Psychoanalysis* 4: 477–98.

—— (1979b) *The Supervisory Experience*, New York: Jason Aronson.

—— (1979c) *The Therapeutic Environment*, New York: Jason Aronson.

—— (1980a) *Interactions: The Realm of Transference and Countertrans-ference*, New York: Jason Aronson.

—— (1980b) 'Some interactional and communicative aspects of resistance', *Contemporary Psychoanalysis* 16: 16–52.

—— (1980c) 'On the properties of an intervention', *Contemporary Psycho-analysis* 16: 460–78.

—— (1980d) 'Supervision and the bipersonal field', in A.K. Hess (ed.) *Psychotherapy Supervision: Theory, Research and Practice*, New York: Wiley.

—— (1980e) 'Truth therapy/lie therapy', *International Journal of Psycho-analytic Psychotherapy* 8: 3–34.

—— (1981a) 'Modes of "cure" in psychoanalysis and psychoanalytic psychotherapy', *International Journal of Psycho-Analysis* 62: 199–214.

—— (1981b) *Resistances and Interventions: The Nature of Therapeutic Work*, New York: Jason Aronson.

—— (1982a) 'Countertransference and the process of cure', in S. Slipp (ed.) *Curative Factors in Dynamic Psychotherapy*, New York: McGraw-Hill.

—— (1982b) 'A new dawn for psychoanalysis', *Voices: The Art and Science of Psychotherapy* 18: 575–612.

—— (1982c) *The Psychotherapeutic Conspiracy*, New York: Jason Aronson.

—— (1982d) *Psychotherapy: A Basic Text*, New York: Jason Aronson.

—— (1982e) 'Supervisory crises and dreams from supervisees', *Contemporary Psychoanalysis* 18: 575–612.

—— (1982f) ' "Feel good" psychotherapy on trial: testimony in Hinckley case shows danger in the technique', *Los Angeles Times* 26 May.

—— (1983) *Unconscious Communication in Everyday Life*, New York: Jason Aronson.

—— (1984a) 'The contribution of the adaptational-interactional approach to psychoanalysis', *Analytic Psychotherapy and Psychopathology* 1: 21–47.

—— (1984b) 'The Irma dream and the origins of psychoanalysis', *Psychoanalytic Revue* 71: 591–617.

—— (1984c) 'Making interpretations and securing the frame: sources of danger for psychotherapists', *International Journal of Psychoanalytic Psychotherapy* 10: 3–23.

—— (1984d) 'The framework of training analyses', *International Journal of Psychoanalytic Psychotherapy* 10: 259–87.

—— (1984e) ' "Transference analysis" and the communicative approach', *Psychoanalytic Inquiry* 4(3): 465–87.

—— (1985a) 'The communicative approach and the future of psycho-analysis', *Contemporary Psychoanalysis* 21: 403–23.

—— (1985b) 'A communicative critique: a response to Emmanuel Peter-freund', *Contemporary Psychoanalysis* 21: 620–36.

—— (1985c) *Madness and Cure*, Emerson, NJ: Newconcept Press.

—— (1985d) *Workbooks for Psychotherapists, Vol. 1: Understanding Unconscious Communication*, Emerson, NJ: Newconcept Press.

—— (1985e) *Workbooks for Psychotherapists, Vol. 2: Listening and Formulating*, Emerson, NJ: Newconcept Press.

—— (1985f) *Workbooks for Psychotherapists, Vol. 3: Intervening and Validating*, Emerson, NJ: Newconcept Press.

—— (1985g) 'The first session', *Yearbook of Psychoanalysis and Psycho-therapy* 1: 125–51.

—— (1986a) 'Clinical issues arising from a new model of the mind', *Contemporary Psychoanalysis* 22: 418–44.

—— (1986b) 'Becoming a communicative psychoanalyst', published in Italian as: 'Diventare uno psicoanalista comunicativo', *Psicoterapia e Scienze Umane* 3: 273–7.

—— (1987a) 'A new model of the mind', *Yearbook for Psychoanalysis and Psychotherapy* 2: 3–34.

—— (1987b) 'Psychoanalysis as an Aristotelian science: pathways to Copernicus and a modern-day approach', *Contemporary Psychoanalysis* 24: 555–76.

—— (1987c) 'Clarifying a new model of the mind', *Contemporary Psychoanalysis* 23: 162–80.

—— (1988a) 'The true and the false in psychoanalysis in light of the history of science', published in Italian as: 'Il vero e il falso in psicoanalisi alla luci della storia della scienza', *Psicoterapia e Scienze Umane* 22: 3–16.

—— (1988b) *A Primer of Psychotherapy*, New York: Gardner Press.

—— (1988c) 'Perspectives on psychoanalysis as a late arrival to the family of sciences', *Contemporary Psychoanalysis* 24: 397–419.

—— (1988d) 'Psychotherapy, systems and science', *The Reality Club* 1: 175–92.

—— (1988e) 'Mathematics for psychoanalysis', *British Journal of Psychotherapy* 5: 204–12.

—— (1988f) 'Understanding your dreams', *New Age* July/August.

—— (1989a) 'Reactions of supervisees (and supervisors) to new levels of psychoanalytic discovery and meaning', *Contemporary Psychoanalysis* 25: 76–97.

—— (1989b) 'Models, theory, and research strategies: towards the evolution of new paradigms', *Psychoanalytic Inquiry* 9: 305–31.

—— (1989c) *Decoding Your Dreams*, New York: Henry Holt and Company.

—— (1989d) *Rating Your Psychotherapist*, New York: Henry Holt and Company.

—— (1989e) 'The transformation function in light of a new model of the mind', *British Journal of Psychotherapy* 5(3): 300–12.

Langs, R.J. and Badalamenti, A. (1990) 'Stochastic analysis of the duration of speaker role in psychotherapy', *Perceptual and Motor Skills* 70: 675–89.

Langs, R.J. and Searles, H. (1980) *Intrapsychic and Interactional Dimensions of Treatment: A Clinical Dialogue*, New York: Jason Aronson.

Langs, R.J. and Stone, L. (1980) *The Therapeutic Experience and its Setting*, New York: Jason Aronson.

Lawrence, M.M. and Goggin, K.P. (1990) 'Interactional processes in supervision: a synopsis', *Newletter of the Society for Psychoanalytic Psychotherapy* 4(1): 3–4.

Lothane, Z. (1980) 'The art of listening: a critique of Robert Langs', *Psychoanalytic Review* 67(3): 353–64.

—— (1985) 'Robert Langs', in J. Reppen (ed.) *Beyond Freud: A Study of Modern Psychoanalytic Theorists*, Hillsdale, NJ: The Analytic Press.

Lubin, M. (1984) 'Views on neurosis, listening and cure: a discussion of Gill's comment on Langs', in J. Raney (ed.) *Listening and Interpreting*, New York: Jason Aronson.

—— (1988–9) 'Who are we talking to?', *Newsletter of the Society for Psychoanalytic Psychotherapy* 3(4) and 4(1): 8–9.

Migone, P. (1987) 'Review of Langs's *Madness and Cure*', *Psicoterapia e Scienze Umane* 21(3): 95–8.

Neuhaus, M. (1984) 'Communicative psychotherapy and object-relations theory', in J. Raney (ed.) *Listening and Interpreting*, New York: Jason Aronson.

Osman, M.P. (1981) 'Review of *The Listening Process* by R. Langs', *Journal of the American Academy of Psychoanalysis* 9: 319–23.

Quinn, B. (1989) 'Clients' unconscious communications as the basis for establishing the framework of treatment: a response to articles by Schamess and Saari', *Clinical Social Work Journal* 17(1): 79–85.

Raney, J. (1982) 'The payment of fees for psychotherapy', *International Journal of Psychoanalytic Psychotherapy* 9: 147–81.

—— (ed.) (1984a) *Listening and Interpreting: The Challenge of the Work of Robert Langs*, New York: Jason Aronson.

—— (1984b) 'Narcissistic defensiveness and the communicative approach', in J. Raney (ed.) *Listening and Interpreting*, New York: Jason Aronson.

—— (1984c) 'Chronological bibliography of the writings of Robert Langs', in J. Raney (ed.) *Listening and Interpreting*, New York: Jason Aronson.

—— (1986) 'The effect of fees on the course and outcome of psychotherapy and psychoanalysis', in D.W. Krueger (ed.) *The Last Taboo: Money as Symbol and Reality in Psychotherapy*, New York: Bruner Mazel.

—— (1987) 'Discussion: The well-tempered supervisor', *Yearbook of Psychoanalysis and Psychotherapy* 2: 85–94.

Rowan, J. (1990) Review of *Decoding Your Dreams* by R. Langs, *Self and Society* 18(4): 41–2.

Rubinstein, H. (1987) 'Discussion: The development of a personal identity as a psychotherapist', *Yearbook of Psychoanalysis and Psychotherapy* 2: 186–200.

Schaus, H.S. (1990) 'The adaptive context – revisited', *Bulletin of the Society for Psychoanalytic Psychotherapy* 5(3): 35–7.

Shapiro, D. (1987) 'Learning by the book: review of *Workbooks For Psychotherapists* by R. Langs', *Changes* 5(5): 314–15.

Silverstein, E.A. (1984) 'Langsian theory and countertransference', in J. Raney (ed.) *Listening and Interpreting*, New York: Jason Aronson.

Simon, E. (1987) 'Forbidden transitions', *Contemporary Psychoanalysis* 23(1): 123–9.

Smith, D.L. (1987a) 'On asking too much of the therapist', *Changes* 5(4): 407–11.

—— (1987b) 'The communicative approach to supervision', *Counselling* 62: 3–5.

—— (1987c) 'Formulating and evaluating hypotheses in psychoanalytic psychotherapy', *British Journal of Medical Psychology* 60(4): 313–17.

—— (1988a) 'Clinical commentary by a communicative psychoanalytic psychotherapist', *British Journal of Psychotherapy* 5(1): 121–4.

—— (1988b) 'The challenge of Robert Langs', *Free Associations* 11: 51–8.

—— (1989) 'An interview with Robert Langs', *Changes* 7(4): 117–21.

Solomon, R. (1974) Review of *The Technique of Psychoanalytic Psychotherapy*, Vol. 1, by R. Langs, *American Journal of Psychiatry* 131: 1054.

Trawinski, C.J. (1990) 'An analysis of a shift in intervention style', *Bulletin of the Society for Psychoanalytic Psychotherapy* 5(3): 5–19.

Troise, F.P. (1985) 'Frame deviations and dreams in psychoanalytic psycho-therapy', *Yearbook of Psychoanalysis and Psychotherapy* 1: 189–201.

Trombi, G. (1987) 'La teoria della tecnica di Robert Langs: L'approccio "communicativo" ', *Psicoterapia e Scienze Umane* 20(3): 55–93.

Trombi, G. and Meacci, M.G. (1989) 'Il lavoro psicoterapeutico in seduta: La "grammatica" . . . e la "practica" ', *Il Ruolo Terapeutico* 50: 85–8.

Vlosky, M. (1984) 'Community mental health, clients' rights and the thera-peutic frame', in J. Raney (ed.) *Listening and Interpreting*, New York: Jason Aronson.

Weisberg, I. (1990) 'Translating theory into the emotional discovery of self: an eleven year overview of the making of communicative analysts', *Bulletin of the Society for Psychoanalytic Psychotherapy* 5(3): 38–9.

Name index

Subject index

Communicative Publications Since the First Edition

Badalamenti, A. & Langs, R. (1990) An empirical investigation of human dyadic systems in the time and frequency domains. *Behavioral Science,* 36: 100-114.

----- (1992) Stochastic analysis of the duration of the speaker role in the psychotherapy of an AIDS patient. *American Journal of Psychotherapy,* 46: 207-225.

----- (1992) The three modes of the science of psychoanalysis. *American Journal of Psychotherapy,* 46: 163-182.

----- (1992) The thermodynamics of psychotherapeutic communication. *Behavioral Science,* 37: 157-180.

----- (1992) Work and force in psychotherapy. *Journal of Mathematical and Computer Modeling,* 16: 3-17.

----- (1992) The progression of entropy of a five-dimensional psychotherapeutic system. *Systems Research,* 9: 3-28.

----- (1992) Some clinical consequences of a formal science for psychoanalysis and psychotherapy. *American Journal of Psychotherapy,* 46: 611-619.

----- (1994) A formal science for psychoanalysis. *British Journal of Psychotherapy,* 11: 92-104.

Badalamenti, A.; Langs, R.; & Cramer, G. (1993) The non-random nature of communication in psychotherapy. *Systems Research,* 10: 25-39.

Badalamenti, A.; Langs, R.; Cramer, G.; & Robinson, J. (1994) Poisson evolution in word selection. *Mathematical and Computer Modeling,* 19: 27-36.

Badalamenti, A.; Langs, R.; & Kessler, M. (1992) Stochastic progression of new states in psychotherapy. *Statistics in Medicine,* 11: 231-242.

Badalamenti, A.; Langs, R.; & Robinson, J. (1993) Lawful systems dynamics in how poets choose their words. *Behavioral Science,* 39: 46-71.

Berns, U. (1994) Die Übereinstimmungsdeutung – Ein Ergebnis der Evaluationsanalyze. *Forum der Psychoanalyze,* 10: 226-244.

----- (1996) Is sound communicative psychotherapy possible given the conditions of the German National Health System? *International Journal of Communicative Psychoanalysis and Psychotherapy,* 11(1-2): 3-11.

----- (1998) Zur deutungstheorie und –technik des Kommunikativen Ansatzes in der Psychoanalyse Ziele, Struktur und Validierung psychoanalytischer Deutung. *Electronic Journal of Communicative Psychoanalysis, 1(1)* *

Blumenthal, S. L. (1992) Ethics, resistance & economics: Difficulties in the practice of communicative psychotherapy. *International Journal of Communicative Psychoanalysis and Psychotherapy*, 7(3-4): 139-141.
Bonac, V. A. (1992) Clinical evidence and the communicative model of the mind. *International Journal of Communicative Psychoanalysis and Psychotherapy*, 7(2): 47-61.
----- (1993) Clinical issues in communicative psychoanalysis: Interactional aspects of requests for premature termination as reflections of secured-frame anxiety in adult and child psychotherapy. *International Journal of Communicative Psychoanalysis and Psychotherapy*, 8(2-3): 67-78.
----- (1994) Clinical issues in communicative psychoanalysis: Premature securing of patients' breaks in psychotherapy frame as expression of therapists' countertransference difficulty with containing patients' projective identifications. *International Journal of Communicative Psychoanalysis and Psychotherapy*, 8(4): 115-121.
----- (1994) A communicative psychoanalytic theory of human development: Part one – introduction, methodology and theorums. *International Journal of Communicative Psychoanalysis and Psychotherapy*, 9(4): 99-105.
----- (1996) The bountiful mother and the fate of transference in times of managed care. *International Journal of Communicative Psychoanalysis and Psychotherapy*, 10(3): 59-72.
----- (1996) The problem with human nature: Reflections on communicative psychoanalysis. *International Journal of Communicative Psychoanalysis and Psychotherapy*, 11(1-2): 21-23.
----- (1996) Perception or fantasy: A new clinical theory of transference. *International Journal of Communicative Psychoanalysis and Psychotherapy*, 11(3-4): 45-59. Republished as 'Perception or fantasy? A new clinical theory of transference' in . *Electronic Journal of Communicative Psychoanalysis.* 1(1)*.
----- (1999) Moments of mystery and confusion: Transference interpretation of acting out. In *Unconscious Communication in Practice.* Ed. E. M. Sullivan. London: Open University Press.
Bucci, W. (1997) *Psychoanalysis and Cognitive Science: A Multiple Code Theory.* New York: Guilford Press.
Bruner, J. (1986) *Actual Minds, Possible Worlds.* Cambridge, MA: Harvard University Press.
Donald, M. (1991) *Origins of the Modern Mind: Three Stages in the Evolution of Culture and Cognition.* Cambridge, MA: Harvard University Press
Dorpat, T. L. (1991) The primary process revisited. *Bulletin of the Society for Psychoanalytic Psychotherapy*, 6(1): 5-22.

Dorpat, T. L. (1991) Primary process meaning analysis. *International Journal of Communicative Psychoanalysis and Psychotherapy,* 6(2): 3-11.

----- (1992) Doctor abuse and the interactional dynamics of graduate-medical training. *International Journal of Communicative Psychoanalysis and Psychotherapy,* 7(1): 39-40.

----- (1993) The Type C mode of communication – An interactional perspective. *Bulletin of the Society for Psychoanalytic Psychotherapy,* 8(2-3): 47-54.

----- (1995) An interactional perspective on Freud's analysis of Dora. *International Journal of Communicative Psychoanalysis and Psychotherapy,* 10(1-2): 9-18.

Gatti-Doyle, F. (1999) *Dream psychotherapy and a fragment from a continuing story.* In *Unconscious Communication in Practice.* Ed. E. M. Sullivan. London: Open University Press.

Goodheart, W. (1993) Between Freud and Charcot: Beginning steps from psychoanalysis and folk psychology towards an interactional science of emotional cognition and communication. *International Journal of Communicative Psychoanalysis and Psychotherapy,* 8(1): 3-15.

Gunton, G. (1999) Therapist illness: A communicative exploration of an interrupted therapy. In *Unconscious Communication in Practice.* Ed. E. M. Sullivan. London: Open University Press.

Haskell, R. (1987a) 'Giambattista Vico and the discovery of metaphor.' In: R.E. Haskell. (Ed.). *Cognition and Symbolic Structures.* Norwood, New Jersey: Ablex Publishing. 67-82

_____ (1987b) 'A Phenomenology of metaphor: A praxis study into metaphor and its cognitive movement through semantic space.' In R.E. Haskell (Ed.) *Cognition and Symbolic Structures.* Norwood, New Jersey: Ablex Publishing. 257-292

_____ (1987c) 'Social cognition and the non-conscious expression of racial ideology,' *Imagination, Cognition and Personality.* 6 (1) 75-97.

_____ (1988) 'Small group 'fantasy theme' analysis: Anthropology and psychology: A comparative study of a psychosocial structure of a ritual ceremony.' *Journal of Psychohistory,* 16. 61-78.

_____ (1989a) 'Analogical transforms: A cognitive theory of the origin and development of equivalence transformation, Part I,' *Metaphor and Symbolic Activity,* 4, 247-259.

_____ (1989b) 'Analogical transforms: A cognitive theory of origin and development of equivalence transformation. Part II,' *Metaphor and Symbolic Activity,* 4. 257-277.

_____ (1990) 'Cognitive operations and non-conscious processing in dream and waking reports.' *Imagination, Cognition and Personality,* 10, 65-84.

Haskell, R. (1991) 'An analogical methodology for the analysis and validation of anomalous cognitive and linguistic operations in small group(fantasy theme)' Reports. *Small Group Research,* 22: 443-474.

_____ (1999) *Between the Lines: Unconscious Meaning in Everyday Conversation.* New York: Plenum/Insight.

_____ (1999) 'Maintaining boundaries in psychotherapy: A view from evolutionary psycho-analysis.' In C. Feltham (ed.) *Controversies in Psychotherapy and Counselling.* London: Sage.

Hodges, A. G. (1998*) A Mother Gone Bad: The Hidden Confession of JonBennet's Killer.* Birmingham, AL: Village House Publishers.

----- (1994) *The Deeper Intelligence.* Nashvill,TN: Thomas Nelson.

Holmes, C. A. V. (1991) The wounded healer. *Bulletin of the Society for Psychoanalytic Psychotherapy,* 6(4): 33-36.

----- (1998) *There is no such Thing as a Therapist.* London: Karnac.

----- (1999) Confessions of a communicative psychotherapist. In *Unconscious Communication in Practice.* Ed. E. M. Sullivan. London: Open University Press.

Kahl-Popp, J. (1994) Ich bin Dr. Deutschland: Rechtsradikale Phantasien als verschluesselte Kommunikation in der analytischen Psychotherapie eines Jugendlichen. *Praxis der Kinderpsychologie und Kinderpsychiatrie,* 43: 266-272.

Kessler, M. (1994) What gets people better: The need for verification. *International Journal of Communicative Psychoanalysis and Psychotherapy,* 9(1): 11-19.

Langs, R. (1991) *Take Charge of Your Emotional Life.* New York: Henry Holt & Company.

----- (1992) Towards building scientifically based mathematical models of psychotherapeutic paradigms. In *Analysis of Dynamic Psychological Systems, Vol. 2.* Ed. Levine, R. & Fitzgerald, H. New York: Plenum.

----- (1992) *Science, Systems and Psychoanalysis.* London: Karnac.

----- (1992) *A Clinical Workbook for Psychotherapists.* London: Karnac.

----- (1992) 1923: The advance that retreated from the architecture of the mind. *International Journal of Communicative Psychoanalysis and Psychotherapy,* 7: 3-15.

----- (1992) The self-processing class and the psychotherapy situation: A comparative study. *American Journal of Psychotherapy,* 46: 75-90.

----- (1992) Teaching self-processing. *Contemporary Psychoanalysis,* 28: 97-117.

----- (1993) *Empowered Psychotherapy.* London: Karnac.

----- (1993) *Psychoanalysis: Narrative myth or narrative science?* Contemporary Psychoanalysis, 29: 555-594.

----- (1994) *Doing Supervision and Being Supervised.* London: Karnac.

----- (1994) *The Dream Workbook.* Brooklyn, NY: Alliance.

Langs, R. (1995) *Clinical Practice and the Architecture of the Mind.* London: Karnac.

----- (1995) Psychoanalysis and the science of evolution. *American Journal of Psychotherapy*, 49: 47-58.

----- (1995) *The Daydream Workbook.* Brooklyn: Alliance.

----- (1995) Mental Darwinism and the evolution of the hominid mind. *American Journal of Psychotherapy*, 50: 103-124.

----- (1996) *The Evolution of the Emotion-Processing Mind, With an Introduction to Mental Darwinism.* London: Karnac.

----- (1997) *Death Anxiety and Clinical Practice.* London: Karnac.

----- (1998) *Ground Rules in Psychotherapy and Counselling.* London: Karnac.

----- (1998) Afterward. In *Current Theories of Psychoanalysis.* Ed. Langs, R. Madison, CT: International Universities Press.

----- (1999) *Dreams and Emotional Adaptation.* Phoenix, AZ: Zeig, Tucker & Co.

----- (1999) On becoming a psychoanalytic myth maker. In *Why I Became a Psychotherapist.* Ed. Reppen, J. Northvale, NJ: Jason Aronson.

Langs, R. & Badalamenti, A. (1990) Quantitative studies of the therapeutic interaction quided by consideration of unconscious communication. In *Psychotherapy Research: An International Review of Programmatic Studies.* Ed. Butler, L. E. & Crago, M. Wahington D.C.: American Psychological Association.

----- (1991) Statistics and mathematics in psychotherapy research. *Bulletin of the Society for Psychoanalytic Psychotherapy,* 6:13-21.

----- (1991) Beyond Decoding Your Dreams. *Bulletin of the Society for Psychoanalytic Psychotherapy,* 6(4): 41-42.

----- (1992) Boundaries and frames: Non-transference in teaching. *International Journal of Communicative Psychoanalysis and Psychotherapy,* 7(3-4): 125-130.

----- (1994) Psychotherapy: The search for chaos, the discovery of determinism. *Australian and New Zealand Journal of Psychiatry,* 28: 68-81.

----- (1994) Response to Burgoyne and Harris, the discussants of 'A formal science for psychotherapy'. *British Journal of Psychotherapy,* 11(2): 303-306.

----- (1996) Response to Joseph Schwartz. *British Journal of Psychotherapy,* 12(3): 376-378.

Langs, R; Badalamenti, A. & Bryant, R. (1991) A measure of linear influence between patient and therapist. *Psychological Reports,* 69: 355-368.

Langs, R.; Badalamenti, A.; & Cramer, G. (1992) The formal mode of the science of psychoanalysis: Studies of two patient-therapist systems. *American Journal of Psychotherapy,* 46:226-239.

Langs, R.; Badalamenti, A.; & Savage-Rumbaugh, S. (1996) Two mathematically defined expressive language structures in humans and chimpanzees. *Behavioral Science*, 41: 124-135.

Langs, R.; Badalamenti, A.; & Thompson, L. (1996) *The Cosmic Circle*. Brooklyn, NY: Alliance.

Langs, R.; Rapp, P.; Thompson, L.; Pinto, A.; Cramer, G.; & Badalamenti, A. (1992) Three quantitative studies of gender and identity in psychotherapy consultations. *American Journal of Psychotherapy*, 46: 183-206.

Langs, R.; Udoff, A.; Bucci, A.; Cramer, G.; & Thompson, L. (1993) Two methods of assessing unconscious communications in psychotherapy. *Psychoanalytic Psychology*, 10: 1-13.

Meacci, M. G. (1991) Some notes on the patient-therapist (p-t) system in the communicative model. *Bulletin of the Society for Psychoanalytic Psychotherapy*, 6(2): 23-29.

----- (1992) Communicative and psychoanalytic psychotherapy models: Similarities and differences in data and technique. *International Journal of Communicative Psychoanalysis and Psychotherapy*, 8(2-3): 95-103.

Meacci, M. G.; Luciano, G.; & Rossati, A. (1991) Papers from the Turin conference. *Bulletin of the Society for Psychoanalytic Psychotherapy*, 6(4): 37-40.

----- (1993) Issues in communicative psychotherapy. *International Journal of Communicative Psychoanalysis and Psychotherapy*, 8(2-3): 79-84.

Myers, P. (1996) Sándor Ferenczi and patients' perceptions of analysis. *British Journal of Psychotherapy*, 13(1): 26-37.

----- (1998) Reconsidering communicative psychoanalysis. *Electronic Journal of Communicative Psychoanalysis*. 1(1). <http://www.mortimer.com/psychoanalysiscom/>

Oaten, G. (1999) Brief communicative therapy and the fixed altered frame. In *Unconscious Communication in Practice*. Ed. E. M. Sullivan. London: Open University Press.

Paivio, A. (1986) *Mental Representation: A Dual Coding Approach*. New York: Oxford University Press.

Petersen, M-L. (1998) Traumatic moments in the psychoanalytic discourse. *Electronic Journal of Communicative Psychoanalysis*. 1(1)*.

----- (1999) Dream interpretation from a communicative perspective. In *Unconscious Communication in Practice*. Ed. E. M. Sullivan. London: Open University Press.

----- (1999) The informative value of erroneous questions. In *Unconscious Communication in Practice*. Ed. E. M. Sullivan. London: Open University Press.

du Plock, S. (1992) The communicative concept of validation and the definition of science. *International Journal of Communicative*

Psychoanalysis and Psychotherapy, 7(3-4): 113-118.

Quinn, B. P. (1992) Interpreting patients' unconscious needs for seeking modifications of the psychotherapy frame. *International Journal of Communicative Psychoanalysis and Psychotherapy,* 7(1): 35-38.

----- (1995) Testing communicative postulates. *International Journal of Communicative Psychoanalysis and Psychotherapy,* 10(1-2):19-28.

Rapp, P.; Jimcnez-Montano, M.; Langs, R.; Thompson, L.; & Mees, A. (1991) Towards a quantitative characterization of patient-therapist communication. *Mathematical Biosciences,* 105: 207-227.

Simon, E. (1991) The 'anguish' of termination. *Bulletin of the Society for Psychoanalytic Psychotherapy,* 6(3): 29-32.

----- (1994) On the curative factors in communicative psychoanalysis. *International Journal of Communicative Psychoanalysis and Psychotherapy,* 9(3): 67-71.

----- (1994) Maternal instinct as the fundamental organizing principle of human nature: Reconciling communicative therapy with attachment theory. *International Journal of Communicative Psychoanalysis and Psychotherapy,* 9(4): 107-113.

Slopak, C. E. (1995) An introduction to understanding child sexual abuse and the communicative approach to the treatment of those involved. *International Journal of Communicative Psychoanalysis and Psychotherapy,* 10(1-2): 3-7.

Smith, D. L. (1991) Psychoanalysis and dogmatism: a reply to Patrick Casement. *British Journal of Psychotherapy,* 7(4): 416-423.

----- (1991) The psychopathology of everyday therapy. *Changes,* 9(2): 74-81.

----- (1992) A revised communicative model of the mind'. *Society for Psychoanalytic Psychotherapy Bulletin,* 6(4): 3-19.

----- (1992) Mind, models and scientific reasoning: a reply to Vesna A. Bonac. *International Journal of Communicative Psychoanalysis and Psychotherapy,* 7(2): 63-70.

----- (1992) Where do we go from here? *International Journal of Communicative Psychoanalysis and Psychotherapy,* 7(1): 17-26..

---- (1994) 'Riding shotgun for Freud: A reply to Ernesto Spinelli', *Journal of the Society for Existential Analysis,* 5: 142-156. Reprinted in. *Existential Challenges to Psychotherapeutic Theory and Practice.* Eds. Cohn, H.W. & Du Plock, S. London: Society for Existential Analysis, 1995.

----- (1994) Psychoanalysis, lies and videotape: The problem of dishonesty in psycho-therapy, *International Journal of Communicative Psychoanalysis and Psychotherapy,* 8(4): 109-113.

----- (1994) The concept of transference: Fact or fantasy? *International Journal of Communicative Psychoanalysis and Psychotherapy,* 8(4): 99-103.

Smith, D.L. (1995) "It sounds like an excellent idea": Part four of a psychological cliff-hanger. *Journal of the Society for Existential Analysis*, 6(1): 149-160.

----- (1996) 'Communicative supervision'. In *In Search of Supervision*. Ed. Jacobs, M. London: Sage, 1996.

----- (1996) Reply to Joseph Schwartz. *British Journal of Psychotherapy*, 12(3): 272-276.

----- (1996) Should psycho-analysts believe what they say? *British Journal of Psychotherapy*, 13(1): 64-75.

----- (1996) The communicative approach to supervision. In Dainow, S. (ed.) *The BAC Reader*. London: Open University Press.

----- (1996) Towards a post-Darwinian psychoanalysis. Introduction to Robert Langs' *The Evolution of the Emotion Processing Mind*. London: Karnac.

----- (1997) Essay review of Langs, R. and Badalamenti, A. (with Thomson, L.) The Cosmic Circle: The Unification of Mind, Matter and Energy *British Journal of Psychotherapy*, 13(2): 285-291.

----- (1998) Communicative psychoanalysis. In *Current Psychoanalytic Theories*. Ed. Langs, R. New York: International Universities Press.

----- (1998) Free associations and honeybee dancers: The unconscious and its place in nature. *The Electronic Journal of Communicative Psychoanalysis*, 1(1)*

----- (1998) Ferenczi, Langs and scientific reasoning: a reply to Martin Stanton. *British Journal of Psychotherapy*, 14(3): 348-353.

----- (1998) 'Understanding patients' countertransferences'. In M. Sullivan (ed.) *Unconscious Communication in Practice*. London: Open University Press.

----- (1999) *Approaching Psychoanalysis: An Introductory Course*. London: Karnac

----- (1999) Communicative psychoanalysis without tears. *Unconscious Communication in Practice*. Ed. E. M Sullivan London: Open University Press.

----- (1999) Maintaining boundaries in psychotherapy: a view from evolutionary psycho-analysis. In *Controversies in Psychotherapy and Counselling*. Ed. Feltham, C. London: Sage.

----- (1999) Understanding patients' countertransferences, In *Unconscious Communication in Practice*. Ed. Sullivan, E. M. London: Open University Press.

Smith, W. (1994) Survivors of sexual abuse and post-traumatic stress disorder: A communicative perspective. *International Journal of Communicative Psychoanalysis and Psychotherapy*, 9(1): 3-11.

Stuttman, G. (1991) Insurance reimbursements: The impossible necessity. *Bulletin of the Society for Psychoanalytic Psychotherapy*, 6(3): 3-10.

Stuttman, G. (1992) Ethics and practice survey: ISCPP. International Journal of Communicative Psychoanalysis and Psychotherapy, 7(3-4): 131-138.

Sullivan, E. M. (ed.) (1999) *Unconscious Communication in Practice.* London: Open University Press.

----- (1999) Madness and reason: Shakespeare's King Lear and the psychoanalytic frame. In *Unconscious Communication in Practice.* Ed. E. M. Sullivan. London: Open University Press.

----- (1999) Stories, settings and supervision: Final thoughts and questions. In *Unconscious Communication in Practice.* Ed. E. M. Sullivan. London: Open University Press.

Thorpe, I. (1999) Two parts of myself: Decoding a video-recorded session between 'Kathy' and Rogers. In *Unconscious Communication in Practice.* Ed. E. M. Sullivan. London: Open University Press.

Trivers, R. (1985) *Social Evolution. Menlo Park,* CA: Benjamin/Cummings.

Troise, F. P. (1992) A re-examination of the universal framework concept in communicative psychoanalysis. *International Journal of Communicative Psychoanalysis and Psychotherapy,* 8(2-3): 105- 111.

----- (1993) Freud's research understanding of transference. *International Journal of Communicative Psychoanalysis and Psychotherapy,* 8(2-3): 55-64.

Trombi, G. (1991) On the communicative approach: Some notes from an Italian psychotherapist. *Bulletin of the Society for Psychoanalytic Psychotherapy,* 6(3): 21-25

Warburton, K. (1995) Student counselling: A consideration of ethical and framework issues. Psychodynamic Counselling, 1(3): Republished in *Unconscious Communication in Practice.* Ed. E. M. Sullivan. London: Open University Press.

Warren, M. P. (1991) An introduction to death. *Bulletin of the Society for Psychoanalytic Psychotherapy,* 6(3): 27-29.

----- (1994) The missing link: The role of empathy in communicative psychoanalysis. *International Journal of Communicative Psychoanalysis and Psychotherapy,* 9(2): 35-39.

Weisberg, I. (1991) Breaking the frame in working with a dying patient. *Bulletin of the Society for Psychoanalytic Psychotherapy,* 6(3): 33-34.

----- (1993) Brief, time-limited psychotherapy and the communicative approach. *International Journal of Communicative Psychoanalysis and Psychotherapy,* 8(4): 105-109.

----- (1993) Transference and countertransference vs. evocation and response: A commentary on the writings of Frank P. Troise. *International Journal of Communicative Psychoanalysis and Psychotherapy,* 8(2-3): 65-66.